T0394739

Special Issues in Early Childhood Mathematics Education Research

Mathematics Teaching and Learning

VOLUME 5

The titles published in this series are listed at *brill.com/mtal*

Special Issues in Early Childhood Mathematics Education Research

Learning, Teaching and Thinking

Edited by

Amal Sharif-Rasslan and Dina Hassidov

BRILL

LEIDEN | BOSTON

All chapters in this book have undergone peer review.

Library of Congress Cataloging-in-Publication Data

Names: Sharif-Rasslan, Amal, editor. | Hassidov, Dina, editor.
Title: Special issues in early childhood mathematics education research : learning, teaching and thinking / edited by Amal Sharif-Rasslan and Dina Hassidov.
Description: Leiden ; Boston : Brill, [2022] | Series: Mathematics teaching and learning, 2589-6016 ; volume 5 | Includes bibliographical references and index.
Identifiers: LCCN 2021058294 (print) | LCCN 2021058295 (ebook) | ISBN 9789004446274 (paperback) | ISBN 9789004446281 (hardback) | ISBN 9789004510685 (ebook)
Subjects: LCSH: Mathematics--Study and teaching (Early childhood)
Classification: LCC QA135.6 .S63 2022 (print) | LCC QA135.6 (ebook) | DDC 372.7/044--dc23/eng/20220126
LC record available at https://lccn.loc.gov/2021058294
LC ebook record available at https://lccn.loc.gov/2021058295

Typeface for the Latin, Greek, and Cyrillic scripts: "Brill". See and download: brill.com/brill-typeface.

ISSN 2589-6016
ISBN 978-90-04-44627-4 (paperback)
ISBN 978-90-04-44628-1 (hardback)
ISBN 978-90-04-51068-5 (e-book)

Contents

PART 6
Conclusion

Preface

It is with great pleasure that we present the current book, *Special Issues in Early Childhood Mathematics Education Research*, which we believe offers some new and interesting perspectives in the field of early childhood mathematics education.

Grey Duncan, Northwestern University Tarry Professor of Education and Social Policy and a faculty fellow at the Institute for Policy Research wrote: "Mastery of early math skills predicts not only future math achievement, it also predicts future reading achievement .... Early math skills have the greatest predictive power, followed by reading and then attention skills .... The paramount importance of early math skills – of beginning school with a knowledge of numbers, number order, and other rudimentary math concepts – is one of the puzzles coming out of the study". We, too, believe, that giving young children mathematical skills will make a great contribution to their future: not only in the realm of mathematics, but also throughout their lives.

The purpose of writing this book was to present a cohesive yet far-reaching review of the current research being done in this field. Overall, we trust that this book presents a balanced set of research papers that reflects the essence of various aspects in early childhood mathematics education.

We believe that this book will be of interest to a broad audience: mathematics education researchers, teacher educators, mathematics teachers, kindergarten teachers, psychologists, and graduate students who are interested in early childhood mathematics.

We hope this book will contribute to the academic and educational world by not only emphasizing the importance of mathematics education in early childhood but in presenting ways and means of effecting that education.

Finally, we would like to thank Dr. Rina Hershkowitz, from the Weizmann Institute, Rehovot, Israel, for her constructive notes, comments, and invaluable help.

Figures and Tables

Figures

Tables

Notes on Contributors

Abraham Arcavi
is a faculty member in the Department of Science Teaching, Weizmann Institute of Science. He is engaged in the research and development of learning materials for students and teachers, as well as mathematics learning and teaching processes for secondary schools. He worked on a special project regarding mathematics education for elementary school that was the result of an evaluation project of the Chief Scientist combined with a fascinating partnership with Dr. Rina Hershkowitz.

Juhaina Awawdeh Shahbari
heads the mathematics education program at the Al-Qasemi: Academic College of Education. Her main area of research deals with cognitive processes in learning and teaching mathematical concepts and exploring processes involved in handling realistic and modeling activities. She has also researched various aspects of the professional development of teachers. She worked for several years as a pedagogical instructor for pre-service childhood teachers, the experience of which led to the rationale behind the research included in this book: an exploration of the weak points that pre-service teachers in an Arabic-speaking college have in mathematical-pedagogical knowledge.

Ruthi Barkai
is a faculty member at Kibbutzim College of Education and a researcher and lecturer at Tel Aviv University in the Department of Education in Math, Science and Technology. Her main areas of interest are mathematical and didactic aspects of proofs for mathematical arguments, mathematical thinking of young children (aged 3–6) and the professional development of pre- and inservice mathematics teachers. In recent years, she has focused, among other things, on comprehensive research in the field of mathematical thinking at young ages and the professional development of preschool teachers in the field.

Douglas H. Clements
is Distinguished University Professor and Kennedy Endowed Chair in Early Childhood Learning at the University of Denver, Colorado, U.S.A. He has published over 146 refereed research studies, 26 books, 90 chapters, and 300 additional publications. on the learning and teaching of early mathematics; creating, using, and evaluating research-based curricula; and taking interventions to scale. He co-authored reports by the National Research Council on

early mathematics, President's National Mathematics Advisory Panel, and Common Core State Standards.

Bat-Sheva Eylon

is a faculty member in the Department of Science Teaching at the Weizmann Institute of Science. She directed the Agam Program since its inception and has been engaged in the research, development and operation of this program. She carries out research in the fields of learning and teaching physics, and the professional development of teachers and educational mentors for physics and science. She is developing and researching methodologies for cultivating thinking and creativity, including strategies based on embodiment theory. In 2015, she was awarded the EMET Prize for Science, Art and Culture for her contribution to education. She is a fellow of the American Association for the Advancement of Science (AAAS).

Dina Hassidov

is a faculty member of Talpiot Academic College, Department of Mathematical Education. Her main areas of interest are mathematical and didactic aspects of the understanding and use of mathematical symbols, mathematical thinking in young children (ages 3–6) and the professional development of pre-service mathematics teachers for preschool and up. In recent years, she has focused on the concept that the professional training of preschool teachers should take place in the preschool itself. She developed and led a national program to train and integrate professional mentors as to advance teaching mathematics in preschools. These mentor specialists have enhanced the professional mathematical knowledge of preschool teachers and, as a result, the preschoolers. This model has been implemented in many preschools around the country and accompanied by extensive research. An additional area of her research is the incorporation of advanced technologies in teaching and learning mathematics.

Dr. Hasidov worked in the Center for Educational Technology (CET-Matach) for many years and managed their operations in the northern district. She was involved in initiating educational programs and activities throughout the country, and integrating and implementing computers in education, especially in mathematics education. She was involved in developing curricula for schools, training teachers for mathematics and integrating them into the education system. She has served on inter-ministerial public committees in the field of education and employment that have led to decision-making processes and their implementation on a national scale. She also worked for the Open University, founding and managing their extended campus in Haifa, and has served as a scientific advisor for the Ministry of Education in a number of areas.

Rina Hershkowitz

is a member of the Mathematics Group in the Department of Science Teaching at the Weizmann Institute of Science since its inception. With colleagues she moved from intensive activity of design, development and implementation, towards basic research on learning and teaching mechanisms within the learning topics of visualization, geometry, functions and probability. This led to a theoretical and methodological research concerning abstraction in context (AiC), research of socio-cognitive processes, like knowledge shifts, knowledge agents and collective creativity in the mathematics classroom.

Lea Ilani

trains and mentors preschool and elementary school mathematics teaching staff. She collaborates in writing study materials and in training teachers in the Department of Science Teaching at the Weizmann Institute of Science. She was a staff member of the Agam Program.

Bat-Sheva Ilany

has been involved in mathematics and mathematics education in teacher training colleges, the Open University, Mishbetzet Publishing, and more. She supervises Master and Ph.D. theses in Hemdat Hadarom College and Hebrew University of Jerusalem. She has collaborated in the writing, development, consulting, and editing of study materials and books on a number of subjects intended for preschools, schools, and teacher training programs, among them: *Developing Young Children's Mathematical Thinking: Theory, Research and Practice in Teachers' Training* (MOFET, 2008; in Hebrew); *Ratio and Proportion: Research and Teaching in Mathematics Teachers' Education* (Sense Publishers, 2012); *and Change and Invariance: A Textbook on Algebraic Insight into Numbers and Shapes* (Sense Publishers, 2016). In addition, Dr. Ilany has published math study materials, research papers, and books in Israel and around the world.

Candace Joswick

is a Research Project Director at Marsico Institute of Early Learning and James C. Kennedy Institute for Educational Success at the University of Denver's Morgridge College of Education. In this role, she participates in various research projects and is focused on testing learning trajectories with children and developing teachers' capacity to use learning trajectories as teaching and assessment tools. She previously worked as a middle and high school mathematics teacher, as an education faculty member at Ohio Dominican University, and as a researcher on numerous education projects at The Ohio State University. Joswick recently completed her dissertation titled "Investigating the Relationship between Classroom Discourse and Concept Development in Geometry Learning". She has presented at numerous local, state, national, and international conferences on classroom interactions, learning progressions, teacher preparation and teacher knowledge, mathematics coaching, and non-native English speaking students' mathematics classroom participation. She has also provided state-level professional development for elementary mathematics teachers and mathematics coaches.

Esther Levenson

is a senior lecturer and researcher at Tel Aviv University, Department of Education in Math, Science and Technology. Her main areas of interest are promoting mathematical creativity among students and teachers, the role that examples and explanations play in learning and teaching mathematics, and developing the mathematical thinking of young children (ages 3–6) and preschool teachers. In recent years, she has focused, among other things, on preschool mathematics and the professional development of preschool teachers.

Zvia Markovits

works in the field of early childhood and in elementary school mathematics. She is a member of the Faculty of Sciences at the Kibbutzim College of Education. Her research deals with teacher beliefs about mathematics, mathematics and gender, and number sense. She served as chairperson of the Israeli Ministry of Education's committee that prepared the mathematics curriculum for preschool. She was a staff member of the Agam Program.

Zemira Mevarech

is Professor Emerita of Education at Bar Ilan University. She was Chief Scientist in the Ministry of Education. At Bar Ilan University, she served as Head of the School of Education, Vice Rector, and Dean of the Faculty of Social Sciences. Her research areas are the teaching of mathematics and meta-cognition. She has published dozens of studies in leading journals.

Joanne Mulligan

is Professor of Education in the Department of Educational Studies, Faculty of Human Sciences Macquarie University, Sydney, Australia. She has conducted a range of research projects focused on early mathematics learning including the development of children's representations, multiplicative reasoning, early algebraic thinking and spatial reasoning. She has conducted Australian Research Council funded projects: The Pattern and Structure Mathematics

Awareness Project with children aged 4 to 8 years and Connecting mathematics learning through spatial reasoning with Grades 3 to 5.

Sherman Rosenfeld

works in the Department of Science Teaching at the Weizmann Institute of Science, the Center for Educational Technology (CET), and other institutions in Israel. He was a staff member of the Agam Program, since its inception. His areas of interest include the professional development of science and technology teachers, qualitative research, and Project-Based Learning (PBL) across all disciplines and age groups. He was the chairperson of the Israeli Ministry of Education's pedagogical committee that prepared the guide, "Towards Developing a Culture of Inquiry in Schools", published in 2017.

Flavia Santamaria

is Associate Professor in the School of Mathematics Teaching in Comahue National University, Argentina. She holds a Master degree in Science Teaching and a Teacher degree in Mathematics from Comahue National University. She is also a Primary School teacher. Her research and teaching activity deals with learning and teaching mathematics in primary and secondary education. She is currently completing her Ph.D. in Mathematics Education, with the study of the development of numerical knowledge and learning skills in first grade.

Julie Sarama

is Kennedy Endowed Chair in Innovative Learning Technologies and Distinguished University Professor at the University of Denver. She has taught high school mathematics, computer science, middle school gifted mathematics and early childhood mathematics. She directs projects funded by the NSF and IES and has authored over 77 refereed articles, 6 books, 55 chapters, and over 80 additional publications. Her interests include development of concepts and competencies, implementation and scale-up of interventions, and professional development models' influence on student learning.

Nora Scheuer

is Principal Investigator at CONICET (National Council of Scientific and Technological Research), in Comahue National University, Argentina. She has a PhD in Psychology from the University of Geneva. She collaborates with researchers from several fields (education, mathematics, communication, linguistics, and biology) to study how children take up and make sense of notational practices and systems, and how this learning impacts on their thought and communication. These works have been published in English, Spanish, and Portuguese in various countries.

Amal Sharif-Rasslan

currently heads the Department of Mathematics in the Academic Arab College of Education, Haifa, where she focuses on teaching mathematics to students in advanced studies in scientific education. She has extensive experience teaching maths for preschool teachers at the Academic Arab College and at Oranim Academic College of Education.

Dr. Sharif-Rasslan has served as a member of the Ministry of Education committee for writing the math curriculum for grades 1–6, and as a member of the steering committee of the Israeli National Center for Elementary Teachers of Mathematics at the University of Haifa.

She is involved in and has published articles in a variety of fields of research, including: (1) elementary mathematics, elementary combinatorics, and proofs without words; (2) advanced mathematical thinking, the development of the number concept historically versus developmentally, and decision making among preschool children; (3) innovative digital pedagogy and the use of computerized models in teaching mathematics; and (4) developing mathematical models for medical studies in the field of cardiology.

Tal Sharir

is a Ph.D. student at Bar Ilan University and researches the tendency to focus spontaneously on mathematical structures (Recognition of Mathematical Structures-ROMS) in early childhood and elementary school age, and the impact of a metacognitive intervention program on the tendency to focus spontaneously on mathematical structures. She is an academic lecturer on the relationship between movement and learning and the impact of movement on learning skills. She manages the unit for dynamic regulation of unique regional schools in the R&D for Experiments and Initiatives Division in the Ministry of Education.

Dina Tirosh

is a faculty member of the Department of Math, Science and Technology Education at Tel Aviv University. Her main areas of interest are intuition and the concept of infinity and the intuitive rules theory. In recent years her main focus is on mathematical thinking in young children (3–6) and on the professional development of teachers in the field.

Pessia Tsamir

is a faculty member at the Department of Math, Science and Technology Education at Tel Aviv University. Her main areas of interest are intuition and the concept of infinity, the intuitive rules theory, and the use of errors in teaching and learning mathematics. One of her main focus of interest, in recent years, is mathematical thinking of young children (3–6) and the professional development of teachers in mathematics education.

Ana Clara Ventura

is Assistant Investigator at CONICET (National Council of Scientific and Technological Research) and Lead Teaching Assistant in the Psychology Department, in Comahue National University, Argentina. She is Managing Editor of *Infancia y Aprendizaje/Journal for the Study of Education and Development*. She has a Ph.D. in Psychology from Mar del Plata National University. Her research interests focus in learning and teaching processes in specific domains. She currently studies metacognitive development in early and middle childhood in the fields of number and writing.

Introduction

Amal Sharif-Rasslan and Dina Hassidov

Special Issues in Early Childhood Mathematics Education Research is a scientific research book that focuses on the three main issues in mathematics education research: learning, teaching, and thinking. The aim of this book is to focus on and discuss research concerned with learning, teaching, and thinking in early-childhood mathematics education research, and to introduce some original studies in this field.

Mathematics plays an important, essential part in scientific thinking, both in the practical and communicative aspects of everyday life and in the development of higher-level thinking. Children essentially begin "practicing" mathematics from the day they are born, and these children are the citizens of tomorrow. In order to give these future citizens a well-founded cognitive basis, it is crucial to encourage the cultivation and practice of mathematics from early childhood, the years that are considered the period of promise for the development of thinking in general and mathematics in particular.

Mathematics education in early childhood is an important, fundamental field that deals with the quantitative and spatial aspects in daily life. The practice of early childhood mathematics education is supported by scientific research. To this end, a number of theories have been advanced that advocate appropriate basic and curricular mathematical knowledge for preschool children. Appropriate learning materials have been developed, and educators that specialize in mathematical education from early childhood have been trained.

Twenty-three international researchers in the field of early childhood mathematics education have collaborated to write the original and innovative chapters presented in this book which reflect the diverse areas of current research. Each chapter presents an area of research relevant to the field of early childhood mathematics, and presents a special issue or idea that relates to its domain. The book comprises six sections. The sections in the book have been orderd so as to begin with those focusing on specific domains, numbers, geometry and patterns and structures. The following section dealt with reasoning and explanations in early childhood. The following section then examines aspects of early childhood mathematics teachers' knowledge and their professional development. The final section focused on holistic analysis and conclusion of the book.

The following is a brief summary of the thirteen chapters in the book.

1   **Part 1: The Number Concept Development in Early Childhood: Cognition, Metacognition and More**

This part deals with various aspects of numbers and comprises three chapters. Chapter 1, by Amal Sharif-Rasslan, discusses the more rudimentary mathematical concepts and terms that are common to the initial development of mathematical literacy and numerical reasoning in both the human species and in infants and young children. She also shares her perspective of how understanding the development of quantitative and numerical thinking can move from the particular to the general, and vice versa.

Chapter 2, by Ana Clara Ventura, Flavia Santamaria, and Nora Scheuer, deals with the development of the number in the child's early years, and examines the claim that this development requires metacognitive perception. The chapter presents the multiple metacognitive processes that young children can use when thinking and communicating numerically.

Chapter 3, by Ruthi Barkai, Esther Levenson, Pessia Tsamir and Dina Tiroh, analyses 18 tablet applications in terms of their affordances and limitations when promoting object counting. Visual, auditory, and gestural aspects are considered. It also presents a case study of one mother-child cohort interacting with one of the applications.

2   **Part 2: Geometry: Learning, Thinking and Teaching**

This part comprises two chapters.

Chapter 4, by Douglas H. Clements, Julie Sarama, and Candace Joswick, examines computerized classroom environments that promote problem-solving approaches, and discusses the benefits of developing mathematical concepts and processes (e.g., reasoning, problem-solving, communication, and representations). In this chapter, the authors briefly review research on young children's concepts and learning of geometry and then focus on the results of several research projects grounded on that research.

Chapter 5, by Zvia Markovits, Rina Hershkowitz, Sherman Rosenfeld, Lea Ilani, and Bat-Sheva Eylon, deals with "The Agam Program for the Development of Visual Thinking". The program is based on the vision of artist Jacob Agam, who believes that visual thinking should be developed already at an early age. In this chapter, the authors relates to definitions of visual thinking and to the importance of developing visual thinking at a young age. Then, describe the Agam Program for developing visual thinking and a visual language; present the program's aims and content, the way they are contextualized in the teaching units for kindergarten teachers and school teachers, and the accessories kit that accompanies the program. Moreover, the authors discuss the unique pedagogical approach of the program and refer to the potential benefits of the program (i.e. to develop the children's visual thinking, problem solution skills and creativity). For this description authentic examples are used from four teaching units: Circle, Square, Patterns and Numerical Intuition. In addition, this chapter includes research findings to illustrate that children's visual thinking can be developed through of the Agam Program.

3   Part 3: Patterns and Structures

This part contains two chapters.

Chapter 6, by Joanne Mulligan, describes an Australian project on models and structures, including a series of related studies that facilitated the development of an assessment interview and pedagogical program for children aged four to eight. In this chapter an overview of the learning pathways of the Pattern and Structure Mathematics Awareness Program (PASMAP) pathways, five structural groupings and the pedagogical approach is described. The PASMAP is articulated through two exemplars of children's representations of structuring grids and hundreds charts. Implications for further research, teaching and learning and professional development are raised.

Chapter 7, by Tal Sharir and Zemira Mevarech, examines the extent to which young children choose to describe their surroundings in mathematical terms, despite the fact that they were not asked to do so. In particular, the authors aim to test what kinds of mathematical structures are recognized by these young children and the extent to which children who recognize and describe the mathematical features that appear around them score higher on mathematical reasoning than children who focus on other features in their environments. These issues were addressed by focusing on numerosity, multiplication patterns and arithmetic series, each represented in both verbal and nonverbal modes.

4   Part 4: Early Childhood Mathematical Thinking and Cognition:
Reasoning and Explanations

This part contains two chapters.

Chapter 8, by Amal Sharif-Rasslan, discusses the relationship between quantifiers and deductions in pre-schoolers. The author regards natural language as the basis for interpersonal communication. Understanding the relationship between natural language, mathematical language, and children's attitudes to quantifiers and logical deductions contributes greatly to mathematics education in early childhood. This understanding emphasizes the importance of addressing quantifiers and logical deductions as a significant part of mathematical education. It also emphasizes the importance of cooperation between parents and preschool teachers. This chapter also discusses decision making while handling logical deductions, characteristics of reasoning created by pre-schoolers, and the link between decision-making and logical deductions that children create.

Chapter 9, by Rina Hershkowitz and Abraham Arcavi, examines the ability of students to explain their solutions and traces the characteristics of the explanations provided by those students. Furthermore, the study examines factors that affect the explanations or the failure to supply such by the students. The authors stress the teacher's important, central role in "orchestrating" and developing class culture regarding providing explanations.

5   Part 5: Early Childhood Mathematics Teachers' Knowledge and Professional Development

This part deals with the knowledge of preschool teachers, teachers and student teachers.

Chapter 10, by Bat-Sheva Ilany and Dina Hassidov, deals with the conception of the relational concepts (<, >, =) among preschool and pre-service teachers from the numerical aspect. It deals with the questions: how and in what ways do preschool and pre-service teachers perceive and use the relational signs (<, >, =) between numbers and operations, and what are the differences between preschool and pre-service teachers in terms of how they themselves perceive and use the signs in the context of the natural language? This chapter emphasizes that, like any language, mathematical language has its own laws and symbols (numbers, operation signs, relational signs, etc.) that allow the language to endure. Consequently, proper comprehension should be reinforced among those involved in teaching mathematics.

Chapter 11, by Juhaina Awawdeh Shahbari, reports on a study carried out in an early childhood education track at a college for Arabic speakers. It examines whether the training for teaching math and geometry in first and second grades provides pre-service teachers with the appropriate components of knowledge, and it reports on the level of mathematical and pedagogical content knowledge for the curricula for first and second grades that had been given to pre-service teachers.

Chapter 12, by Dina Hassidov and Bat-Sheva Ilany, deals with the professional development and advancement of mathematical knowledge for early-childhood math instructors and preschool teachers. The chapter presents an instructor-training program and describes the contribution that the program had to advance the mathematical knowledge of both the instructors and preschool teachers. It also reports on the cooperation between instructors and teachers during joint activities. The chapter describes the instructors' position regarding teaching mathematics in kindergarten, their contribution to the advancement of mathematical and professional knowledge among preschool teachers through modeling, and a classification of the types of professional collaboration between math instructors and preschool teachers.

6 Part 6: Conclusion

Finally, Chapter 13, by Amal Sharif-Rasslan, presents a synthesis based on mathematics early childhood curricula that wraps up all the chapters in this book.

PART 1

The Number Concept Development in Early Childhood: Cognition, Metacognition and More

∴

CHAPTER 1

Comparing the Development of Numerical and Quantitive Ability Historically and in Children

Does One Reflect the Other?

Amal Sharif-Rasslan

Abstract

This chapter presents an overview of the development of 'number' in various cultures, including an exploration of the development of numbering systems, words (spoken), and symbols (written). Moreover, the chapter discusses and compares this initial development of mathematical literacy and numerical reasoning in both the human species and in infants and young children. To this end, some observations from case studies with children under the age of four who were carried out, analysed and compared the childrens' behaviour when coping with some basic activities attached to the concept of numbers. These activities included expressing a quantity, writing basic symbolics for numbers, and comparing quantities. Some perspective basing on the 'fractal' concept is used to understand the development of a mathematical concept, in particular quantitative and numerical thinking, can move from the particular to the general and vice versa.

Keywords

number – number development – numerical reasoning – history – early childhood – fractal – cauliflower

1   Introduction

About two decades ago, I was in the waiting room of a children's dental clinic that was equipped with toys, puzzle games for children, writing tools, colours, drawing papers, etc. A little boy of about three, accompanied by his mother, was there. The child was preoccupied with drawing. After a while, the boy turns to his mother, waves a page upon which he has drawn and says 'One'. He then waves another page and says 'Two' and then waves another page and says 'Three'. Then he picked up and waved a fourth page saying 'lotsss'. This incident happened before I had become involved in mathematical education in general and early childhood mathematical education in particular. At that point, I was studying pure mathematics, but that child's words intrigued me, gave me much food for thought, and led me to a myriad of questions about mathematical development.

Numeric ability seems to be something that is unique to humans. Is it innate? And what about animals? Do they have any numerical ability, and if so, how does it differ from that of humans?

This led to other questions: How and why were numbers invented? Who invented numbers? When were numbers first used? With respect to mathematical development in children, is there a common development process with regard to numbers for children in one culture? In all cultures? Does the development pattern in children echo the development pattern throughout history (and prehistory) and if so, might it be possible to learn about the development of the concept of number among children from its historical development and vice versa?

In this chapter, I shall explore these and related aspects in depth. In particular, I shall discuss the more rudimentary mathematical concepts and terms that are common to the initial development of mathematical literacy and numerical reasoning in both the human species and in infants and young children. To this end, I offer an overview of the development of 'number' in various cultures, including an exploration of the development of numbering systems, words (spoken), and symbols (written). Following this is a review of some documented studies regarding the development of numerical ability in children alongside my own observations from case studies with children under the age of four who were asked to carry out some basic activities attached to the concept of numbers. These included expressing a quantity, writing basic symbolics for numbers, and comparing quantities. But I shall start by sharing my perspective on how understanding the development of a mathematical concept, in particular quantitative and numerical thinking, can move from the particular to the general and vice versa.

2   A Metaphorical View – The Cauliflower

Throughout this chapter, I shall discuss and compare the development of oral and object counting from two perspectives: universal/historical and early childhood.

In 1986, Hughes referred to such a comparison by saying 'The idea that aspects of children's development should be parallel to the evolution of the human species is by no mean new'. Hughes suggested a metaphorical view '... ontogeny recapitulates phylogeny', he explained, '... that is, development within an individual (ontogeny) will both mirror and incorporate the development of the species (phylogeny)' (1986, p. 79). In this chapter, the main argument of our metaphorical aspect is that the 'universal/historical perspective' applies to all the peoples in the world, beginning with prehistoric times and then developing within the various cultures.

In this context, we may divide all humanity into sub-groups, i.e., 'nations', and then divide each nation into a collection of smaller 'societies', each of which is comprised of 'clans', which are comprised of large 'family groups', which are comprised of a number of nuclear families, which are, finally, comprised of individuals. This decomposition can be viewed as the 'small being a smaller version of the large, and the large being a larger version of the small'. This perspective can be equated to the concept of 'fractals', which are patterns that repeat at any dimension: no matter at what magnification we look at them, the same shape is revealed.

The fractal-like breakdown of a cauliflower (see Figure 1.1) can be a metaphor for the description of 'all humanity'. A whole cauliflower (Figure 1.1a) can be broken down into parts that appear to be 'smaller cauliflowers' comprised of 'even smaller cauliflowers' (Figure 1.1c), and so on. In other words, the patterns for both the structure of humanity and the cauliflower repeat themselves at the micro level as well as at the macro level. Observing Figures 1.1a and 1.1d side by side allows us to see how one seems to be a greater/smaller version of the other. In other words, a basic organizing principle of fractals is self-similarity: fractals maintain their form regardless of the scale on which they are observed. Researchers in other fields have used the fractal metaphor. For example, Rosenhouse (2017) compared 'fractals' and some of their features to language development, and Forouharfar (2019) explained the concept of organizational power by using the fractal metaphor.

Based on this analogy, it is possible to compare common human development – which includes the development of the concept of numbers – to a

(a)   (b)   (c)   (d)

FIGURE 1.1   Breakdown of a cauliflower: (a) Whole; (b) Cut in half; (c) A large individual floret; (d) Smallest floret

cauliflower. The complete cauliflower (Figure 1.1a) represents all the development of 'all humanity' since prehistory, while the floret (Figure 1.1d) represents the development of an individual (in our case, a typical baby or pre-schooler). Both evolve along a similar time-axis with respect to the development of the concept of number and quantitative reasoning. This comparison illustrates similarities and differences between the development of this concept for humanity as a whole and for a child, the differences being that the timespan involved (clearly, development for humanity took longer) and there are more parameters for 'humanity' than the parallel development among children.

Since this chapter deals with pre-schoolers, it addresses only the very first historical stages of this development, which will be seen to be almost identical to the development of the concept of number for all (normal) babies and pre-schoolers (Dehaene, 1997; Harris, 1987).

Because the child represents one component of its society (analogous to Figures 1.1a and 1.1d), their thinking (along the time-axis) will be representative of the thinking among the whole of society (albeit over a shorter timeframe). Based on this perspective and taking into account specific differences between the development of the child and humanity as a whole, the development pattern of quantitative thinking in a child in a particular society may illuminate the development of numerical thought in that society in general. Conversely, how the concept of number developed in a particular culture should emulate its process of development among children in that culture.

3 The Historical Development of Numbers: From Concept to Words to Symbols

3.1 *Numerical Ability in Animals and Humans*

Studies on animals including birds, fish, and mammals (Agrillo, Dadda, Serena, & Bisazza, 2008, 2009) have demonstrated that animals can indeed distinguish between small quantities (one, two, three, and, perhaps, four). However, they do not have the ability to distinguish beyond this quantity and with respect to larger numbers (five and more), they have only a sense of 'approximately'. Studies with infants (see, for example, Marmasse, Bletsas, & Marti, 2000) have shown that infants develop basic numeric capabilities with small amounts well before developing language ability, and Starkey and associates (Starkey, Spelke, & Gelman, 1983) have shown that infants between four and seven-and-a-half months can distinguish between quantities up to three but cannot distinguish between four and six items. Dehaene (1997), a French brain researcher, claimed that a baby comes into the world equipped with the ability to make analogous distinctions between small quantities, but beyond the quantities of one, two, or three, the distinctions are only approximate.

In the same study, Dehaene demonstrated notable differences between the cognitive abilities of humans and those of animals: in contrast to animals, humans have (a) an inborn ability to develop symbol systems, including mathematical language; (b) the ability to express their intellectual thoughts through language, enabling them to share them with others; and (c) the ability to form complex ideas based on retrospective memory of previous events and prospective memory for future possibilities.

Researchers in mathematical education have reported that infants possess an innate quantitative (numerical) ability (Dehaene, 1997; Rips, Bloomfield, & Asmuth, 2008) and Gallistel and Gelman (1992) showed that human beings possess a pre-verbal quantifying mechanism. Dehaene claims that this innate numerical ability, what is called 'numerical insight', allows a person to eventually grasp what the quantity of a given group is and to connect this to an abstract symbol. This innate ability may be further developed in a person (through learning), but at the very least, it remains intrinsic (Rips, Asmuth, & Bloomfield, 2008).

3.2   *The Concept of the Number*

Numbers (as a concept) were discovered (or invented, depending on one's philosophical point of view) before recorded history (Harris, 1987). This probably occurred when humans needed to *subitize*: that is to know 'how many' (objects were in a small set) without actually 'counting'. In fact, thousands of years ago, the only number words were 'one' and 'two'.

It is interesting to note that even today, there are tribes that still adhere to the 'one, two, three, a lot' method of counting. For example, the Pirahã tribe in Brazil do not have any words to describe numbers in their language.[1] In fact, they do not even have a word that is the equivalent of 'number', and the only quantitative words are 'an amount that is close to one', 'an amount that is close to two', and 'many'. Similarly, there are no numbers greater than three in the (ancient) language of the Australian Aboriginals (Brandenstein, 1970, p. 13; Dixon, 1980, pp. 107–108; Blake, 1981, pp. 3–4).

The members of the Pirahã tribe use the words '*ba´aiso*' (everything), '*gɩ´ia T*' (part), and "*aaɩ´ba*' (many), with the latter two words being used to express the numbers 'one' and 'two' (Everett, 2005). Perhaps there was no need for a formal number system until people began to live in tribes, villages, or towns and began to engage in trade (Everett, 2005).

3.3   *The Evolution of Number Words*

Once the concept of 'how many' had arisen, people developed a method for orally expressing specific numerical values, and as language (and writing) progressed, more complex 'number word systems' were created to allow the expression of quantities greater than the limited words initially available (i.e., 'one', 'two', 'more'). The various ways that the terminologies for numbers evolved is a fascinating study and some examples are described below.

3.4   *From One to Ten*

The first development in any particular language was, obviously, the creation of basic number words (called 'numerals' in mathematical language) to express larger quantities.

On an island in Australia (in the Torres Strait) lived a tribe with no written language. In speech, they used only two numerals: '*urapun*' (one) and '*okosa*' (two), and combinations of the two were used express quantities larger than two. For example, the number 'three' was expressed as '*okosa-urapun*', 'four' as '*okosa-okosa*', 'five' as '*okosa-okosa-urapun*', and 'six' as '*okosa-okosa-okosa*'. But this is as far as they got: any other number greater than six was expressed as '*ras*' (Haddon, 1890).

However, this is unique. The counting system of many peoples – in fact most cultures – is based on the decimal ('ten') system thanks to our natural anatomical abacus – our fingers (Burton, 2011). Thus, in most cultures, the first ten numbers were given 'basic' names that were then used to further develop patterns for numbers beyond ten. For example, in Mandarin Chinese, the words for the numbers 1 to 10 are '*yī, èr, sān, sì, wǔ, liù, qī, bā, jiǔ*, and *shí*'[2] (the marks over the words indicate the appropriate tone). These words form the basis of all the rest of the number words exactly in their basic form. For example, 11 to 19 are all expressed as ten plus the unit ('*shí yī, shí èr*', and so on).

Other languages follow this concept to a point. Take Hebrew and Arabic as examples. In Hebrew, the words '*ahad, shtayim, shalosh, arba ... tesha, eser*'[3] and in Arabic, '*wāḥid, ithnān, thalāthah, arba ..., tisʻah, ʻashrah*'[4] correspond to the English words for 'one, two, three, ..., nine, ten'. To express numbers greater than ten, a combination of the basic words is used. For example, this quantity – ♣ ♣ ♣ ♣ ♣ ♣ ♣ ♣ ♣ ♣ ♣ ♣ ♣ ♣ – is expressed as a combination of the words for 'four' and 'ten': in Hebrew it is '*arba assar*' (ארבע עשר), in formal Arabic it is '*arba ashar*' (أربع عشر), and in spoken Arabic it is '*arbetash*' (أربعطاش).[5]

It is fascinating to observe that in many languages, the words for the 'teen numbers' and multiples of ten are not always exactly a combination of the basic numbers, nor do they follow a consistent pattern. In English, 'fourteen' is pretty close to the original words and 'thirteen' and 'fifteen' less so, but this can be attributed to the evolution of the language. But English has the words 'eleven' and 'twelve' and not 'one-teen' and 'two-teen'.[6] A similar pattern appears in various European languages. For example, in French and Italian, the words for 11–19 start out in one pattern but then 'reverse' at some point.[7] These anomalies tend to lead to a difficulty among European-language-speaking children (including English) when they want to use numbers larger than ten (Geary, 2006).

Similar to this is the problem that the difference between formal and spoken Arabic raises: in formal Arabic, the 'teens' are combinations of the 'digits' whereas in *spoken* Arabic, the words reflecting the numbers 11–19 may be quite different, making it difficult for children to remember them in succession. (For example, 15 in formal Arabic is 'h'msata A'ashar', which reflects the 5 [h'msa] and the 10 [A'ashara]). However, in spoken Arabic it is 'h'mistash', which includes the five [h'msa], but 'tash' does not resemble the word for ten).

3.5   *From Ten to 100 and Beyond*

The words for higher multiples of ten generally follow a pattern using the basic unit plus a change to indicate multiples.

In Mandarin Chinese, for example, they follow a very regular pattern using the number of multiples followed by the word for ten: 20, 30, 40 ... are 'èr shí', 'sān shí', 'sì shí', and so forth. Expressing hundreds is done by simply adding the unit word to the word 'bǎi', leading to 'yībǎi' (100), 'èrbǎi' (200), and so forth. The number 70 is expressed in Hebrew as 'shivim' (שבעים), which reflects a plural seven, and in Arabic as 'sabeun' (سبعون), which recall the word for 'seven'. In English, of course, we have 'thirty', 'forty',[8] ... 'seventy', etc.

French, again, offers some significant anomalies: the words to express multiples of ten from 30 on[9] *start out* related to the respective unit word ('*trente, quarante, cinquante, soixante*' for 30, 40, 50, and 60) but the numbers following are expressed very differently: 70 is '*soixante-dix*' (60 plus 10), 80 is '*quatre-vingts*' (four 20s) and 90 is '*quatre-vingt-dix*' (four 20s plus 10).

3.6   *Oops, What about the Zero?*

The concept of 'nothingness', '*lo klum*', '*shum davar*' in Hebrew (לא כלום', 'שום דבר') and '*lachya'a*' in Arabic ('لا شيء') is an intuitive concept that was known to prehistoric humans and is known even in the most primitive societies. Boucenna (2013) named this concept 'intuitive zero'. Clearly, if a farmer starts out with a quantity of wheat and uses it all up, he is aware that he has 'nothing' left. Boyer (1994) claimed that there can be no unique answer to the query 'who discovered zero' as a concept. However, the actual designation of a specific term for 'zero' as a number to indicate 'nothing' is a fairly sophisticated cognitive ability, and this probably first occurred in ancient India in the 7th century AD, if not earlier. It certainly appears in the writings of Indian mathematician Brahmagupta (598–668) (Boucenna, 2013).

With respect to the mathematical history of 'zero' as a word (in all languages), it is possible to assume that the concept is, indeed, intuitive, and the use of other number words predated the actual word for 'nothing'. Perhaps this is because 'three apples' can be indicated with three fingers, but it is hard to indicate 'zero' with fingers. Yet, an actual symbol for 'zero/nothing' appeared relatively late in the evolution of number systems, and the concept itself has a reputation for being hard to grasp, even in our culture (Hughes, 1986).

Besides providing a word to express 'a void set', the digit '0' also is used as a placeholder when writing large numbers. For example, in '407', the '0' indicates that there are no tens. The Babylonians originally used an empty space to symbolize 'nothing'. Later, with the introduction of the decimal system, the zero was used as the placeholder (Burton, 2011). Hughes (1986) highlighted the difficulty in the use of zero as placeholder, in the sense of the previous example (407).

The etymological evolution of the word 'zero' is interesting. According to Musa (2014), the Arabic word determined for zero was 'sifr' ('صفر'). This word was adopted, with minor changes, into the European languages, metamorphosing over time from 'sifr' into 'cypher' (French), 'zefiro' (Latin) and finally to 'zero' and variations in English and other languages (e.g., 'zero' in Italian and 'cero' in Spanish).[10]

3.7 Fractions

To complete the picture, we shall address the concept of the fraction. Thousands of years ago, the Babylonians and the Egyptians, independently, divided up the land so that people would pay taxes. That was the beginning of the concept of fraction. What is interesting is that the word equivalents for 'fraction' in various languages are often based on the word for 'to break': in Hebrew, 'shever' (שבר); in Arabic, 'kaser' ('كسر'); and in Latin, 'fractio' (the precursor of the English 'fraction', Italian 'frazione', and Spanish 'fracción'). Even in Sanskrit the word for fraction is 'bhinna', which also means 'break' (Sýkorová, 2010). It should be noted that the concept of the fraction was mentioned in the Holy Books (both the Quran and Scriptures). In the Bible, for example, there are many fractions mentioned, such as half, quarter, fifth, sixth, and tenth.

However, it is most probable that the concept of the fraction did not originate at the dawn of human history but rather only after people began dealing with divisions, since the etymology reflects this concept in all languages.

3.8 Counting: Recitation (Oral Counting) and Enumeration (Object Counting)

Having words for numbers is, obviously, a requirement if a person wants to 'count' in both aspects of the word, that is to say, recitation (oral counting: reciting the words for numbers in the correct order, 'one, two, three, ...') or enumeration (object counting: expressing a quantity, which may or may not use the equivalent number word for that quantity). Enumeration also includes expressing the order of objects (i.e., the use of ordinal numbers, 'first, second, third, ...') to indicate the arrangement of objects or entities. This is also the action performed to answer the question 'how many?' In other words, one must appreciate the difference between the concept of counting to deliberately recite the numbers in order and the concept of counting to express quantity. Researchers claim that the more complicated the semantics of the numeric system, the more difficult it will be for children (or people learning the language) to correctly recite the numbers in order, leading to difficulty in object counting (Marmasse et al., 2000).

3.8.1 Bijective Correspondence

Even before language developed, prehistoric man developed object counting based on one-to-one (bijective) correspondence, that is to say, the perfect pairing between the items in two different groups. For example, when a prehistoric tribal chief wanted to count the number of people in a particular village, he assigned a stone for every person in the village. The size of the pile of stones indicated the number of people in the village. Similarly, this method was used to count his flock and determine whether it had returned in its entirety from pasture (Burton, 2011). For each sheep that went out, he placed a stone in a pile; for each sheep that returned, he removed a stone. If there were any stones left, he knew that some sheep were missing.

3.9 The Development of Numerical Symbols

The use of body parts to create number systems was the province of many peoples and this was often much more complex than the 'simple' use of the fingers only. For example, the numbering system used by the Oksapmin tribe in Papaya-New Guinea was based on 27 organs of the body as depicted in Figure 1.2: one begins with the thumb on one hand and enumerates 27 positions around the upper periphery of the body, ending with the little finger of the opposite hand (Saxe, 1982). To count further, one continues up to the wrist, forearm, and around the body (Saxe & Esmonde, 2004). The use of the ten fingers was the province of other peoples, such as the ancient Greeks, the Romans, and others,

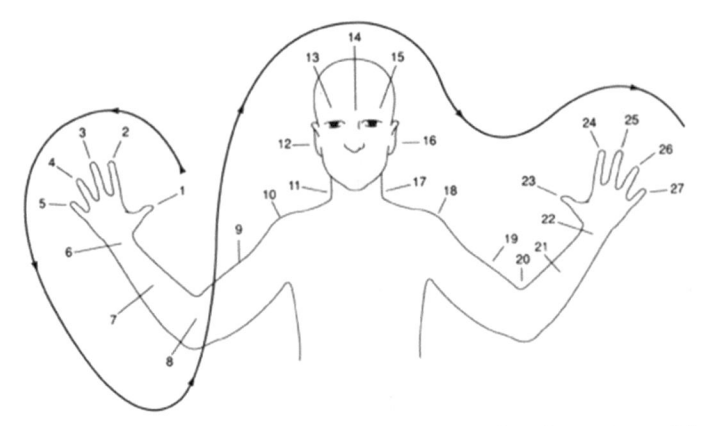

FIGURE 1.2   The counting system of the Oksapmin is based on 27 parts of the body
(from Saxe, 1982)

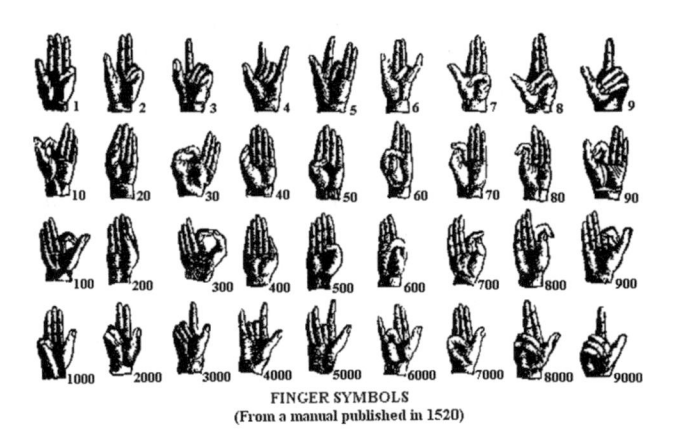

FINGER SYMBOLS
(From a manual published in 1520)

FIGURE 1.3   Finger symbols (from Dantzig, 1954, p. 2)

who could use the fingers to symbolize numbers even past 8000! One ancient finger system is shown in Figure 1.3.

Before recorded history, primitive man used concrete items such as fingers, stones, or sticks to represent quantities. This method is considered appropriate for object counting but not for oral counting.

3.10   *Representing Numbers: Symbolization*

The development of writing systems by different societies required the development of a system of symbols to represent numbers. These developments depended on time and place, and, undoubtedly, the properties of these representations facilitated or inhibited the development of numerical insight (Marmasse et al., 2000). Nataraj and colleagues (2009) directs our attention to the fact that the term 'written' numbers have different connotations in the Old World and the New World.

The tally stick – a piece of wood (or other material) marked with grooves to symbolize quantities – was the first apparatus invented to register quantities (Burton, 2011). The earliest object of this kind found is the Ishango bone (from more than 9000 years ago), upon which are engravings meant to record quantities. This bone was discovered near the shores of the Nile River in Zaire and contains etchings arranged in three columns running the length of the tool on both sides. In 1937, a wolf bone containing fifty-five similar-sized etchings arranged approximately in fives was found in Czechoslovakia. Grouping items in fives – ⲎⲎⲎ – is an efficient method of marking numbers and is still practiced today (Burton, 2011).

Smith and Ginsburg (1971) pointed out that the Ancient Egyptians and Babylonians and then the Greeks and Romans (thousands of years later) depicted the word for 'one' with the symbol '|'. A similar symbol is found in many cultures. This may be linked to the act of lifting one finger to show the amount of 'one', which is the most natural method to express an individual item. They also pointed out that another method for symbolizing the concept of 'one' was with a bead or pebble or a horizontal line (—), which symbolized a stick. In the same way, 'two' can be expressed with two fingers or sticks and thus symbolized | | or =.

In many cultures, the symbols used to express the numbers 'one', 'two', and 'three' use such lines (|, | |, | | | or —, =, ≡). The Roman numeral system is one, and it can also be explained by the use of the fingers (Hooper, 1945).[11] The numerals I, II, and III are clearly similar to the position of the fingers to express the amounts 1, 2, and 3, respectively. The V can be compared to the right hand held upright with the fingers pointing up and the thumb pointing outward and ten might come from an image of crossing both thumbs to indicate both hands: X. The numbers 6–8 represent a combination of the right and left hands: 6 (V, I), 7 (V, II), 8 (V, III). One might expect that the number four would be expressed by ||||, but the Romans modified the system to include a subtraction rule for writing four, nine, and similar numbers (forty, four hundred, etc.) and thus reduced the number of symbols needed. Thus 4 is written as 'one before five' (IV) and 9 is 'one before ten' (IX).

Logical thinking served humanity for symbolizing larger numbers. Sticks and fingers are only useful for writing numbers from one to ten. For example, for '5', the Egyptians used the symbol 'I' five times: $\frac{III}{II}$ – and so on until the number 9. But beyond that, it was difficult to subitize. Egyptians thus assigned special hieroglyph symbols for the powers of ten: 10 by a horseshoe (∩); 100, a coil of rope (ℰ); 1,000, a lotus (𓏼); 10,000, a pointing finger (𓂭); 100,000, a tadpole (𓆐); 1,000,000, a person raising his hand in surprise (𓁨), and 10,000,000, by (apparently) a shining sun. These symbols, along with the symbol for '1' and the principle of addition, formed the basis for writing every other number.

The Egyptian number system is based on the 'natural' base-ten decimal system. The additive writing principle meant that there was no importance to the order of the symbols, although often the numbers with greater value were written on the right.

Approximately 2000–3000 BC, the Babylonians developed another method for writing large numbers based on the value of the 'location' of the symbol. This is called the positional number system. In the case of the Babylonians, the base of the system was 60: a perpendicular stake, $\mathbf{T}$, represented the numbers 1, 60, 60^2, 60^3 and so on, and could be used up to 9 times. A horizontal stake, $\mathbf{<}$, represented the number 10 and could be used up to five times. This positional method was used in other systems too. For example, the ancient Chinese number system used nine different symbols to write numbers; the Maya number system (2000 years ago), used base 20, with one-to-four dots symbolizing 1 to 4, respectively, and a short, horizontal line to represent 5. These two symbols, along with the 'clam' to represent 'zero', was used to write all the rest of the numbers. The Roman system and eventually the Indio-Arabic number system also were positional, the latter being the one currently in use in most of the world.

One must not overlook the Greek system used in the 5th century BC. They used the twenty-four Greek letters and another three letters borrowed from the Phoenician alphabet ('*digma*', '*coba*' and '*sampi*' to represent 6, 90, and 900, respectively) (Burrton, 2011, p. 16). However, the Greek writing system was additive (not positional).

4   How Young Children Develop the Concept of Numbers

In this section we will examine how infants and pre-schoolers develop the concept of 'number' early in their lives. This includes the concepts of number sense, object counting, oral counting, and symbolization. As we will see, it develops along a progression that is similar to the historical process.

4.1   *Number Sense*

For many years, the term 'number sense' was a basic one in mathematics education. The first use of this term was by Dantzig (1954), who wrote,

> Man, even in the lower stages of development, possesses a faculty which, for want of better name, I shall call number sense. This faculty permits him to recognize that something has changed in a small collection when, without his direct knowledge, an object has been removed or added to the collection. (p. 1)

Many researchers have tried to define this term but without complete success (Sayers & Andrews, 2015; Berch, 2005; McIntosh, Reys, Reys, Bana, & Farrell, 1997). Whitacre, Henning, and Atabaş (2020) perused a sample of 140 research articles that focused on number sense and settled on three constructs for it: innate, early, and mature. As noted above, Dehaene (1997, 2011) has mentioned 'innate number sense', and has claimed that it is based on certain neurological abilities that are common to humans and even some animals, and that it involves perception and discrimination of magnitudes rather than explicit knowledge of number words or symbols. Other researchers (e.g., Jordan et al., 2006; Sayers & Andrews, 2015) consider 'early number sense' to include skills that are learned relatively early in life (which may be based upon innate abilities) such as counting. These skills are well-aligned with school mathematics, especially in the early childhood years (preschool to Grade 2).

Sayers and Andrews suggested three distinct but related stages of early number sense, which they labeled 'preverbal', 'foundational', and 'applied'. Preverbal number sense concerns those number insights innate to all humans and comprises an understanding of small quantities that allow for comparison. For example, young babies can discern 1:2 ratios but not 2:3 ratios (see also, Feigenson et al., 2004). Foundational number sense are understandings that precede applied number sense, typically forming during the first year of school and requiring instruction (see also, Ivrendi, 2011; Jordan & Levine, 2009). Applied number sense concerns those number competences related to arithmetical flexibility that prepare learners for an adult world (see also, McIntosh et al., 1992).

According to Whitacre and colleagues (2020), in addition to innate and early number senses, there is also a third stage that they term 'mature' number sense. This is described in terms of its components, which include conceptual structures and habits of mind, such as flexibility rather than skills (e.g., McIntosh et al., 1992; Reys & Yang, 1998). Furthermore, whereas early number sense is well aligned with school mathematics, mature number sense is often contrasted with school mathematics: students who competently perform computations using standard algorithms may not always exhibit mature number sense (Reys & Yang, 1998; Reys et al., 1999).

Since this chapter focuses on early childhood, we will focus on the innate and early number sense constructs. Thus, number sense includes the children's skills related to counting, recognizing number patterns, comparing numbers, and estimating (this follows Dyson et al., 2013). In 2009, Clements and Sarama noted that young children progress at different rates in the development of their number sense, and individual differences can be observed during these years. They further noted that early numerical development depends on four interrelated foundational skills: (a) subitizing, (b) using conventional number words to count in a constant order, (c) enumerating collections of objects, and (d) numbering (i.e., using cardinal numbers). Note that Yilmaz (2017) has claimed that children start to develop number sense well before they start school.

4.2 Object Counting: Counting Using Fingers

Researchers in mathematical education have addressed the terminologies used by young children for object counting. Geary (2006) attaches great importance to learning the culture of 'counting numbers' in connection with children's mathematical development. If a child knows the series of number words, then he can develop numerical representations for numbers greater than three or four (Gelman & Gallistel, 1978; Wynn, 1990). Armed with this knowledge, the child develops counting methods based on the ten fingers (Figure 1.4), similar to the methods noted above that are based on the body's organs. It is natural that children learn to count with the help of their ten fingers. Fayol and Seron (2005) observed that finger counting is considered to be a 'mediator' between an inner rough number sense and a developed, symbolically represented, number concept.

Children also use the 'bundle of sticks' method to count quantities, especially when using an abacus. In addition, when children begin to engage in two-digit and three-digit numbers, they use the position terminology method to describe the tens and the hundreds.

Gelman and Galistel (1978) described five principles of the object counting process that can be divided into 'how to count' and 'what to count' as listed below.

4.3 The Three Principles of "How" to Count

1. The one-to-one (bijective) correspondence principle: Linking words for numbers with the counted objects. In other words, labelling while pointing. This requires the ability to distinguish between what has already been counted and what has not yet been counted.

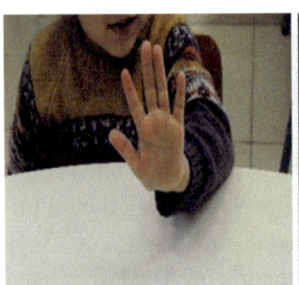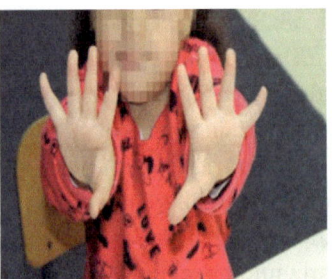

FIGURE 1.4   Examples of children using fingers to represent numbers

2. The stable-order principle: Each word occurs only once and always in the same place.
3. The cardinal principle: The last word voiced represents the quantity of the objects.

4.4 The Two Principles of 'What' to Count

1. The abstract principle: Any set of discrete objects can be counted, that is, understanding that it does not matter what you count because how you count remains the same. Indeed, even imaginary things can be counted.
2. The order-irrelevance principle: The order in which items are counted is irrelevant. It does not matter whether the counting procedure is carried out from left to right, from right to left, or from anywhere else, as long as every item in the collection is counted once and only once.

Some researchers in mathematical education (Baroody & Willkins, 1999; Fuson, 1988) have investigated the nature of the errors that children make when object counting. Typically, younger children point their fingers while counting. This serves two roles: to connect the number words to the actual objects and as a tool by which the child can physically separate the objects that have already been counted from those that have not. Fuson noted that in the early stages of counting, children frequently err with respect to this one-to-one correspondence principle, as they may have difficulty separating the objects already counted from those remaining (even if the objects are arranged in a single row). Typical errors are either to skip (one or more) objects or to count an object more than once. This object-pointing error indicates a lack of spatial coordination and not assigning one unique word for each object. Such errors are uncommon after the age of four. Also, older children can point without actually touching the objects (Wynn, 1992).

Studies have also shown that children who know how to properly count orally do not always understand its connection to object counting or how to use it for various purposes (Cowan, 1987; Fuson, 1988; Baroody et al., 1999; Wynn, 1992; Sarnecka & Carey, 2008; Negen & Sarnecka, 2015). For example, when asked to compare two groups of objects, some children, even though they can 'recite the numbers' well, cannot use this skill to answer the question 'which group has more objects?' For this purpose, they needed to use one-to-one correspondence between the groups.

4.5 Children's Concepts of Zero and Fractions

4.5.1 Zero

What about a child's development of the concept of 'zero'? Several researchers have investigated this and found that in the context of mathematical education, the concept of 'zero' is one of the hardest for a child to comprehend (Wheeler & Feghali, 1983; Wheeler, 1987; Carpenter, Franke, & Levi, 2002). Merritt and Brannon (2013) emphasized that the concept of 'zero' may present unique developmental and conceptual challenges for children because, unlike other integers, zero does not represent the *presence* of a specific quantity but rather the *absence* of a quantity.

Wellman and Miller (1986) suggest that there are three stages in a child's understanding of the symbol 'zero': (a) First, children learn to identify (and name) the symbol for zero without understanding the symbol's significance; (b) Second, children learn that zero represents 'none' or 'nothing'. However, they still do not understand that zero is a numerical value on the numerical continuum; (c) finally, children learn the relationship between zero and other numbers on the continuum. A study by Wellman et al. (1986) showed that the progress of this development is fairly slow: four-year-old children are usually not at the first stage, and only six-year-old children will have reached the final stage.

In another study, Hughes (1986) presented children between approximately three-and-a-half to almost eight years of age with paper and pencil and placed a quantity of bricks on a table. First, the children were asked to make a mark on the paper to represent the number of bricks they saw on the table. Next, the table was cleared of bricks and the children were asked to make a mark on the paper to show that there were no bricks. He found that *many* of the children responded to this task with a puzzled look, not understanding what they were supposed to do.

In another experiment (same study), Hughes gave each child (this time between the ages of approximately three to six) four identical tins, each containing a different number of bricks (3, 2, 1, or none) and asked them to pick out 'the tin with one/two/three/no bricks' and mark on a piece of paper something to show how many bricks were in the tin. For the first three tins, the children made three, two, or one mark, as required. In the case of the tin with no bricks, the most common action was to leave the paper blank (often with a comment such as 'I won't put any writing on it because there are no bricks in the tin'. A later study also found evidence that, for preschoolers, understanding zero was no harder than understanding positive integers (Bialystock & Codd, 2000).

Nevertheless, although children under the age of six can competently use the words from 'one' up to 'ten' (and frequently higher), the use of the word 'zero' comes only when they are almost seven, when they understand what it means to have 'nothing'. At this age, children will use and understand sentences such as 'I have no marbles left', 'I have nothing on my plate', and 'this box is empty'. It seems that this development echoes the development of humanity in terms of the word 'zero', which came later than the cardinal numbers.

Furthermore, it has been noted that children understand the use of zero as a placeholder only from the age of seven or above (Blake & Verhille, 1985), a concept that also developed later in human history.

4.5.2   Fractions

It is likely that the use of the term 'fraction' becomes legitimate in the child's world only when they begin to develop and understand the concept of 'dividing something up'. At about four years, children begin to understand the concept of dividing an apple into two or into four and it is only then that he or she begin to understand the meaning of equal division, which leads to the use of terms such as 'half' or 'quarter'.

Siegler, Fazio, Bailey, and Zhou (2013) have suggested that to be able to understand the development of fraction knowledge, one must understand the distinctions between conceptual and procedural knowledge and between non-symbolic and symbolic knowledge. *Conceptual knowledge* includes understanding the properties of fractions: magnitudes, principles, and notations; *procedural knowledge* involves fluency with the four arithmetic operations performed on fractions. *Non-symbolic knowledge* involves competence with concrete stimuli (e.g., which set has a higher proportion of blue dots); *symbolic knowledge* involves competence with conventional representations (which is greater, 2/3 or 4/9?). Since the non-symbolic and symbolic distinctions are more relevant to our discussion about early childhood, we will concentrate on these distinctions.

Non-symbolic understanding. McCrink and Wynn (2007) have indicated that infants possess a basic non-symbolic understanding of fractions. For example, when they presented six-month-old infants a picture with a 2:1 ratio of yellow to blue dots and then presented them with a picture with the dots in 4:1 ratio, they noticed that the infants were dishabituated after the switch. This suggests that the infants could discriminate between the two ratios. Goswami (1989, 1995) has suggested that by the age of three years, children can draw analogies between pairs of non-symbolic fractions (e.g., ½ of a square: ½ of a circle; 3/4 of a square: 3/4 of a circle). Furthermore, Spinillo and Bryant (1991, 1999) have suggested that older children will use '½' as a reference point when matching non-verbal representations of fractions. For example, when asked which of two partially filled rectangles represent 'a third', six- and seven-year-olds are more accurate when the two options are on opposite sides of ½. For example, when matching ⅜, participants are more accurate when the options presented represent ⅜ and ⅝ than when they represent ⅜ and ⅛.

Symbolic understanding. Symbolic understanding of fractions develops later than non-symbolic (Singer-Freeman & Goswami, 2001; Bialystock & Codd, 2000).

For example, four-years-olds will respond accurately when asked to give a doll half a cookie, but cannot do so for ¼ and 3/4 until age seven. Also, it is only at this age that children comprehend that sharing a quantity of objects with more people reduces the number of objects each person receives, regardless of the number of people or the size of the set (Wing & Beal, 2004).

4.6   Case Study

To complete the picture, we present here some observations from a study carried out by this author in which preschool children were given three separate tasks concerning numbers as concepts (understanding), as symbols (representing), and for object counting (which group has more). Two groups of preschool children (toddlers) participated: a younger group with six children aged 30–32 months and an older group of five children aged 32–38 months. In each group, the children came from a variety of socio-economic backgrounds.

Each child was asked to perform several tasks dealing with numbers up to three. First, they were provided with a selection of coloured beads and small toys and were asked to demonstrate 'one', 'two', or 'three' when they heard the appropriate word. For the second task, they were provided with paper and crayons and asked to 'put something appropriate on the paper' when they heard the words 'one', 'two', or 'three'. For the third task, they were given four blue beads and six red beads scattered on the table and were asked which kind of bead there were more of.

These tasks were chosen based on the universal development of the concept of the number and quantitative reasoning: first, names are assigned to the concept of specific quantities (which is actually quantitative reasoning), next comes representing the number words by some symbolic representation, and lastly comes the concept of having to compare groups (Hughes, 1986; Burton, 2011).

The analysis of the tasks was based on semiotic terminology, which is the study of signs, symbols, and signification (Berger, 2000, 2004). Semiotics is based on three constructs: (a) a 'sign', which anything used to communicate and is made up of a signifier and a signified, (b) the 'signifier', which is the *form* that the sign takes, and (c) the 'signified', which is the *concept* that the signifier represents. In the semiotic terminology introduced by Charles Sanders Peirce (Peirce, 1931, in Wiese, 2003), three kinds of signs are distinguished: symbolic, index, and icon. The link between symbolic signs and the object is established by convention (as in the case of human language or the abstract forms of numbers to represent quantity); index signs are related to the object by some physical or temporal relation (e.g., a skull to indicate 'poison'), and icons are signs that share some physical features with its referent (e.g., a photograph of an object to signify that object, a smiling emoticon to signify happiness) (Wiese, 2003).

4.7 *Task Number One: Demonstrating the Number Words*

Each child in turn was asked the following questions: *Can you show me 'one'? Please show me 'two'. Please show me 'three'.* The children were allowed to respond without any intervention or prompting whatsoever. In fact, the researchers insisted that the interviewers not give any input whatsoever and leave it up to the children themselves to decide what is being asked for.

4.7.1 Children's Responses

All the children (in both groups), without exception, used their fingers to indicate the number. Figures 1.5a, 1.5b, and 1.5c show children in the first group and Figures 1.5d, 1.5e, and 1.5f in the older group, for 'one', 'two', and 'three' respectively.

4.8 *Task One: Analysis, Commentary, and Discussion*

Look carefully at Figure 1.5a and note that two of the three children raised their index finger (the signifier) to express 'number one' (the signified), whereas the middle child used the index fingers of both hands close to one another. Figure 1.5d shows one child in the older group, who also used his index finger to

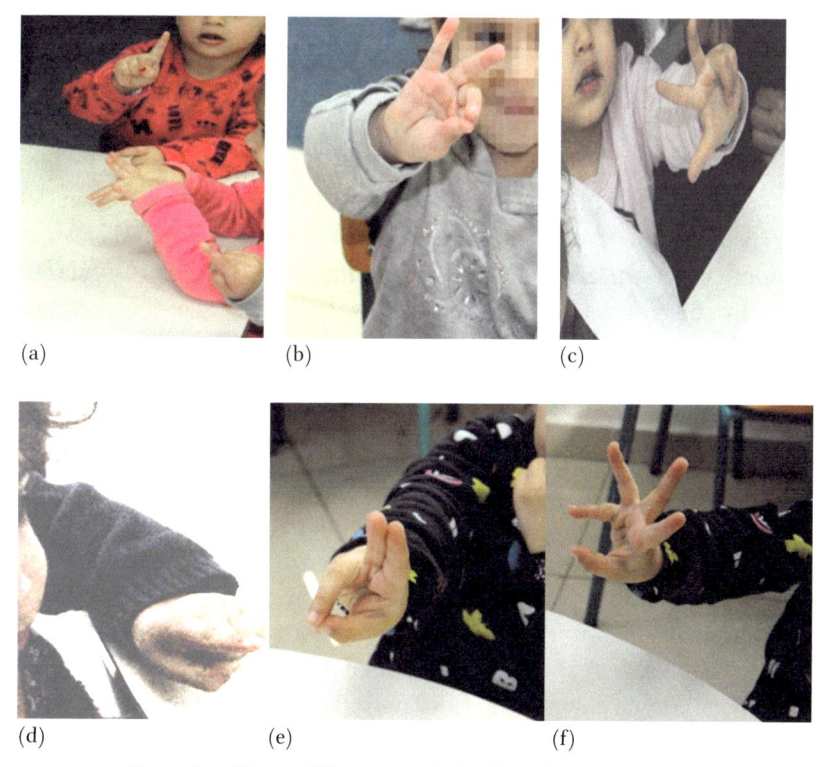

(a)   (b)   (c)

(d)   (e)   (f)

FIGURE 1.5   Examples of how toddlers responded to the Task 1

express 'number one'. Expressing 'number two' is shown in Figures 1.5b and 5e: the signifiers are two adjacent fingers. The younger child used her little and ring fingers while the older child used her index and middle fingers. Note that the older child has her fingers pressed together, while the younger one does not, perhaps because it is difficult for her to hold these two fingers tightly together. Figures 1.5c and 5f show the signifiers for 'three', which are three fingers: the younger child is holding up the thumb, index finger, and middle finger, while the older child is holding up the index, middle, and ring fingers. Again, we may note that not all children can hold the fingers tightly together. These children's responses may be classified as *symbolic*, because they were established by the convention of the human language.

To sum up, all the children used symbolic 'number patterns' to demonstrate the numbers 'one', 'two', and 'three' by lifting one, two, or three fingers, respectively. The literature talks about this attribute: Baroody and colleagues (1999), for example, pointed out that 'number patterns' are natural and powerful methods for representing numbers. In addition, Pixner, Kraut and Dresent (2017) have reported that counting skills are based on the use of the fingers. Di Luca and Pesenti (2011) have argued that finger numeral representations are symbolic (i.e., some conventional meaning shared with other individuals). On the other, toddlers will use fingers and gestures to communicate numerical and mathematical concepts prior to acquiring proficiency in speech production (Lee, Kotsopoulos, Tumber, & Makosz, 2014). Note that that Nishiyama (2013) has pointed out that '[c]ounting using the fingers differs according to region, ethnicity, and historical period'. This may explain the differences between the signifiers used for the same signified between the children in this task.

The number pattern method used by the children in this task is similar to how primitive men began expressing numbers: 'The evidence of finger-counting is so widespread that we are forced to conclude that it has been a universal practice' (Flegg, 1984, p. 14). In other words, the children's behaviour corresponds to the historical development of how numbers were represented by the fingers among different peoples.

4.9 Task Number Two: Graphical Representation of Number Words
The children were asked to put something on a piece of paper to *show* the number words 'one', 'two', and 'three' (in succession). Note that the children were not asked *to write/draw* the number but rather *to show the number* so as to offset any possibility that the child had been exposed to the term 'write' or 'draw' by their parents or any other third party. We presumed that if the child was asked to 'show' the numbers on the paper, it would let us understand his real behaviour.

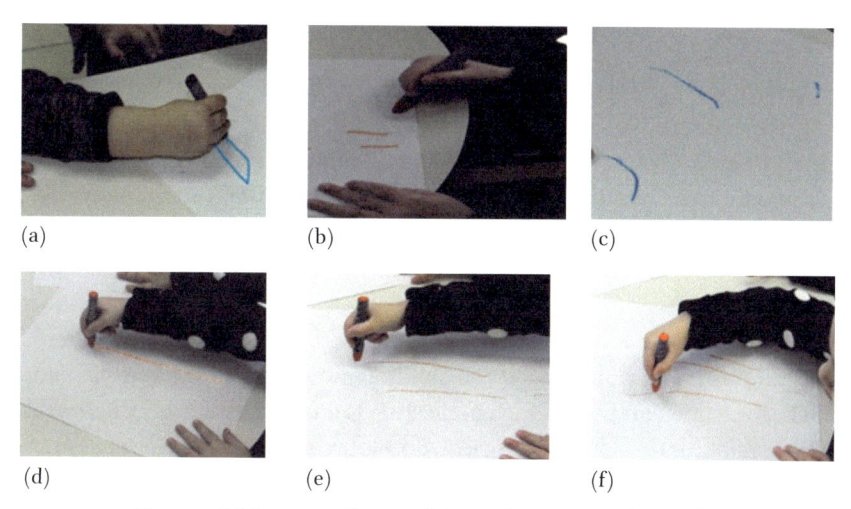

FIGURE 1.6   The way children up to the age of 38 months represent the numbers '1', '2', and '3' in writing

4.9.1   Children's Responses

Figures 1.6a, 1.6b, and 1.6c show examples of the responses of the younger children, and Figures 1.6d, 1.6e, and 1.6f the responses of the older group. As can be seen, all the children used marks (lines) to indicate the number they had heard. It is worth noting that the younger children were able to mark lines only for the number one and two; in the case of 'three', they made three marks which were not lines (Figure 1.6c).

4.10   *Task Two: Analysis, Commentary, and Discussion*

The children in both groups (except for one child in the younger group who drew three marks but no lines for 'three') produced exactly as many lines as the number word they heard. This response is an iconic one, as the sign shares some feature with its related referent, which is the number word. The response of the young child who drew three marks (not lines) is also an iconic response because he did draw three 'signs' when he heard the word 'three'.

These responses were similar to those obtained in Hughes's (1986) analysis of children's responses when they were asked to represent the quantities one, two, three, four, five, and six. In Hughes's experiment, the children were provided with paper and pencil, and a quantity of bricks was placed in the table in front of them. They were asked 'Can you put something on the paper to show how many bricks are on the table?' Hughes classified the children's responses into four types: idiosyncratic (inability to discover regularities in the child's representation for the number of presented objects); pictographic (the child tried to represent the number by representing the appearance of what was in front of them); iconic (the child used a discrete mark of his own to represent each brick); and symbolic (the child used conventional symbols such as '1', '2', etc., to represent the quantity of bricks).

Analysing the children's quantitative reasoning behaviour echoes the real-world model based on the universal triad of number word, number symbol, and quantity, each of which complements the other (Fuson, De La Cruz, Smith, Lo Cicero, Hudson, & Ron, 2000). In all instances, what the children showed (drew) was directly related to the word in that the number of lines drawn expressed the word (except in the case of 'three' for younger children).

It is interesting to note that all the children drew descending vertical lines, similar to the lines on the Ishango bone. This is another example of how children's development echoes historical development. This was also demonstrated in Hughes's (1986) study.

4.11   Task Three – Comparing Sets (Which Set Has More)

Four blue beads and six red beads were placed on the table, and each child in turn was asked whether there were more blue beads or more red beads.

4.11.1   Children's Responses

The younger group could not cope with the task at all. They started playing with the objects or talking about their colours or other aspects. They seemed not to comprehend the question at all.

In the older group, two children responded by attempting to count (although inaccurately) the items of each colour, two began to arrange the objects in two groups according to colour (one-to-one correspondence), and one child did not respond at all.

Figure 1.7 demonstrates one child's process of using one-to-one correspondence: she arranged the objects in parallel lines, first taking one red bead and matching it with a blue bead, then continuing with a second red bead and a second blue bead, and so on. Finally, she quietly said: 'There are more red beads'.

4.12   Task Three: Analysis, Commentary, and Discussion

In this task, the child depicted in Figure 1.7 arranged the blue beads in a row (Figure 1.7, steps 1–3). Focal analysis gives us a detailed picture of the child's communication/conversation on the level of its immediate mathematical content and makes it possible to assess the effectiveness of communication (Sfard & Kieran, 2001). It reveals that the child's intentions were mathematical in nature when she created the first group of blue beads so as to be able to use one-to-one correspondence to determine which group of beads had more.

Step 1   Step 2   Step 3

Step 4   Step 5   Step 6

FIGURE 1.7   Demonstration of how one three-year-old coped with task three

After arranging the set of blue beads, she matched a red bead to each, (Figure 1.7, steps 4 and 5), finally continuing to arrange the 'extra' red beads in their row.

The focal analysis of this utterance indicated that the child was creating the second group (red beads) at the same time she was building the one-to-one correspondence between the two groups, which ultimately led her to decide that there are more red beads. This child's *mental device*, which was precisely one-to-one correspondence, not only provided a means for comparing the groups but also allowed her to manipulate several numbers, even without knowing how to count or name the quantities involved. In this context, Ifrah (2000) claimed that '[a]t about fifteen or sixteen months, infants go beyond the stage of simple observation of their environment and become capable of grasping the principle of one-for-one [sic] correspondence, and in particular the property of mapping' (p. 10). Box and Scott (2004) wrote 'This correspondence [one-to-one correspondence] was used in many ways by primitive people ...'. Thus, the behaviour of the child depicted in Figure 1.7 is reminiscent of the method used by primitive man to check if all his sheep had returned from pasture, as described above.

It is interesting to observe that the two children who tried to answer the question by counting were unable to correctly solve the problem. There are two reasons for this. First, they did not count the objects properly: they skipped some items or used incorrect terms (a phenomenon supported by the literature, see Fuson, 1988). Second, even if they properly counted the items 'out loud', they did not understand the significance of their 'findings', another phenomenon observed in the literature (Cowan, 1987).

5   Comparing Universal and Early Childhood Numerical and Quantitative Thinking

Observing how the children dealt with the given tasks provides some insight into the question posed at the beginning of this chapter: 'Does the pattern of the development of the concept of number (and other mathematical concepts) in children echo its development throughout history (and prehistory) and, if so, can one learn about the one from the other and vice versa?'.

It seems that, yes, it can.

First, it must be noted that, throughout history, the development of the concept of number in various peoples or societies followed the exact same course. First was the pre-language stage, when man was occupied with identifying quantities, mainly small ones. Then came the post-language stage and the creation of words for the numbers (required when conducting a dialogue). This was followed by the development of symbols for the numbers when men had developed the ability to record (i.e., write).

It is interesting to note that 'primitive' man 'invented' number words when he felt the 'need' for it. Thus, we may claim that first came the invention of numbers and then all 'primitive men' in the same society 'learned' to use these numbers.

Similarly, a baby at first is inarticulate. However, infants even in the first few months of their lives can identify small quantities (Dahaene, 1997, p. 48). As they develop, they become aware of and are able to identify larger quantities. Around three years old, most children have already acquired language skills, and now these children can associate words and numbers. Some may have also learned to recite the numbers in order (having learned this from their surroundings in rhymes, etc. even before they actually comprehend the meaning of the words). Eventually, they all learn the meaning of the number words and begin to learn how to count items by matching the quantity to the appropriate word.

6   Continuing Forward

Although the progression of the development of number concepts (both through history and by individual age) was analysed in the previous section along a time axis, I will share with you another aspect of this issue based – once again – on the analogy between the fractal natures of humanity and the cauliflower. Thus, we can finally answer the original question set forth in this chapter: 'Is the universal historical development of numerical and quantitative thought similar to its development in a (normal) human being?'

First, Hughes (1986) did mention the idea of comparing the development of number concepts between children and their historical development:

> There are a number of fascinating parallels between the representations of young children and systems developed by various other cultures .... It seems that there are important similarities in the ways in which people in different situations cope with the problem of producing written representations of number and arithmetical operations. (p. 94)

Second, it would be logical to assume that one might also be able to find a similar parallel with respect to the development of mathematical concepts beyond the stages dealt with in this chapter, that is to say, the development of the numbers using the basic words and symbols, and then the development of more sophisticated concepts such as (besides zero and fractions) the arithmetic operations (addition and subtraction, followed by multiplication and division), and then, even later, more complicated concepts of numbers such as rational, irrational, negative, and complex numbers.

Likewise, the development of an individual's mathematical knowledge follows this progression. First, as we have discussed above, they acquire the concept of number, then the words for the numbers, then symbols for the words. The first symbols are simple marks to illustrate the number. Later, at the age of six or seven, children begin to use the conventional abstract symbols common to their culture and to count based on the decimal system (Baroody et al., 1999; Fuson et al., 2000). At a relatively young age, children also develop an arithmetic sense of addition and subtraction of small quantities (Gellman et al., 1978), and subsequently the concepts of multiplication and division (for example, dividing an apple into parts). As children progress, they further develop the basic arithmetic operations and build for themselves schemas, which help them learn algorithms for performing the arithmetic operations with numbers of more than one digit. Adolescents are exposed to more advanced concepts – negative numbers, rational and irrational numbers – and a small portion (usually advanced pupils) continue on to the more advanced concepts such as complex numbers.

In conclusion, the fractal example represented by the cauliflower and its analogy to humanity underscores that if we take a closer and closer look at universal numerical and quantitative development (overall population, culture, people, family, person ...), we will see the same order of development repeating itself every time on a different scale.

In view of the above, it is possible to conclude that numerical and quantitative reasoning among young children is a miniature version of numerical and quantitative reasoning of a particular culture, as it is a miniature version of the development of quantitative and numerical thinking over history. Conversely, universal quantitative reasoning is a magnified version of the child's quantitative and numerical thinking.

Notes

1   The Pirahã are the descendants of the Mura family, who formerly ruled over considerable parts of the Amazon.
2   一, 二, 三, 四, 五, 六, 七, 八, 九, 十.
3   שלוש ,.... שניים, אחד. Note that Hebrew is written from right to left.
4   'واحد، اثنان، ثلاثة، .... تسعة، عشرة'. Note that Arabic is written from right to left.
5   Formal Arabic is an academic and literary language and is the same in all Arab countries; spoken Arabic is colloquial with a variety of accents depending on country.
6   Nataraj and Thomas (2009) claim that the source of the word 'eleven' comes from expression 'ein lifon' which means 'one left over' while the number 'twelve' comes from 'twe lif', meaning 'two left over'.
7   French 11–19: *onze, douze, treize, quatorze, quinze, seize, dix-sept, dix-huit, dix-neuf.* Italian 11–19: *undici, dodici, tredici, quattordici, quindici, sedici, diciassette, diciotto, diciannove.*
8   Another problem for learners, as it is 'forty' and not 'fourty', compared with four, and fourteen.
9   As in English, twenty, vingt, is in a different form.
10 It is interesting that in contrast to many other words that are similar in Arabic and Hebrew, the terms for 'o' are not. In Hebrew, '*efes*' is based on words mentioned in the Bible that mean 'only' or 'nothing'.
11 Hopper also presents two other explanations, but they are not relevant to this current chapter.

References

Agrillo, C., Dadda, M., Serena, G., & Bisazza, A. (2008). Do fish count? Spontaneous discrimination of quantity in female mosquitofish. *Animal Cognition, 11*(3), 495–503. doi:10.1007/s10071-008-0140-9

Agrillo, C., Dadda, M., Serena, G., & Bisazza, A. (2009). Use of number by fish. *PLOS ONE, 4*(3), e4786. doi:10.1371/journal.pone.0004786

Baroody, A. J., & Wilkins, J. L. M. (1999). The development of informal counting, number, and arithmetic skills and concepts. In J. V. Copley (Ed.), *Mathematics in the early years* (pp. 48–65). National Association for the Education of Young Children.

Berch, D. (2005). Making sense of number sense. *Journal of Learning Disabilities, 38*(4), 333–339.

Berger, A. A. (2000). Semiotic analysis. In A. A. Berger (Ed.), *Media and communication research methods* (pp. 35–51). Sage.

Berger, A. A. (2004). Semiotic analysis. *Media Analysis Techniques, 3*, 3–42.

Bialystock, E., & Codd, J. (2000). Representing quantity beyond whole numbers: Some, none and part. *Canadian Journal of Experimental Psychology, 54*, 117–128.

Blake, B. J. (1981). *Australian Aboriginal languages.* Angus and Robertson.

Blake, R., & Verhille, C. (1985). The story of o. *For the Learning of Mathematics, 5*(3), 33–47.

Boucenna, A. (2013). *Origin of the numerals: Zero concept.* Department of Physics, Faculty of Sciences, Ferhat Abbas University, Sétif, Algeria. Retrieved December 18, 2018, from https://arxiv.org/ftp/arxiv/papers/0707/0707.3579.pdf

Box, K., & Scott, P. (2004). Early concepts of number and counting. *Australian Mathematics Teacher, 60*(4), 2–6.

Boyer, C. B. (1994). Zero: The symbol, the concept, the number. *National Mathematics Magazine, 18*(8), 323–330.

Brandenstein, C. G. Von. (1970). What next in Aboriginal Australian linguistics? *The Etruscan, 19*, 11–15.

Burton, D. M. (2011). *The history of mathematics: An introduction* (7th ed., International ed.). McGraw-Hill.

Carpenter, T., Franke, M., & Levi, L. (2002). *Thinking mathematically: Integrating arithmetic and algebra in elementary school.* Heinemann.

Clements, D. H., & Sarama J. (2009). *Learning and teaching early math: The learning trajectories approach.* Routledge.

Cowan, R. (1987). When do children trust counting as a basis for relative number Judgments? *Journal of Experimental Child Psychology, 43*, 328–345.

Dantzig, T. (1954). *Number: The language of science.* MacMillan.

Dehaene, S. (1997). *The number sense: How the mind creates mathematics* (1st ed.). Oxford University Press.

Dehaene, S. (2011). *The number sense: How the mind creates mathematics.* Oxford University Press. (Original work published 1997)

Di Luca, S., & Pesenti, M. (2011). Finger numeral representations: more than just another symbolic code. *Frontiers in Psychology, 2*(272), 272. doi:10.3389/fpsyg.2011.00272

Dixon, R. M. W. (1980). *The languages of Australia.* Cambridge University Press.

Dyson, N., Jordan, N. C., Beliakoff, A., & Hassinger-Das, B. (2015). A kindergarten number-sense intervention with contrasting practice conditions for low-achieving children. *Journal for Research in Mathematics Education, 46*(3), 331–370.

Dyson, N. I., Jordan, N. C., & Glutting, J. (2013). A number sense intervention for low-income kindergartners at risk for mathematics difficulties. *Journal of Learning Disabilities, 46*, 166–181. doi:10.1177/0022219411410233

Everett, D. L. (2005). Cultural constraints on grammar and cognition in Pirahã. *Current Anthropology, 46*(4), 621–646.

Fayol, M., & Seron, X. (2005). About numerical representations: insights from neuropsychological, experimental and developmental studies. In J. I. D. Campbell (Ed.), *Handbook of Mathematical Cognition*. Psychology Press.

Feigenson, L., Dehaene, S., & Spelke, E. (2004). Core systems of number. *Trends in Cognitive Sciences, 8*(7), 307–314.

Flegg, G. (1984). *Numbers: Their history and meaning*. Penguin Books Ltd.

Forouharfar, A. (2020). The anatomy and ontology of organizational power as a fractal metaphor: A philosophical approach. *Cogent Business & Management, 7*, 1. doi:10.1080/23311975.2020.1728072

Fuson, K. C. (1988). *Children's counting and concepts of numbers*. Springer-Verlag.

Fuson, K. C., De La Cruz, Y., Smith, S. T., Lo Cicero, A., Hudson, K., & Ron, P. (2000). Blending the best of the 20th century to achieve a mathematics equity pedagogy in the 21st century. In M. Burke & F. R. Curcio (Ed.), *Learning mathematics for a new century*. National Council of Teachers of Mathematics.

Gallistel, C. R., & Gelman, R. (1992). Preverbal and verbal counting and computation. *Cognition, 44*, 43–74.

Geary, D. C. (2006). Development of Mathematical understanding. In D. Kuhn, R. S. Siegler, W. Damon, & R. M. Lerner (Eds.), *Handbook of child psychology: Cognition, perception, and language* (pp. 777–810). John Wiley & Sons, Inc.

Gelman, R., & Gallistel, C. R. (1978). *The child's understanding of number*. Harvard University Press.

Goswami, U. (1989). Relational complexity and the development of analogical reasoning. *Cognitive Development, 4*, 251–268 29.

Goswami, U. (1995). Transitive relational mappings in three- and four-year-olds: the analogy of Goldilocks and the Three Bears. *Child Development, 66*, 877–892.

Haddon, A. C. (1890). The ethnography of the western tribes of Torres Straits. *Journal of the Anthropological Institute of Great Britain and Ireland, 19*, 297–437.

Harris, J. (1987). Australian Aboriginal and Islander mathematics. *Australian Aboriginal Studies, 2*, 29–37.

Hooper, A. (1945). *The river mathematics*. Holt.

Hughes, M. (1986). *Children and numbers: Difficulties in learning mathematics*. Blackwell Publishing.

Ifrah, G. (2000). *The universal history of numbers*. John Wiley & Sons, Inc.

Ivrendi, A. (2011). Influence of self-regulation on the development of children's number sense. *Early Childhood Education Journal, 39*(4), 239–247.

Izard, V., Streri, A., & Spelke, E. S. (2014). Toward exact number: Young children use one-to-one correspondence to measure set identity but not numerical equality. *Cognitive Psychology, 72*, 27–53.

Jordan, N. C., Kaplan, D., Olah, L. N., & Locuniak, M. N. (2006). Number sense growth in kindergarten: A longitudinal investigation of children at risk for mathematics difficulties. *Child Development, 77*(1), 153–175. doi:10.1111/j. 1467-8624.2006.00862.x

Jordan, N. C., & Levine, S. (2009). Socioeconomic variation, number competence, and mathematics learning difficulties in young children. *Developmental Disabilities Research Reviews, 15*(1), 60–68.

Lee, J., Kotsopoulos, D., Tumber, A., & Makosz, S. (2014). Gesturing about number sense. *Journal of Early Childhood Research, 13*(3), 263–279. doi:10.1177/1476718X13510914

Lema, J., & Petty, K. (2018). Developing number sense and counting skills in prekindergarten. *Texas Child Care Quarterly, 42*(2).

Marmasse, N., Bletsas, A., & Marti, S. (2000). *Numerical mechanisms and children's concept of numbers*. Retrieved November 15, 2018, from http://alumni.media.mit.edu/~stefanm/society/som_final.html

McCrink, K., & Wynn, K. (2007). Ratio abstraction by 6-month-old infants. *Psychological Science, 18*, 740–745.

McGuire, P., Kinzie, M., & Berch, D. (2012). Developing number sense in pre-k with five frames. *Early Childhood Education Journal, 40*(4), 213–222. doi:10.1007/s10643-011-0479-4

McIntosh, A., Reys, B., & Reys, R. (1992). A proposed framework for examining basic number sense. *For the Learning of Mathematics, 12*(3), 2–8.

Musa, A. (2014). Origin of modern mathematical numeral – 0, 1, 2, 3, 4, 5, 6, 7, 8, 9: The Hindu-Indian-Brahmagubta, the Islamo-Arabic or the West? *Research & Reviews: Discrete Mathematical Structures, 1*(2), 36–55.

Nataraj, M. S., & Thomas, M. O. J. (2009). Developing understanding of number system structure from the history of mathematics. *Mathematics Education Research Journal, 21*(2), 96–115.

Negen, J., & Sarnecka, B. W. (2015). Is there really a link between exact-number knowledge and approximate number system acuity in young children? *British Journal of Developmental Psychology, 33*, 92–105. doi:10.1111/bjdp.12071

Nishiyama, Y. (2013). Counting with the fingers. *International Journal of Pure and Applied Mathematics, 85*(5), 859–868.

Peirce, C. S. (1931). Collected papers. In C. Hartshorne & P. Weiss (Eds), *Vol. II (Elements of logic), Ch. 2 ('Division of signs')*. Harvard University Press.

Pixner, S., Kraut, C., & Dresen, V. (2017). Early predictors for basic numerical and magnitude competencies in preschool children – are they the same or different regarding specific subgroups? *Psychology, 8*, 271–286. doi:10.4236/psych.2017.82016

Reys, R. E., Reys, B., McIntosh, A., Emanuelsson, G., Johansson, B., & Yang, D. C. (1999). Assessing number sense of students in Australia, Sweden, Taiwan, and the United States. *School Science and Mathematics, 99*(2), 61–70. doi:10.1111/j.1949-8594.1999.tb17449.x

Reys, R. E., & Yang, D. (1998). Relationship between computational performance and number sense among sixth- and eighth-grade students in Taiwan. *Journal for Research in Mathematics Education, 29*(2), 225–237. doi:10.2307/749900

Rips, L. J., Asmuth, J., & Bloomfield, A. (2008). Do children learn the integers by induction? *Cognition, 106*, 940–951.

Rips, L. J., Bloomfield, A., & Asmuth, J. (2008). From numerical concepts to concepts of number. *Behavioral and Brain Sciences, 31*(6), 632–642.

Rosenhouse, J. (2017). Fractals as a metaphor in dialectology. *International Journal of Design & Nature and Ecodynamics, 12*(3), 385–395.

Sarnecka, B. W., & Carey, S. (2008). How counting represents number: What children must learn and when they learn it. *Cognition, 108*, 662–674. doi:10.1016/j.cognition.2008.05.007

Saxe, G. B. (1982). The development of measurement operations among the Oksapmin of Papua New Guinea. *Child Development, 53*, 1242–1248.

Saxe, G. B., & Esmonde, I. (2004). Making change in Oksapmin trade stores: A study of shifting practices of quantification under conditions of rapid shift towards a cash economy. *South Pacific 9999*.

Sayers, J., & Andrews, P. (2015). Foundational number sense: Summarising the development of an analytical framework. In *CERME 9-Ninth Congress of the European Society for Research in Mathematics Education, Prague, Czech Republic, February 2015* (pp. 361–367).

Sfard, A., & Kieran, C. (2001). Cognition as communication: rethinking learning-by-talking through multifaceted analysis of students' mathematical interactions. *Mind, Culture, and Activity, 8*(1), 42–76. doi:10.1207/S15327884MCA0801_04

Siegler, R. S., Fazio, L. K., Bailey, D. H., & Zhou, X. (2013). Fractions: The new frontier for theories of numerical development. *Trends in Cognitive Sciences, 17*(1), 13–19.

Singer-Freeman, K. E., & Goswami, U. (2001). Does half a pizza equal half a box of chocolates? Proportional matching in an analogy task. *Cognitive Development, 16*, 811–829. doi:10.1016/S0885-2014(01)00066-1

Smith, D. E., & Ginsburg, J. (1971). *Numbers and numerals* (9th ed.). USA National Council of Teachers of Mathematics.

Spinillo, A. G., & Bryant, P. E. (1991). Children's proportional judgments: The importance of 'half'. *Child Development, 62*, 427–440.

Spinillo, A. G., & Bryant, P. E. (1999). Proportional reasoning in young children: Part-part comparisons about continuous and discontinuous quantity. *Mathematical Cognition, 5*, 181–197.

Starkey, P., Spelke, E. S., & Gelman, R. (1983). Detection of intermodal numerical correspondences by human infants. *Science, 222*, 179–181.

Sýkorová, I. (2010). Fractions in ancient Indian mathematics. In J. Safrankova & J. Pavlu (Eds.), *WDS'10 proceedings of contributed papers, Part 1* (pp. 133–138). Matfyz Press.

Wheeler, M. (1987). Children's understanding of zero and infinity. *Arithmetic Teacher, 35*(5), 42–44.

Wheeler, M. M., & Feghali, I. (1983). Much ado about nothing: Preservice Elementary school teachers' concept of zero. *Journal for Research in Mathematics Education, 14*(3), 147–155.

Whitacre, I., Henning, B., & Atabaş, Ş. (2020). Disentangling the research literature on number sense: Three constructs, one name. *Review of Educational Research, 90*(1), 95–134.

Wiese, H. (2003). Iconic and non-iconic stages in number development: The role of language. *Trends in Cognitive Sciences, 7*(9), 385–390.

Wing, R. E., & Beal, C. R. (2004). Young children's judgments about the relative size of shared portions: the role of material type. *Mathematical Thinking and Learning, 6*, 1–14.

Wynn, K. (1990). Children's understanding of counting. *Cognition, 36*, 155–193.

Wynn, K. (1992). Children's acquisition of the number words and the counting system. *Cognitive Psychology, 24*, 220–251. https://doi.org/10.1016/0010-0285(92)90008-P

Yilmaz, Z. (2017). Young children's number sense development: Age related complexity across cases of three children. *International Electronic Journal of Elementary Education, 9*(4), 891–902.

Young Children's Metacognitive Processes in a Variety of Challenging Number Tasks

Ana Clara Ventura, Flavia Santamaria and Nora Scheuer

Abstract

Based on a fluid approach to metacognition in real-time situations, young children's communication and regulation of their own numerical cognition was investigated. Sixty school children (20 in each of the following years: K4, K5 and Y1) participated in an individual interview which integrated a variety of multimodal number tasks with open-ended questions and requirements. A situated, in-depth qualitative analysis of childrens' verbal, gestural and graphic participation and productions was conducted. Results firstly provide a fine-grained repertoire of numerical metacognitive processes: fifteen indicators regard communicating the own number activity, and other fifteen regard regulating it. Next, results delve into the dynamics of those multiple metacognitive processes in the domain of number, in terms of four statements. We state that: (i) children deployed metacognitive processes both when they exhibited conventional number knowledge and when they displayed partial or idiosyncratic approximations; (ii) the metacognitive processes deployed varied across number tasks that entail different affordances and challenges; (iii) communication and regulation of the own cognitive activity were intertwined; and (iv) prospective, ongoing and retrospective temporal frames formed a continuous flow. The dynamics captured by each statement is illustrated with excerpts from children's interviews. These findings may contribute to teachers', administrators' and researchers' understanding of early number development as a reflective and self-regulated process and, hopefully, may highlight the importance of promoting young learners' agency in mathematics learning.

Keywords

fluid approach – repertoire – communication – regulation – dialogical interview

1 Introduction

This chapter is devoted to flesh out the view of young children as agentive and reflective learners of mathematics. Previous studies analysing four- to seven-year-old school children's numerical thinking and communication show that by the time children begin to explore and use numbers, they also display related metacognitive processes (Santamaria, 2015; Scheuer, de la Cruz & Iparraguirre, 2010; Scheuer & Germano, 2005; Siegler, 2005). For instance, they set their own goals and manage strategies to attain them, express awareness of their own achievements and difficulties, identify sources of support, and recognize origins, limitations and changes of their emerging number knowledge.

However, the view of early number learning as an agentive and reflective process is in striking contrast with the ways in which school mathematics are pervasively taught in many schools around the world. There is a remarkable lack of fit between school practices and children's tendency to actively construct their learning. It seems that Sophian's warning (1992, p. 34) is still in force:

> We need to be sensitive to the danger of unintentionally teaching children to give up sense-making when it comes to school mathematics, to view it as a world of its own (…). Children are likely to be deterred from trying to make sense of school mathematics when activities are presented without any explanation of their purpose, when lessons consist of a rapid succession of unrelated activities, and when the emphasis in the classroom is on getting work done quickly rather than on reflection.

As long as school mathematics continues to be experienced as a world of its own, students faced with mathematical tasks may not be able to anticipate lines of action or estimate reasonable results, not to say devise and explore creative solutions, monitor their actions on task with respect to a meaningful plan, and assess their outcomes. Paradoxically, these kinds of exploratory and metacognitive processes are at the very heart of mathematical thinking (Schoenfeld, 1992).

The enhancement of metacognitive processes from the beginning of early school years requires thorough knowledge about the ways in which such processes intervene in young children's numerical thinking and communication. Our study deals precisely with this issue, by contributing with a fine-grained picture of young children's metacognitive processes in a variety of challenging number tasks.

The plan of the chapter is as follows: a review of number development in the first years of life, and a justification of the argument that this development entails a metacognitive stance. Next, a review of the field of metacognitive studies which establishes conceptual and methodological contrasts between the "componential" and "fluid" research programs. This study adopts a fluid approach, developed in order to integrate the interplay between two main functions of metacognition (communication and regulation), and among its temporal frames of reference (ongoing, retrospective and prospective). The qualitative study presented next intended to underscore the multiple metacognitive processes young children can deploy when they think and communicate numerically. This allowed for the construction of a repertoire of metacognitive processes evidenced by children as they performed diverse multimodal numerical activities. The analysis of the way this repertoire operates at an intra-individual level is presented. This leads to the proposal of four statements about the deployment of such metacognitive processes, illustrated with excerpts from children's interviews. Finally, the findings of this study are summarized, limitations are pointed out, and educational implications are drawn.

1.1   *Number Development in the First Years of Life*

Since 1980, laboratory studies (Starkey & Cooper, 1980) have provided growing evidence that well before babies are able to manipulate objects, produce intentional gestures or articulate verbal speech, they react in systematic ways to certain variations in the quantity of items in visual collections or auditory sequences (for reviews, see Leibovich, Katzin, Harel & Henik, 2017; Rodríguez & Scheuer, 2015). But, what is it that enables the young child to go beyond the set of fixed reactions to quantity that operates shortly after birth, in order to become numerate? Numeracy is anchored in children's bodily experience, action with objects, and reflective abstraction (Piaget & Szeminska, 1941), all of them mediated by socio-cultural processes (Nunes & Bryant, 1996). Children's immersion in number practices, or number enculturation (Bishop, 1991), is supported by more knowledgeable others, who pay attention to number properties, segment and itemize entities, engage in numerical goals, carry out numerical procedures and use number signs, guide and encourage children in taking part in this kind of activities.

Studies of young children's number related activity in natural contexts (Cavalcante & Rodríguez, 2015; Droz, 1992; Mix, Huttenlocher & Cohen Levine, 2002; Scheuer & Sinclair, 2009; Sinclair, 2005) have shown that between the ages of two and three years old, children begin to use gestures and number words to enumerate items (be them objects, events, actions, or movements), designate the cardinality of small sets, comment on quantitative differences between two or more sets or even keep track of changes in the size of a set.

The model of early number development elaborated by Saxe, Guberman and Gearhart (1987) explains these different achievements in terms of the interplay between numerical functions and numerical forms, at both the social and the individual levels. Functions are the socially set goals for number practices (i.e., enumeration, quantification, number comparison and arithmetical operations). Numerical forms are the semiotic systems and procedures that are carried out in order to attain such goals. Numerical forms displayed in the first five or six years of life include: one-to-one correspondence among pointing gestures and objects; diverse counting procedures supported by parts of the body, speech and tallies; finger patterns to convey quantity; number words and written number signs, or numerals, as those composing the base-10 hindu arabic system (see Ifrah, 1998).

This picture of numeracy underscores that semiosis is at the core of number knowledge and development – as philosophers, mathematicians, anthropologists, linguists and psychologists have repeatedly highlighted. For instance, Hurford (1987) has stated: "Without language, no numeracy" (p. 305), meaning that by virtue of (verbal) semiotic systems human cultures have become able to represent the cardinality of collections beyond the limit of subitization which supports the understanding of number structure. Based on a multimodal approach to representation and communication (Kress, 2010), the above statement should be expanded to include gestures with different parts of the body, particularly fingers (Fuson, 1992; Scheuer & Sinclair, 2009; Teubal & Dockrell, 2005), objects and artifacts, graphic marks such as tallies or icons, and structured notations, all of which pervade number practices in everyday and academic environments.

Numeracy is sociocultural not only because its progress depends on social interaction, semiotic systems and cultural practices, but also because it is experienced by children as a way of participating in a shared culture (Scheuer, de la Cruz & Iparraguirre, 2010; Teubal & Guberman, 2014). In this process, children become emotionally engaged (Droz, 1992) and make deliberate efforts to understand the signs and practices that make part of their world (Tolchinsky, 2003). The understandings attained in the course of their numerical sense-making does not necessarily match conventional knowledge. However, even non-canonical behaviours and understandings are part of the sense-making process, allowing children to establish new connections, become aware of convergences and contradictions, explore new solutions and push forward their intuitions and strategies. Moreover, children recurrently revise and refine their comprehension and strategies, seeking further levels of canonicity, coherence, accuracy and autonomy (Brizuela, 2004; Dockrell & Teubal, 2007; Santamaria, 2015; Tolchinsky, 2003).

As young children attempt to appropriate the number domain, they develop certain awareness of their cognitive activity, thus becoming increasingly able to regulate their attempts, procedures and outcomes. Many studies have shown the relationships between conceptual and procedural knowledge in several strands of numerical activity. The strategies children implement to count objects tell us a lot about their understanding of cardinality. For instance, if not enough care is taken to count each object once, the resulting number value may not lead to the correct cardinality. It is particularly informative to ask children to count a collection, add further elements and then repeat the question "How many there are now?" Kindergartners frequently count-all the objects from one. However, counting-on from the first added object suggests they have grasped that larger cardinalities include smaller ones.

Similarly, young children's notational strategies to record numbers and quantities on paper (Dockrell & Teubal, 2007; Hughes, 1986) and to solve additive problems (Baroody, 1987; Siegler, 2005) have been studied as a window to children's efforts to appropriate and organise the number system. Overall, these studies show that by the time they enter Kindergarten, children may use varied strategies to solve problems involving quantification and addition – whether in the oral mode, using objects, fingers, pencil and paper, or combining these different semiotic means. Some children can even comment on the requirements and relative usefulness of particular strategies. Thus, children's deployment of strategies on task gives clues not only of their conceptual understanding, but also of their metacognition. In addition, as children become immersed in number practices and knowledge at home and school, they also become aware of the origins and variations in their knowledge (Scheuer, de la Cruz & Iparraguirre, 2010). This awareness shapes the goals children set for themselves, as well as the means to achieve them.

1.2   *Metacognition in Early Cognitive Development: From a Componential towards a Fluid Research Program*

Nowadays, the field of metacognition lacks a unified theoretical framework that encompasses the different research programs and associated terms such as monitoring, control, regulation, cognition, motivation, behavior, and knowledge (Reder, 1996). The most common definition of metacognition is "cognition about cognition" or "thinking about thinking" (Veenman, Van Hout-Wolters & Afflerbach, 2006).

According to the influential research program, which we term "componential" here, metacognition includes three components: (i) *metacognitive knowledge*, (ii) *metacognitive regulation* and (iii) *metacognitive experiences* (Flavell, 1979).

Metacognitive knowledge refers to what people know about cognition. This strand includes knowledge or beliefs about one's own and other people's cognition, about cognitive tasks and strategies. Metacognitive knowledge stands on the understanding that people (including oneself) have a mind storing knowledge and memories that can be retrieved, extended and modified. According to a *copy* theory of mind, usual among Kindergartners, mental contents are generated and modified due to exposure to external information. Instead, an *interpretive* theory of mind, prevalent in middle childhood, underscores personal agency and reflection in knowledge acquisition, growth and change (Weimer, Dowds, Fabricius, Schwanenflugel & Woon Suh, 2017; Wellman, 1990).

In addition, metacognitive knowledge referring specifically to one's own cognition reminds us of aspects of Dienes & Perner's (1999) model of knowledge explicitation. Namely, the explicitation on the part of the knower of his[1] own attitudes and self. Explicitation of attitude entails awareness of the relationship one establishes with an object of knowledge. Typically, explicitation of attitude is evidenced through the use of mental verbs (i.e., "I know that x is a fact"). Instead, self as knower is made explicit when the person represents in speech (or another semiotic mode) autobiographical continuities and/or changes regarding herself as knower.

Metacognitive regulation includes verbalizations and behaviours related to planning, monitoring, control and evaluation of cognition and its products (Whitebread et al., 2009). In recent years, efforts have been made to include emotional regulation related to learning and problem-solving. Last, *metacognitive experiences* accompany and pertain to cognitive activities (Flavell, 1979), including metacognitive feelings and judgements (Efklides, 2008).

According to this research program, the three components are linearly connected, so that "a necessary prerequisite for choosing a strategy is basic metacognitive knowledge about which learning strategies are beneficial for long-term memory" (McCabe, 2011, p. 462). In this sense, metacognitive knowledge is considered as the acquisition of mental states, conceived of in a rather fixed way, while metacognitive experiences and regulation are considered as processes. Metacognitive regulation is seen as unfolding sequentially (Cleary, Callan & Zimmerman, 2012) or cyclically (Zimmerman, 2002) along prospective, ongoing and retrospective temporal frames. That is, as if metacognitive regulation events typically began by planning, continued by monitoring and control, and ended with assessment.

From a methodological perspective, this relationship has been investigated predominantly through correlational analysis (as pointed out by Kuvalja, Verma & Whitebread, 2014). On such basis, some studies suggest that the three components of metacognition may develop at different ages. For example, metacognitive regulation would emerge around 8 to 10 years of age, and expand during the years thereafter (Berk, 2003; Veenman & Spaans, 2005; Veenman, Wilhelm & Beishuizen, 2004). Moreover, certain metacognitive regulation processes, such as monitoring and evaluation, appear to develop later on than others such as planning (Veenman, Van Hout-Wolters & Afflerbach, 2006).

A contrasting research program, which we term "fluid" approach, considers that the relation among metacognitive knowledge, regulation and experiences takes place in real-time situations, that is, that these kinds of processes are deployed in a continuous temporal flow (Molenaar, 2014) and interact with each other during cognitive activities. For example, Johnson, Azevedo & D'Mello (2011) showed that planning activities occur frequently in advanced moments of a learning task. There is great variation of the degree to which the different metacognitive processes at play are explicit (both from the standpoints of the learner and of the researcher), accurate and effective regarding the transformation of the course of cognitive activity. According to this program, efforts to support children's metacognitive development in context must consider research methods capable of capturing adequate variability in the phenomena under study and account for child-environment interdependencies (Kuvalja, Verma & Whitebread, 2014; McClelland, Geldhof, Cameron & Wanless, 2015). Working in this direction, Whitebread and colleagues (Bryce, Whitebread & Szűcs, 2015; Whitebread et al., 2009) have shown that 4- and 5-year-old children may reveal forms of monitoring and control when the task is appropriate to their interests and understandings.

We take Pramling's studies on "content-and-context-dependent" metacognition (1983) as an original contribution to the fluid approach. According to Pramling, as children learn something, they also become aware of *what* and *how* they learn it. Three main ways of conceiving of learning have been identified among 3- to 8-year-old children: learning as being capable of doing, as knowing, and as understanding. In order to understand a phenomenon, children must become aware of certain features of its learning. Conversely, developing learning awareness enables a more developed understanding of the object of knowledge. These studies, carried out in educational settings, show that children's situated metacognition can be fostered by facilitating first-person experience, reflection and dialogue with peers and teachers, regarding content of knowledge as well as ways of knowing.

1.3   *A Fluid Approach of Metacognitive Processes: Interplay of Functional and Temporal Dimensions*

We consider that the fluid approach captures dynamism, the property that defines the ontology of processes (Whitehead, 1978) more appropriately than what is achieved when processes are set apart into disjoint – albeit interconnected – components. In addition, this approach allows to view metacognitive knowledge, such as metacognitive comments (Whitebread et al., 2009) and explicitation of the own knowledge attitudes and self (Dienes & Perner, 1999), in terms of emerging activity. Further grounding for a genuinely dynamical understanding of metacognition can be found in contributions of *multimodality* (Kress, 2010), the *resources-based* perspective to cognition (Hammer, Elby, Scherr & Redish, 2005) and the *commognitive* framework (Sfard, 2008), all of them proposing that cognition and communication are interrelated activities consisting in shaping and reshaping meaning, rather than in accessing previously stored representations or skills. Even if these contributions have not directed their attention specifically to mathematics in early childhood, they allow to put forward that the interplay between communication and thought is fostered in this area when children engage in cognitive tasks that combine familiarity, meaningful purposes and assistance in open-ended multimodal endeavours where the level of difficulty can be calibrated by the learner (Carr, Peters & Young-Loveridge, 1994).

A graphic representation of metacognition as a fluid process is presented in Figure 2.1 by means of a bidimensional loop. Its vertical dimension accounts for the interaction between the two main functions of metacognition: *communication* and *regulation* of the own cognitive activity. The horizontal dimension of the loop shows the flow across temporal frames of reference. *Ongoing* reference draws on the current cognitive activity, either occurring at the very moment or taking place along a more extended interval that is subjectively experienced as the ordinary, present state of affairs. *Retrospective* reference draws on close or distant previous activity, while *prospective* reference regards

FIGURE 2.1   A fluid approach of metacognitive processes: Interplay of
             functional and temporal orientations

anticipated activity to be carried out sooner or later, or consisting in possible but uncertain project.

2   The Study

2.1   *Aims*

The aim of the study is to capture the qualitatively different ways in which metacognition is evidenced in children's verbal, gestural and notational production when they think and communicate numerically. In addition, the study seeks to understand how children deploy the identified metacognitive processes in real time in their numerical activity.

2.2   *Participants*

Thirty children attending public schools in Río Negro, Argentina, participated in this study. They were equally distributed in K4 (M = 54 months; SD = 3 months), K5 (M = 66 months; SD = 4 months) and Y1 (M = 78 months; SD = 5 month). In each educational level, half the children were girls and half were boys. All participants had provided personal (oral) and family (in writing) consent to participate.

In Argentina, at the time the study took place, Kindergarten education was compulsory from the age of four (K4). Primary education starts at age six (Y1). According to regional curricular guidelines, Y1 teaching focuses in solving diverse problems with numbers up to 100 in the oral and notational modes. Manipulatives are often used. Kindergarten guidelines establish expectations only for the complete educational level, in terms of fluency with numbers up to 20.

2.3   *Procedure, Tasks, and Materials*

Participants were individually interviewed in dedicated rooms at their schools, based on a semi-structured script of open questions (Scheuer, Santamaria & Echenique, 2016). The script was carefully designed in order to give children a wide range of opportunities to think and express their thinking in relation to numbers. To this end, a variety of magnitudes, semiotic modes, referents and cognitive-communicative demands was deliberately included, children's responses were not valued in terms of "right" or "wrong", and special interest was dedicated to the paths children took to arrive to solutions, as well as to their comments, doubts and questions.

The interviewer (INT) introduced herself by saying: "I know children have great ideas about numbers and I would like to know more about them. Would you help me by sharing your ideas with me?" On the whole, the eight sets of tasks (see Appendix 1) required to represent numbers and collections of objects of different magnitudes in three semiotic modes (oral, with manipulatives, and notational), in relation to diverse referents (number series, manipulable identical physical objects, imagined and evoked objects, years of age). In addition, different kinds of cognitive-communicational demands were considered: demonstrating knowledge and achieving solutions regarding number tasks; justifying own numerical ideas and procedures; reconstructing origins of own knowledge, learning experiences and everyday uses of numbers, as well as projecting future learning goals.

In the context of the different tasks, INT said: "I am sure you can think of a way to do it with your own ideas, even if you have not been taught this yet". Most tasks were playful in that they promoted self-confidence, imagination and exploration. Tasks allowed for various procedures. No time limitations were set. In all tasks, if the child (CH) did not respond to the first formulation of the question or request, or seemed not to understand it, INT repeated it, thus offering a further opportunity. If CH looked uncertain or doubtful with respect to her response, INT asked: "Do you wish to try again? Go ahead".

Materials consisted of thirty 2.5 cm diameter circles made of green EVA rubber, blank paper (a new sheet for each notational task) and pencil. Interviews lasted approximately 40 minutes and were videotaped and transcribed verbatim. Actions and gestures were also informed.

3 Analysis and Results

3.1 A Repertoire of Children's Numerical Metacognitive Processes

Constructing a repertoire appeared as a most appropriate instrument to grasp the multiple metacognitive processes young children can deploy when they think and communicate numerically. A repertoire, defined as "the full range of things that someone (…) can do" (MacMillan, 2017), is a form of description that is especially apt to capture a person's skills in terms of the variety and plasticity of her resources (Blommaert & Backus, 2011). The interest of conceptualising the different ways in which a phenomenon appears does not stem from their rate within a corpus or sample, since a variant occurring only rarely might lead to significant insights, or entail a rich potential for developing understanding, learning and teaching (Blommaert & Bakus, 2011; Pramling, 1983).

Category analysis was based on a Grounded Theory Approach (Strauss & Corbin, 1990). Thus, categories for identifying metacognitive processes in children's speech, gestures, actions and notational production were informed by prior research and adapted when necessary, in an iterative process that continued until new data did not change the categories. Similar categories were grouped in order to allow the visualisation of certain trends of psychological and educational interest. The categories composing the resulting repertoire were applied to the full transcription of children's complete responses to all of the tasks reported in Appendix 1. Two researchers independently coded all interviews. They later controlled for agreement. In instances in which coding was not aligned, re-reading and discussing the transcripts allowed to resolve the discrepancy. If disagreement persisted, a conservative criterion was applied and the category under discussion was not allocated.

The repertoire of metacognitive processes identified in participants' verbal, gestural and graphic productions is informed in Table 2.1. As argued in the section about the fluid approach of metacognitive processes, metacognitive processes deployed in cognitively engaging settings necessarily articulate communicative and regulatory orientations. However, *each* of the occurrences of number-related metacognitive processes in children's participation in the interview is predominantly oriented *either* to communicating the child's own cognitive activity, *or* to regulating its course. In what follows, the repertoire of metacognitive processes will be presented in certain detail. Examples from the interviews are provided in the second section of Analysis and Results, dedicated to understanding the interplay *among* occurrences of metacognitive processes during children's activity.

3.1.1 Metacognitive Processes Oriented to Communicating Own Cognitive Activity with Numbers

In order to identify metacognitive processes oriented to communicating own cognitive numerical activity, contributions from three trends of research in the above review of the metacognition literature were taken into account: (i) the metacognitive knowledge component regarding one's own cognition, task and strategies, (ii) development of theory of mind in childhood, especially as the use of mental verbs and the distinction between a copy and an interpretive theory of mind are concerned, and (iii) Dienes and Perner's (1999) distinction between explicitation of own mental attitudes and of own self as knower. Fifteen categories that established further distinctions than the available ones and pertained to the number domain were developed.

In this way, within the metacognitive processes directed mainly at communicating own cognitive activity – to the interviewer or/and to oneself – comments on *epistemic attitudes, affective attitudes,* or *self in relation to own autobiography as learner of number,* and *number tasks* were identified. Children's comments

TABLE 2.1   A repertoire of children's metacognitive processes oriented to communicating or regulating the own cognitive activity

Communication dimension

Categories	Indicators: Child comments, mentions or refers to
Epistemic attitudes	
C1. that he knows numbers or numerical activities:	a. in general or absolute terms, as when child says he knows to count, or he knows many numbers; b. in specific terms, as when child says he knows to count up to x, or how many chips there are on the table; c. in contextual terms, child know how to carry out a number activity when he is in the company of his father.
C2. that she does not know a given numerical content:	a. in general or absolute terms; b. by specifying unknown aspects or threshold of ignorance, as when she says that she does not know numbers beyond x, or how to note a number in a conventional way; c. in contextual terms.
C3. that she remembers numbers or how to carry out numerical activities:	a., b. and c. as those informed for C1.
C4. that he does not remember, is confused or unsure in regard to a given numerical content:	a., b. and c. as those informed for C2.
C5. gaps in own cognition related to a given numerical content, regarding:	a. knowledge vs ignorance (know vs. does not know); b. teaching vs learning (as when child mentions he has been taught x but didn't learn it); c. expectation vs. outcome (as when child says he wants to solve x but does not succeed); d. environments (as thinking about or using numbers at home vs. doing so at school); e. being able to vs not being able to (as when child says that sometimes he can solve x and sometimes he cannot).
Affective attitudes	
C6. preference, fondness or interest for a given numerical activity.	
C7. dislike, lack of interest or boredom toward a given numerical activity.	
C8. other feelings or bodily sensations in relation to numerical task or activity.	

(*cont.*)

TABLE 2.1   A repertoire of children's metacognitive processes oriented to communicating or
             regulating the own cognitive activity (*cont.*)

Communication dimension

Categories	Indicators: Child comments, mentions or refers to

Self, autobiography as learner of number

C9. changes over time in own knowledge, skills, interests or views.

C10. origins of own knowledge in terms of:	a. when, where, with whom, or with what artifacts she has accessed knowledge; b. how she has accessed knowledge; c. specific numerical content.

C11. what she wishes or plans to learn or know but has not learnt yet.

Number task

C12. difficulty/easiness to perform a given numerical task.

C13. strategies, procedures or reasoning involved in a numerical task.

C14. productions or results in relation to a numerical task.

C15. goals, motivations or uses of a numerical task:	a. fulfill a task set by teacher or parent; b. play; c. solve a numerical problem; d. learn; e. teach or help another person.

Regulation dimension

Categories	Indicators: Child explicitly
R1. seeks help from INT in order to:	a. check own understanding of task; b. carry out task; c. check or evaluate progress or production.
R2. anticipates goal or production.	
R3. anticipates actions or strategies.	
R4. makes a pause to think.	
R5. in order to respond an ongoing task, looks for/takes up:	a. previous productions in the interview; b. previous strategies in the interview; c. daily life experience.
R6. guides or supports own numerical activity through:	a. gestures; b. speech; c. actions with objects; d. actions with notation.
R7. evaluates progress on task in relation to goal.	
R8. modifies strategy based on monitoring.	

(cont.)

TABLE 2.1   A repertoire of children's metacognitive processes oriented to communicating or regulating the own cognitive activity (*cont.*)

Regulation dimension

Categories	Indicators: Child explicitly
R9. adjusts responses according to own knowledge, skills and goals.	
R10. changes course of action based on emotional awareness.	
R11. becomes aware of:	a. a new idea; b. a mistake.
R12. corrects own response by:	a. crossing it out; b. overwriting a previous response; c. completing a response; d. substituting a response by starting again from scratch; e. modifying a response or procedure without leaving any trace of the previous response.
R13. repeats a procedure to check quality of result or to reconstruct the result.	
R14. refuses:	a. to perform task; b. to continue on task; c. interrupt own activity on task; d. to modify.
R15. evaluates own performance or productions as:	a. positive; b. negative; c. intermediate.

on *epistemic attitudes* included explicitation of: being knowledgeable (C_1), recalling mentally stored information or experiences (C_3), as well as the opposite subjective states of not being knowledgeable (C_2) or not succeeding to recover stored knowledge (C_4). Children expressed these four basic kinds of epistemic attitudes in three ways, which seem to indicate different tacit views of the mind. Frequently, children expressed that they knew, remembered, ignored or did not remember numbers or numerical activities in general or absolute terms (indicator a), as if epistemic states regarding number were a matter of all-or-nothing. Children expressed epistemic states also in relatively precise or aspectual terms, when they informed the scope and limits of the own knowledge or memory contents (b). Here, they spoke of epistemic states regarding specific objects or intervals within the domain of numbers. Only rarely, children expressed these epistemic states as context-dependent (c). This way of communicating epistemic attitudes denotes some awareness of the situated nature of subjective cognitive states; mind appears as connected with environment. Comments on own cognitive gaps (C_5) explicitly drew two opposing states together, marking a contrast between them. In these cases, children communicated their joint or double awareness of knowing x and not knowing y (indicator a); spoke about a mismatch between teaching and learning, or between expectations and outcomes (b and c respectively); commented on the cognitive difference of carrying out an activity in one or another context (d), or the distance between what they could and couldn't manage to do or solve (e). Children's explicit comments on cognitive gaps might indicate that they realized that number knowledge, learning, thinking or skills are not mastered at once or for once and for all, so that contrasting cognitive states may coexist in oneself.

As children responded to the proposed number tasks, they also commented on their own *affective states*, mostly in terms of being interested or fond of a numerical content (C6) or, on the contrary, disliking it or being uninterested about it (C7). A few comments on their feelings in relation to a task (C8) also arose, such as feeling anxious or nervous, having fun or being delighted, or experiencing fatigue. Children also made a few comments about themselves as knowers, bringing forth their autobiographies as learners of number in some way. They spoke about changes over time in their epistemic states or ways of relating to number knowledge, skills, interests or views (C9), the origins or sources of their knowledge (C10), and also traced goals for their number learning in the future (C11). Thus, children explicitly drew connections among various mental states and autobiographical episodes in the realm of number.

The last group of categories for metacognitive processes directed at communicating their own cognitive activity assembles comments making reference to solving a particular *number task*. Children talked about the degree of difficulty/easiness posed by the task (C12) or about the strategies they had applied, were applying or should have applied (C13); named or described an outcome without assessing its quality (C14). Children frequently spoke about the motivations, uses or purposes of number tasks (C15). Several indicators were identified within this category: number tasks as compulsory assignments set by others (mostly teachers, indicator a), or as directed at personal goals such as playing (b), solving problems (c), learning (d), helping or teaching someone else (e). This last variant indicates the child considers herself more knowledgeable or competent than the addressee, as well as perceiving number knowledge as valuable and necessary – for this reason, she presents herself as teaching or assisting someone who is considered less numerate than herself.

The 15 categories of metacognitive processes directed mostly at communication referred to any of the three temporal frames of metacognitive reflection:

ongoing, past or future cognition. Overall, most occurrences referred to present cognition, be it ongoing, or extending during a continuous, ordinary present time (especially for C_1 to C_4, C_6 to C_8, C_{12}, C_{15}). There were also many instances of metacognitive processes communicating recent past cognitive activity, which had just taken place in the frame of the task (especially for C_{13} and C_{14}). By definition, comments on self (C_9 to C_{11}) amalgamated at least two different times (two past moments; past and present; present and future). Comments on their own cognitive gaps (C_5) regarded any temporal frame *per se* or connected any two temporal frames to one another.

3.1.2 Metacognitive Processes Oriented to Regulating Their Own Cognitive Activity with Numbers

This group of categories of metacognitive processes adapted and extended the detailed scheme devised to code children's metacognitive regulation in the area of visuo-spatial construction (Whitebread et al., 2009), in the terms presented in the second block of Table 2.1. All these metacognitive processes, which are directed at regulating children's own cognitive activity are on-task, i.e. they regard the cognitive activity (or its products) in relation to a task that is being carried out, is about to be carried out, or has just been completed.

For the sake of clarity, we begin with metacognitive processes oriented prospectively, continue with those directed at ongoing cognitive activity, and end up with metacognitive processes directed at activity or products that have just been produced. This order of presentation does not intend to convey that the coded processes occur in such a linear order in real-time, as will become clearer in the second section of Analysis and Results. Specifically, our adaptation of Whitebread and colleagues' (2009) original coding scheme consisted in opening a few variants within existing categories, and introducing new categories. The categories which were opened and the new ones are informed in Appendix 2.

3.2 Children's Deployment of Metacognitive Processes on Task

In order to provide the readers with a sense of *how* children deployed the identified metacognitive processes in real time and on task, four foci will be successively adopted. Namely, the relations between children's deployment of metacognitive processes and: (1) children's conventional and emerging number knowledge, (2) the affordances and challenges of different number tasks, (3) communicative and regulatory functions, and (4) present, past and future temporal frames of reference. This leads us to the formulation of four statements.

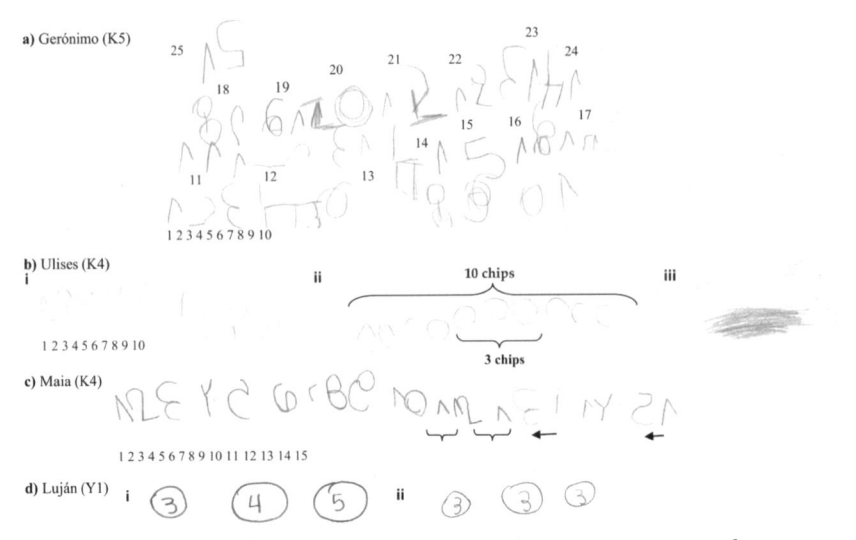

FIGURE 2.2   Examples of notational production for each statement. Note: In order to support
readers' understanding of children's notational intentions, we added the
conventional numeral it stood for when it could be helpful.

Each statement is presented and illustrated based on selected passages of
the dialogic interviews. In these illustrations, oral speech is reported in italics.
When CH or INT referred in speech to a notation (the whole numeral or composing digits), the number word is spelt within single quotation marks. References to numerals actually produced in the interview are typed in boldface.
Coding of children's verbal, gestural and notational production according to
the repertoire is indicated in square brackets, according to labels in Table 2.1.
Children's related notations are presented in Figure 2.2.

*Statement 1. Children can deploy metacognitive processes when they exhibit
either conventional number knowledge, or non conventional approximations to
number.* This statement is illustrated by taking a detailed look into the (liter-
ally speaking!) constructive process whereby Gerónimo [G] (K5) achieved to
note down the number series up to 25. G progressed in his series step by step,
by combining numerals, number-like notations (Teubal & Dockrell, 2005) and
blank spaces (see Figure 2.2a). During his efforts, G frequently sought for INT's
help [R1]. Just after he had produced the first digit, he left a blank space and
continued with the third digit. A few minutes later, once G had reached 11 and
was seeking to build the notation for 12, we had the opportunity to discover
that his omission of 2 had been deliberate.

G: *I don't know all the numbers* [C2a]. *I don't know number 'two'* (leaving a black space between 1 and 3) [C2b, R7, R6d]. *Six, seven, eight, nine.* (He enunciates these number words as he writes out 6 and 7 only, thus indicating that he is supporting his notational activity in two ways: by dictating himself and by anticipating the 8 and 9 to be noted down later on) [R6b, R2]. (G stops and looks at the vertically and horizontally inverted 4 he has produced). *The 'four' is like a chair* [C14].
[...]

G: *Six, seven* [R13]. (Looking at INT) *What comes after seven?* [R1b]. *Eight* (G says the number word himself, without waiting for INT's response and produces a simile-8) [R2]. *Next, nine?* [R1c].

INT: *Yes, nine after eight.*

G: (silently goes on noting 10 and 11). *After the ...* [R4]. *I don't know, and I don't know any more* (numerals) *because I don't know how to make the 'two'* [C2b, R7, R9, R14b, R15c].

INT: *Don't you know how to make the 'two'? Do you want me to show you how it is?*

G: (nods)

INT: *I'll show it to you on another piece of paper* (writes 2 out) ... *It's like this, look.*

G: *Then, I'll make it here.* (G produces a simile-2 in the blank space between 1 and 3) [R2, R3, R12c].

G went on noting reversed numerals and number-like notations, one by one up to 14, with the scaffolding provided by the dialogical interaction with INT. In order to note 15, he asked INT for help. Similarly, as happened with 2, based on the information obtained in the frame of the dialogical interaction, G went back to the blank he had left between his 4 and 6 and completed it with a simile-5. Here, the operation was even more complex than what had occurred for 2. G began by mentally breaking up 15 into its composing digits, next looked at his 2 and mentally rotated it to achieve a 5, which he firstly used to complete the space he had left for 5, and only then turned to produce 15 at the end of his series.

G: *After the 'one', which one ...?* (Making reference to the fact that bi-digit numerals for the teens are formed by an initial 1 and followed by another digit) [R4, R6b]. (Without waiting for INT to respond, G says:) *The fifteen!* [R2].

INT: *Fifteen, fine!*

G: *The 'one' and the 'five'?* [R1c, R2]

INT: *Yes.*

G: *And what about the 'five', how is it like?* [R1b] *Is it like this one?* (Pointing
       at 2 and looking to INT). *Or is it with the mouth open looking to the other
       side?* (referring to the inverse orientation of 2 and 5) [R1b, R5a, R5b]. (G
       writes down 5 on the blank space between his 4 and 6) [R6d, R12c].

INT: *Fine. You had said "eleven, twelve, thirteen, fourteen" and now you were
       going to write down the fifteen. Do you remember?*

G: (Goes on with his number-like notations for 15, 16 and 17).

INT: *How did you think about that?*

G: *Because I know how to count* [C1a, C15c]. *And after seventeen, which one
       comes next?* [R1b, R14c]. *Let's see, (I'll make it) alone!* [R3, R6b]. *One, two,*
       (enunciates all the numbers up to) *eighteen* [R8, R13]. *Eighteen* [C14].

G continued in this way up to 22. After rereading the whole series and writ-
ing down his name, he announced: *Now I will put down more numbers on paper*
[R7, R3, C15c]. This initiative indicates that G refused to interrupt the task
[R14c], in order to add more number-like notations to his series [R12c].

Overall, the selected passages highlight that children's inaccurate numerical responses may contain a wealth of productive ideas. This is the reason we
chose to refer to this kind of responses as "approximations to conventions",
instead of as "non conventional". Even if at first G was not capable of noting 2
and 5 down, he was well aware of his specific lack of knowledge. He found his
way to represent on paper not only the numerals he knew, but also those he did
not know yet, by means of the deliberate action of leaving a blank space. These
blanks and their successive completions help us to visualise the paths children
may take on their way to appropriate the conventional notational system. G's
particular path took shape in a dialogical context, where the adult gave the
child enough time, as well as cognitive and graphic space, for his knowledge
to emerge as an exploratory and constructive process. It is noteworthy that at
times, the sole possibility of asking INT for information triggered G's self-re-
sponses. In fact, just posing his questions aloud to a receptive partner, enabled
G to retrieve a helpful answer himself. As Veraksa and colleagues (2016) have
pointed out, in dialogical interviews child's spoken out thoughts should be
taken as a kind of communication directed both to the adult and to self. In
other instances, INT's help consisted in providing a piece of graphic information G could swiftly make use of (as occurred with 2). In this kind of context,
the transition from lack of knowledge to exhibiting conventional knowledge
may depend on a single opportunity. If the adult had been only interested in
checking G's purely conventional knowledge of the number series, she might
have concluded that G was capable of noting the first digit in the series without

skipping any (because of the initial *I do not know 'two'*), as well as a few ordered pairs (such as **6, 7** or **10** and **11**, granted horizontal orientation and strict proportionality are not required).

Statement 2. A variety of number tasks entails multiple affordances and challenges, which in turn set the ground for a wide range of metacognitive processes. The trajectory of Ulises [U] (K4) throughout the different tasks makes this statement clear. In the tasks related to the number series, U displayed a conventional oral series up to nineteen and noted down the first ten numerals conventionally (see Figure 2.2b-i). In the task requiring to quantify a collection of 3 chips, he said that there were *three* – based on a rapid visual appreciation of quantity: *Because there were three* – and represented this quantity by drawing three circles. To quantify 10 chips, U counted all of them, starting from the first chip again (in spite of the fact that he had just counted the first three chips). Instead, in order to note 10 chips on paper, he used the three circles he had produced to note 3 chips [R5a], so that he had to draw seven new circles only (instead of ten). That is, while U's oral quantification relied on a counting-all strategy, his notation for the same collection was based on the more sophisticated and economical counting-on strategy (see Figure 2.2b-ii). When he was presented with 30 chips, U instantly anticipated: *I won't count them* [R14a, R3]. Upon INT's insistence, U succeeded to count 20 out of the 30 chips, and refused to note this collection down [R14a], probably because he was aware of this "failure". Interestingly, when in a further task U was asked to imagine and to note a large number of chips (without any physically present referent), he succeeded to produce a notational response, which consisted in drawing sixteen circles. His achievement might have been related to the fact that the task involved an indefinite quantity. In contrast, when faced to a definite quantity made up of physically present objects, as the collection of 30 chips was, U needed to count *all* of them in order to be able to note them on paper, rather than activating an approximate response.

When asked to note down that "there are no chips", U initially proposed *not to draw anything* [R2], indicating that for him a strict correspondence between graphic signs and the designed items is to be kept. This is the reason why if there is nothing, nothing will be drawn. Confronted to INT's questioning: *Then, how do you realize that there is no anything?* U expressed doubts [R4], and after looking at INT, he drew a circle [R12b]. When requested to reread what he had produced, he seemed to be unsatisfied with his production [R15b]. In order to represent "many stars" on paper he drew four stars. Next, in order to represent "a few stars" he slightly crossed out his drawings of four stars, in such a way they nevertheless remained visible. When asked to represent that "no stars can be seen in the sky", he firmly crossed out one of the stars until it could almost not be seen any longer (see Figure 2.2b-iii). Adding strikes to the original notational production [R5a] in the form of layers was his way of showing successive subtractive operations. It is noteworthy that U dismissed the first two strategies he had suggested to note the absence of chips (not noting anything and drawing one single circle). In the task requesting to note the absence of stars, he developed new strategies on the basis of his notational production for the inverse situation: seeing many stars in the sky [R8].

Overall, it seems that the variety of tasks enabled U's deployment of multiple metacognitive processes – anticipating, monitoring, adjusting and correcting, evaluating – and, by the hand, fostered refining the kinds of solutions for the number problems presented in the interview. It should be noted that the variety of metacognitive processes displayed by U was inscribed in a microhistory (Tartas, Perret-Clermont & Baucal, 2016), so that the metacognitive and notational processes implemented previously set the grounds for the deployment of the subsequent ones.

Statement 3. Metacognitive processes involving communication and regulation interact in cognitive activities. Analysing how Maia [M] (K4) demonstrated her knowledge and achieved solutions in the notational number series task provides a rich picture of the reciprocal interplay between communicating and regulating own cognitive activity. As will be seen below, M began by using her own speech to support her notational activity. When she found herself in trouble, she turned to INT's help. Then, M spontaneously commented on the origins of her number knowledge and, as complementary and physically available sources to retrieve information, she took up a previous notation of hers to devise the next numeral in the series. She also supported her numerical activity by pointing gestures, and even succeeded to orally deconstruct a notational strategy that she had previously applied in silence. Here is the excerpt:

INT: *Would you put down on this sheet of paper the numbers you have just said?*

M: (Notes all the numerals and from 1 to 12, see Figure 2.2c, fluently one after another as she speaks out the corresponding number words) *one, two* (all the number words up to:) *twelve* [R6b]. (Then, she turns to INT). *And the 'thirteen'?* [R1b]

INT: *How might the 'thirteen' look like? How can you put it together?*

M: *It looks to me as if I have seen it in the books at home* [R5c].

INT: *What might it be like? Perhaps with the 'one' that you have already written?*

M: (Spontaneously rereads her notational series starting from the 10). *The 'one' and ...* [R5a, R13].

INT: 'Cause, let's see, how did you make the 'ten'?
M: (Points at 11) [R6d]
INT: Afterwards, how did you make the 'eleven'?
M: With two 'ones' [C14].
INT: And is this twelve? The 'two' and the 'one'? (Pointing at M's 21 for 12).
M: Yes.

Based on her attentive analysis (scaffolded by INT) of the three bidigit numerals she had already achieved autonomously (10, 11 and 21 for 12), M became able to generate notations for 13, 14 and 15. In her efforts to extend her notational number series, M deployed a cumulus of metacognitive processes, with regulative and communicative ones contributing to each other. A remarkable case of intertwinement is her anticipation regarding how to make up the notation for 13, which she dismissed even before setting pencil to paper! Following, M commented on her strategy to identify the mistake she had only performed at an anticipatory level.

INT: And then, how can 'thirteen' be?
M: The 'one' and the 'forty' [R2].
INT: Let's see.
M: No, not like this [R11b, R15b]. It should be with the three [R12e] (and notes down 03).
INT: And how did you realize it was with the three?
M: Cause I saw it [C13, C10a]. (M replaces 0 with 1). And I already know how to make 'fourteen' [C1b].
INT: How is it?
M: The 'four' and the 'one' [R2] [...] (notes down 14 and in addition, achieves 15).
INT: Do you feel like going on?
M: No [R14b].
INT: Not the sixteen?
M: No [R14b].

In spite of having found her way to note the first six bidigits, M chose not to continue beyond 15. This highlights the need to take the child's goals into account, as well as the extent to which she is willing to take risks as she solves a task. M's refusal to continue, similarly as what happened with U at a certain point, suggests that in a dialogical setting for cognitive activity, the permission to explore alternatives might be just as important as the permission to leave the task when the child feels she has reached a certain threshold she is not willing to surpass. This is the reason why certain refusals have been considered as indicators of self-regulation.

Statement 4. Metacognitive processes referring to prospective, ongoing and retrospective temporal frames are deployed in a continuous flow. In the task requesting to quantify and note on collections of manipulatives on paper, Luján [L] (Y1) deployed metacognitive processes referring to retrospective and prospective temporal frames references. Such processes pivoted on the ongoing notational activity, and as shown in the following excerpt, enhanced such a notational activity, allowing L to shift from purely iconic notation to the inclusion of a few numerals.

INT: *Can you put down here that the girl has got three chips?*
L: (L draws three circles; see Figure 2.2d-i) *Oh no, I made them* (too) *big!* [R15b]
INT: *Don't worry. Tell me, what did you put down here?*
L: *I made three.*
INT: *And with one number, is it possible to say that she has three chips?*
L: *Yes.*
INT: *Let's see, how?*
L: *'three'* (writes 3 inside the chip at the left) [R2, R5a, R6d].

Following, L continued to show a fluid movement between attention to what she was about to solve, to what she was carrying out, as well as to the products she had just achieved. As noted in Statement 2, *per se*, the notational activity sets a privileged ground for this kind of metacognitive temporal shifts, especially as (retrospective) reviewing is concerned.

L: *And now, may I put down 'four'?* (She asks INT for permission to write another numeral in her drawing for the second chip) [R1b, R7].
INT: *As you like.*
L: (She introduces 4 in her second circle) *'Four'* [C14].
INT: *'Four'. And will you put anything in the other one?*
L: (Notes 5 down).
INT: *'Five'. Well, you put a number inside each chip. Could you show that the girl has three by using only one number, outside the chips?*
L: (She nods)
INT: *Show me how.*
L: *May I put another, another 'three' here, and may I put 'three' and 'three'?* [R2, R3, R8, R9].

INT: *Oh, 'three' and 'three'! Do you know how it is?*
L: *Look, shall I make it for you here?* [R1b, R3].
INT: *Sure.*
L: *Or shall I make ...?* (keeps silent and still) [R4].
INT: *Can you put down that she has three chips by using numbers?*
L: (L draws three circles and writes a 3 inside each of them; see Figure 2.2d-ii) *'Three' and 'three'* [C14].

Finally, L put retrospective references into play, in terms of comments about her production as well as her strategies used to conduct the task, as when she looked at her notations and said: *the numbers must be there* [C13].

In sum, L deployed her activity by continuously shifting her attention from what she had just achieved (and how she had managed to do so), to what (and how) she was about to do, or asked to do. This fluid back and forth metacognitive movement kept her going, both at a motivational level and at figuring out solutions to challenges that fell slightly beyond her numerical zone of comfort.

4   Final Remarks

Based on a fluid view of metacognition, young children's communication and regulation of their own numerical cognition was investigated. The current study has adopted what in our eyes is a powerful methodology, based on a situated and in-depth analysis of dialogical interviews in which K4, K5 and Y1 children were encouraged to represent and communicate numbers in a variety of challenging and multimodal tasks. In this setting, children were able to develop their ideas and strategies, as well as to try new ones out and reflect about their learning experiences in the field of number. Compared to methods that use self-report summated scales and correlational analyses, such as those pervasive in componential approach studies to metacognition (as pointed out in Kuvalja, Verma & Whitebread, 2014), our viewpoint allowed to capture metacognitive processes as unfolding in interactional contexts, rather than as prepacked skills, ready to be activated in any situation.

Within the scope of an exploratory and qualitative design, a fine-grained repertoire of numerical metacognitive processes has been evidenced. This repertoire differs from existing models in developmental psychology (Berk, 2003; Veenman & Spaans, 2005; Veenman, Van Hout-Wolters & Afflerbach, 2006; Veenman, Wilhelm & Beishuizen, 2004; Whitebread et al., 2009) in several aspects. First, it allows to integrate processes pertaining to communication and regulation about own cognition in a common framework. Second, it broadens the categories traditionally studied and introduces new ones. In addition, the repertoire enables to capture such metacognitive processes in the specific field of early numerical thinking with more subtlety than prior studies (Santamaria, 2015; Scheuer, de la Cruz & Iparraguirre, 2010; Scheuer & Germano, 2005; Siegler, 2005).

The metacognitive processes which constitute this repertoire should be understood as emerging within supportive and challenging activities. Supportive, insofar as the sociocognitive space the interview deliberately sought to generate was characterised by a tissue of mutually cooperating features. Namely, children were encouraged to share their partial approximations to number principles and conventions, even if they were not fully canonical or accurate. In addition, children could count on different semiotic modes both to construct an understanding of tasks and to devise their ways to solve them, as well as on a more knowledgeable partner in order to clarify tasks, obtain information, check trials and results. Besides, children were stimulated to comment on their ideas, concerns, doubts and even bring about connected autobiographical episodes, rather than pressed to give a straightforward single response. Another feature to be highlighted is that children were allowed to calibrate the magnitudes involved in their numerical representation and communication, as well as how long they wished to continue on task. Last but not least, the presented activities were challenging because they were open-ended and shifted from familiar, middle-sized magnitudes, to very large ones and to the absence of quantity, combining concreteness and imagination.

The dynamics of the metacognitive processes revealed by the repertoire became visible as four statements. Children were found to deploy metacognitive processes: (i) when they exhibited conventional number knowledge, but also when they displayed approximations to number knowledge; (ii) that varied as they responded to a broad variety of number tasks that entail different affordances and challenges; (iii) by intertwining communication and regulation of their own cognitive activity; and (iv) that interwove prospective, ongoing and retrospective temporal frames in a continuous flow. Such dynamics should be valued in the light of a resources approach to human cognition and communication and, as a fall out, to child development and education. According to this approach, knowledge in its different forms is not a mental posession that, once achieved, is ready to be applied in any setting and for any purpose (Hammer et al., 2005). Rather, and just as occurs with any "commognitive" (Sfard, 2008), or representational/communicational process (Kress, 2010), young children's metacognitive processes are continuously shaped and reshaped in the frame of ongoing interactive situations.

Therefore, the theoretical contribution of the present study, in line with the set of previous works that are inscribed in what we have termed a "fluid and agentive" vision of numerical metacognition, consists in discussing some of the pillars of the Component Research Program. Specifically, we question that conventional numerical knowledge is a necessary prerequisite for the deployment of metacognitive processes, as proposed by McCabe (2011). Likewise, our analyses do not support that the functional relations between regulation and communication of cognitive activity unfold linearly, or that prospective, ongoing and retrospective regulation processes follow each other in a fixed sequence, as Cleary, Callan and Zimmerman (2012) have proposed.

However, this is only a preliminary study. It is still necessary to obtain a systematic description of the ways in which children bring metacognitive processes into play vary according to their progress in numerical thinking, to the extent to which their mathematical education is oriented to foster an agentive and reflective stance on the part of the learner, as well as to particular task and interaction features. Another significant contribution would be to explore children's deployment of metacognitive processes in authentic school settings, where children could count on the support of interacting with their teachers and peers. In spite of being aware of the limitations of this first study, we hope that its findings contribute to expand teachers', administrators' and researchers' understanding of early number development as a reflective and self-regulated process and, hopefully, highlight the importance of promoting learners' agency in mathematics learning.

In the daily classroom environments, teachers can create conditions where meaning-making and negotiation are possible and children's questions and answers are taken seriously and dealt with as equally important. In addition, teachers could explore together with students the variety of strategies students perceive as relevant for their engagement in the educational context for pursuing different goals. Such an open dialogue would reveal to educators students' ideas, strategies and preoccupations, as well as the contingencies entailed by adopting certain purposes and employing certain strategies in particular classroom and task contexts.

Acknowledgements

We thank the schools that participated in this study. This research counted on support by Universidad Nacional del Comahue (C-130), ANPCYT (PICT 2017-0627) and CONICET (PIP 0122) of Argentina and Ministerio de Economía y Competitividad of Spain (grant number EDU2013-47593-C2-2-P). We are grateful to Eva Teubal and María Silvina Márquez for their thoughtful review-ing of a preliminary version of this chapter.

Note

1   We vary the use of gender personal pronouns along the text.

References

Baroody, A. J. (1987). *Children's mathematical thinking: A developmental framework for preschool, primary, and special education teachers.* Teacher's College Press.

Berk, L. E. (2003). *Child development* (6th ed.). Allyn and Bacon.

Bishop, A. (1991). *Mathematical enculturation: A cultural perspective on mathematics education.* Kluwer Academic Publishers.

Blommaert, J., & Backus, A. (2011). *Repertoires revisited: 'Knowing language' in super-diversity.* Working Papers in Urban Language & Literacies, Paper 67. King's College London.

Brizuela, B. M. (2004). *Mathematical development in young children: Exploring nota-tions.* Teachers College Press.

Bryce, D., Whitebread, D., & Szűcs, D. (2015). The relationships among executive func-tions, metacognitive skills and educational achievement in 5 and 7-year-old chil-dren. *Metacognition and Learning, 10*(2), 181–198.

Carr, M., Peters, S., & Young-Loveridge, J. (1994). Early childhood mathematics: Finding the right level of challenge. In J. Neyland (Ed.), *Mathematics education: A handbook for teachers* (Vol. 1, pp. 271–282). Wellington College of Education.

Cavalcante, S., & Rodríguez, C. (2015). The understanding of die as an object that has numerical functions. A longitudinal study using two children from the ages of 24 to 36 months interacting with an adult. *Estudios de Psicología, 35*(2), 48–70.

Cleary, T. J., Callan, G., & Zimmerman, B. J. (2012). Assessing self-regulation as a cycli-cal, context-specific phenomenon: Overview and analysis of SRL microanalytic pro-tocols. *Education Research International,* 1–19.

Dienes, Z., & Perner, J. (1999). A theory of implicit and explicit knowledge. *Behavioral and Brain Sciences, 22,* 735–808.

Dockrell, J., & Teubal, E. (2007). Distinguishing numeracy from literacy: Evidence from children's early notations. In E. Teubal, J. Dockrell, & L. Tolchinsky (Eds.), *Notational knowledge. Developmental and historical perspectives* (pp. 113–134). Sense.

Droz, R. (1992). The multiple roots of natural numbers and their multiple interpreta-tions. In J. Bideaud, C. Meljac, & J. P. Fischer (Eds.), *Pathways to number: Children's developing numerical abilities* (pp. 229–243). Lawrence Erlbaum Associates.

Efklides, A. (2008). Metacognition. Defining its facets and levels of functioning in relation to self-regulation and co-regulation. *European Psychologist, 13,* 277–287.

Flavell, J. H. (1979). Metacognition and cognitive monitoring: A new area of cognitive–developmental inquiry. *American Psychologist, 34*(10), 906–911.

Fuson, K. C. (1992). Relationships between counting and cardinality from age 2 to age 8. In J. Bideaud, C. Meljac & J. P. Fischer (Eds.), *Pathways to number: Children's developing numerical abilities* (pp. 127–149). Lawrence Erlbaum Associates.

Hammer, D., Elby, A., Scherr, R. E., & Redish, E. F. (2005). Resources, framing, and transfer. In J. Mestre (Ed.), *Transfer of learning from a modern multidisciplinary perspective* (pp. 89–120). Information Age Publishing.

Hughes, M. (1986). *Children and number.* Basil Blackwell.

Hurford, J. R. (1987). *Language and number: The emergence of a cognitive system.* Blackwell.

Ifrah, G. (1998). *The universal history of numbers: From prehistory to the invention of the computer.* Harvill Press.

Johnson, A. M., Azevedo, R., & D'Mello, S. K. (2011). The temporal and dynamic nature of self-regulatory processes during independent and externally assisted hypermedia learning. *Cognition and Instruction, 29*(4), 471–504.

Kress, G. (2010). *Multimodality: A social semiotic approach to contemporary communication.* Routledge.

Kuvalja, M., Verma, M., & Whitebread, D. (2014). Patterns of co-occurring non-verbal behaviour and self-directed speech; a comparison of three methodological approaches. *Metacognition and Learning, 9*(2), 87–111.

Leibovich, T., Katzin, N., Harel, M., & Henik, A. (2017). From 'sense of number' to 'sense of magnitude' – The role of continuous magnitudes in numerical cognition. *Behavioral and Brain Sciences, 40,* 1–62.

McCabe, J. (2011). Metacognitive awareness of learning strategies in undergraduates. *Memory and Cognition, 39,* 462–476.

McClelland, M. M., Geldhof, G. H., Cameron, C. E., & Wanless, S. B. (2015). Development and Self-Regulation. In W. F. Overton & P. C. Molenaar (Eds.), *Handbook of child psychology and developmental science* (pp. 523–565). Wiley.

MacMillan. (2017). *MacMillan collocations dictionary.* MacMillan Education.

Mix, K. S., Huttenlocher, J., & Cohen Levine, S. (2002). *Quantitative development in infancy and early childhood.* Oxford University Press.

Molenaar, I. (2014). Advances in temporal analysis in learning and instruction. *Frontline Learning Research, 6,* 15–24.

Nunes, T., & Bryant, P. (1996). *Children doing mathematics.* Blackwell.

Piaget, J., & Szeminska, A. (1941). *Lagenesedu nombrechez l'enfant* [*The child's conception of number*]. Delachaux et Niestle.

Pramling, I. (1983). *The child's conception of learning.* Acta Universitatis Gothoburgensis.

Reder, L. M. (1996). Different research programs on metacognition: Are the boundaries imaginary? *Learning and Individual Differences, 8*(4), 383–390.

Rodríguez, C., & Scheuer, N. (2015). The paradox between the numerically competent baby and the slow learning of two- to four-year-old children. *Estudios de Psicología, 36*(1), 18–47.

Santamaria, F. I. (2015). Year-one children thinking about and writing 'large' quantities. *Estudios de Psicología, 36*(1), 113–137.

Saxe, G., Guberman, S., & Gearhart, M. (1987). Social processes in early number development. *Monographs of the Society for Research in Child Development, 52*(2), 3–162.

Scheuer, N., de la Cruz, M., & Iparraguirre, M. S. (2010). El aprendizaje de distintos dominios notacionales según niños de preescolar y primer grado. *Revista Latinoamericana de Ciencias Sociales, Niñez y Juventud, 8*(2), 1083–1097.

Scheuer, N., & Germano, A. (2005). Conocimientos matemáticos de niños de cuatro a siete años en entornos de alfabetización limitada. In B. Brizuela & M. Alvarado (Eds.), *Las notaciones matemáticas en la escuela primaria* (pp. 109–145). Paidós.

Scheuer, N., Santamaria, F., & Echenique, M. (2016). Exploring children's thinking with and about numbers from a resources-based approach. *Early Child Development and Care, 187*(7), 1123–1137.

Scheuer, N., & Sinclair, A. (2009). From one to two. Observing one child's early mathematical steps. In C. Andersen, N. Scheuer, M. del P. Pérez Echeverría, & E. Teubal (Eds.), *Representational systems and practices as learning tools* (pp. 19–37). Sense Publishers.

Schoenfeld, A. H. (1992). Learning to think mathematically: Problem solving, metacognition and sense making in arithmetics. In D. A. Grouws (Ed.), *Handbook of research on arithmetics teaching and learning. A project of the national council of teachers of arithmetics* (pp. 334–370). Simon & Schuster Macmillan.

Sfard, A. (2008). *Thinking as communicating. Human development, the growth of discourses, and mathematizing.* Cambridge University Press.

Siegler, R. S. (2005). Children's learning. *American Psychologist, 60*, 769–778.

Sinclair, A. (2005). Mathematics and imitation from age one to three. *Infancia y Aprendizaje, 28*(4), 377–392.

Sophian, C. (1992). Learning about numbers: Lessons for mathematics education from preschool number development. In J. Bideaud, C. Meljac, & J. P. Fischer (Eds.), *Pathways to number: Children's developing numerical abilities* (pp. 19–40). Lawrence Erlbaum.

Starkey, P., & Cooper, R. (1980). Perception of numbers by human infants. *Science, 210*, 1033–1035.

Strauss, A. L., & Corbin, J. (1990). *Basics of qualitative research: Grounded theory procedures and techniques.* Sage.

Tartas, V., Perret-Clermont, A., & Baucal, A. (2016). Experimental micro-histories, private speech, and a study of children's learning and cognitive development. *Infancia y Aprendizaje, 39*(4), 772–811.

Teubal, E., & Dockrell, J. E. (2005). Children's developing numerical notations: The impact of input display, numerical size, and operational complexity. *Learning and Instruction, 15,* 257–280.

Teubal, E., & Guberman, A. (2014). *Graphic texts literacy enhancing tools in early childhood.* Sense Publishers.

Tolchinsky, L. (2003). *The cradle of culture and what children know about writing and numbers before being taught.* Lawrence Erlbaum Associates.

Veenman, M. V. J., & Spaans, M. A. (2005). Relation between intellectual and metacognitive skills: Age and task differences. *Learning and Individual Differences, 15,* 159–176.

Veenman, M. V. J., Van Hout-Wolters, B. H. A. M., & Afflerbach, P. (2006). Metacognition and learning: Conceptual and methodological considerations. *Metacognition and Learning, 1,* 3–14.

Veenman, M. V. J., Wilhelm, P., & Beishuizen, J. J. (2004). The relation between intellectual and metacognitive skills from a developmental perspective. *Learning and Instruction, 14,* 89–109.

Veraksa, N., Shiyan, O., Shiyan, I., Pramling, N., & Pramling-Samuelsson, I. (2016). Communication between teacher and child in early child education: Vygotskian theory and educational practice. *Infancia y Aprendizaje, 39*(2), 221–243.

Weimer, A. A., Dowds, S. J., Fabricius, W., Schwanenflugel, P., & Woon Suh, G. (2017). Development of constructivist theory of mind from middle childhood to early adulthood and its relation to social cognition and behavior. *Journal of Experimental Child Psychology, 154,* 28–45.

Wellman, H. M. (1990). *The child's theory of mind.* MIT Press.

Whitebread, D., Coltman, P., Pino Pasternak, D., Sangster, C., Grau, V., Bingham, S., Almeqdad, Q., & Demetriou, D. (2009). The development of two observational tools for assessing metacognition and self-regulated learning in young children. *Metacognition and Learning, 4*(1), 63–85.

Whitehead, A. N. (1978), *Process and reality. An essay in cosmology.* Free Press.

Zimmerman, B. J. (2002). Becoming a self-regulated learner: an overview. *Theory into Practice, 42*(2), 64–70.

Appendix 1

Script Used in the Interviews

Tasks		Mode			Demand		
		O	M	N	D	J	R
Oral number series	*Do you know how to count? Would you show me?* If CH stopped counting or incorrectly said one or several numbers, INT repeated the last numbers CH had correctly stated and asked: *Which one comes next? And after that?*	X			X		
	How did you learn to count? How have you been taught, so that you could learn? When do you count? What do you count for?	X				X	X
Notational number series	*Could you write down all the numbers you just said?*			X	X		
	Please read me *what you wrote here.* (pointing at CH's previous graphic response)	X		X	X		
	When do you note numbers down? How was it that you began to note numbers on paper? How were you taught? And what do you do in order to learn?	X				X	X
Quantification of 3, 10 and 30 chips in a casual array.	*How many chips are there?* INT adds 7 chips and requests CH to quantify the whole amount. Finally, INT adds another 20 chips and repeats the previous requests.	X	X		X		
	After each quantification: *What did you do in order to know how many there are?*	X	X			X	
Notation of the quantities made of 3, 10 and 30 chips	*Can you note down how many chips the child has got?*		X	X	X		
	Let's see, can you tell me what you have noted here?	X		X	X	X	
Expression of own age	*How old are you? How would you note down your age?*	X		X	X		

Tasks		Mode			Demand		
		O	M	N	D	J	R
Expression of large quantities *We'll play the game of enlarging and shrinking numbers. Do you feel like playing?*	CHIPS: *Let's imagine that the child now has got many, many chips. How would you note down a very large number of chips?* AGE: *How would you note down the age you will be when you grow into an elderly person?* STARS: *Let's imagine the sky on a clear night, full with stars. Can you note down the number of all the stars you can see?*	X		X	X		
	After notation for each large quantity: *What have you noted down? How did you manage to note it?*	X		X	X	X	
Expression of absence of quantity	CHIPS: *How would you note down that she has none, not a single chip?* STARS: *What if it's so cloudy that not even a single star can be seen?*	X		X	X		
Closing and farewell	*Do you think that you can go on learning about noting down numbers? What would you like to keep learning noting down numbers? How could you do that?*	X					X

Note: Semiotic modes. O: oral, M: with manipulatives, N: notational. Cognitive-communicative demands: D: demonstrating knowledge and achieving solutions regarding number, J: justifying own numerical ideas and procedures; R: reconstructing the origins of the own knowledge and learning experiences and projecting future learning goals.

Appendix 2

Note on Categories of Children's Metacognitive Processes Oriented to Regulating Their Own Cognitive Activity with Numbers

Here we detail the innovations we introduced in our adaptation and extension of the scheme proposed by Whitebread et al. (2009) to code children's metacognitive regulation in the area of visuo-spatial construction. The categories which were opened and the new ones are the following:

– *seeking help* (R1) was distinguished in function of its purpose: to check own understanding of task (a), to carry out task (b), to check or evaluate progress or product (c);

- *anticipating* (planning in Whitebread et al., 2009) was distinguished according to its object: goal and productions (R2), or actions and strategies (R3);
- *taking up* a previous: production (R5a), strategy (R5b) or daily life experience (R5c) as a cognitive resource;
- *supporting own thinking* (R6) was distinguished according to the semiotic modes involved: gestures (a), speech (b), actions with objects (c), actions with notations (d);
- *becoming aware of* (R11) is not limited to realizing a mistake has been made (R11b) but also considers conscience of the emergence of a new idea (R11a).
- *correcting own response* (R12) was opened up into: crossing out (a), overwriting (b), completing a response (c), substituting a response by starting again from scratch (d), modifying a response or procedure without leaving any trace of the previous response (e);
- *evaluating own performance or productions* (R15), included a mixed or imprecise assessment (c), going beyond clearcut binary judgments.

The new categories are: CH makes a pause to think (R4); adjusts response according to own knowledge, skills and/or goals (R9); refuses to perform task, to continue on task, to interrupt own activity on task or to modify own response (R14).

CHAPTER 3

Playing with Counting 'Games' on the Tablet

Ruthi Barkai, Esther Levenson, Pessia Tsamir and Dina Tirosh

Abstract

More and more young children are spending time engaging with game-like applications on touch-screen tablets. This paper analyzes 18 tablet applications in terms of their affordances and limitations when promoting counting objects. Visual, auditory, and gestural aspects are considered. A case study of one mother-child cohort interacting with one of the applications is also presented. Findings indicated that verbal counting and one-to-one correspondence are given more attention than cardinality. Suggestions are offered for adults and educators wishing to make use of tablet applications when promoting children's counting competencies.

Keywords

counting – enumerating – set comparison – tablet applications

1 Introduction[1]

The importance of fostering mathematical development during the early years is supported by studies reporting early mathematics competencies are predictors of later school success (e.g., Duncan et al., 2007). While several countries have instated mandatory mathematics curricula for preschools (for example, the *Israel National Mathematics Preschool Curriculum* (INMPC) (Ministry of Education, 2010)), studies suggest that for children to take advantage of the academic opportunities provided at preschool, some level of support from the home environment, such as toys that stimulate learning number and shapes, is necessary (Anders et al., 2012).

This study came about as we were planning a program for adults (not kindergarten teachers) that would promote their knowledge of young children's early number conceptions and encourage them to engage young children with mathematics. As part of the program, we wished to present activities to the participants that could promote early number skills, such as verbal and object counting, and assessing the numerical equivalence of sets (in short, set comparison). Taking into account the growing use of tablet applications (apps) in education (e.g., Moyer-Packenham, Salkind, & Bolyard, 2008), we also searched for appropriate 'game' apps. This search led to a need for a systematic way of analyzing the mathematical affordances and limitations of such apps.

Several studies have analyzed the use of iPads, tablets, and touch-screen technology in early childhood (ages 4–7) mathematics education. Some focused on game apps that are not specifically directed at practicing mathematics skills, but may still afford opportunities to engage with mathematics (Lange & Meaney, 2013). Other studies focused on using virtual manipulatives, which may be defined as "computer based renditions of common mathematics manipulatives and tools" (Dorward, 2002, p. 329). Specifically related to counting, Sinclair and SedaghatJou (2013) designed an instrument for the iPad based on the approach that "mathematical thinking is centrally constituted by bodily activity" (p. 2201). Similarly, Tucker and Johnson (2020) also found a strong relationship between finger use and how children were thinking of numbers.

In this study, we analyze game-like applications that are specifically designed to engage the young child with counting, both verbal and object counting, and with set comparison. Touch-screen technology offers users a possible combination of visual, audio, and gestural (e.g., tapping, dragging, and swiping) experiences. Different gestures, such as tapping and dragging, may impact differently on learners' understanding of mathematical concepts (Dubé & McEwen, 2015). Accordingly, the first aim of this study is to analyze how the design of an app may promote or limit the learning of verbal counting, object counting, and set comparison. Stein, Grover, and Henningsen (1996) noted that "... tasks can change their character once unleashed in real classroom settings (p. 460). Similarly, the design of an app may be influenced by an adult's guidance and a child's engagement. Thus, the second aim of this study is to investigate if and how theoretical affordances and limitations of an app come to be realized in practice, as a child-adult cohort engages with one of the apps.

2   Counting, Enumerating, and Assessing Equivalence of Sets

Counting objects, also called enumerating, involves several skills. First, there are the three "how-to-count" principles: the stable-order principle, the one-to-one principle, and the cardinal principle (Gelman & Gallistel, 1978). The stable-order principle refers to saying the number words in the proper order and knowing the principles and patterns in the number system as coded in one's natural language (Baroody, 1987). When learning to count verbally, children go through two distinct but overlapping phases (Fuson, 1988). The first is the acquisition phase, where children not only learn the conventional number words, but learn to produce them in order and consistently. A common error of children in this phase is to recite the conventional number names, in a consistent fashion, but not in order. For example, reciting 1, 2, 5, 3, 4 and when asked to count again, repeating the numbers 1, 2, 5, 3, 4 as before. The second phase is the elaboration phase when children become aware that the chain of numbers can be broken up and that parts of the chain may be produced starting from a number other than one.

The one-to-one principle involves assigning one count word to each object. Common mistakes related to this principle occur when an object is skipped over, and not counted, or when one object is assigned more than one count number (Fuson, 1988). One-to-one correspondence is a skill that may also be used when assessing the numerical equivalence of sets. By matching each item of one set with an item of another set, one may discern if the sets have an equal number of items. Yet, one-to-one matching is easier among some sets than others. Children find it rather easy to carry out one-to-one matching when two sets contain identical heterogeneous items (e.g., a toy car, pencil, doll, and button), or when items contextually belong together, such as baby animals to adult animals (Greenfield & Scott, 1986). Indeed, when investigating the number knowledge of young children in the beginning of their preparatory year of school, over 90% were able to place one straw in each of five glasses placed on the table (Clarke et al., 2006). These authors suggested that due to children's familiarity with placing straws in cups, the task may have been too simple to truly assess one-to-one correspondence. They theorized that it might have been more appropriate and challenging for children to place one teddy-bear on each counter.

Comprehension of the one-to-one correspondence principle can also play a role in children's ability to compare sets. In an experiment involving children between the ages of 2 and 3 years (Izard et al., 2014), five or six puppets were placed each on one of six branches of a toy tree, stressing one-to-one correspondence. After removing and hiding the puppets, and then requesting the children to return the puppets to the branches, children searched longer for all of the puppets when the initial amount of puppets matched exactly the number of branches. The researchers concluded that children were able to take advantage of a one-to-one correspondence situation when discriminating between the amount of elements belonging to each set.

The third "how-to" principle is cardinality, knowing that when counting objects in a set, the last number mentioned represents the number of objects in that set. A child who has not yet understood this principle, may state any number when asked how many objects are in a set, or recount the objects which have just been counted (Fluck & Henderson, 1996). Comprehending the cardinality principle allows children to use the results of counting to compare amounts in two sets.

In addition to the three "how-to-count" principles, there are two "what-to-count" principles: the abstraction principle, and the order-irrelevance principle (Gelman & Gallistel, 1978). The abstraction principle means that any set of discrete objects can be counted. The order-irrelevance principle includes knowing that one may enumerate the objects in any order (e.g., from right to left, from left to right, etc.) and that enumerating objects in different ways results in the same cardinality. According to Baroody (1987), kindergarten children readily accept that objects may be enumerated in several ways, but have difficulty accepting that their cardinality stays the same. Notably, children may show knowledge of one principle while violating another principle; for example, erring with regard to the one-to-one correspondence principle, but showing understanding of cardinality (Fuson, 1988).

Counting objects also involves skills not necessarily related to the counting principles stated by Gelman and Gallistel (1978). One skill is being able to keep track of what was counted and what was not, which may be affected by how the objects to be counted are laid out. For example, one study compared children's ability to count items placed in a row versus items placed in a circle (Tirosh, Tsamir, Barkai, & Levenson, 2018). While all children were able to count the items placed in row, only half correctly counted the items when they were placed in a circle. The most common error was over or under-counting by one. Moreover, when the items were placed in a circle, some children did not even attempt to count them. The authors suggested that children may not have experience counting objects that are not arranged in a specific order. Spatial arrangements of objects can also affect ability to subitize (Arp & Fagard, 2005). Sarama and Clements (2009) differentiated between perceptual subitizing and conceptual subitizing. Perceptual subitizing refers to recognizing a number without knowingly employing other mental processes, and then naming the number. Conceptual subitizing refers to recognizing a set of objects as two (or more) collections via perceptual subitizing. For example, when shown five dots, a child may say five, because he sees three and two (Sarama & Clements, 2009). Similarly, young children see finger patterns as a recognition of the cardinality of a set (Kullberg & Björklund, 2020). Recently, Tucker and Johnson (2020) investigated a digital mathematics game where children indicated the number of items on the screen by using the corresponding number of fingers to simultaneously touch the screen. The authors stated that this all-at-once gesture was conceptually congruent to subitizing. Subitizing also supports advanced counting strategies, such as counting on. For example, when shown seven dots, a child may subitize three, and then count, four, five, six, and seven. Sarama and Clements (2009) also point out that the "counting out" (e.g., taking out six candies from a bag containing 30 candies) is more challenging than simply counting six candies set on the table.

Taking into consideration the complexity of object counting, and the various sub-skills involved, it is important to offer children various opportunities to practice these skills. In this study, we investigate the theoretical affordances and limitations of different tablet apps to promote object counting and set comparison. We then investigate an adult-child cohort as they engage in one of those apps, assessing how those theoretical affordances and limitations are experienced in practice.

3   Methodology

The first part of this two-part study investigated affordances and limitations of apps, and the second investigated a child-adult cohort playing with one of the apps. For the first part, we used a document analysis methodology (Bowen, 2009), analyzing eighteen game-like apps that were available for free on Android tablets. We chose to use freely available apps recognizing that most parents and other interested adults would be more apt to download a free app, than one they would have to buy. Because there are so many more apps available in English than in Hebrew (our native language), we chose four Hebrew apps, and the rest were in English.

Our analysis began by investigating the ways in which apps may support or constrain verbal counting, one-to-one correspondence, the cardinality principle, and comparison of sets. For example, did the app say the number words out loud so that children could hear the counting words in order? Did the app ask children to compare the number of items in different sets? A second analysis was directed at the ways in which the objects to be counted or compared, were presented. For example, were the objects static or moving? Were they placed in an organized manner? Did the organization of the objects promote the use of subitizing? For each type of analysis, we considered both perceptual, auditory, and motor experiences that may contribute or limit to a child's enumerating and comparison skills.

For the second part of the study, we focused on one child-adult cohort playing with a set comparison app. We chose this app because it afforded us a chance to investigate opportunities for verbal counting, object counting, as well as set comparison. The adult videoed the child playing with app. For most of the video, the focus is on the tablet, allowing us to see the child's gestures and the movements seen on the app. This video was transcribed, recording all utterances and gestures made by the child and the adult, as well as all sound and movements seen on the tablet. The data was then analyzed in terms of how the cohort took advantage of opportunities afforded by the app and how limitations constrained opportunities. The approaches of the adult to interacting with an app were analyzed in accordance with the three approaches identified by Hundeland, Erfjord, and Carlsen (2013): the assistant approach (e.g., assisting children with minor issues such as starting the app and switching screens); the mediator approach (e.g., supporting children in interpreting the screen and making them aware of crucial elements of the screen); and the teacher approach (e.g., asking questions and making comments regarding the children's interactions with the app).

4 Analysis of Apps

This section presents the findings according to the first three "how-to-count" principles of Gelman and Gallistel (1978). It then analyzes the presentation of objects on the screen, taking into consideration the two "what-to-count" principles.

4.1 Verbal Counting

In general, apps that promote verbal counting for non-readers are apps that say out loud the counting numbers, from one to some number, supporting the stable-order principle. In most of the apps surveyed, verbal counting accompanied some action on the part of the player, for example, placing tomatoes in a basket. As the player drags each tomato to the basket, the app counts out loud, 1, 2, 3, and so forth. For other apps, as the child touches an object, the app says out loud the counting words. We found eight apps that did not say out loud the number words. For example, when placing eight ostriches in a truck, the movement of the ostriches from the zoo to the truck was not accompanied by the sound of verbal counting.

Counting from some number other than one, was possible in some of the apps. For example, when counting eight fish, placing three fingers on three fish, caused the app to say three, and then, when touching one fish at a time, you hear 4, 5, 6, 7, 8. However, if one first touched three fish, and then two, and then three, you would hear 3, 5, 8. Thus, counting by ones may not necessarily be promoted. While none of the apps specifically promoted skip counting, in apps that allow touching two or three objects at a time (as described above),

TABLE 3.1   Frequency of apps which promote verbal counting skills (N = 18)

	Saying out loud the numbers from 1	Skip counting	Counting from some number other than one	Counting backwards
Frequency	10	–	2	1

skip counting could be promoted. Regarding counting backwards, one of the apps placed items in a row and when touching each item from left to right, you would hear the numbers from one to the number of items on the screen, and when touching the items in order from right to left, you would hear the numbers in backwards order. Thus, it may be said, that this app could promote counting backwards. However, if you touched the third item from the left, and then the fourth item from the left, and then the first, and then the second, you would hear the numbers 3, 4, 1, 2. In other words, each item was given an ordinal number, based on its place starting from the left. Table 3.1 summarizes the frequency of apps which supported different verbal counting skills. The apps in the first column include the apps from the last two columns.

4.2   One-to-One Correspondence

Apps that supported one-to-one correspondence offered some type of feedback when an item on the screen was touched. Fourteen apps supported this principle. In general, the player only needed to tap an object, and the tablet responded, while in two apps, the player needed to drag the object from one place on the screen to another (e.g., dragging a bee to a flower).

There were several types of perceptual feedback to touching an object, all letting the player know that the object had been touched: the object changed color or brightness; the numeral corresponding to the order in which the object was touched appeared on the object itself; the object moved and changed its place; the object disappeared entirely. Figure 3.1 shows an example of four trees, which when touched become faded, and a number appears on the tree that was touched, in the order that it was touched. All of these perceptual changes can assist the child in keeping track of what was counted, and what still needs to be counted. They also emphasize that for each touch there is one and only one corresponding reaction. Specifically, if the child touches an object that was already touched (i.e., counted) the object does not change again. In two of the apps, you could touch more than one object at a time, but different fingers had to be used for each object (e.g., I can use three fingers to touch three trees).

FIGURE 3.1   Counting four trees

FIGURE 3.2
Are there more bees or flowers?

As a component of enumeration, one-to-one correspondence means assign-ing one counting word to one, and only one, object. All apps, except three, responded to touch with a number assignment, either by visually showing the appropriate number symbol (see Figure 3.1) and/or by saying the number out loud (auditory feedback) in coordination with the visual change in the object. The other three apps responded to touch by moving the object, but did not assign the movement a corresponding number.

A more general notion of one-to-one correspondence, not related to enu-meration, entails assigning one item in a set, to one and only one item in a sec-ond set. Two apps promoted this general one-to-one correspondence, one app which promoted counting and one which promoted set comparison. In the counting app, the child paired, for example, one sun, with one plant (see Fig-ure 3.6). In the set comparison app, the child was able to drag one bee to one flower, which then opened up as the bee hovered above. In this way, one-to-one correspondence allowed the child to see if there were more bees or more flowers, determining which set, bees or flowers, contained more, less, or the same number of items (see Figure 3.2).

Table 3.2 summarizes the number of apps which promoted aspects of one-to-one correspondence. The apps in the first column include those in the other two columns.

4.3   *Cardinality*

Regarding cardinality, we differentiate between apps that promote children's understanding of the cardinality principle (10 apps) and apps where children can or must be able to apply the cardinality principle to complete a different

TABLE 3.2 Frequency of apps which promote one-to-one correspondence (N = 18)

	Touch/drag an item and receive feedback	One word to one and only one item	Matching one item in a set to one item in a different set
Frequency	14	11	2

task (8 apps). In the first category were apps that displayed on the screen the numeral corresponding to the amount of items on the screen, and where the user is encouraged to touch each of the items. Having the numeral representing cardinality displayed on the screen, as the user touches each item, can reinforce the idea that the last number said represents the amount of items touched. That being said, we found three different ways in which the numeral, representing cardinality, was displayed. The first was found on one app which had instructions on the screen, "Touch eight creatures". However, as the creatures were touched, the statement changed to "one touched, two touched", and so on, and as the last creature is touched, the screen immediately changes. Thus, the numeral representing cardinality is not displayed as the user touches the last creature. The second type of display was found on seven apps, which displayed the numeral representing cardinality throughout the user's play. For example, see Figure 3.4, where the numeral 8 stays on the screen as the user colors each fish. The third type of display was found in two apps, where the numeral representing cardinality only appeared after all items on the screen were touched. In one of those apps, the user is asked, for example, "how many rabbits appear on the screen", and when the user touches each rabbit, the tablet counts aloud each touch, and after touching all of the rabbits, sums up by voicing "There are 10 rabbits".

In the second category were three types of activities where the cardinality principle can be applied. The first type (found in two apps) was a *counting out* activity, e.g., dragging five ostriches from a whole bunch of ostriches to a waiting truck (see Figure 3.3). This requires the child not only to count one at a time, but also to recognize when to stop. The second type of activity was set comparison (found in two apps), where a child has to recognize the cardinality of each set and then indicate which is bigger. The third type of activity was matching the number of items displayed on the screen with the corresponding numeral (see Figure 3.5). Four apps required the user to choose a numeral, from among several numerals displayed on the screen, corresponding to the amount of items shown on a screen.

FIGURE 3.3   Counting-out five (initial position, three out of five, five)

4.4   *What-to-Count*

The what-to-count principle relates to how objects are presented in the specific task. A basic task (found in 16 apps) is requesting the user to count objects or compare the number of objects in two sets, and presenting only those objects to be counted or compared (see Figures 3.1 and 3.2). A more complex task, is counting out, requiring the player to count n objects, when being presented with more than n objects (see Figure 3.3). In that case, the extra objects may be identical to those which need to be counted, or different. Two such tasks were found.

4.5   *The Abstraction Principle*

In all the apps we analyzed, except one, items to be counted were identical. That is, if the player was requested to count fish, the fish were exactly the same shape, color, size, and, in the case when the pictures were static, they even faced the same way. Even in the comparison tasks, the items in each set were identical, that is, when comparing the number of bees to flowers, all the bees were identical and all the flowers were identical. In only one app, the items to be counted were not identical, although they were of the same general type (e.g., they were all fish, but different kinds of fish – see Figure 3.4). Even when the task was counting out, the objects to be counted were identical. For example, faced with an assortment of vegetables, if the player was asked to count out three tomatoes, those tomatoes were identical.

Another important aspect of object presentation is the way objects are organized on the screen. This is related to the order-irrelevance principle in that organization might impact on the order in which a player counts the objects. However, regardless of the way objects were presented, all the apps allowed the player to tap or drag objects in any order. In one of the apps (mentioned in Section 4.1), which seemed to assign an ordinal number to each object, one could touch each item in any order, but would then hear the numbers assigned to that item, not necessarily in numerical order. Thus, the order-irrelevance principle was not promoted in that app, and may even lead one to believe that counting must be carried out from left to right.

FIGURE 3.4   Eight fingers and eight fish   FIGURE 3.5   Subitizing butterflies

Regarding initial presentation, either objects were arranged in rows, some-times with an equal number of objects in each row, and sometimes not, or objects were spread out in no particular way (see Figure 3.3 where the ini-tially the ostriches are spread out). When objects were spread out, they were sometimes arranged in small groups of two or three, promoting subitizing (see Figure 3.5). As mentioned previously, with some apps, touching the object changed its position on the screen, resulting in a new organization. In all the apps, when the objects were initially spread out, they ended up in rows (e.g., Figure 3.3, where the ostriches stand in a row in the truck). There was one app where the objects were initially in rows, moved together to a bunch (e.g., all the tomatoes ended up in a basket), and after being touched again, ended up once again in rows (e.g., on the supermarket shelf).

Three apps offered the player an opportunity to enumerate the same amount of objects using different objects each time. For example, one app encouraged the user to count four suns, for four plants, and then count four tomatoes (see Figure 3.6). A different app presented a number of objects to be counted (in rows), while on the screen was a picture of hands holding up the appropriate number of fingers (see Figure 3.4). Thus, two different representations of the number were present at the same time. In one of the comparison tasks, chil-dren were able to count different objects, and in the case where the number of objects was the same, were able to see different representations of the same amount. In all other apps, the number of objects to be counted kept on chang-ing with each new screen, without offering the opportunity to visualize more than one presentation of the number.

FIGURE 3.6   Four suns and four plants, become four tomatoes, all in a basket

4.6   Discussion: Affordances and Limitations of the Apps

The first aim of this study was to analyze how the design of an app may promote or limit the learning of verbal counting, object counting, and set comparison. In this section, we summarize our findings, taking into consideration how adults may take advantage of affordances and overcome limitations.

Regarding verbal counting, almost all the apps counted out loud in sync with the user's touch, offering repeated auditory opportunities for hearing the counting words in order. However, in addition to counting by ones, several mathematics curricula recognize the importance of promoting skip counting (e.g., Israel National Preschool Mathematics Curriculum [INPMC], 2010). While, no specific promotion of skip counting was found in the apps, an adult sitting with a child might suggest that the child specifically touch two objects at time (where the app allows this), affording the child to hear skip counting by twos. We found only one app that afforded opportunities for counting backwards, an important skill that can support subtraction (Sarama & Clements, 2009). Here too, an adult might find opportunities to count backward with the child when, for example, the tomatoes are taken out of the basket.

Perhaps the most supported competency was one-to-one correspondence. However, only two apps supported the more general notion of one-to-one correspondence (e.g., by matching one sun to one plant). Adults may seek additional ways of supporting this competency, for example, by engaging children with activities such as setting the table, one plate in front of each chair (INPMC, 2010). Another issue, as mentioned in the background, is that children find it difficult to keep track of what was and was not counted (Fuson, 1988). Most of the apps do this, for example, by shading the object counted. In essence, by doing so, the apps limit children's opportunities for developing tracking schemes of their own. Here, as in Dubé and McEwen's (2015) study, we take note of the difference between tapping an object and dragging it. Dragging an object from one spot to another, mimics the action a child may take when trying to keep track of physical objects to be counted, and thus might support such a strategy in the future. Keeping track of items is also made easier or more difficult by their organization. An adult might at first choose an app where the objects are arranged neatly in rows, and then move on to apps that present objects spread out. A few of the apps grouped items in such a way as to support subitizing. Recall also that one app presented finger representations of numbers (Figure 3.4). In line with Kuller and Björklund (2020), children could be encouraged to copy finger patterns, such as those they see on the app, supporting their conceptualization of part-whole relations. An adult sitting with a child might also point out such groupings, and in doing so, promote more advanced counting strategies, such as counting-on. None of the apps specifically arranged objects in a circle, a challenging arrangement for children (Tirosh, Tsamir, Barkai, & Levenson, 2018). As opposed to the focus on finger coordination found in other apps (Tucker & Johnson, 2020), none of the apps in this study specifically promoted finger configurations as a way to enhance children's number sense.

The principle of cardinality was marginally supported. Indeed, several of the apps seem to implicitly rely on children's acceptance of this principle, without necessarily promoting this competence. Recall that one app placed the counted items in a bunch (e.g., in a basket – see Figure 3.6). At this point, not being able to actually see how many items are in the basket, an adult may ask the child, how many items are in the basket. Not being able to actually see how many there are, may strengthen the notion that the last number said when putting them in, represents the amount of items in the basket. Taking them out and placing them on the shelf may be used as a way of checking the answer to the question of how many.

All the apps except one supported the order-irrelevance principle, in that objects could be touched and counted in any order. However, none actually promoted it. An adult sitting with a child may focus on this principle by requesting the child to play the same 'game' again, but this time request the child to count the objects in a different order. Asking questions, such as, "if we now count from here, how many will there be?" could also support this principle. None of the apps could be said to support the abstraction principle, in that all the items to be counted were identical. Furthermore, continuously counting only identical items may reinforce the erroneous conception that sets must contain items that have an explicit common property (Linchevski & Vinner, 1988). Adults should be aware of this limitation.

After theoretically investigating several apps, we now present a case study of one cohort's interaction with a set-comparison app.

5 Interacting with an App: Ben and Mom

Ben (a pseudonym) was five years old at the time of the study. His mother, Mom, was participating in a workshop to promote adults' knowledge of children's mathematical competencies. During the workshop, adults were encouraged to engage their children with various apps, video these engagements, and discuss them during the workshop. No explicit instructions were given to the adults regarding if and how to intervene during the children's playing with the app. We chose to present Ben's engagement with a set-comparison app because the app offers opportunities for verbal counting, object counting, as well as set comparison. First, we describe the app and present an a-priori analysis of its affordances and limitations. We then describe in detail, gestures and utterances, of Ben playing with the app, and Mom's comments. Finally, we analyze if and how the theoretical affordances and limitations of the app come to be realized in practice, as Mom and Ben engaged with the app.

5.1 Comparing the Number of Bees to Flowers: An A-Priori Analysis

This app presents a number of identical flowers in a row, and a number of identical bees that are bunched randomly together, hovering somewhere on top of the screen, in the "sky". On the bottom of the screen are three icons: an equals sign, a picture of the same identical flower, and a picture of the same identical bee (see Figure 3.2). The app asks out loud, "Are there more flowers, or more bees, or an equal number of each?" If the child touches the appropriate icon, then a burst of stars appears on the screen, and a new screen appears. If the child touches an incorrect icon, then the app moves the bees such that one bee hovers over each flower. If there is one-to-one correspondence between bees and flowers, then the amount of bees and flowers are equal. If there is an unequal amount, either one or more flowers will be left without a bee or vice versa. After moving the bees to the flowers, the app waits for the user to touch one of the icons on the bottom of the screen. The user is given a last opportunity to touch the correct icon, before the app presents the correct answer. The app also allows the user to drag the bees from place to place on the screen. If the bee is dragged to a flower and left there, then the flower opens up, and the bee stays on top of the flower. If the bee is dragged to any other place on the screen and left there, it will not stay there, but will move back to its original position among the other bees. At random intervals, the app demonstrates that a bee may be moved to a flower and left there, but this demonstration is not consistently presented each time the user begins playing with the app.

Regarding affordances, the app displays flowers and bees in different ways, the flowers in a row and the bees in a bunch, affording children a chance to practice object counting in simpler and more complicated formations. One-to-one correspondence is promoted by allowing the user to drag one, and only one, bee to each flower and having it sit on that flower. Regarding limitations, the app does not say counting words out loud (i.e., there is no promotion of verbal counting). Also, the principle of cardinality is not explicitly promoted. However, if the user chooses to count the items in each set, then the user applies cardinality when deciding which set has more items.

5.2 Six Episodes of Ben Playing with the App

The following six episodes occurred in Ben and Mom's house, in the order in which they appear here, in the same sitting.

Episode 1 – On the screen are four flowers in a row and three bees hovering above. Ben uses his finger to count the bees, counting out loud as he touches each one, "one, two, three", and then counts the flowers (also with his finger and also counting out loud – "one, two, three, four"). Mom then asks, "So which has more?" Ben touches the icon of the flower on the bottom of the screen, correctly indicating that there are more flowers than bees, and Mom says, "well done".

Episode 2 – On the screen are five flowers and five bees. Ben drags one of the bees and uses that bee to count each flower, without picking up his finger in between, and counts out loud, "one, two, three, four, five". In other words, he uses the bee as a pointer to count each flower. He lifts his finger from the bee and it goes back to where it was in the beginning. He then wants to count the bees, and again chooses one of the bees, dragging it to each of the other bees, saying out loud, "one, two, three, four". He touches the icon of the flower on the bottom of the screen to indicate that there are more flowers. At this point, the app recognizes the mistake and the bees move so that one bee hovers over each flower. Mom then says, "Not right. See, the app explains to you that they are equal. You missed one (bee). Never mind". At this point Ben touches the icon of the equal sign and a new screen appears.

From the above two episodes, we learn that Ben can count out loud at least till five. He also exhibits understanding of the one-to-one principle as he assigns one counting number to each flower or bee. It seems also that he is aware of the cardinality principle; he counts the items and then chooses the icon representing the set which, according to his enumeration, has more items.

In the first episode, Mom does not intervene other than her encouragement at the end. In the second episode, she does intervene, but only after Ben chooses the incorrect icon. That being said, she takes the mediator approach (Hundeland, Erfjord, & Carlsen, 2013) by interpreting what happened on the screen when Ben touched the incorrect icon. She does not explicitly explain to Ben what happened on the screen, nor does she ask Ben if he understands what happened. She also does not wait and give Ben a chance to understand what the app is trying to show him. Instead, she refers to his counting of the bees, saying that he "missed one", perhaps reinforcing enumeration as a method for set comparison. Furthermore, she does not point out how his mistake occurred, that if he had not used the bee as a pointer, he might have answered correctly. Finally, we cannot know if Ben touched the equality icon because his mother said that the sets were equal or because he understood now, perhaps from the bee-to-flower correspondence displayed on the screen, that the sets were indeed equal.

Episode 3 – On the screen are four flowers and five bees. Ben again uses a bee as an Episode 3 – On the screen are four flowers and five bees. Ben again uses a bee as a pointer, dragging it to each flower and counting out loud, "one, two, three, four". He then lifts his finger, and the bee returns to its former place. Ben again uses a bee to count the other bees, saying out loud, "one, two, three, four ... they are equal", and immediately presses the equal icon. As the app then moves each bee to each flower (leaving one bee in the sky), Mom says: "Equal? Look. What do you see? So, what is there more of? Who has one left over? Who has more?" Ben replies by pressing on the bee icon, indicating that there are more bees, while answering his Mom, "bees". It seems that Ben understands that if every flower is matched to one bee, and there are still bees left over, then that means that there are more bees than flowers.

When comparing Mom's intervention here with the intervention in the second episode, we notice a few differences. First, in the second episode, Mom states facts, while in the third episode, she asks questions. In the second episode, Mom tells Ben the answer. Here she does not. In the second episode, she does not refer to the flower-to-bee correspondence shown on the screen, while in the third episode, she explicitly points to the bee left hovering over the flowers. It seems that in the third episode Mom has transitioned to more of a teacher approach (Hundeland, Erfjord, & Carlsen, 2013). On the other hand, in both episodes she does not refer to Ben's use of the bee as a pointer as the apparent cause of his mistakes.

Episode 4 – On the screen are six flowers and six bees. Ben once again starts by taking one of the bees to use as a pointer when counting the flowers. As he drags the bee his Mom says, "You don't have to take it (the bee) with you". Here, Mom is taking the assistant approach (Hundeland, Erfjord, & Carlsen, 2013), helping Ben to use the app correctly. Ben then lets go of the bee, and uses his finger to count each bee, saying out loud "one, two, three, four, five, six". After counting the bees, Mom says, "Good". Ben then uses his finger to count the flowers, again saying out loud, "one, two, three, four, five, six". He then says, "Equal", and presses the equals sign. Mom says "good job", and the screen changes.

Episode 5 – On the screen are seven flowers and seven bees. Ben counts correctly the flowers, using his finger. He then counts the bees, counting one of the bees twice and thus reaching eight. He clicks on the bee (incorrectly) and the app moves the bees so that one bee hovers over each flower. Ben then presses the equals sign. Mom does not comment at all. Without assistance, it seems that Ben understands that if there is one-to-one correspondence there must be an equal amount of items in each set.

Episode 6 – On the screen are four flowers and two bees. Ben counts the flowers with his finger, then the bees, and correctly presses the flower icon.

Summarizing the first six episodes, we note that Ben always counts the flowers correctly, but only counts the bees correctly when there are two or three bees. In the beginning, he uses a bee to count the other bees, but does not include that pointer bee in the set of bees. However, even when this mistake is corrected, he miscounts the bees when there are seven, yet correctly counts seven flowers. Recall, that the flowers are laid out in a row, while the bees are not in any order. This might have contributed to Ben's difficulty in keeping track of which bees he already counted.

5.3 Discussing Ben and Mom

The second aim of this study was to investigate if and how theoretical affordances and limitations of an app come to be realized in practice, as a child-adult cohort engages with one of the apps. Although this particular app did not specifically promote verbal counting or cardinality, Ben was able to practice these skills while counting the bees and flowers and choosing which had more elements. Mom offered general feedback in her response of "well done", but not explicit feedback regarding these skills. On the other hand, the app specifically promoted one-to-one correspondence by allowing the user to drag one, and only one, bee to each flower and having it sit on that flower. Yet, Ben did not realize that he could drag each bee to a flower, nor did his mother assist him in using the technology. Thus, although the app provided two ways of comparing sets (one-to-one correspondence and counting), Ben only uses the counting method.

Several educators suggest that solving a problem in multiple ways may promote flexibility, as well as advanced mathematical thinking (Leikin, 2007; Silver, 1997). Even at a young age, children are able to solve a problem in more than one way (Tsamir, Tirosh, Tabach, & Levenson, 2010). While Mom, at this point in the workshop, was familiar with Gelman and Gallistel's (1978) counting principles, it could be that she was less aware of the importance of being able to solve a problem using different methods. It could also be that she related one-to-one correspondence to enumeration, not realizing its usefulness when comparing sets. That being said, when Ben touched an incorrect icon, the app moved the bees, visually showing one-to-one correspondence between bees and flowers. With Mom interpreting the screen for Ben, Ben was able to understand from this visual presentation if the sets are equivalent or not.

6 Conclusions

As shown in this study, different apps have different ways of supporting various competencies, along with different limitations. The analysis carried out in this study can be used to help early childhood educators choose apps that can support counting and enumeration. Taking into consideration the affordances and limitations of such apps, as well as how these affordances may be taken advantage of, adults can plan how to use the apps when interacting with children. The study also demonstrates the importance of adult intervention. While Ben's mother helped him overcome some obstacles, more could have been gained. As teacher educators, we are aware of the need to enhance teachers' mathematics knowledge as well as their pedagogical content knowledge (Shulman, 1986). Similarly, but perhaps using different methods, if we wish the home environment to contribute to children's mathematical growth, and we wish parents to download apps wisely and engage with their children on these apps, we also need to seek ways to enhance adults' mathematics knowledge and pedagogical knowledge. Studies such as these are a step in this direction.

Acknowledgment

This research was supported by The Israel Science Foundation (grant No. 1631/18).

Note

1   Parts of this study were presented at the SEMT'19 conference in Prague.

References

Anders, Y., Rossbach, H. G., Weinert, S., Ebert, S., Kuger, S., Lehrl, S., & von Maurice, J. (2012). Home and preschool learning environments and their relations to the development of early numeracy skills. *Early Childhood Research Quarterly, 27*(2), 231–244.

Arp, S., & Fagard, J. (2005). What impairs subitizing in cerebral palsied children? *Developmental Psychobiology: The Journal of the International Society for Developmental Psychobiology, 47*(1), 89–102.

Baroody, A. J. (1987). *Children's mathematical thinking: A developmental framework for preschool, primary, and special education teachers*. Teacher's College Press.

Bowen, G. (2009). Document analysis as a qualitative research method. *Qualitative Research Journal, 9*(2), 27–40.

Clarke, B., Cheeseman, J., & Clarke, D. (2006). The mathematical knowledge and understanding young children bring to school. *Mathematics Education Research Journal, 18*(1), 78–102.

Dorward, J. (2002). Intuition and research: Are they compatible? *Teaching Children Mathematics, 8*(6), 329–332.

Dubé, A. K., & McEwen, R. N. (2015). Do gestures matter? The implications of using touchscreen devices in mathematics instruction. *Learning and Instruction, 40,* 89–98.

Duncan, G. J., Dowsett, C. J., Claessens, A., Magnuson, K., Huston, A. C., Klebanov, P., et al. (2007). School readiness and later achievement. *Developmental Psychology, 43*(6), 1428–1446.

Fluck, M., & Henderson, L. (1996). Counting and cardinality in English nursery pupils. *British Journal of Educational Psychology, 66,* 501–517.

Fuson, K. C. (1988). *Children's counting and concepts of number.* Springer-Verlag.

Gelman, R., & Gallistel, C. (1978). *The child's understanding of number.* Harvard University Press.

Greenfield, D. B., & Scott, M. S. (1986). Young children's preference for complementary pairs: Evidence against a shift to a taxonomic preference. *Developmental Psychology, 22*(1), 19.

Hundeland, P. S., Erfjord, I., & Carlsen, M. (2013). Use of digital tools in mathematical learning activities in the kindergarten: Teachers' approaches. In B. Ubuz, Ç. Haser, & M. A. Mariotti (Eds.), *Proceedings of the Eighth Congress of European Research in Mathematics Education* (pp. 2108–2117). Middle East Technical University and ERME.

Israel National Preschool Mathematics Curriculum (INPMC). (2008). Retrieved April 7, 2009, from http://meyda.education.gov.il/files/Tochniyot_Limudim/KdamYesodi/Math1.pdf

Izard, V., Streri, A., & Spelke, E. S. (2014). Toward exact number: Young children use one-to-one correspondence to measure set identity but not numerical equality. *Cognitive Psychology, 72,* 27–53.

Kullberg, A., & Björklund, C. (2020). Preschoolers' diferent ways of structuring part-part-whole relations with finger patterns when solving an arithmetic task. *ZDM Mathematics Education, 52*(4), 767–778.

Lange, T., & Meaney, T. (2013, February). iPads and mathematical play: A new kind of sandpit for young children. In B. Ubuz, C. Haser, & M. A. Mariotti (Eds.), *Proceedings of the Eighth Congress of the European Society for Research in Mathematics Education* (pp. 2138–2147). Middle East Technical University and ERME.

Leikin, R. (2007). *Habits of mind associated with advanced mathematical thinking and solution spaces of mathematical tasks* [Paper presentation]. The Working Group on Advanced Mathematical Thinking – CERME-5, Cyprus.

Linchevski, L., & Vinner, S. (1988). The naive concept of sets in elementary teachers. In *Proceedings of the 12th International Conference for the Psychology of Mathematics Education* (Vol. 2, pp. 471–478). Veszprém, Hungary.

Ministry of Education. (2010). *Israel National Mathematics Preschool Curriculum (INMPC)*. Ministry of Culture and Education.

Moyer-Packenham, P. S., et al. (2015). The role of affordances in children's learning performance and efficiency when using virtual manipulative mathematics touchscreen apps. *Mathematics Education Research Journal, 28,* 79–105.

Sarama, J., & Clement, D. (2009). *Early childhood mathematics education research: Learning trajectories for young children*. Routledge.

Shulman, L. S. (1986). Those who understand: Knowledge growth in teaching. *Educational Researcher, 15*(2), 4–14.

Sinclair, N., & SedaghatJou, M. (2013). Finger counting and adding with TouchCounts. In B. Ubuz, C. Haser, & M. A. Mariotti (Eds.), *Proceedings of the Eighth Congress of the European Society for Research in Mathematics Education (CERME 8)* (pp. 2198–2207). Middle East Technical University and ERME.

Silver, E. A. (1997). Fostering creativity through instruction rich mathematical problem solving and problem posing. *ZDM The International Journal of Mathematics Education, 29*(3), 75–80.

Stein, M. K., Grover, B. W., & Henningsen, M. (1996). Building student capacity for mathematical thinking and reasoning: An analysis of mathematical tasks used in reform classrooms. *American Educational Research Journal, 33*(2), 455–488.

Tirosh, D., Tsamir, P., Barkai, R., & Levenson, E. (2018). Engaging young children with mathematical activities involving different representations: Triangles, patterns, and counting objects. *Center for Educational Policy Studies Journal, 8*(2), 9–30.

Tsamir, P., Tirosh, D., Tabach, M., & Levenson, E. (2010). Multiple solution methods and multiple outcomes – is it a task for kindergarten children? *Educational Studies in Mathematics, 73*(3), 217–231.

Tucker, I. S., & Johnson, N. T. (2020). Developing number sense with Fingu: A preschooler's embodied mathematics during interactions with a multi-touch digital game. *Mathematics Education Research Journal.* https://doi.org/10.1007/s13394-020-00349-4

PART 2

Geometry: Teaching Learning and Thinking

∵

CHAPTER 4

Learning and Teaching Geometry in Early Childhood

Douglas H. Clements, Julie Sarama and Candace Joswick

Abstract

Geometry is an essential topic in mathematics and helps build a foundation for learning other mathematical topics and advanced mathematics study as well as for other subject matter areas, such as science, technology, engineering, and cartography. Furthermore, geometry and spatial thinking are fundamental to young children's mathematical *development*. However, in many countries, including the United States, geometry does not play a significant role in research or educational policy and praxis. We briefly review research on young children's concepts and learning of geometry and then focus on the results of several research projects grounded on that research.

Keywords

geometry – spatial thinking – young children – early childhood education – preschool

1 Introduction

Geometry is an essential topic in mathematics and helps build a foundation for learning other mathematical topics and advanced mathematics study. Geometry also builds a foundation for other subject matter areas, such as science, technology, engineering, and cartography (Cheng & Mix, 2012; Clements & Battista, 1992; Kell, Lubinski, Benbow, & Steiger, 2013; N. Newcombe, 2010; Olkun & Sarı, 2016; Sarama & Clements, 2009b; The Spatial Reasoning Study Group, 2015; Vallortigara, 2012; Verdine, Golinkoff, Hirsh-Pasek, & Newcombe, 2017; Zacharos, Antonopoulos, & Ravanis, 2011; Zorzi, Priftis, & Umiltà, 2002) and, thus, "is an integral part of our cultural experience being a vital component of numerous aspects of life from architecture to design" (Jones, 2002, p. 122). Research indicates the importance of geometry and spatial thinking to children's mathematical development (Clements & Battista, 1992; Maričić

& Stamatović, 2017; Olkun & Sarı, 2016; The Spatial Reasoning Study Group, 2015; Vallortigara, 2012; Zacharos, Antonopoulos, & Ravanis, 2011; Zorzi, Priftis, & Umiltà, 2002). However, in many countries, including the United States, geometry does not play a significant role in research or educational policy and praxis (e.g., Clements & Sarama, 2021; Klim-Klimaszewska & Nazaruk, 2017), although it has begun to re-emerged in some (Woolcott, Logan, Marshman, Ramful, Whannell, & Lowrie, 2020). In this chapter, we briefly review research on young children's concepts and learning of geometry and then focus on the results of several research projects grounded on that research.

2 Young Children's Geometric Thinking

Geometric shape is a fundamental construct in mathematics, and also in cognitive development. For example, very young children form initial categories for everyday objects via similarity among instances in shape (Jones & Smith, 2002).

Turning to learning about geometric shapes themselves, the influential van Hiele theory (1986) posits that there are levels of thinking. Two are relevant to the early years. At the visual-holistic level, children view shapes only as "wholes" and, asked to justify why a shape is a rectangle, may reply, "It looks like a door". At the second, descriptive/analytic, level, children learn about the properties of shapes, such as rectangles having equal and opposite length sides and all right angles. Several modifications has been suggested to this overarching theory, such an initial "pre-recognition" level (Clements & Battista, 1992).

Subsequent research shows children begin forming conceptual understanding of geometric figures in the early childhood years. Experiences children have regarding concepts such as the names of shape classes (Vinner & Hershkowitz, 1980) tend to stabilize by the age of 6 years (Gagatsis & Patronis, 1990), so 3- to 6-years of age may be a particularly significant period for learning about geometric figures (Clements, Swaminathan, Hannibal, & Sarama, 1999; National Research Council, 2009).

Analysis of children's identification of geometric figures is aided by defining specific subcategories of examples (members of the class of shapes) and nonexamples (nonmembers of the class of shapes). We classify geometric figures used in research assessments into four subcategories (Clements & Sarama, 2021) illustrated in Figure 4.1 with examples for the classes of triangles and rectangles. Geometric figures are categorized as either members of the class (correct selections on shape identification items) or non-members, called distractors. Each of these categories is further categorized into those

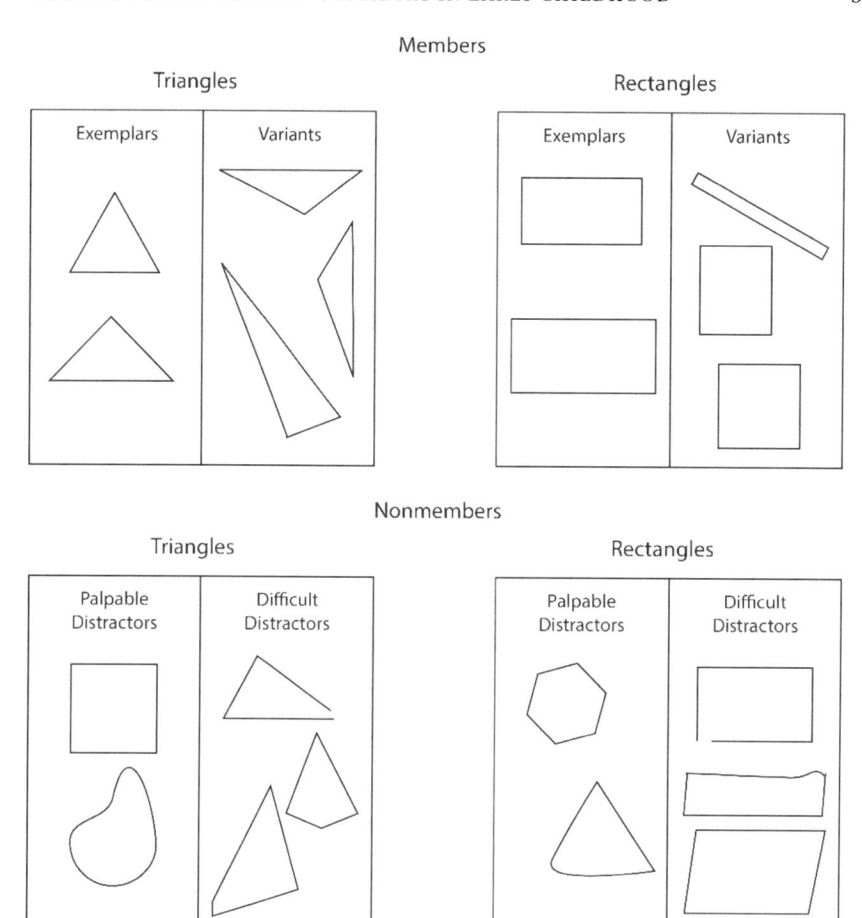

FIGURE 4.1   Subcategories of geometric shapes

more and less representative of that category. Exemplars are theoretically- and empirically-determined prototypes of the class – that is, the often traditional, common representations of shapes like equilateral triangles with a horizontally-oriented base. Variants are other members of the class that differ from these exemplars, or are less common or traditional representations used in young children's instruction and storybooks. Palpable distractors do not have an overall resemblance to members of the shape class (e.g., curved shapes for the triangle selection item). Difficult distractors are highly visually similar to members but lack at least one defining attribute (e.g., a triangular shape with a slight gap).

The basis for this categorization is simultaneously mathematical and psychological. Mathematically, of course, members are those geometric figures that possess all defining attributes of the shape classes, whereas non-members do not. Psychological studies validate the other subcategories: exemplars vs. variants, and palpable distractors vs. difficult distractors. For instance, research suggests inborn or early developing geometric competences and tendencies to form specific mental prototypes such as the exemplars in Figure 4.1 (Dillon, Huang, & Spelke, 2013; Dillon & Spelke, 2015; Newcombe & Huttenlocher, 2000; Sarama & Clements, 2009b). Culture influences these preferences, such as the ubiquitous presentation in the United States and other countries of so-called "basic" shapes (often circles, squares, rectangles, triangles) in limited prototypical forms (Aslan & Aktas-Arnas, 2007a). Such forms are directly reflected in children's behaviors (e.g., Clements et al., 1999). For example, 4- to 5-year olds considered non-horizontally and vertically oriented squares no longer the same shape or even same size (Vurpillot, 1976). Similarly, 6- to 7-year-olds retained shapes' characteristics, but lost their category and name; for example, a square rotated 45° was no longer a square to them, and instead was frequently named a "diamond". Only by 8- to 9 years of age did students achieve invariance of such shapes (Vurpillot, 1976) and without high-quality instruction many students do not achieve this until much later. This may reflect systematic bias for horizontal and vertical shape sides and line segments and a need for perceptual learning and flexibility, but restricted exposures exacerbate such restrictions. Research indicates that without high-quality geometry experiences, such rigid visual prototypes dominate children's concepts and dominate children's visual and geometric thinking throughout their lives (Fuys, Geddes, & Tischler, 1988; Kabanova-Meller, 1970; Vinner & Hershkowitz, 1980; Zykova, 1969).

Research has identified specific prototypes children develop, with similar results in Singapore, Turkey, and the U.S. (Aktas-Arnas & Aslan, 2004; Aslan & Aktas-Arnas, 2007b; Clements et al., 1999; Yin, 2003). Preschoolers (about 4 years old) identify circles accurately, with only a few children choosing an ellipse and other "curved" shapes (those are difficult distractors). Most children describe circles as "round", but few could offer any description. Children also identified squares fairly well, with some choosing nonsquare rhombi (again, difficult distractors).

Children were less accurate at recognizing triangles and rectangles (except in Turkey, Aslan, & Aktas-Arnas, 2007b). Aslan found that children correctly identified triangles whose examples are, of course, more visually diverse than circles, squares, or rectangles, about 60% of the time. Data from both the U.S. and Singapore revealed a phase in which children chose more triangle examples and palpable distractors, then restricted their criteria to omit some palpable distractors but also some members – essentially over-sharpening their concepts of triangle class members. In particular, the children's visual prototype seemed to be of an isosceles triangle with a horizontal base. Turkish children found triangles the most difficult class of shapes to classify (Aslan & Aktas-Arnas, 2007b). Asked to select rectangles, young children tended to also accept "long" parallelograms or right trapezoids along with rectangle shapes. Thus, children's visual prototype of a rectangle seems to be a four-sided figure with two long parallel sides and "close to" square corners. Striking across the U.S. studies is the lack of significant change from the preschool years to sixth grade (Clements et al., 1999). Indeed, children ages 3 to 6 were asked to sort a variety of manipulative forms (Clements, Swaminathan, Hannibal, & Sarama, 1999). Certain characteristics irrelevant to mathematical shape classification affected children's categorizations: skewness, aspect ratio, and, for certain situations, orientation. When sorting manipulatives, orientation had the least effect. Children may ignore orientation for manipulatives, knowing intuitively that they can be easily turned. Most children accepted triangles even if their base was not horizontal. Skewness, or lack of symmetry, had more influence on their identifications. Many children rejected triangles because "the point on top is not in the middle". Turkish children were also highly influenced by lack of symmetry and showed the same pattern (Aslan & Aktas-Arnas, 2007b). For rectangles, on the other hand, many children accepted non-right parallelograms and right trapezoids.

Also important was aspect ratio. Children preferred an aspect ratio near one for triangles; that is, about the same height as width. Children described other forms as "too pointy" or "too flat" (see the later section on Shape Makers). Children rejected both triangles and rectangles that were "too skinny" or "not wide enough". These same factors (with an additional one of size in some cases) similarly affected children's judgments in Turkey (Aslan & Aktas-Arnas, 2007b).

In another study, children of 3, 4, 5, 7, and 9 years of age, and adults, were asked to sort shapes (Satlow & Newcombe, 1998). A substantial change occurred between 4- and especially 5-years of age to 7 years, with older children relying more on rule-based definitions and less on perceptual similarity (early concept images) than younger children. Younger children were more likely to accept palpable distractors with characteristic features and reject variants. Development regarding recognition of variants was incremental, but identification of palpable distractors showed sudden improvement. Consistent with research discussed, shapes with multiple variants, such as triangles, were more difficult. The authors state that this evidence disconfirms theories of general development, including Piaget's or the van Hieles'. However, the shift itself is consistent with our hierarchic interactionalism reinterpretations of these theories (Sarama & Clements, 2009b).

3 Teaching and Learning about Shapes

Geometry does not play a significant role in the practice of early mathematics education in the U.S. and some other countries (Clements, 2004; National Research Council, 2009; N. Newcombe, 2010; Ng, 2011; Sarama & Clements, 2009b; The Spatial Reasoning Study Group, 2015). Instead, both research and practice is dominated by number and arithmetic operations (Clements & Sarama, 2011; Clements et al., 1999; Dağlı & Halat, 2016; Flevares & Schiff, 2014). In fact, geometry is one of the mathematical domains least understood by teachers of young children in many countries (e.g., Clements & Sarama, 2011; Fujita & Jones, 2006; Lee, 2010; Ng, 2011; Turgut, Yenilmez, & Anapa, 2014) with negative effects (Firmender, 2011; van der Sandt, 2007). Such neglect is inconsistent with research indicating the importance of geometry and spatial thinking to children's mathematical development (Clements & Battista, 1992; Olkun & Sarı, 2016; The Spatial Reasoning Study Group, 2015; Vallortigara, 2012; Zacharos, Antonopoulos, & Ravanis, 2011; Zorzi, Priftis, & Umiltà, 2002). To contribute to research that can guide early geometry teaching and curriculum, we review research on young children's learning of shape from recent interventions. We first describe an early intervention because it contributed to several of these.

3.1 The Agam Program

The Agam program was designed to teach young children "visual literacy" (Eylon & Rosenfeld, 1990; Razel & Eylon, 1986). An artist, Yaacov Agam, and collaborating educational researchers designed the Agam program to develop the visual language of children ages 3 to 7 years. This visual language is composed of basic elements and their interrelationships. Like verbal language, visual language is based on a symbol system and it can be applied to thinking and problem-solving in many areas. For these reasons, the researchers and practitioners who have implemented this curriculum believe that "teaching visual language should be viewed as 'a basic' and should commence, within the formal school system, at a young age" (Razel & Eylon, 1990, p. 12).

The activities begin by building a visual alphabet. For example, the activities introduce horizontal lines in isolation. Then, they teach relations, such as parallel lines. In the same way, activities introduce circles, then concentric circles, and then a horizontal line intersecting a circle. The curriculum also develops verbal language, but always following a visual introduction. Combination rules involving the visual alphabet and ideas such as large, medium, and small, generate complex figures. As words combine to make sentences, the elements of the visual alphabet combine to form complex patterns and symmetric forms. The Agam approach is structured, with instruction proceeding from passive identification to memory to active discovery, first in simple form (e.g., looking for plastic circles hidden by the teacher), then in tasks that require visual analysis (e.g., finding circles in picture books, see Flevares & Schiff, 2014). Only then does a teacher present tasks requiring reproduction of combinations from memory. The curriculum repeats these ideas in a large number of activities featuring multiple modes of representation, such as physical activity, group activity, and auditory perception.

The authors believed that "the generative nature of the visual language developed in the experimental children would allow children to extend the language learned to new situations and help them to solve problems in which no prior training was given" (Razel & Eylon, 1990). The results of using the program, especially with children for consecutive years, supported this hypothesis. Children gained not only geometric and spatial skills and showed pronounced benefits in the areas of arithmetic and writing readiness (Razel & Eylon, 1990, 1991). Those children who participated in the curriculum instruction for 2 years benefited more than those who participated for 1 year or not at all. Razel and Eylon (1990) concluded that these two findings point to the educational potential of the Agam approach of systematic long-term instruction in the domain of visual cognition in early childhood.

3.2   *The Agam Program Adapted for USA Kindergartens*

Compared to children who have participated in the Agam program in Israel, children of ages 5 and 6 in the U.S. experience limited instruction or guidance in geometry learning beyond informal experiences. This is unfortunate, as the aforementioned research has indicated that understanding spatial skills and geometry concepts, in addition to visual cognition, results in positive effects on general intelligence and school readiness of children entering the first grade. Therefore, we adopted and adapted the Agam program for use in a kindergarten (Clements, Sarama, Swaminathan, Weber, & Trawick-Smith, 2018; Swaminathan, Clements, & Schrier, 1995). Findings confirmed the positive effects. In the area of shape identification, the Agam group was significantly better in identifying squares and triangles. For example, only 95% of the Agam group recognized "rotated" squares compared to only 20% of the comparison group. The Agam group also more frequently referred to the geometric attributes in justifying their decisions. They showed more growth in geometric patterning and in reproducing patterns from memory, indicating an enhancement in mental visual cognition.

3.3   *The Building Blocks Curriculum*

Building Blocks was a U.S. National Science Foundation (NSF)-funded mathematics curriculum development project, designed to comprehensively address recent standards for early mathematics education for all children (Sarama &

Clements, 2002). Previous articles describe the research-based design model that guided its development in further depth (Clements, 2007; Sarama & Clements, 2002). Here we review the design, then give geometric examples.

3.3.1   The Center of Building Blocks: Research-Based Learning Trajectories

All components of the Building Blocks curriculum (Clements & Sarama, 2013) are based on learning trajectories for each core topic. Learning trajectories are descriptions of the paths of children's thinking and learning in a specific mathematical domain, and a related, conjectured route through a set of instructional tasks. They have three interrelated components, (a) a goal, (c) a developmental progression of levels of thinking, and (c) instructional activities correlated to each level. To attain a certain mathematical competence in a given topic or domain (the goal), students learn each successive level (the developmental progression), aided by tasks (instructional activities) designed to build the mental actions-on-objects that enable thinking at each higher level. The design process for the Building Blocks learning trajectories had three distinct steps. First, each topic was examined to ensure it was appropriate and important – mathematically and generative of future learning. Second, empirically-based models of children's thinking and learning were synthesized to create a developmental progression of levels of thinking in the goal domain (Clements & Sarama, 2004; Clements, Sarama, & DiBiase, 2004; Cobb & McClain, 2002; Gravemeijer, 1999; Simon, 1995). Third, sets of activities were designed to engender those mental processes or actions hypothesized to move children through the developmental progression. This resulted in seven *learning trajectories* for early geometry.

For geometric shapes (both two- and three-dimensional) and spatial reasoning, the process revealed distinct levels of geometric thinking for different topics that built upon, but extended, early work (Clements, 1992; Van den Heuvel-Panhuizen & Buys, 2005; van Hiele, 1986), which produced developmental progressions – the core of learning trajectories – for each topic (Clements & Sarama, 2021; Sarama & Clements, 2009b). For example, the progression for knowledge of geometric figures moves from increasingly sophisticated comparing (matching) through levels of recognizing and naming (including variants and difficult distractor, Figure 4.1), identification of the components of figures, to the understanding of properties of shapes, and finally the use of those properties when classifying and analyzing sets of geometric figures. Instruction was designed to help students gain competencies at each successive level of the learning trajectory. Every Building Blocks instructional activity is also based on research. As an example, activities incorporate body movement, from tracing and walking the contours of shapes to building them, because even recognizing shapes involves more than static visual perception (Clements & Sarama, 2021; Piaget & Inhelder, 1967). In fact, research recommends that even books on shapes should follow research, because most trade books on shapes are woefully inadequate (Flevares & Schiff, 2014; Nurnberger-Haag, 2016).

To provide a more illustrative example, consider the related topic of shape composition. Composition of two-dimensional geometric figures was determined to be significant for children in two ways (similar for 3D shapes, which we do not discuss here). First, it is a basic geometric competence, growing from preschoolers' building with shapes to sophisticated interpretation and analysis of geometric situations in high school mathematics and above. Second, the concepts and actions of creating and then iterating units and higher-order units in the context of constructing patterns, measuring, and computing are established bases for mathematical understanding and analysis (Clements, Battista, Sarama, & Swaminathan, 1997; Reynolds & Wheatley, 1996; Steffe & Cobb, 1988).

The developmental progression was born in observations of children's explorations (Sarama, Clements, & Vukelic, 1996) and refined through a series of clinical interviews and focused observations, then validated by comparing to previous studies (Mansfield & Scott, 1990; Razel & Eylon, 1986; Sales, 1994; Vurpillot, 1976). From a lack of competence in composing geometric shapes (called the Separate Shapes Actor: Foundations level) children gain abilities to use individual shapes to make a picture but with each shape playing a unique semantic role (Piece Assembler) and then to combine shapes – initially through trial and error (e.g., Picture Maker), concatenating shapes to form a component of a picture but not necessarily conceptualizing these creations as geometric shapes. At the Shape Composer level, children develop competence with angles and anticipatory imagery and thus compose shapes to intentionally create superordinate shapes, or shapes that are compositions of other shapes.

A main instructional task of Building Blocks requires children to solve outline puzzles with shapes off and on the computer, a motivating activity (Eylon & Rosenfeld, 1990; Razel & Eylon, 1986; Sales, 1994; Sarama, Clements, & Vukelic, 1996, note Building Blocks borrowed many other aspects and activities from the Agam program, with permission). For example, in on- and off-computer activities, they solve geometric puzzles. The objects are shapes and composite shapes and the actions include creating, duplicating, positioning (with geometric motions like "turn" and "flip"), combining, and decomposing both individual shapes (units) and composite shapes (units of units). The characteristics of the tasks require actions on these objects corresponding to each level in the learning trajectory. For example, the puzzles for the Piece Assembler level scaffold children's growing ability to match shapes without, and then with sides touching. Those for the Picture Maker level increasingly require that children must compose shapes and those for Shape Composer have larger areas in which angles must be attended to. Teachers are guided to use the cognitive model of each level (Sarama & Clements, 2009b) to guide formative assessment, identifying children's level of thinking and interacting with them to help them develop thinking at the subsequent level. Ample opportunity for student-led, student designed, open-ended projects are included in each set of activities. Problem posing on the part of students appears to be an effective way for students to express their creativity and integrate their learning (Brown & Walter, 1990; Kilpatrick, 1987; van Oers, 1994), although few empirical studies have been conducted, especially on young children. The computer can offer support for such projects (Clements, 2000). For "Piece Puzzler", students design their own puzzles with the shapes; when they click on a "Play" button, their design is transformed into a shape puzzle that either they or their friends can solve. More details for all seven of the learning trajectories for early geometry and spatial thinking are provided in Clements & Sarama (2021) or at *Learning and Teaching with Learning Trajectories* (including videos for each level of the developmental progression and of many instructional activities).[1]

3.3.2   Results from Multiple Studies – What Did Children Learn in Geometry from Building Blocks?

In an early comparison study involving only four classrooms, effects on geometry were large (Clements & Sarama, 2007). Examining specific topics, the relative effects on turn and congruence were small. Effects on construction of shapes and spatial orientation were large. The largest relative gains in geometry were achieved on shape identification and composition of shapes (gains in composition were four times as large as those of the control group, Clements & Sarama, 2007). A qualitative study of children's learning in the Building Blocks classrooms showed that children felt quite powerful knowing and applying definitions of triangles (Spitler, Sarama, & Clements, 2003). One preschooler said, "That's not a triangle! It's too skinny!" However, his Building Blocks friend responded, "I'm telling you, it is a triangle. It's got three straight sides, see? One, two, three! It doesn't matter that I made it skinny" (see similar results in Section 3.5.1).

A second study was a randomized-trials evaluation involving 36 preschool classrooms randomly assigned to one of three conditions: experimental (Building Blocks), comparison (a different preschool mathematics curriculum) or control (Clements & Sarama, 2008). The Building Blocks group scored significantly higher than the comparison group (effect size, .47) and the control group score (effect size, 1.07). On geometry, both intervention groups scored higher than the control group, with little difference between them, on identifying shapes and constructing shapes, although the Building Blocks group increased in the frequency of completely correct constructions more than the other two groups (again, these comparisons involved descriptive statistics only, not inferential tests. The Building Blocks group scored higher than both the comparison and control groups on comparing shape and on shape composition, again mostly due to the Building Blocks group generating fully correct solutions. They also increased substantially more than the other groups in using more sophisticated strategies, such as rotating shapes into the correct orientation before placing them on the puzzle, searching for specific shapes with intentionality, and, in general, solving puzzles systematically, immediately, and confidently.

Finally, we also evaluated Building Blocks' effectiveness in a larger cluster randomized trial design involving 42 schools serving 1,375 preschoolers in 106 classrooms (Clements, Sarama, Spitler, Lange & Wolfe, 2011). Teachers implemented the intervention with adequate fidelity. The overall positive effect was moderate to large (.72 SD); we did not analyze its effects on geometry separately. For this paper, we calculated effects for the geometry sections of the assessment. Hierarchical Linear Modeling analyses revealed a significant difference for the experimental versus comparison conditions (beta = .273, $p < .05$, effect size, .61). Children experiencing Building Blocks demonstrated higher ability scores on geometry than control children.

3.3.3   General Discussion of Building Blocks Research

Supporting previous studies, emphasis on the learning trajectory for geometric topics in the Building Blocks curriculum led to effects, some equivalent to benefits often found for individual tutoring. In the second study, the Building Blocks curriculum made the most substantial gains compared to both a non-treatment and another preschool math curriculum in shape composition and several other topics. Especially because the other curriculum also included all these geometric topics, such as shape composition activities, we believe that the greater gains caused by the Building Blocks curriculum can be attributed to its explicit use of the sequenced activities developed from, and the teachers' knowledge of, learning trajectories. These learning trajectories explicate the mathematical concepts, principles, and processes involved in each level of the trajectory and the relationships across levels, including the components of geometric shapes (e.g., correct definition of "side") as well as relationships between components (e.g., sides forming a right angle) and shape classes (e.g., a square as a subcategory of rectangle and justification for this based on properties). The learning trajectories are also designed to develop teachers' knowledge of students' developmental progressions in learning that content (moving from intuitively recognizing shapes as unanalyzed visual wholes, to recognizing components of shapes, to hierarchically classifying shape categories) and to inform teachers of the rationale for the instructional design of each (e.g., why certain length sticks are provided to children with the challenge to build specific shapes).

3.4   *Educational Technology for Early Geometry*

Research indicates that well-designed educational technology, with its visual, dynamic, and interactive elements, can have a positive effect on young children's learning of geometry. For example, one of the largest predictors of child gain in the Building Blocks research was use of the software (that combined computer-assisted instruction, or CAI, with computer manipulatives, as described in the following section, Clements et al., 2011). Studies of CAI, usually include simple tutorials and practice-with-feedback, from around the world with CAI has an extensive history of success teaching early geometry (e.g., Almohtadi, Aldarabah, & Jwaifell, 2019; Clements & Sarama, 2003; Putri, 2020; Sarama & Clements, 2020; Zaranis, 2018). The following sections focus on approaches that go beyond simple CAI.

3.4.1   Computer Manipulatives and the Learning and Teaching of Shape

In an earlier study that influenced the design of the software in Building Blocks and LearningTrajectories.org, we investigated the role of a computer manipulative in the development of children's geometric thinking. The theoretical foundation for the study was our constructivist-based belief that both physical and computer manipulatives can aid mathematical activity, each in specific ways (Clements & McMillen, 1996). We believe that software design can and should have an explicit theoretical and empirical foundation, beyond its genesis in someone's intuitive grasp of children's learning, and it should interact with the ongoing development of theory and research – reaching toward the ideal of testing a psychological theory of children's mathematical development by testing the software that reflects the objects and processes of this theory (Clements & Battista, 2000).

In the first version of the software, called *Shapes,* kindergarten children engaged in both on- and off-computer activities involving pattern blocks (Sarama & Clements, 2016; Sarama, Clements, & Vukelic, 1996). The software and its many descendants were designed to offer specific practical and pedagogical benefits as well as mathematical and psychological benefits. Our goal was to gain insight into the role on- and off-computer manipulatives can serve in the development of geometric ideas. Both the pedagogical/practical benefits and mathematical/psychological benefits were explored, as well as the children's conceptualization of angle, shape properties, and patterning.

3.4.1.1 Practical/Pedagogical Benefits

P1. *Provides another interaction medium, configurations can be stored and retrieved.*

Unlike physical shapes, which must be put away most of the time, children's work can be saved and worked on again and again (and the supply of shapes is infinite for all children). Therefore, careful development can take place day after day.

P2. *Provides manageable, clean, and flexible manipulatives.*

Unlike physical manipulatives, computer shapes are more manageable and "clean" insomuch as they always snap into correct position even when filling an outline and they stay where they're placed. Software manipulatives often offer greater control and flexibility to children and are just as meaningful as physical manipulatives yet are easier to use for learning (Clements & McMillen, 1996; Sarama & Clements, 2016). Figure 4.2a shows a child turning the last rhombus of a picture she invented into place, which snaps into position and stays there.

P3. *Provides extensible manipulatives.*

Certain constructions are easier to make with software than with physical manipulatives. For example, building triangles (of all types) by partially occluding shapes with other shapes and making right angles by combining and occluding various shapes.

P4. *Records work and thus work can easily be extended.*

Children's explorations might be printed, making instant record-your-work, take-it-home, paper copies. The process of recording work with templates or cut-outs is less time consuming.

P5. *Allows teachers and children to build their own activities.*

Outline puzzles, "draw the other half" mirror challenges, and other similar activities easily and quickly. By pressing the arrow at the bottom right (Figure 4.2a), the girl created a puzzle for her friend to solve (Figure 4.2b).

3.4.1.2 Mathematical/Psychological Benefit

Perhaps the most powerful feature of this genre of software is that the actions possible can embody the processes we want children to develop and internalize as mental processes.

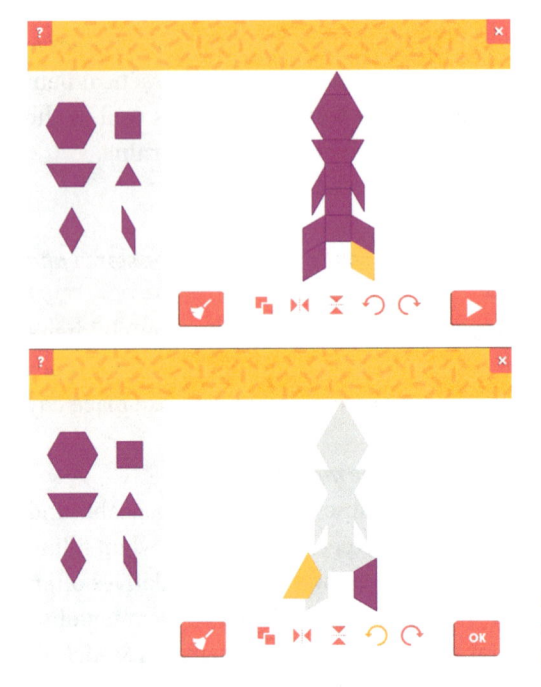

FIGURE 4.2
Shape Puzzles software from
LearningTrajectories.org

M1. *Engenders mathematical ideas and processes.*

Built-in turn and flip tools are a good way to bring geometric motions to an explicit level of conscious awareness and explicate these motions (along the bottom of Figure 4.2).

M2. *Changes the very nature of the manipulative.*

The flexibility of the computer manipulatives allows children to explore geometric figures in ways not available with physical shape or pattern sets. For example, in many software environments, children can change the size of any or all computer shapes.

M3. *Allows for composition and decomposition processes.*

Software encourages composition and decomposition of shapes with processes that would be difficult to duplicate with physical manipulatives.

M4. *Allows creating and operating on units of units.*

More advanced versions of such software allow the construction of *units of units* in children's tilings and linear patterns. For example, a set of ungrouped objects can be turned together, though, each shape will turn separately. When those objects are grouped together, though, they would turn as a unit. Thus, the actions children perform on the computer are a reflection of the mental operations we wish to help children develop (Clements & McMillen, 1996).

M5. *Allows patterns to be abstracted and extended.*

Children can use "duplication" tools to copy a shape or composite shape that they have constructed. They can move this unit with the slide, flip, and turn tools.

M6. *Allows for the exploration of symmetry dynamically.*

Some software has built-in "mirrors" which allow children to explore symmetry dynamically and which are easier to use and understand than a physical mirror or Mira because the computer does the "reflecting". Further, the software allows you to act on the shape and see the results unfolding dynamically; thus, symmetry can be seen as process rather than just static "reflection" through this illustration. In fact, for symmetry, computer activity should actually precede activity with physical manipulatives.

M7. *Develops visualization and higher-level spatial representation constructions.*

Tools and features help children develop visualization capabilities and construct higher-level spatial representations. Further, the combination of these features is powerful mathematically. For example, children might build a shape that they think is symmetric by combining any number of other shapes and gluing them together. They can then duplicate this new shape, flip it, and slide it over the original to check congruency. Again, these embody the mental processes that we want children to develop.

M8. *Connects space/geometry to number learning.*

One of the most powerful benefits of the computer is how it aids children in their linking of ideas and processes about number and arithmetic to their ideas and processes about shape and space. In fact, geometric models are used ubiquitously to teach about number.

3.4.1.3 *Findings on the Software*

Qualitative analyses showed that children experienced the specific practical/pedagogical and mathematical/psychological benefits we had posited. A discussion of each follows; space constraints allow us to provide only limited examples, all from the original research with the *Shapes* software using our original hypothesized benefits (Sarama & Clements, 2016; Sarama, Clements, & Vukelic, 1996).

P1. *Shapes provides another interaction medium, configurations can be stored and retrieved* and P2. *Shapes provides manageable, clean, and flexible manipulatives.*

As a group of children were working on a pattern with physical manipulatives, and wanted to move it slightly on the rug, two girls (four hands) tried to keep the design together, but were unsuccessful. Marissa asked Leah to "fix" the design. But in re-creating the design, Leah inserted two extra shapes and the pattern wasn't the same and the girls experienced considerable frustration at their inability to get their "old" design back. Had they been able to save their design, or move their design and keep the pieces together, as *Shapes* allows, their group project would have continued.

While working on the *Shapes* software, the children quickly learned to glue the shapes together and move them as a group when they needed more space to continue their designs. They also could leave them on the screen (or save the file) while they left to get a friend or teacher without fear of someone destroying their design.

P3.   *Shapes provides extensible manipulatives.*

Matthew, working with the physical manipulatives (off-computer), filled in an outline of a man using all rhombuses as best as possible. He was left with a space that only a green triangle would fit, and said, "If I was on computer I could make it all blue". Upon further questioning, it was revealed that the child knew that the two shapes were not the same, but that 2 green triangles (occluded) is the same as (or congruent to) one blue rhombus. He also understood that on the computer, unlike with physical manipulatives, he could use a blue diamond, allowing half of it to cover other shapes, thus filling the outline with shapes of all the same color. *Shapes*, and the flatness of the screen or lack of tangible third dimension, allows for such "building up" and thus explorations of these types of relationships.

P4.   *Shapes records work and thus work can easily be extended.*

Carl, who always built extensive designs off computer, was usually frustrated by having his designs destroyed when it was time to clean up. When he started a fairly complex pattern on computer, of which several of his classmates were watching and giving him advice, it became time to move on to another activity. Carl was finally able to return to and complete this complex design because his teacher saved the pattern for him. Marisssa and Leah's work, described previously, also provide support for this principle.

In sum, the hypothesized practical/pedagogical benefits were supported by the data, with one exception. No data was collected relevant to P5.

M1.   *Shapes engenders mathematical ideas and processes.*

When working off-computer, Mitchell quickly manipulated the pattern block pieces to fill an outline, resisting answering any questions as to his intent or his reasons. When he finally paused, a researcher asked him how he had made a particular piece fit. He struggled with the answer and then finally said that he "turned it". When working on-computer he again seemed very sure of himself and quickly manipulated the shapes, avoiding answering the questions. However, he seemed more aware of his actions, in that when asked how many times he turned a particular piece, he said, "Three", without hesitation.

M2.   *The very nature of the manipulative is changed with Shapes.*

The example of Matthew wanting to make an all blue man, recognizing that he could overlap the rhombuses and be able to exactly cover a triangle space, also serves as to support this benefit as well.

M3. *Shapes allows for composition and decomposition processes.*
Mitchell started making a hexagon out of triangles. After placing two, he counted with his finger on the screen around the center of the incomplete hexagon, imaging the other triangles. He announced that he would need four more triangles to complete the hexagon. After placing the next one, he said, "Whoa! Now, three more!" Whereas off-computer, Mitchell had to check each placement with a physical hexagon, the intentional and deliberate actions on the computer lead him to form mental images (decomposing the hexagon imagistically) and predict each succeeding placement.

M4. *Units of units can be created and operating on in Shapes* and M5. *Patterns can be abstracted and extended in Shapes.*
When Monica finished making a unit for a pattern on the computer, she glued the pieces together and moved the group to the side. She then finished making a row of that unit and stated that now she had to "glue them". When asked how many she was going to have to glue, she pointed to each hexagon (a hexagon was the center piece of her unit) and counted to six. She had built and operated on a *unit of units* as a unique entity. In many other cases, and only in the computer environment, children glued to create a unit of units and referred to it as a single entity.

M7. *Interaction with Shapes develops visualization and higher-level spatial representation constructions.*
The example of Mitchell visualizing the triangles filling a hexagon applies here as well.

The students in this study were not presented with the opportunity to engage in software activities relevant to benefits M6 and M8. In sum, the hypothesized mathematical/psychological benefits were supported in those cases for which data were collected.

In summary, in those cases for which data was collected, it supported the hypothesized benefits of the program. The children showed evidence of growth in their spatial thinking while working through the activities. Children explicated their ideas about and actions involving motions only in the computer environment. Further, only on the computer did children differentiate between the geometric motions turn and flip.

Other studies have confirmed the benefits of using such computer manipulatives (see Sarama & Clements, 2016). For example, third-grade students' exposure to virtual manipulatives was linked to improved conceptual knowledge and procedural knowledge (statistically significant improvement from pre to posttest) and enhanced enjoyment of mathematics learning (attitude surveys and interviews), especially due to the elimination of paper-and-pencil methods (Reimer & Moyer, 2005). Further, the children noted that the meaningfulness and timeless of feedback given during mathematical exploration was improved over traditional teacher-provided feedback.

3.4.2   The Geometric Turtle

One of the most heavily researched computer environments involve "turtle geometry", first widely available in the computer programming language Logo and now also in other environments such as Scratch[2] or Snap![3] Spatial learning with physical and computer movements can be particularly meaningful because it can be consistent with young children's way of moving their own bodies (Papert, 1980). With the geometric turtle, for example, young children can abstract and generalize directions and other map concepts, learning geometry and related spatial skills. Giving the turtle directions such as forward 10 steps, right turn, forward 5 steps, children learn orientation, direction, and perspective concepts, among others.

Turtle geometry in these environments can be evocative in generating thinking about shapes. In one large study (Clements, Battista, & Sarama, 2001), in response to their work with Logo some kindergartners formed their own concept, saying, "it's a *square rectangle*". This concept was applied only in certain situations: squares were still squares, and rectangles, rectangles, unless you formed a square while working with procedures – on the computer or in drawing – that were designed to produce rectangles. The concept of a "square rectangle" (a square produced with rectangle procedures) was strongly visual in nature, and no logical classification per se, such as class inclusion processes, should be inferred. The creation, application, and discussion of the concept, however, were arguably a valuable intellectual exercise.

Many researchers have studied the effects of turtle geometry on students' understanding of 2D geometric shapes in general (Clements, Battista, & Sarama, 2001; Clements & Sarama, 1997; Sarama & Clements, 2016, 2017). Guided experience can significantly enhance students' concepts of 2D figures (Butler & Close, 1989; Clements, 1987). When asked to describe geometric shapes, students with turtle geometry experience give more statements overall and more statements that explicitly mention geometric properties of shapes than students with no such experience (Clements & Battista, 1989, 1990; Lehrer & Smith, 1986). In one study, students were able to apply their knowledge of geometry better than a comparison group, but there was no difference in their knowledge of basic geometric facts. The researchers concluded that the use of turtle geometry influenced the way in which students mentally represented their knowledge of geometric concepts (Lehrer, Randle, & Sancilio, 1989).

Similarly, turtle geometry experience appears to significantly affect students' ideas about angle. Responses of control students in one study reflected no knowledge of angle or common usage, such as describing an angle as "a line tilted". In comparison, the Logo students indicated more mathematically oriented conceptualizations, such as describing an angle as "Like where a point is. Where two lines come together at a point" (Clements & Battista, 1989). Several researchers have reported that turtle geometry experience has a positive effect on students' angle concepts (Clements & Battista, 1989; du Boulay, 1986; Frazier, 1987; Kieran, 1986a; Kieran & Hillel, 1990; Noss, 1987; Olive, Lankenau, & Scally, 1986). However, in some situations, benefits do not emerge until students have more than a year of such experience (Kelly, Kelly, & Miller, 1986–1987).

On the other hand, Logo experiences may also foster some unintended conceptions of angle measure. For example, students may confuse angle measure with the amount of rotation along the path (e.g., the exterior angle in a polygon) or the degree of rotation from the vertical (Clements & Battista, 1989). In addition, concepts generated while working with turtle geometry do not replace previously-learned concepts of angle measure. For example, students' conceptions about angle measure and difficulties they have coordinating the relationships between the turtle's rotation and the constructed angle have persisted for years, especially if not properly guided by their teachers (Clements, 1987; Cope & Simmons, 1991; Hoyles & Sutherland, 1986; Kieran, 1986a; Kieran, Hillel, & Erlwanger, 1986). In general, however, appropriately designed turtle geometry experience appears to facilitate understanding of angle measure. After working with turtle geometry, students' concepts of angle size are more likely to be mathematically correct, coherent, and abstract (Clements & Battista, 1989; Kieran, 1986b; Noss, 1987), while showing a progression from van Hiele visual level to the abstract/relational level in the span of the turtle geometry instruction (Clements & Battista, 1989). If turtle geometry experiences emphasize the difference between the angle of rotation and the angle formed as the turtle traces a path, confusion regarding the measure of rotation and the measure of the angle may be avoided (Clements & Battista, 1989; Kieran, 1986b).

Generally, then, studies support the use of turtle geometry as a medium for learning and for teaching mathematics, especially for learning and teaching geometry (Barker, Merryman, & Bracken, 1988; Butler & Close, 1989; Clements & Meredith, 1993; Hoyles & Noss, 1987; Kynigos, 1991; Miller, Kelly, & Kelly, 1988; Salem, 1989). However, not all research has shown positive outcomes. First, few studies report that students "master" the mathematical concepts that are the teachers' goals for instruction. Second, some studies show no significant differences between turtle geometry and control groups (Johnson, 1986). Without teacher guidance, mere "exposure" to turtle geometry often yields little learning (Clements & Meredith, 1993). Third, some studies have shown limited transfer. One reason is that students do not always think mathematically, even if the turtle geometry environment invites such thinking (Noss & Hoyles, 1992). For example, some students rely exclusively on visual/spatial cues and avoid analytical work (Hillel & Kieran, 1988). This visual approach is not related to an ability to create visual images but to the role of the visual "data" (i.e., the students' perceptions) of a geometric figure in determining students' turtle geometry constructions. Although helpful initially, this approach inhibits students from arriving at mathematical generalizations if overused. Further, there is little reason for students to abandon visual approaches unless tasks that can only be resolved using an analytical, generalized, mathematical approach are presented. Finally, dialogue between teacher and students, and student-to-student, is essential for encouraging predicting, reflecting, and higher-level reasoning.

In sum, studies showing the most positive effects involved carefully planned sequences of turtle geometry activities. Appropriate teacher mediation of students' work with those activities was necessary for students to construction geometric concepts successfully. This mediation helped students forge links between turtle geometry and other experiences and between procedural knowledge and more traditional conceptual knowledge (Clements & Battista, 1989; Lehrer & Smith, 1986). Care must be taken that such links are not learned by rote (Hoyles & Noss, 1992).

A large project addressed these concerns with a carefully sequenced curriculum in turtle geometry (Clements, Battista, & Sarama, 2001). The findings were clear that turtle geometry can help students construct elaborate knowledge networks (rather than mechanical chains of rules and terms) for geometric topics. One main effect was increasing students' ability to describe, define, justify, and generalize geometric ideas. Students' greater explication and elaboration of geometric ideas within the environments appear to facilitate their progression to higher van Hiele levels of geometric thinking. For example, in programming the turtle, there is a need to analyze and reflect on the components and properties of geometric shapes and to make relationships explicit. In addition, the necessity of building Logo procedures encourages students to build understandable, implicit definitions of these shapes. Students construct more viable knowledge because they are constantly using graphical manifestations of their thinking to test the viability of their ideas. There is also support for the linkage of symbolic and visual external representations.

In a similar vein, there was a positive effect on students' consideration of multiple geometric properties. As we previously hypothesized (Clements & Battista, 1994), computer environments can allow the manipulation of specific screen objects in ways that assist students to view them as geometric (rather than visual/spatial) and to recognize them as representatives of a class of geometric objects. The power of the computer is that students simultaneously confront the specific and are concrete with the abstract and generalized (as represented by code). Students treat a figure both as having characteristics of a single shape and as one instance of many such figures.

Logo environments and their progeny, including Scratch, Snap!, and robots such as Beebot, CHERP (Flannery & Bers, 2013), and Nao and KindSAR (Keren & Fridin, 2014) appear to demand and thus facilitate precision in geometric thinking. In contrast, there is imprecision when students work with paper and pencil, and they can be distracted by the actual effort of drawing. The need in turtle geometry environments for more complete, exact, and abstract explication may account for students' creation of richer concepts. That is, by using turtle geometry students have to specify steps with thorough specification and detail to a noninterpretive agent. The results of these commands can be observed, reflected on, and corrected; the computer serves as an explicative agent. In noncomputer manipulative environments, a student can make intuitive movements and corrections without explicit awareness of mathematical objects and actions. For example, even young children can move puzzle pieces into place without conscious awareness of the geometric motions that can describe these physical movements. In noncomputer environments, attempts are sometimes made to promote such awareness. Still, descriptions of motions tend to be generated from, and interpreted by, physical action of students (Johnson-Gentile, Clements, & Battista, 1994). This interpretation of the results is consonant with previous research indicating prolonged retention and continuous construction of early computational schemes for geometric concepts (Clements, 1987).

3.5 *Dynamic Geometry Environments*

Significant improvement in students' geometric learning has also been linked to the use of dynamic geometry environments (DGEs, e.g., Cabri, GeoGebra, Sketchpad, see Almeqdadi, 2007; Dixon, 1996; Lester, 1996; Yousef, 1997). Dynamic geometry environments allow for the investigation and exploration of geometric phenomena in a flexibly structured environment, often through the use of specifically-designed "micro-worlds", or lessons and curricula. DGEs allow for replicas of physical, concrete manipulatives, like shapes, as virtual manipulatives of both static and *dynamic* types.

Although much more research has been conducted with older students, some studies show that constructing shapes with DGEs benefits younger children as well. For example, using a DGE to draw buildings, Malaysian 5- to 6-year olds drawing learned concepts in geometry such as geometric transformations (Seloraji & Eu, 2017).

Another team of researchers show that dynamic geometry can help young children build more robust and accurate geometry concepts. For example, 4 to 5-year-old children worked with a DGE, making continuous transformations (e.g., moving vertices dynamically) to extend their concepts of triangles. Children did grow in the diversity of shapes that they recognized as members of the class of triangles, showing signs of moving from the visual-holistic level to the descriptive/analytic level of geometric thinking (Sinclair & Moss, 2012). A related study similarly showed students moving from informal descriptions, such as "If I move that one, that one also moves" to mathematical properties such as "the angles are staying the same" as well as to more generalized statements (Kaur, 2014, p. 418).

The efficacy of DGE has also been demonstrated for specific geometric concepts. For example, children ages 5 to 7 years used DGE to decide if two lines that they knew continued (but they could not see the continuation) would intersect (Sinclair & Jones, 2009). Children moved from a visual description to a more theoretical and abstract one, suggesting that young children can engage in deductive reasoning. Also, students in grades 1 to 3 learned reflectional symmetry in a dynamic geometry environment, the "Symmetry Machine" (Ng & Sinclair, 2015). Students developed dynamic and embodied ways of thinking about symmetry and moved from distinguishing symmetrical and asymmetrical figures statically to generalising about *properties* of symmetry, shown by their representations of symmetric movement through words, gestures and diagrams both during the computer-based lessons as well as in the follow-up paper-and-pencil tasks. This supports our previous hypothesis (Sarama, & Clements, 2016; Sarama et al., 1996) that in some cases, symmetry being one, experience with technology might beneficially come *before* other modes of engagement (e.g., paper and pencil or physical manipulatives).

3.5.1   Shape Makers

A specific type of DGE, *Shape Makers* consists of seven quadrilateral "Shape Makers" or virtual manipulative shape-making objects. The constructions of Shape Makers within *The Geometer's Sketchpad* dynamic geometry application constrain Shape Maker movements to create only the named class of shapes. Additionally, the inquiry-based geometry curriculum *Shape Makers* is designed to encourage and support students' development of geometric reasoning about shapes, promoting learning through the first two van Hiele levels (1986) – visual-holistic thinking about shapes and descriptive/analytic properties of shapes.

3.5.1.1   *The Shape Makers Microworld*

The "Parallelogram Maker", for example, is a virtual version of a quadrilateral that can be manipulated – by dragging its vertices and sides – and that is constrained to always have *opposite sides parallel*. Accordingly, the Parallelogram Maker, no matter the manipulated state, is always a *parallelogram*. And, similar to some of the conceptualizations built by children with experience in turtle geometry, with Shape Makers, such as the Parallelogram Maker, children can build conceptualizations of both the parts and properties of the shape and the class of shapes, including hierarchical classification or interrelationships between shapes and classes. For instance, children can manipulate the Parallelogram Maker to discover that is can make "square parallelograms" or "rectangle parallelograms" to use the language of turtle geometry children.

In *Shape Makers*, children actively participate in the process of doing geometry (Battista, 2002). Visual inspection and manipulation of Shape Makers encourages and supports abstraction of the structure of the different types of quadrilaterals (Battista, 1998). Thus, through exploration, reflection, and abstraction, children discover the parts and properties of shapes, and coordinate the relationships between shapes. Further, they build mental models that are "refined through a recursive spiral of abstraction" (Battista, 2015) – initial models might only be recalled when the physical artifact is also present. Later, more sophisticated models can be used without the physical artifact present and may be "used to stimulate never-performed actions on phenomena".

An initial *Shape Maker* activity tasks children to create a picture, like free play, with their seven Shape Makers, thus becoming familiar with the virtual manipulation process and exploring the movement possibilities of each Shape Maker. Then, children duplicate a picture, using each Shape Maker only once, but having to manipulate them to cover the picture in entirety. Such an activity draws children's attention to possible manipulated states of each Shape Maker given that the constraints on each Shape Maker allow for a finite set of Shape Maker-shape pairing possibilities for completing the puzzle. Both of these example activities promote thinking at van Hiele visual-holistic level. Shape Maker activities that promote reasoning at van Hiele descriptive/analytic properties of shapes, like "Predict and Check", come later in the curriculum. In that activity, students are given a set of six static shapes, asked to predict if a particular Shape Maker can or cannot make each of those shapes, reason why, then test those predictions. Continued progress through the activities helps children make sense of properties of each Shape Maker and class of shape, preparing them for thinking at the van Hiele abstract relational level.

3.5.1.2 *Findings from Shape Makers*

Pre-*Shape Makers* instructional assessments showed that the majority children in a grade 5 classroom had insufficient property-based information to specify a shape. Students' progress through the levels and activities has been described in *Shape Makers* studies elsewhere (Battista, 2001, 2007, 2008), and for space constraints, will only briefly be illustrated here. Reasoning visual holistically, student MI said, "The Square [Maker] would only get bigger and twist around – so it can't make a rectangle" (Battista, 2001). He had been unable to make a non-square rectangle, and used his observations of the dynamic nature of the Square Maker to reason why. Similarly, JD reasoned that a rectangle could not be made by the Square Maker because "when you change one side, they all change" (Battista, 2007). Though, JD's peer, ER, said, "All the sides are equal". This shows progress towards more formal and precise property-based reasoning, descriptive/analytic van Hiele level.

Post-assessment data showed nearly all students, for all shapes, provided sufficient property-based information as definitions. Indeed, 83% were judged at the descriptive/analytic level or higher (Battista, 2011, p. 548). Further, students could apply their property-based reasoning to make inferences and correct conjectures about classes of shapes and relationships between shapes and shape properties post-*Shape Makers*. For example, a student may say that they could describe a parallelogram as a 4-sided shape with opposite sides equal length and parallel, but that it is only necessary to state that the opposite sides are parallel (knowing that the equal length property is inherent). Or, a student may reason that squares, rhombuses, and rectangles are all types of parallelograms because each of those shapes have opposite sides parallel. Many students reached the van Hiele abstract relational level, and while they did not perhaps fully attain this level, they surpassed *Shape Makers* researcher and curricular intentions.

In sum, Battista (2001, 2007) has illustrated individual and small groups of students' progresses along the van Hiele learning progression when using *Shape Makers*, characterized by students' actions and reflections-upon-actions of their manipulation of the shapes. He concluded that the geometry learning with *Shape Makers* was "much richer and more powerful than that which occurs in many traditional curricula" (Battista, 2007, p. 875).

Although *Shape Makers* has been used most widely in late primary and elementary grades settings (e.g., U.S. grade 5), young children have successfully engaged with initial *Shape Makers* activities (though not studied at scale to our knowlege) – those target visual/holistic and early property-based van Hiele levels of thinking and reasoning. The environment allows children to personally construct mathematical ideas, consistent with research on children's mathematics learning.

4   Conclusions and Implications

The studies discussed here show that young children are capable of learning geometric ideas and processes to a surprising degree and depth (e.g., Maričić &

Stamatović, 2017). We find that children can learn richer concepts about shape if their educational environment includes six features: varied examples and nonexamples, a wider variety of shape classes, and a broad array of geometric tasks, movement from "Sensory-Concrete" to "Integrated-Concrete" cognition (Clements, 1999; Clements & McMillen, 1996; Sarama & Clements, 2009a, 2016; Sarama, Clements, & Vukelic, 1996), discussions about shapes and their attributes, the teacher's use of learning trajectories, and the appropriate inclusion of educational technology. We discuss each of these in turn.

1. Educators should ensure that children experience many different examples of a type of shape, so that they do not form narrow ideas about any class of shapes. Playing with building blocks and other geometric toys is important and useful (Park, Chae, & Boyd, 2008; Ramani, Zippert, Schweitzer, & Pan, 2014; Verdine et al., 2014), but a variety of shapes should be included (similar for books, Flevares & Schiff, 2014). Use of prototypes may bootstrap initial learning, but examples should become more diverse as soon as possible. Showing nonexamples and comparing them to similar examples help focus children's attention on the critical attributes of shapes and prompts discussion. This is especially important for classes that have more diverse examples, such as triangles.

2. Curricula and educational activities in the USA should include a wide variety of shape classes. Early childhood curricula traditionally introduce shapes in four basic level categories: circle, square, triangle, and rectangle. The idea that a square is not a rectangle (or that these shapes are distinct and unrelated) is rooted by age five. We suggest presenting many examples of squares and rectangles, varying orientation, size, and so forth, including squares as examples of rectangles. Perhaps even the use of dynamic rectangles, that can be manipulated into squares, is appropriate. If children say, "that's a square", teachers might respond that it is a square, which is a special type of rectangle, and they might try double naming ("it's a square-rectangle"). Older children can discuss "general" categories, such as quadrilaterals and triangles, counting the sides of various figures to choose their category. Also, teachers might encourage them to describe why a figure belongs or does not belong to a shape category. Then, teachers can say that because a triangle has all equal sides, it is a special type of triangle, called an equilateral triangle. Children might also "test" right angles on rectangles with a "right angle checker". including but not limited to semi-circles, quadrilaterals, trapezoids, rhombi, and hexagons.

3. Educators should challenge children with a broad array of interesting tasks. Experience with manipulatives and computer environments are often supported by research, if the experiences are consistent with the implications just drawn. Activities that promote reflection and discussion might include building models of shapes from components. Matching, identifying, exploring, and even making shapes with computers is particularly motivating (Clements & Sarama, 2003).

4. Children should be guided to progress from Sensory-Concrete to Integrated-Concrete cognition (Clements, 1999; Clements & McMillen, 1996; Sarama & Clements, 2009a, 2016; Sarama, Clements, & Vukelic, 1996). The studies cited here, such as those from the Agam program and researched-based learning trajectories, support development from Sensory-Concrete implicit levels at which perceptual supports are necessary and fundamental to later learning (i.e., building strong concept images, Vinner & Hershkowitz, 1980), and reasoning may be restricted to limited cases, to more explicit, verbally-enhanced generalizations and abstractions that characterize Integrated-Concrete understandings (involving internalized mental imagery and linked verbal schemes that generate operations and abstractions that are increasingly sophisticated and powerful).

5. Educators should encourage children's descriptions while encouraging the development of language. Visual (prototype-based) descriptions should, of course, be expected and accepted, but attribute and property responses should also be encouraged. They may initially appear spontaneously for shapes with stronger and fewer prototypes (e.g., circle, square). Again, they should be especially encouraged for shape categories such as triangles. Children can learn to explain why a shape belongs to a certain category – "It has three straight sides" or does not belong ("The sides aren't straight!"). Eventually, they can internalize such arguments; for example, saying, "It is a weird, long, triangle, but it has three straight sides!" Further, math talk occur throughout the day. However, research shows talk about geometry can be difficult for teachers, as it is infrequent and stilted. However engaging in good-fit math talk (interactions that match children's need in terms of content, context and levels of guidance) that discusses shapes' attributes significantly impacts children's growth. (Clements, Sarama, Swaminathan, Weber, & Trawick-Smith, 2018).

6. Teachers should understand and teach with learning trajectories, which connect mathematical goals, children's thinking and learning levels, and instruction. They support formative assessment, helping teachers identify children's level of thinking and interact with them to maximize their learning.

7. Educational technology, such as the use of software such as *Shapes*, turtle geometry, and *Shape Makers*, has been shown to enhance all six of these features. They engender both spatial and geometric explorations, attention to geometric attributes, and explication of geometric concepts and procedures.

In sum, computer and classrooms environments that promote a problem-solving approach to education appear to have benefits for the development of both mathematical concepts and processes (e.g., reasoning, connecting, problem-solving, communicating, and representing). They seem especially beneficial for developing student competence in solving complex problems. Further, because students test ideas for themselves, computers can aid them to move from naive to empirical to logical thinking and encourage them to make and test conjectures. Thus, it can be argued that high-quality implementations of Logo-like experiences places as much emphasis on the spirit of mathematics – exploration, investigation, critical thinking, and problem solving – as it does on geometric ideas. We believe that it has the potential to develop valid geometric thinking in students (Clements, Battista, & Sarama, 2001).

In these ways, children move through developmental progressions, building intuitions and perceptually-based competencies and then explicating these early developments through math talk to connect verbal and abstract thinking – building integrated concrete knowledge of geometry and spatial reasoning. Throughout the early childhood years, it seems not only appropriate, but essential, to introduce, expand, and guide children through this learning process.

Acknowledgments

This research was supported in part by the Institute of Education Sciences, U.S. Department of Education through Grants R305K05157 and R305A110188, the National Science Foundation through Grant DRL-1313695, the Gates Foundation, and the Heising-Simons Foundation. The opinions expressed are those of the authors and do not represent views of these agencies.

Notes

1   See https://learningtrajectories.org
2   See https://scratch.mit.edu
3   See https://snap.berkeley.edu

References

Aktas-Arnas, Y., & Aslan, D. (2004). The development of geometrical thinking in 3 to 6 years old children group. In O. Ramazan, K. Efe, & G. Güven (Eds.), *1st International Pre-School Education Conference* (Vol. I, pp. 475–494). Ya-Pa Yayıncılık.

Almeqdadi, F. (2007). The effect of using The Geometer's Sketchpad (GSP) on Jordanian students' understanding of geometrical concepts. In *Proceedings of the International Conference on Technology in Mathematics Education*. ERIC Document Reproduction Service No. ED 477317.

Almohtadi, R., Aldarabah, I. T., & Jwaifell, M. (2019). Effectiveness of instructional electronic games in acquisition of geometry concepts among kindergarten children. *Research on Humanities and Social Sciences, 9*(12). doi:10.7176/RHSS

Aslan, D., & Aktas-Arnas, Y. (2007a). Okul öncesi egitim materyallerinde geometrik sekillerin sunulusuna iliskin icerik analizi [Content analysis of the ways geometrical shapes represented in early childhood education materials]. *Cukurova Universitesi Sosyal Bilimler Enstitüsü Dergisi [Journal of Cukurova University Institute of Social Sciences], 16*(1), 69–80.

Aslan, D., & Aktas-Arnas, Y. (2007b). Three-to six-year-old children's recognition of geometric shapes. *International Journal of Early Years Education, 15*(1), 81–101.

Barker, W. F., Merryman, J. D., & Bracken, J. (1988, April). *Microcomputers, math CAI, Logo, and mathematics education in elementary school: A pilot study.* New Orleans.

Battista, M. T. (1998). *Shape makers: Developing geometric reasoning with the geometer's sketchpad.* Key Curriculum Press.

Battista, M. T. (2001). Shape makers: A computer environment that engenders students' construction of geometric ideas and reasoning. *Computers in the Schools, 17*(1), 105–120.

Battista, M. T. (2002). Learning geometry in a dynamic computer microworld. *Mathematics Teacher, 8*(6), 333–339.

Battista, M. T. (2007). The development of geometric and spatial thinking. In F. Lester (Ed.), *Second handbook of research on mathematics teaching and learning* (pp. 843–908). National Council of Teachers of Mathematics.

Battista, M. T. (2008). Development of the shape makers geometry microworld: Design principles and research. In G. Blume & K. Heid (Eds.), *Research on technology in the learning and teaching of mathematics: Case and perspectives* (Vol. 2, pp. 131–156). NCTM/Information Age Publishing.

Battista, M. T. (2011). Conceptualizations and issues related to learning progressions, learning trajectories, and levels of sophistication. *The Mathematics Enthusiast, 8,* 507–570.

Battista, M. T. (2015). *Students' construction of geometric properties in an instructional computer microworld* [Unpublished draft].

Brown, S. I., & Walter, M. I. (1990). *The art of problem posing.* Erlbaum.

Butler, D., & Close, S. (1989). Assessing the benefits of a Logo problem-solving course. *Irish Educational Studies, 8,* 168–190.

Cheng, Y.-L., & Mix, K. S. (2012). Spatial training improves children's mathematics ability. *Journal of Cognition and Development, 15*(1), 2–11. doi:10.1080/15248372.2012.725186

Clements, D. H. (1987). Longitudinal study of the effects of Logo programming on cognitive abilities and achievement. *Journal of Educational Computing Research, 3,* 73–94.

Clements, D. H. (1992). Elaboraciones sobre los niveles de pensamiento geometrico [Elaborations on the levels of geometric thinking]. In A. Gutiérrez (Ed.), *Memorias del Tercer Simposio Internacional Sobre Investigatcion en Educacion Matematica* (pp. 16–43). Universitat De València.

Clements, D. H. (1999). 'Concrete' manipulatives, concrete ideas. *Contemporary Issues in Early Childhood, 1*(1), 45–60.

Clements, D. H. (2000). From exercises and tasks to problems and projects: Unique contributions of computers to innovative mathematics education. *Journal of Mathematical Behavior, 19*, 9–47.

Clements, D. H. (2004). Geometric and spatial thinking in early childhood education. In D. H. Clements, J. Sarama, & A.-M. DiBiase (Eds.), *Engaging young children in mathematics: Standards for early childhood mathematics education* (pp. 267–297). Erlbaum.

Clements, D. H. (2007). Curriculum research: Toward a framework for research-based curricula. *Journal for Research in Mathematics Education, 38*, 35–70.

Clements, D. H., & Battista, M. T. (1989). Learning of geometric concepts in a Logo environment. *Journal for Research in Mathematics Education, 20*, 450–467.

Clements, D. H., & Battista, M. T. (1990). The effects of Logo on children's conceptualizations of angle and polygons. *Journal for Research in Mathematics Education, 21*, 356–371.

Clements, D. H., & Battista, M. T. (1992). Geometry and spatial reasoning. In D. A. Grouws (Ed.), *Handbook of research on mathematics teaching and learning* (pp. 420–464). Macmillan.

Clements, D. H., & Battista, M. T. (1994). Computer environments for learning geometry. *Journal of Educational Computing Research, 10*(2), 173–197.

Clements, D. H., & Battista, M. T. (2000). Designing effective software. In A. E. Kelly & R. A. Lesh (Eds.), *Handbook of research design in mathematics and science education* (pp. 761–776). Erlbaum.

Clements, D. H., Battista, M. T., & Sarama, J. (2001). Logo and geometry. *Journal for Research in Mathematics Education* (Monograph series, Vol. 10). National Council of Teachers of Mathematics. doi:10.2307/749924

Clements, D. H., Battista, M. T., Sarama, J., & Swaminathan, S. (1997). Development of students' spatial thinking in a unit on geometric motions and area. *The Elementary School Journal, 98*, 171–186.

Clements, D. H., & McMillen, S. (1996). Rethinking "concrete" manipulatives. *Teaching Children Mathematics, 2*(5), 270–279.

Clements, D. H., & Meredith, J. S. (1993). Research on Logo: Effects and efficacy. *Journal of Computing in Childhood Education, 4*, 263–290.

Clements, D. H., & Sarama, J. (1997). Research on Logo: A decade of progress. In C. D. Maddux & D. L. Johnson (Eds.), *Logo: A retrospective* (pp. 9–46). Haworth Press.

Clements, D. H., & Sarama, J. (2003). Strip mining for gold: Research and policy in educational technology – A response to "Fool's Gold". *Educational Technology Review, 11*(1), 7–69.

Clements, D. H., & Sarama, J. (2007). Effects of a preschool mathematics curriculum: Summative research on the Building Blocks project. *Journal for Research in Mathematics Education, 38*(2), 136–163.

Clements, D. H., & Sarama, J. (2008). Experimental evaluation of the effects of a research-based preschool mathematics curriculum. *American Educational Research Journal, 45*, 443–494. doi:10.3102/0002831207312908

Clements, D. H., & Sarama, J. (2011). Early childhood teacher education: The case of geometry. *Journal of Mathematics Teacher Education, 14*, 113–148.

Clements, D. H., & Sarama, J. (2013). *Building Blocks, Volumes 1 and 2.* McGraw-Hill Education.

Clements, D. H., & Sarama, J. (2021). *Learning and teaching early math: The learning trajectories approach* (3rd ed.). Routledge.

Clements, D. H., & Sarama, J. (Eds.). (2004). Hypothetical learning trajectories [Special issue]. *Mathematical Thinking and Learning, 6*(2).

Clements, D. H., Sarama, J., & DiBiase, A.-M. (2004). *Engaging young children in mathematics: Standards for early childhood mathematics education.* Erlbaum.

Clements, D. H., Sarama, J., Spitler, M. E., Lange, A. A., & Wolfe, C. B. (2011). Mathematics learned by young children in an intervention based on learning trajectories: A large-scale cluster randomized trial. *Journal for Research in Mathematics Education, 42*(2), 127–166. doi:10.5951/jresematheduc.42.2.0127

Clements, D. H., Sarama, J., Swaminathan, S., Weber, D., & Trawick-Smith, J. (2018). Teaching and learning geometry: Early foundations. *Quadrante, 27*(2), 7–31.

Clements, D. H., Swaminathan, S., Hannibal, M. A. Z., & Sarama, J. (1999). Young children's concepts of shape. *Journal for Research in Mathematics Education, 30*, 192–212.

Cobb, P., & McClain, K. (2002). Supporting students' learning of significant mathematical ideas. In G. Wells & G. Claxton (Eds.), *Learning for life in the 21st century: Sociocultural perspectives on the future of education* (pp. 154–166). Blackwell.

Cope, P., & Simmons, M. (1991). Children's exploration of rotation and angle in limited Logo microworlds. *Computers in Education, 16*, 133–141.

Dağlı, U. m. h. Y. i., & Halat, E. a. (2016). Young children's conceptual understanding of triangle. *EURASIA Journal of Mathematics, Science & Technology Education, 12*(2), 189–202. doi:10.12973/eurasia.2016.1398a

Dillon, M. R., Huang, Y., & Spelke, E. S. (2013). Core foundations of abstract geometry. *PNAS, 110*(35), 14191–14195.

Dillon, M. R., & Spelke, E. S. (2015). Core geometry in perspective. *Dev Sci, 18*(6), 894–908. doi:10.1111/desc.12266

Dixon, J. (1996). English language proficiency and spatial visualization in middle school students' construction of the concepts of reflection and rotation used the GSP. *Dissertation Abstract International*. DAI-A 56111.

du Boulay, J. B. H. (1986). Part II: Logo confessions. In R. Lawler, B. du Boulay, M. Hughes & H. Macleod (Eds.), *Cognition and computers: Studies in learning* (pp. 81–178). Ellis Horwood Limited.

Eylon, B.-S., & Rosenfeld, S. (1990). *The Agam project: Cultivating visual cognition in young children*. Department of Science Teaching, Weizmann Institute of Science.

Firmender, J. M. (2011). *A study of teachers' pedagogical content knowledge and instructional practices during and after implementation of advanced primary mathematics curriculum* [Doctoral dissertation]. University of Connecticut. Available from UMI ProQuest database (UMI No. 3475520).

Flannery, L. P., & Bers, M. U. (2013). Let's dance the "Robot Hokey-Pokey!": Children's programming approaches and achievement throughout early cognitive development. *Journal of Research on Technology in Education, 46*(1), 81–101.

Flevares, L. M., & Schiff, J. R. (2014). Learning mathematics in two dimensions: A review and look ahead at teaching and learning early childhood mathematics with children's literature. *Frontiers in Psychology, 5*(459), 1–12. doi:10.3389/fpsyg.2014.00459

Frazier, M. K. (1987). *The effects of Logo on angle estimation skills of 7th graders* [Master's thesis]. Wichita State University.

Fujita, T., & Jones, K. (2006). Primary trainee teachers' understanding of basic geometrical figures in Scotland. In J. Novotná, H. Moraová, M. Krátká, & N. Stehlíková (Eds.), *Proceedings 30th conference of the International Group for the Psychology of Mathematics Education (PME30)* (Vol. 3, pp. 129–136). The International Group for the Psychology of Mathematics Education (PME).

Fuys, D., Geddes, D., & Tischler, R. (1988). The van Hiele model of thinking in geometry among adolescents. *Journal for Research in Mathematics Education Monograph Series, 3*, 1–198.

Gagatsis, A., & Patronis, T. (1990). Using geometrical models in a process of reflective thinking in learning and teaching mathematics. *Educational Studies in Mathematics, 21*, 29–54.

Gravemeijer, K. P. E. (1999). How emergent models may foster the constitution of formal mathematics. *Mathematical Thinking and Learning, 1*, 155–177.

Hillel, J., & Kieran, C. (1988). Schemas used by 12-year-olds in solving selected turtle geometry tasks. *Recherches en Didactique des Mathématiques, 8*(1.2), 61–103.

Hoyles, C., & Noss, R. (1987). Synthesizing mathematical conceptions and their formalization through the construction of a Logo-based school mathematics curriculum. *International Journal of Mathematics Education, Science, and Technology, 18*, 581–595.

Hoyles, C., & Noss, R. (1992). A pedagogy for mathematical microworlds. *Educational Studies in Mathematics, 23*, 31–57.

Hoyles, C., & Sutherland, R. (1986). *When 45 equals 60*. University of London Institute of Education, Microworlds Project.

Johnson, P. A. (1986). *Effects of computer-assisted instruction compared to teacher-directed instruction on comprehension of abstract concepts by the deaf* [Doctoral dissertation]. Northern Illinois University.

Johnson-Gentile, K., Clements, D. H., & Battista, M. T. (1994). The effects of computer and noncomputer environments on students' conceptualizations of geometric motions. *Journal of Educational Computing Research, 11*, 121–140.

Jones, K. (2002). Issues in the teaching and learning of geometry. In L. Haggarty (Ed.), *Aspects of teaching secondary mathematics: Perspectives on practice* (pp. 121–139). Routledge Falmer.

Jones, S. S., & Smith, L. B. (2002). How children know the relevant properties for generalizing object names. *Developmental Science, 2*, 219–232.

Kabanova-Meller, E. N. (1970). The role of the diagram in the application of geometric theorems. In J. Kilpatrick & I. Wirszup (Eds.), *Soviet studies in the psychology of learning and teaching mathematics* (Vol. 4, pp. 7–49m). University of Chicago Press.

Kaur, H. (2014). Two aspects of young children's thinking about different types of dynamic triangles: *Orototypicality and inclusion. ZDM Mathematics Education, 47*(3), 407–420. doi:10.1007/s11858-014-0658-z

Kell, H. J., Lubinski, D., Benbow, C. P., & Steiger, J. H. (2013). Creativity and technical innovation: Spatial ability's unique role. *Psychological Science*. doi:10.1177/0956797613478615

Kelly, G. N., Kelly, J. T., & Miller, R. B. (1986–1987). Working with Logo: Do 5th and 6th graders develop a basic understanding of angles and distances? *Journal of Computers in Mathematics and Science Teaching, 6*, 23–27.

Keren, G., & Fridin, M. (2014). Kindergarten social assistive robot (KindSAR) for children's geometric thinking and metacognitive development in preschool education: A pilot study. *Computers in Human Behavior, 35*, 400–412. doi:10.1016/j.chb.2014.03.009

Kieran, C. (1986a). Logo and the notion of angle among fourth and sixth grade children. In C. Hoyles & L. Burton (Eds.), *Proceedings of the tenth annual meeting of the International Group fore the Psychology in Mathematics Education* (pp. 99–104). City University.

Kieran, C. (1986b). Turns and angles: What develops in Logo? In G. Lappan & R. Even (Eds.), *Proceedings of the eighth annual meeting of the North American Chapter of the International Group for the Psychology of Mathematics Education* (pp. 169–177). East Lansing, MI: Michigan State University.

Kieran, C., & Hillel, J. (1990). "It's tough when you have to make the triangles angles": Insights from a computer-based geometry environment. *Journal of Mathematical Behavior, 9,* 99–127.

Kieran, C., Hillel, J., & Erlwanger, S. (1986). Perceptual and analytical schemas in solving structured turtle–geometry tasks. In C. Hoyles, R. Noss, & R. Sutherland (Eds.), *Proceedings of the Second Logo and Mathematics Educators Conference* (pp. 154–161). University of London.

Kilpatrick, J. (1987). Problem formulating: Where do good problems come from? In A. H. Schoenfeld (Ed.), *Cognitive science and mathematics education* (pp. 123–147). Erlbaum.

Klim-Klimaszewska, A., & Nazaruk, S. (2017). The scope of implementation of geometric concepts in selected kindergartens in Poland. *Problems of Education in the 21st Century, 75*(4), 345–353.

Kynigos, C. (1991). Can children use the turtle metaphor to extend their learning to include non-intrinsic geometry? In F. Furinghetti (Ed.), *Proceedings of the 15th annual meeting of the International Group for the Psychology of Mathematics Education* (Vol. II, pp. 269–276). Program Committee, 15th PME Conference.

Lee, J. (2010). Exploring kindergarten teachers' pedagogical content knowledge of mathematics. *International Journal of Early Childhood, 42*(1), 27–41.

Lehrer, R., Randle, L., & Sancilio, L. (1989). Learning pre-proof geometry with Logo. *Cognition and Instruction, 6,* 159–184.

Lehrer, R., & Smith, P. C. (1986). *Logo learning: Are two heads better than one?* American Educational Research Association.

Lester, M. (1996). The effects of the GSP software on achievement knowledge of high school geometry students. *Dissertation Abstract International.* DAI-A 57106.

Mansfield, H. M., & Scott, J. (1990). Young children solving spatial problems. In G. Booker, P. Cobb, & T. N. deMendicuti (Eds.), *Proceedings of the 14th annual conference of the Internation Group for the Psychology of Mathematics Education* (Vol. 2, pp. 275–282). Internation Group for the Psychology of Mathematics Education.

Maričić, S. M., & Stamatović, J. D. (2017). The effect of preschool mathematics education in development of geometry concepts in children. *Eurasia Journal of Mathematics, Science and Technology Education, 13*(9), 6175–6187. doi:10.12973/eurasia.2017.01057a

Miller, R. B., Kelly, G. N., & Kelly, J. T. (1988). Effects of Logo computer programming experience on problem solving and spatial relations ability. *Contemporary Educational Psychology, 13,* 348–357.

National Research Council. (2009). *Mathematics learning in early childhood: Paths toward excellence and equity.* National Academy Press.

Newcombe, N. (2010). Picture this: Increasing math and science learning by improving spatial thinking. *American Educator, 34*(2), 29–35.

Newcombe, N. S., & Huttenlocher, J. (2000). *Making space: The development of spatial representation and reasoning.* MIT Press.

Ng, D. (2011). Indonesian primary teachers' mathematical knowledge for teaching geometry: Implications for educational policy and teacher preparation programs. *Asia-Pacific Journal of Teacher Education, 39*, 151–164.

Ng, O.-L., & Sinclair, N. (2015). Young children reasoning about symmetry in a dynamic geometry environment. *ZDM Mathematics Education, 47*, 421–434. doi:10.1007/s11858-014-0660-5

Noss, R. (1987). Children's learning of geometrical concepts through Logo. *Journal for Research in Mathematics Education, 18*, 343–362.

Noss, R., & Hoyles, C. (1992). Afterword: Looking back and looking forward. In C. Hoyles & R. Noss (Eds.), *Learning mathematics and Logo* (pp. 427–468). MIT Press.

Nurnberger-Haag, J. (2016). A cautionary tale: How children's books (mis)teach shapes. *Early Education and Development, 28*(4), 415–440. doi:10.1080/10409289.2016.1242993

Olive, J. (1991). Logo programming and geometric understanding: An in-depth study. *Journal for Research in Mathematics Education, 22*, 90–111.

Olive, J., Lankenau, C. A., & Scally, S. P. (1986). *Teaching and understanding geometric relationships through Logo: Phase II. Interim report: The Atlanta–Emory Logo project.* Emory University.

Olkun, S., & Sari, M. H. (2016, July 24–31). *Geometric aspect of number line estimations* [Paper presentation]. 13th International Congress on Mathematical Education.

Papert, S. (1980). *Mindstorms: Children, computers, and powerful ideas.* Basic Books.

Park, B., Chae, J.-L., & Boyd, B. F. (2008). Young children's block play and mathematical learning. *Journal of Research in Childhood Education, 23*, 157–162.

Piaget, J., & Inhelder, B. (1967). *The child's conception of space* (F. J. Langdon & J. L. Lunzer, Trans.). W. W. Norton.

Putri, A. A. (2020). Recognize geometry shapes through computer learning in early math skills. *Jurnal Pendidikan Usia Dini, 14*(1), 43–57. https://doi.org/10.21009/JPUD.141.04

Ramani, G. B., Zippert, E., Schweitzer, S., & Pan, S. (2014). Preschool children's joint block building during a guided play activity. *Journal of Applied Developmental Psychology, 35*(4), 326–336. doi:10.1016/j.appdev.2014.05.005

Razel, M., & Eylon, B.-S. (1986). Developing visual language skills: The Agam program. *Journal of Visual Verbal Languaging, 6*(1), 49–54.

Razel, M., & Eylon, B.-S. (1990). Development of visual cognition: Transfer effects of the Agam program. *Journal of Applied Developmental Psychology, 11*, 459–485.

Razel, M., & Eylon, B.-S. (1991, July). *Developing mathematics readiness in young children with the Agam Program* [Paper]. The fifteenth conference of the International Group for the Psychology of Mathematics Education, Genova, Italy.

Reimer, K., & Moyer, P. S. (2005). Third-graders learn about fractions using virtual manipulatives: A classroom study. *Journal of Computers in Mathematics and Science Teaching, 24*(1), 5–25.

Reynolds, A., & Wheatley, G. H. (1996). Elementary students' construction and coordination of units in an area setting. *Journal for Research in Mathematics Education, 27*(5), 564–581.

Salem, J. R. (1989). Using Logo and BASIC to teach mathematics to fifth and sixth graders. *Dissertation Abstracts International, 50*, 1608A.

Sales, C. (1994). *A constructivist instructional project on developing geometric problem solving abilities using pattern blocks and tangrams with young children* [Master's thesis]. University of Northern Iowa.

Sarama, J., & Clements, D. H. (2002). *Building Blocks* for young children's mathematical development. *Journal of Educational Computing Research, 27*(1&2), 93–110. doi:10.2190/F85E-QQXB-UAX4-BMBJ

Sarama, J., & Clements, D. H. (2009a). "Concrete" computer manipulatives in mathematics education. *Child Development Perspectives, 3*(3), 145–150.

Sarama, J., & Clements, D. H. (2009b). *Early childhood mathematics education research: Learning trajectories for young children.* Routledge.

Sarama, J., & Clements, D. H. (2016). Physical and virtual manipulatives: What is "concrete"? In P. S. Moyer-Packenham (Ed.), *International perspectives on teaching and learning mathematics with virtual manipulatives* (Vol. 3, pp. 71–93). Springer International Publishing.

Sarama, J., & Clements, D. H. (2017). Designing, scaling up, and evaluating comprehensive professional development based on learning trajectories. In P. Sztajn, P. H. Wilson, & C. Edgington (Eds.), *Learning trajectories-based professional development.* Teachers College Press.

Sarama, J., & Clements, D. H. (2020). Promoting a good start: Technology in early childhood mathematics. In E. Arias, J. Cristia, & S. Cueto (Eds.), *Learning mathematics in the 21st century: Adding technology to the equation* (pp. 181–223). Inter-American Development Bank.

Sarama, J., Clements, D. H., & Vukelic, E. B. (1996). The role of a computer manipulative in fostering specific psychological/mathematical processes. In E. Jakubowski, D. Watkins, & H. Biske (Eds.), *Proceedings of the 18th annual meeting of the North America Chapter of the International Group for the Psychology of Mathematics Education* (Vol. 2, pp. 567–572). ERIC Clearinghouse for Science, Mathematics, and Environmental Education.

Satlow, E., & Newcombe, N. S. (1998). When is a triangle not a triangle? Young children's developing concepts of geometric shape. *Cognitive Development, 13*, 547–559.

Seloraji, P., & Eu, L. K. (2017). Students' performance in geometrical reflection using GeoGebra. *Malaysian Online Journal of Educational Technology, 5*(1), 65–77.

Simon, M. A. (1995). Reconstructing mathematics pedagogy from a constructivist perspective. *Journal for Research in Mathematics Education, 26*(2), 114–145. doi:10.2307/749205

Sinclair, N., & Jones, K. (2009). Geometrical reasoning in the primary school, the case of parallel lines. *Proceedings of the British Society for Research into Learning Mathematics, 29*(2), 88–93. https://bsrlm.org.uk/wp-content/uploads/2016/02/BSRLM-IP-29-2-16.pdf

Sinclair, N., & Moss, J. (2012). The more it changes, the more it becomes the same: The development of the routine of shape identification in dynamic geometry environment. *International Journal of Educational Research, 51–52*, 28–44. doi:10.1016/j.ijer.2011.12.009

Spitler, M. E., Sarama, J., & Clements, D. H. (2003, April). *A preschooler's understanding of "Triangle:" A case study* [Paper presentation]. 81th Annual Meeting of the National Council of Teachers of Mathematics.

Steffe, L. P., & Cobb, P. (1988). *Construction of arithmetical meanings and strategies.* Springer-Verlag.

Swaminathan, S., Clements, D. H., & Schrier, D. M. (1995). *The Agam curriculum in kindergarten classes: Effects and processes.* University of Buffalo, State University of New York.

The Spatial Reasoning Study Group. (2015). *Spatial reasoning in the early years: Principles, assertions, and speculations.* Routledge.

Turgut, M., Yenilmez, K. r. a., & Anapa, P. (2014). Symmetry and rotation skills of prospective elementary mathematics teachers. *Bolema, Rio Claro, 28*(48), 383–402. doi:10.1590/1980-4415v28n48a19

Vallortigara, G. (2012). Core knowledge of object, number, and geometry: A comparative and neural approach. *Cognitive Neuropsychology, 29*(1–2), 213–236. doi:10.1080/02643294.2012.654772

Van den Heuvel-Panhuizen, M., & Buys, K. (2005). *Young children learn measurement and geometry: A learning-teaching trajectory with intermediate attainment targets for the lower grades in primary school.* Freudenthal Institute, Utrecht University.

van der Sandt, S. (2007). Pre-service geometry education in South Africa: A typical case? *IUMPST: The Journal, 1*, 1–9. http://www.k-12prep.math.ttu.edu/journal/journal.shtml

van Hiele, P. M. (1986). *Structure and insight.* Academic Press.

van Hiele, P. M. (1986). *Structure and insight: A theory of mathematics education.* Academic Press.

van Oers, B. (1994). Semiotic activity of young children in play: The construction and use of schematic representations. *European Early Childhood Education Research Journal, 2*, 19–33.

Verdine, B. N., Golinkoff, R. M., Hirsh-Pasek, K., & Newcombe, N. S. (2017). Links between spatial and mathematical skills across the preschool years. *Monographs of the Society for Research in Child Development, 82*(1), Serial No. 324. http://onlinelibrary.wiley.com/doi/10.1111/mono.v82.1/issuetoc

Verdine, B. N., Golinkoff, R. M., Hirsh-Pasek, K., Newcombe, N. S., Filipowicz, A. T., & Chang, A. (2014). Deconstructing building blocks: Preschoolers' spatial assembly performance relates to early mathematical skills. *Child Development, 85*(3), 1062–1076. doi:10.1111/cdev.12165

Vinner, S., & Hershkowitz, R. (1980). Concept images and common cognitive paths in the development of some simple geometrical concepts. In R. Karplus (Ed.), *Proceedings of the Fourth International Conference for the Psychology of Mathematics Education* (pp. 177–184). Lawrence Hall of Science, University of California.

Vurpillot, E. (1976). *The visual world of the child*. International Universities Press.

Woolcott, G., Logan, T., Marshman, M., Ramful, A., Whannell, R., & Lowrie, T. (2020). The re-emergence of spatial reasoning within primary years mathematics education. In J. Way, C. Attard, J. Anderson, J. Bobis, H. McMaster, & K. Cartwright (Eds.), *Research in mathematics education in Australasia 2016–2019* (pp. 245–268). Springer.

Yin, H. S. (2003). Young children's concept of shape: Van Hiele visualization level of geometric thinking. *The Mathematics Educator, 7*(2), 71–85.

Yousef, A. (1997). The effect of the GSP on the attitude toward geometry of high school students. *Dissertation Abstract International*. A58105.

Zacharos, K., Antonopoulos, K., & Ravanis, K. (2011). Activities in mathematics education and teaching interactions. The construction of the measurement of capacity in pre-schoolers. *European Early Childhood Education Research Journal, 19*, 451–468.

Zaranis, N. (2018). Comparing the effectiveness of using ICT for teaching geometrical shapes in kindergarten and the first grade. *International Journal of Web-Based Learning and Teaching Technologies (IJWLTT), 13*(1), 50–63. doi:10.4018/IJWLTT.2018010104

Zorzi, M., Priftis, K., & Umiltà, C. (2002). Brain damage – Neglect disrupts the mental number line. *Nature, 417*, 138.

Zykova, V. I. (1969). Operating with concepts when solving geometry problems. In J. Kilpatrick & I. Wirszup (Eds.), *Soviet studies in the psychology of learning and teaching mathematics* (Vol. 1, pp. 93–148). University of Chicago.

CHAPTER 5

Visual Thinking and a Visual Language for Young Children: The Agam Program

Zvia Markovits, Rina Hershkowitz, Sherman Rosenfeld, Lea Ilani and Bat-Sheva Eylon

Abstract

This chapter presents the "Agam Program for the Development of Visual Thinking" designed to actualize this vision. First, we relate to definitions of visual thinking and to the importance of developing visual thinking at a young age. Then, we describe the Agam Program for developing visual thinking and a visual language. We present the program's aims and content, the way they are contextualized in the teaching units for kindergarten teachers and school teachers, and the accessories kit that accompanies the program. We discuss the unique pedagogical approach – "visual pedagogy" – of the program and refer to the potential benefits of the program. The program's potential is to develop the children's visual thinking, problem solution skills and creativity. For this description we use authentic examples from four teaching units: *Circle, Square, Patterns* and *Numerical Intuition*. Later, we include research findings illustrating that children's visual thinking can be developed through of the Agam Program.

Keywords

visual thinking – the Agam Program – visual alphabet – young children – preschool teachers

• • •

All of us are visual illiterates. The education we give to our children causes them to be visually illiterate as well.

YAACOV AGAM (1984)

∴

1   Introduction

The visual dimension of our lives has become more and more important during recent years. We are exposed to visual information almost everywhere and are required to act in a visual world in which understanding and communication are conducted in a 'visual language'. In order to cope effectively with this large amount of visual information, we have to become intelligent consumers of visual information and develop our visual thinking.

Educational systems in Israel and around the world teach the verbal language of each respective country. Moreover, they teach another language – a "foreign language", mostly English – so that graduates of the educational system can cope with this language and communicate in it. Educational systems also invest in languages that are applied in mathematics and science, e.g. the number system, the symbolic language of algebra, and the language of logic.

Given this background, it is incomprehensible and interesting that educational systems hardly engage in the development of visual thinking and a visual language. Moreover, we are taught to express our experiences in a verbal manner that restricts exhaustion of the potential of these experiences (Wileman, 1993). This neglect is probably based on the assumption that visual thinking and a visual language do not need to be taught systematically since children develop them by themselves. But according to the artist, Yaacov Agam (1984), this assumption has no foundation, since we are all "visually illiterate".

Yaacov Agam's vision has been to develop visual thinking already at a young age. He maintains that this can be done by teaching a visual language, similarly to the way we teach verbal language skills and skills associated with the language of mathematics. Agam attributes great importance to the "education of the eye" and to the process of systematic development of visual thinking skills.

2   What Is Visual Thinking?

Visual thinking is a complex concept. In the literature that deals with the visual domain, one can find a variety of concepts associated with visual thinking, such as visual communication, visual problem-solving, dynamic visual thinking, spatial intelligence, spatial thinking, spatial sense, spatial perception and more (Arnheim, 1969; Eylon & Rosenfeld, 1990; Gardner, 1983; Kepes, 1994; Paivio, 1971; Sibbet, 1992).

Gardner (1983) argues that spatial intelligence includes the following abilities: (1) to perceive and recognize various instances of the same element, (2) to transform and manipulate these perceptions, (3) to make mental images and to transform them, and (4) to produce a graphic likeness of spatial information. Gershmehl and Gersmehl (2007) conclude that the parts in the brain that are responsible for the spatial thinking abilities are fully active already at a very young age. According to them, an appropriate intervention at these ages is essential.

Cyrs (1997), basing himself on Wileman (1993), maintains that visual thinking is the ability to continue conceptualizing and presenting thoughts, ideas and data, such as pictures and graphs, while changing a large part of the words we usually use into visual aids in order to communicate. This reference to visual thinking illuminates the fact that visual thinking facilitates a visual presentation of ideas and thoughts, exchanging in this way part of the verbal language usage.

Moore (2005) includes in her article another definition of visual thinking and links visual thinking with creativity. Moreover, she relates to the need for developing visual competences and discusses a 'visual language'.

> Visual competence is frequently perceived as the ability to think in pictures, an ability that explains in fact how we find logic in pictures, identify shapes, think in pictures … Visual competences are necessary in order to read what is called the 'visual language', a language of a 'feeling about shapes', emotions and even concepts. The visual way by which we think is apparently our reservoir of creativity …. (p. 179)

> The research supports the claims that visual thinking is a central meta-cognitive competence in mathematical thinking (Alsina & Nelsen, 2006), in scientific thinking (Gilbert, 2005) and in creative thinking (McKim, 1980). Visual thinking competences are essential for daily activities, in the workplace and in the solution of scientific problems. These competences are necessary for a variety of professions. For example, strategies of visual thinking were applied during the training of nurses. (Moorman, Hensel, Decker & Busby, 2017)

3   Visual Thinking at an Early Age

Recent years have witnessed a growing acknowledgement of the importance of both visual thinking development and the need to integrate visual thinking in curricula in general and in curricula for young children in particular. Studies illustrate that developing visual thinking at a young age enhances basic geometric abilities and mathematical thinking development (Clements & Sarama, 2000; Denton & West, 2002). Moreover, research findings show that it promotes writing capabilities as well as abilities associated with school readiness (Clements & Sarama, 1999, Eylon & Rosenfeld, 1990).

Nevertheless, as indicated above, visual thinking development is neglected in the curriculum for children in kindergarten and elementary school. Studies show that in most cases children do not acquire these capabilities by themselves (Markovits & Hershkowitz, 1997; Markovits, Rosenfeld & Eylon, 2006). Indeed, the report of the American National Research Council (NRC, 2006) recommends including visual thinking as an integral part of the curriculum for all kindergarten and school grades (K-12). The report recommends that visual thinking should be taught systematically in order to evoke interest in this field and to allow children to acquire important skills that will be useful to them throughout their lives.

4   The Agam Program for Visual Thinking Development

The Agam Program is a systematic curriculum, aiming to develop visual thinking of children at a young age. The program was conceived by the artist Yaacov Agam and was translated, re-written, and researched by a team of the Department of Science Teaching at the Weizmann Institute of Science. For this program, Yaacov Agam was awarded in 1996 the UNESCO prestigious Comensius Prize, named after Johannes Amos Comenius (1592–1670), considered as the 'father of modern education'. A guiding feature of the Agam Program is the assumption that visual thinking should be developed from a young age through the development of a visual language. This assumption is grounded in the idea that speaking in an appropriate language helps and affects the development of thinking. The program presents in a modular way visual concepts that are mutually integrated according to appropriate 'grammatical' laws, which is similar to the process of learning a verbal language (Chomsky, 1957). This language-oriented feature of the program reflects the assumption that children trained in the program learn to develop a visual language that can help them solve various kinds of problems.

The Agam Program was introduced and implemented in the Israeli educational system by the Agam staff at the Weizmann Institute of Science during the years 1984–1990, involving children aged 3–8. The implementation was stopped, due to budgetary difficulties, but renewed in 2004, when the Ministry of Education decided to implement the program in about 100 kindergartens throughout the country. The implementation of the program was accompanied by a long-term professional development of kindergarten teachers. During the academic year 2006–2007, the program started to be implemented also in the early grades of elementary school.

4.1   *Teaching Units of the Agam Program*

The Agam Program consists of 36 teaching units that include written and illustrated guidelines for kindergarten teachers. The units are listed below:

1. Circle	13. Variations of Forms	25. White, Black & Grey
2. Square	14. Symmetry	26. Trajectory
3. Patterns	15. Curved Line	27. From the Eye to the Hand
4. Circle &Square	16. Large, Medium, Small	28. Numerical Intuition
5. Flash Identification	17. Angles	29. Composition
6. Horizontal	18. Point	30. First Dimension
7. Vertical	19. Typical Forms	31. Second Dimension
8. Horizontal & Vertical	20. Proportion	32. Third Dimension
9. Oblique	21. Red	33. Fourth Dimension
10. Horizontal, Vertical & Oblique	22. Yellow	34. Letters
11. Triangle	23. Blue	35. Visual Grammar
12. Circle, Square & Triangle	24. Secondary Colours	36. Creativity

These units expose the children to basic visual concepts. Some of the units are basic and create a 'visual alphabet' that can be combined in different ways into units of a higher order. For example, the advanced units (e.g., *Symmetry, Proportions*, and *Numerical Intuition*) can be considered as cornerstones of the mathematical and scientific aspects of visual thinking. The units in the Agam Program can be divided into a number of 'clusters' that create a rich visual language. The clusters are detailed below (number of brochure in brackets):

- *Geometric Shapes*: Circle (1), Square (2), Circle and Square (4), Triangle (11), Circle, Square and Triangle (12), Angles (17).
- *Orientations*: Horizontal (6), Vertical (7), Horizontal and Vertical (8), Oblique (9), Horizontal, Vertical and Oblique (10).
- *Colors*: Red (21), Yellow (22), Blue (23), Secondary Colors (24), White, Black and Grey (25).
- *Size, Relationship and Estimation*: Large, Medium and Small (16), Numerical Intuition (28).
- *Advanced Concepts*: Patterns (3), Symmetry (14), Proportion (20).
- Visual Skills and Creativity: Flash Identification (5), Variations of Shapes (13), Typical Shapes (19), Trajectory (26), From the Eye to the Hand (27), Composition (29), Letters (34), Visual Grammar (35), Creativity (36).
- *Dimensions*: Point (18), Curved Line (15), One Dimension (30), Two Dimensions (31), Three Dimensions (32), Four Dimensions (33).

It is important to note that only some of these units are taught in kindergarten. Other units are designed for the early grades of elementary school, e.g. the unit engaging *Numerical Intuition* (28) is taught in the 3rd grade. The dimension units (*First Dimension, Second Dimension, Third Dimension*, and *Fourth Dimension*) are taught in the 1st and 2nd grades.

Another feature of the program is the initial learning of every visual concept as an isolated concept, after which the concept usually appears in combination with other concepts. During the acquisition of the visual language, the children advance from the simple to the complex. First, they learn the relations between various examples of one visual concept, for example, two circles with a common center, or three parallel vertical lines. At the next stage, they learn the relations between examples of various concepts, e.g., a circle and a square with a common center, or a vertical line that bisects a horizontal line. Similarly to the verbal language, these and other combinations facilitate the building of 'visual words'. Two circles with a common center and two bisecting circles are two different 'visual words' with different visual presentations. It is obviously impossible to learn all the possible visual combinations of these concepts. Nor is it necessary, since children learn to invent by themselves combinations according to their wishes, needs and imagination. It is noteworthy that most educational programs relate to visual concepts in isolation. For instance, a 'square' is taught both in kindergarten and in elementary school as a geometric concept, usually with a uniform presentation. Children do not learn the dynamics of the different visual representations of the square, when it is connected to different circles or to other shapes (Ministry of Education, 2006, 2010). Learning by this dynamic way complies with the rules of 'visual grammar' that help children to create 'visual sentences' and then 'visual stories', namely combinations of visual concepts on a higher level.

4.2 The Manipulatives Included in the Agam Program

In addition to the teaching units, the program offers a kit of manipulatives that constitutes an integral part of the program. These manipulatives include the following items:

- A wide variety of different geometric shapes (circles, squares, triangles, parallelograms, trapezoids, rhombuses, quadrilaterals, ellipses, and other polygons) of different sizes, colors and materials.
- Rods of different colors and lengths for comparing and measuring lengths, as well as for learning the concepts of ratio and proportion.
- Transparencies with lines and geometric shapes of different sizes and colors that illustrate the dynamic relations between the different shapes.
- Memory flash cards for each of the 36 teaching units.

FIGURE 5.1   The children playing freely with the manipulatives

The manipulatives are used in two situations: (1) when the kindergarten teacher teaches a small group or the whole class, and (2) when the children have free play time. All the shapes, rods, transparencies and memory cards are located in the 'Agam Corner' of the kindergarten and are always accessible to the children (see Figure 5.1).

4.3   *Teaching Units That Present Basic Concept in Mathematics and Science*

Many of the teaching units in the program present basic concepts in mathematics and science. For example, the units *Circle*, *Square*, *Patterns*, and *Numerical Intuition* are examples of such basic concepts. The unit *Circle* is the first unit in the program. Through the activities in this unit the children learn this 'first letter' in the 'visual alphabet'. Another 'letter' in the 'visual alphabet' is taught in the second unit, *Square*. In these two units, the children learn to create 'words in the visual language'. Each word consists of several circles or several squares that are connected by a particular connective condition, such as 'bisecting', 'tangent to', and 'inclusion'. After learning these two letters and composing 'visual words', the children learn in the third unit, *Patterns*, to compose 'sentences'. In the Agam Program, a pattern is a repeating series of shapes, in this case, circles and squares. The shapes, colors, sizes and positions of these shapes, as well as the spaces between the shapes, make up each pattern.

The patterns in the unit are linear, that is, they develop along a straight line. Hence, while the repeated cycle is finite, in principle the series can be infinite. The examples of patterns presented in the unit are developed from a very simple series (with few elements) to very complex ones. It is noteworthy that the 3–4 years old children create patterns that are highly complex. For example, Figure 5.2 illustrates examples of two 2-dimensional patterns created by children in the program. One matrix (A) is a series of shapes with the same order of elements (both the columns in the matrix and the main diagonal) and it is a linear series (finite or infinite as one wishes). The other matrix is a

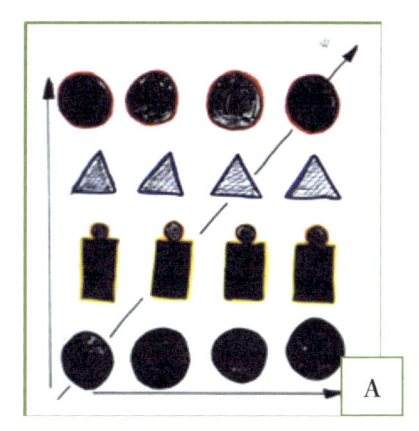 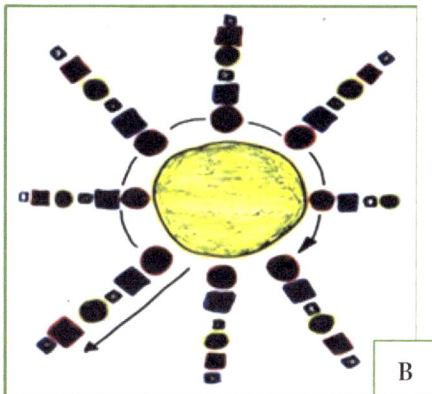

FIGURE 5.2   Examples of creating a 'pattern' by two children aged 3–4

2-dimensional series with the sun in the center and with rays that are all equal linear series (finite or infinite as one wishes) (Hershkowitz & Markovits, 1992). This a wonderful example presenting the Agam program, because the child can come close intuitively to one of the most important concepts in Math and Science by only two visual words.

The unit *Numerical Intuition* consists of activities with flash cards showing different patterns of elements (dots). The children are asked to estimate the total number of elements (dots). The flash cards are presented at a quick pace that does not allow enough time for counting. The purpose behind this quick pace is to force the children to come up with a reasonable answer to the challenge very quickly, in an intuitive way. The activities in this unit aim to develop the ability to make accurate visual estimations quickly, so that the process becomes immediate and intuitive. Several examples of dots on flash cards are presented in Figure 5.3.

4.4   The Pedagogical Approach of the Agam Program – "Visual Pedagogy"

In order to engage children in learning a visual language, the Agam Program has adopted several special pedagogical means:

a.   *Using a systematic approach for teaching every new concept.* Learning the concept starts with its *identification*, when it is first presented by the kindergarten teacher. For example, in the *Circle* unit, the children learn to *identify* the circle. They observe the circle, find out its property (rolling) and distinguish circles from other shapes. Then, they move from the abstract shape to actual objects, i.e., searching for objects with a circle-like shape. They discover the center of the circle and the various combinations of circles as well as the relations between them (circles with a common

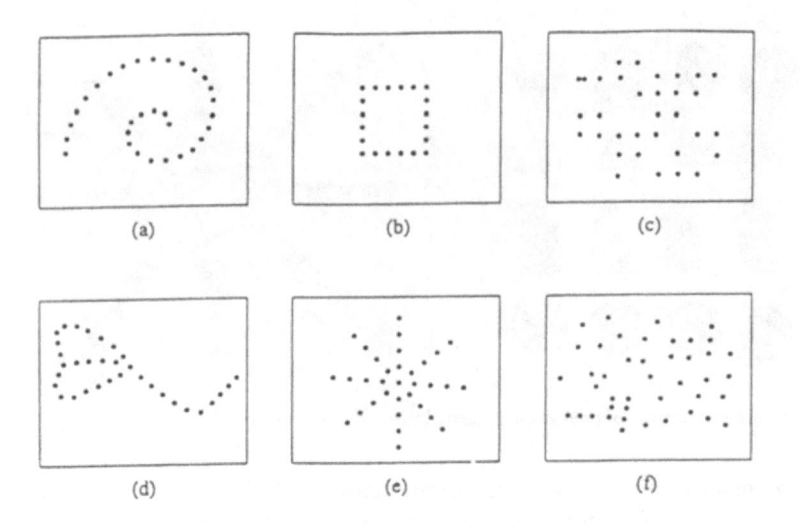

FIGURE 5.3   Several examples of dots on flash cards for training the eye in visual estimation
(see findings in Section 5.2)

center, circles enclosed within other circles, bisecting circles, circles tangent to each other and circles that are independent from each other).

The stage of developing visual *memory* is introduced next, by means of tasks that require identification from memory of combinations based on the concept. For example, in the *Circle* unit, the activities involve the use of flash cards, first including simple combinations of circles and then more complex combinations of these shapes. Additional activities include remembering circles and their location in the visual environment, as well as remembering circle-shaped objects and locating them. The unit of *Numerical Intuition* includes activities that develop memory accompanied by the visual estimation of object groups that gradually increase in number. This unit develops the children's intuition related to quantities of visual objects. This type of estimation is an important element in making spontaneous visual estimations.

The next stage is *reproduction*. In the *Circle* unit, reproduction of the visual concept is performed by various means: reproduction by use of the body, cardboard strips, colorful dough and drawings. The last stage is *reproduction from memory*. For example, in the *Circle* unit, the children observe a model of combined circles, remember it and reconstruct it by means of transparencies or memory cards. The units end with an opportunity for the children to creatively use and express the respective concepts.

b. *Using multiple representations.* The activities in each unit engage the children in the concept through different representations and creative methods. The different representations are visual, auditory and sensory, by means of physical activity and representations in different materials. For instance, in the *Patterns* unit, the children reconstruct a pattern with the shapes, by creating the pattern with objects, wooden beads, and cardboard shapes, and by drawing, cutting and pasting. Moreover, the children reconstruct patterns by using different senses: clapping hands, jumping on a pattern according to a particular beat, marching on a pattern with their eyes closed and according to musical sounds; for example, the child has to choose a circle when hearing the sound of the drum and to choose a square when hearing the sound of the triangle; the child places the appropriate shapes side by side and creates a pattern (Figure 5.4).

c. *Using a progressive presentation strategy.* Combinations of concepts are taught only after the children have mastered each concept separately. For example, in the *Patterns* unit that follows the *Circle* and *Square* units, only circles and squares are used in order to create patterns. This is done despite the fact that the pattern concept is much more general than a pattern made only of circles and squares. In fact, while learning additional units, the concept of patterns is expanded to include other shapes.

FIGURE 5.4   Illustrations from the Patterns unit – the children reconstruct patterns in different ways

d.   *'Intuitive' presentation of visual concepts.* Instead of receiving verbal defi-
     nitions, the children experience each visual concept in a direct visual
     way. Throughout the program, verbal definitions and instructions are
     used in a very limited way. The assumption is that when a visual stimulus
     is accompanied with a flow of words, the children will not sufficiently
     focus on the visual experience. For example, in the *Circle* unit, during
     the first activity, the kindergarten teacher shows the circle to the chil-
     dren without speaking. She presents a big blue circle and the children
     observe it. She moves her hand around the circle in a continuous and
     flowing movement, without any angle or fragmentation of the line, in
     order to illustrate the continuity of the circle's circumference. Then she
     rotates the circle on the floor. The children realize that the circle has been
     rotated but has not changed its shape in relation to the floor, on which
     it rotates. The kindergarten teacher then rolls the circle on the floor and
     the children observe the rolling circle. Until this point the kindergarten
     teacher has not spoken at all. The children's visual discoveries stem from
     observing the movements of both the kindergarten teacher and the cir-
     cle. At the end of this activity progression, the kindergarten teacher says:
     "This is a shape. This is a circle", without any further explanation.

4.5   *Developing Skills of Problem Solving and Providing Opportunities to Develop Thinking*

Developing skills of problem solving and providing opportunities to develop
thinking are integral parts of each unit in the Agam Program. We illustrate this
theme by presenting several design principles found in the first two units – the
Circle and the *Square*.

1.   *Developing the ability to distinguish between examples and non-examples
     of a concept.* For example, in the *Circle* unit, children distinguish between
     circles and other geometric shapes. A similar activity is included in the
     Square unit and is repeated in additional units (with other shapes or
     other concepts). This visual discrimination activity helps the children
     to consolidate their comprehension of the fact that there are two inde-
     pendent groups with regard to a certain concept – the group of the con-
     cept examples (i.e., circle) and the group of all the examples that are not
     included in the concept group (i.e., ellipse, square, triangle.)

2.   *Developing the ability to link the world of mathematical concepts and daily
     life.* For example, in the *Circle* unit the children are challenged to find cir-
     cles in objects, books, and pictures, both inside the kindergarten as well
     as outside in the yard. This activity is repeated in the other units; it helps
     children to translate the abstract visual concepts into tangible objects
     located in the world around them.

3. *Developing the understanding that a shape does not change when its position in space is changed.* For example, one of the first activities in the *Square* unit emphasizes that the square remains a square even if its position changes. A similar activity is repeated in additional units. This principle is extremely important in the development of geometric comprehension. The activity builds children's understanding that the shape, and therefore its name, do not change when its location in space is changed.

4. *Developing the ability to observe relations between geometric shapes. Understanding and naming the possible relations between them.* For example, in the activity in the *Circle* unit, children learn to observe and to name, by means of transparencies, the possible relations between circles: tangent circles, bisecting circles, circles within circles and circles with a common center, and independent circles. Through these activities, children learn the properties of a certain shape as well as the possible relations between them.

5. *While developing memory and observation abilities, comparing and finding the correct item among many similar items.* For example, in one of the activities in the *Circle* unit, 15 memory cards are placed before the children, each card with two to five circles of different sizes. The circles maintain one of the relations indicated above: tangent circles, bisecting circles, etc. At first, the children are shown one of the flash cards for a very short time and then a sequence of flash cards. The children have to identify the same card or the series of cards that were presented. The children must concentrate, observe well, remember what they have seen and compare what they have seen with the cards placed on the table.

6. *Developing creativity.* Developing creativity occurs throughout the entire program. For example, in the *Circle* unit, the children cut circles of different colors and sizes and create a combination of circles according to their will. In another activity in the *Square* unit, the children cut squares from magazines, creating a group or individual collage. In addition, as mentioned above, each unit ends with opportunities for the children to creatively use and express the respective concepts.

7. *Developing the ability to reproduce from memory.* In one of the activities in the *Circle* unit, the children are shown for a short time a flash card with several circles of different sizes. The circles have different relationships between each other. The children have to reproduce the circle combinations with a pencil on a paper page. Reproducing these circles from memory requires the children to understand the shapes and the relations between them, to remember them and then to reproduce them from memory.

FIGURE 5.5
A Hanukkah menorah built by
the children with the rods in the
manipulatives kit

8. *Developing problem solving skills.* The development of these skills occurs when the children play freely in the Agam corner. Below are two examples:

   (a) Children accurately cover a large square by means of smaller squares. This problem has several correct solutions. Each solution requires that the large square is covered without any 'bulge' on the sides and that the smaller squares do not cover another square. In fact, problem-solving in this case requires engagement in the topic of tiling.

   (b) Children have decided to build a Hanukkah menorah from the rods in the kit. They wanted all the candles to be of the same height, except for the ninth holder (the candle used for lighting the other candles) which should be higher. The sticks in the kit are of different lengths. Hence, in order to create candles of equal length, they have to find suitable combinations of the sticks. One result is presented in Figure 5.5.

5 The Effect of the Agam Program on Visual Thinking

In order to investigate the effect of the Agam Program on visual thinking, we conducted two comprehensive studies of kindergarten children and one study of 3rd graders. Moreover, we conducted several studies that focused on the kindergarten teachers who have worked with the program. This section briefly describes the three studies of the children: the first study of kindergarten children conducted during the years 1985–1987; the study of the 3rd graders conducted in 1995; and the study of the kindergarten children conducted during the years 2005–2007. In addition, we present the studies conducted with the kindergarten teachers.

5.1   *Study of Kindergarten Children (1985–1987)*

The first comprehensive study of kindergarten children who were involved in the Agam Program was conducted during the years 1985–1987. This study was conducted in 25 experiment group kindergartens in which the program was implemented, compared to 25 control group kindergartens. Significant differences in visual competencies were found between the children in these two groups, specifically in the topics of visual identification, visual memory and visual reproduction (Razel & Eylon, 1986; Eylon & Rosenfeld, 1990). The systematic observations and the interviews illustrated that the program had been positively received by the kindergarten teachers. Moreover, the findings showed a positive effect on the intelligence and readiness for 1st grade, mainly as far as geometry and writing were concerned. There was also an increase in the children's visual learning ability and in their performance of new assignments (transfer tasks). The program had more of an effect on children who participated in it for two years, as compared to children who joined the program in the second year, indicating that the program made an accumulated impact. These findings show that the approach advocated by the Agam Program has considerable educational potential (Eylon & Rosenfeld, 1990; Razel & Eylon, 1991).

5.2   *Study of 3rd Graders (1995)*

Markovits and Hershkowitz (1997) conducted a study that explored 3rd graders' ability to perform a visual estimate associated with discrete quantities. This ability was measured both prior to the children's learning the unit on this topic (*Numerical Intuition*) as well as after they learned this unit. The study consisted of interviews in which 12 children took part. As part of the study, flash cards with groups of dots were presented to the children for a very short time (see Figure 5.3). The children were asked to give a numerical estimate for each flash card and say how many dots they thought were in each flash card. Moreover, they were requested to describe the strategy by which they arrived at their answer. The first three pictures (Figures 5.3a, 5.3b, 5.3c) were presented in the interview before learning the unit and the three additional pictures (Figures 5.3d, 5.3e, 5.3f) were shown in the interview following the unit. Generally speaking, the children were closer to the accurate answers in the second interview. In the first interview, the average error was 27% as compared to only 14% in the second interview. During the interviews, the children applied four different strategies in order to perform the visual estimate. Below are examples of the children's responses:

– "I counted 2, 4, 6, up to 8 and still many more dots were left". (The *Counting Strategy*).

- "20 – I relied on the previous picture and reduced several dots". (The *Comparison* Strategy).
- "About 30 – the dots are spread about in 4s everywhere; I circled in my head every 4 dots". (The *Groups* Strategy).
- "50! This is what I saw, I did not start counting, I looked! *You simply guessed? I did not guess!* According to what I saw. You can see that there are 50 dots". (The *Global-Visual Perception* Strategy).

Below is a description of these 4 strategies:

1. *Counting* – The children counted as much as they could during the short time that they saw the flash card and then added more dots to their number.

2. *Comparison* – The children compared the number of dots in a certain picture to the number of dots in previous pictures.

3. *Groups* – The children divided (in their heads) the dots into groups, usually with an equal number of dots per group and multiplied by the number of groups that they identified.

4. *Global-Visual Perception* – The children found it hard to explain what they did. They did not use any of the previous strategies. They said that they looked at the picture and intuitively decided on the number of dots.

The research findings show that between the first and second interview, a change occurred in the strategies used by the children. In the *Counting* Strategy that did not 'work' due to lack of time, there was a decrease from 42% in the first interview to 19% in the second interview. In the *Groups* Strategy, there was a slight increase, from 31% in the first interview to 36% in the second. In the *Comparison* Strategy there was no change, 11% in both interviews. In the *Global-Visual Perception* Strategy, there was an increase from 16% in the first interview to 34% in the second interview.

These findings illustrate an improvement in the children's intuitive visual estimation as a result of learning the *Numerical Intuition* unit. This improvement was manifested both by the accuracy in the number of dots in the pictures and by the use of more effective strategies in the second interview, with an increase in the strategy of global-visual perception. It is noteworthy that in the study conducted with 25 kindergarten teachers before starting to work in the Agam Program (Markovits et al., 2006), one of the tasks dealt with visual estimation, in which the kindergarten teachers were shown the first three pictures (Figure 5.3). The findings of that study indicate that the average error of the kindergarten teachers was 25%, very similar to that of the 3rd graders before learning the unit. As far as strategies were concerned, the kindergarten teachers applied the *Counting* Strategy less than the children (6%); they applied the *Groups* Strategy more than the children (53%) and applied much less the *Global-Visual Perception* Strategy (18%). These findings illustrate that the strategy of global-visual estimation does not necessarily improve with age.

5.3   Study of Kindergarten Children (2005–2007)

The second study of kindergarten children was conducted in 20 kindergartens, ten in the experiment group and ten in the control group (Eylon, Hershkowitz, Ilani, Markovits & Rosenfeld, 2014). The control group kindergartens were chosen so that they matched the experiment group kindergartens regarding the children's background. The experiment group, like the control group, consisted each of 310 children about 4 years old. A year later, a visual thinking test was taken again by 45 children from the experiment group who continued working with the Agam Program and 45 children from the control group.

The main research findings support the findings of the earlier 1985–1987 study. They illustrate that in most items, the experiment group children demonstrated higher capabilities than the control group children with regard to visual thinking in the identification and analysis of geometric shapes (such as a circle and a square), both in a simple visual environment and in a complex visual environment. Furthermore, their capabilities were higher with regard to items involving memory and visual problem solution. Regarding some of the items, the findings were statistically significant and in some, the experiment group demonstrated higher capabilities than the control group, albeit with no statistical significance.

5.3.1   Identification of Circles and Squares in a Complex Visual Environment

The instructions given to the children were to mark in red all the circles in the drawing and to mark in blue all the squares in the drawing (Figure 5.6a).

The percentage of the total correct answers to this item ranged between 56–70.

In the test given prior to the unit, no significant statistical differences were found between the two groups. In the post-test given at the end of 2006, significant statistical differences were found in favor of the experiment group (p < 0.005).

5.3.2   Analysis of Shapes in a Complex Visual Environment

The children were told: "Look at the drawing on the left (the interviewer showed what was intended) and choose the shapes on the right (the interviewer showed what was intended) of which the drawing consists" (Figure 5.6b).

This item was not given in the test prior to the program but only in the post-test. The percentage of the total correct answers ranged between 65 and 100. Significant statistical differences were found in the favor of the experiment

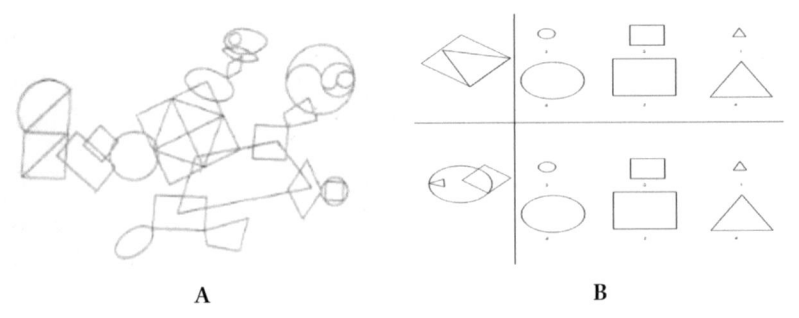

A   B

FIGURE 5.6   Items from the visual thinking test

group in the post-test of 2006 (p < 0.0001). Significant statistical differences were found in favor of the experiment group also in the post-test of 2007 (p < 0.0001).

5.4   *Studies of Kindergarten Teachers Working with the Agam Program*

We conducted three studies of the kindergarten teachers who participated in the Agam Program. One of the studies, which comprised 25 kindergarten teachers before joining the program, explored their visual thinking and beliefs about visual thinking development at a young age (Markovits et al., 2006). Two other studies were conducted for the purpose of examining the kindergarten teachers' perceptions of the Agam Program and its potential contribution to the development of visual thinking. The participants in the study conducted in 2008 were 54 kindergarten teachers and in the study conducted in 2013 the participants were 24 kindergarten teachers (Eylon et al., 2014).

Findings of the first study (2006) illustrated that some of the kindergarten teachers encountered difficulties in performing tasks associated with visual estimation, visual memory and reproduction from memory. As mentioned above, their visual estimation ability was similar to that of the 3rd graders (Markovits & Hershkowitz, 1997). The kindergarten teachers said that they believed visual thinking could be developed by means of an appropriate program. However, they were skeptical about the possibility of developing visual thinking in young children.

The studies conducted with the kindergarten teachers in 2008 and 2013 show that the kindergarten teachers highly appreciated the Agam Program. They pointed out that the program made a considerable contribution to the development of visual thinking in the kindergarten children. Moreover, they mentioned that the children made a transfer of their visual knowledge to situations outside the kindergarten. In addition, the kindergarten teachers indicated that the program enhanced the development of additional abilities in the children, e.g. the ability to concentrate, the development of memory and curiosity, as well as the children's abilities in their transition to 1st grade. An important issue that emerged from the kindergarten teachers' responses was the contribution of the Agam Program to children with linguistic difficulties or with attention deficit. The teachers said that in addition to the contribution to these children, the program also helped them in developing their visual thinking. All the kindergarten teachers specified that they were interested in continuing to work with the program. They wanted to recommend to their friends to take part in this program since it has the potential to develop children's visual thinking, imagination and creativity.

Below are several quotations from the kindergarten teachers as a response to two of the questions included in the study: (a) In your opinion, what is the contribution of the Agam Program to the children in your kindergarten? and (b) Has the Agam Program contributed to you as a kindergarten teacher? If yes, in what way?

(a) In your opinion, what is the contribution of the Agam Program to the children in your kindergarten?

> Developing visual thinking and recognizing geometric shapes and the program is also a source for developing creativity. The program developed the children's ability to persevere and concentrate and it improved their working habits.

> Visual sharpness – children learned to look at many new things: people who come to the kindergarten, various shapes around them and even different weather conditions.

> The contribution of the program to the children with regard to the visual domain is great. I also see great contributions to the children in the area of concentration, attention to details and other competences that the children need at school, not to mention mathematical concepts (mainly in geometry).

> There is a positive contribution to the children who do not speak much, since here they can act and think without many words. In particular, there are immigrant children in my kindergarten who have not yet mastered the language. In addition, the manipulatives are very aesthetic and attract the children to the activities.

> The program improves the children's attention and perseverance since it educates them for silent observation, patience, waiting for their turn, listening without speaking and focusing on shape.

(*b*) *Has the Agam Program contributed to you as a kindergarten teacher? If yes, in what way?*

> The program has contributed a lot to me. First, it made me understand and internalize the expression 'Seeing is better than a thousand words'. Second, it reinforced and increased my confidence in the children's ability to learn, teach, analyze, ask, draw conclusions, etc. Third, it helped me to understand better what makes a curriculum operational and easy to use. Fourth, I greatly enjoyed the experience of not talking.

> The program contributed to me mostly in the visual domain. I feel I have become stronger and can identify shapes much faster, even the small shapes. It developed my eye contact with the children and particularly with each child in a more focused way. I see every movement, identify every whisper. The children and I have developed a language. Through their eyes they can understand what I want them to do.

> I suddenly notice how difficult it is to explain something in words and how much easier it is to show them in a drawing or illustration. I am simply more aware of how many words that we use, while neglecting the visual dimension.

> The Agam Program enabled me to learn how to develop visual perception. How to develop a topic about shapes and especially a circle, since it is familiar to the children.

> I realized that young children can understand complex concepts more that I had thought in the past. Consequently, I expanded other topics to a higher level. The program consists of stages that are built one upon the other and served me as an example about how to build new topics from different domains. The program is an example of how you can learn and internalize without verbal expression.

6   Summary

Developing visual thinking is usually neglected in kindergarten and primary school. Educational systems are still mistaken in making the naive assumption that in some way learners will acquire visual thinking abilities which they could use now and later, when such abilities become necessary. Visual cognition is also very important in mathematics, as demonstrated by many positive responses of mathematics educators to publications describing the Agam Program and its achievements.

Our work with the Agam Program has challenged the assumption related to a 'natural' development of visual cognition. Our research and development work provide strong evidence that visual cognition can be developed by systematic learning that leads learners to enjoy its benefits in a wide range of academic fields. Moreover, our work supports the view that preventing such a systematic development will leave us – and our children – "visually illiterate".

References

Agam, Y. (1984). Seeing is learning – or should be! *Kidma: Israeli Journal of Development, 8*(2), 24–31.

Alsina, C., & Nelsen, R. B. (2006). *Math made visual: Creating images for understanding mathematics.* Mathematical Association of America.

Arnheim, R. (1969). *Visual thinking.* University of California Press.

Chomsky, N. (1957). *Syntactic structures.* Morison.

Clements, D. H., & Sarama, J. (1999). *Preliminary report of building blocks foundations for mathematical thinking, pre-kindergarten to grade 2: Research-based materials development.* State University of New York at Buffalo.

Clements, D. H., & Sarama, J. (2000). Young children's ideas about geometric shapes. *Teaching Children Mathematics, 6,* 482–88.

Cyrs, T. E. (1997). Visual thinking: Let them see what you are saying. *New Directions for Teaching and Learning, 71,* 27–32.

Denton, K., & West, J. (2002). *Children's reading and mathematics achievement in kindergarten and first grade.* National Center for Education.

Eylon, B., Hershkowitz, R., Ilani, L., Markovits, Z., & Rosenfeld, S. (2014). *Educating the eye: The Agam Programme.* Research Report. Department of Science Teaching, Weizmann Institute of Science.

Eylon, B., & Rosenfeld, S. (1990). *The Agam Project: Cultivating visual cognition in young children.* Technical Report. Department of Science Teaching, Weizmann Institute of Science.

Gardner, H. (1983). *Frames of mind: The theory of multiple intelligences.* Basic Books.

Gersmehl, P., & Gersmehl, C. (2007). Spatial thinking by young children: Neurologic evidence for early development and "educability". *Journal of Geography, 106*(5), 181–191.

Gilbert, J. K. (2005). *Visualization in science education.* Springer Publishers.

Hershkowitz, R., & Markovits, Z. (1992). Conquer math concepts by developing visual thinking. *Arithmetic Teacher, 39*(9), 38–41.

Kepes, G. (1994). *Language of vision.* Paul Theobald.

Markovits, Z., & Hershkowitz, R. (1997). Relative and absolute thinking in visual estimation processes. *Educational Studies in Mathematics, 32*(1), 29–47.

Markovits, Z., Rosenfeld, S., & Eylon, B. (2006). Visual Cognition: Content knowledge and beliefs of preschool teachers. In K. Novotna, H. Moraova, M. Kratka, & N. Stehlikova (Eds.), *Proceedings of the 30th PME Conference* (Vol. 4, pp. 145–152). The International Group for the Psychology of Mathematics Education (PME).

McKim, R. H. (1980). *Experiences in visual thinking.* PWS Engineering Publishers.

Ministry of Education. (2010). *Mathematics curriculum for kindergartens in the state and religious-state education.* Pedagogical Secretariat, Section of Curricula Planning and Development. [in Hebrew]

Ministry of Education, Culture and Sport. (2006). *Mathematics curriculum for the 1st–6th grades in all the sectors.* Pedagogical Secretariat, Section of Curricula Planning and Development. [in Hebrew]

Moore, K. (2005). Visual thinking: Hidden truth of hidden agenda? *Journal of Visual Art Practice, 4*(2&3), 177–195.

Moorman, M., Hensel, D., Decker, K. A., & Busby, K. (2017). Learning outcomes with visual thinking strategies in nursing education. *Nurse Education Today, 51,* 127–129.

National Research Council (NRC). (2006). *Learning to think spatially.* National Academies Press.

Paivio, A. (1971). *Imagery and verbal processes.* Holt Rinehart, Winston.

Razel, M., & Eylon, B. (1986). Developing visual language skills; The Agam programme. *Journal of Visual and Verbal Languages, 6*(1), 49–54.

Razel, M., & Eylon, B. (1991). A wise man has his eyes in his head: A cognitive transferral in the Agam program for visual education. *Megamot, 2,* 205–231. [in Hebrew]

Sibbet, D. (1992). *Fundamentals of graphic language.* Grove.

Wileman, R. E. (1993). *Visual communicating.* Educational Technology Publications.

PART 3

Patterns and Structure

∵

CHAPTER 6

Pathways to Early Mathematical Thinking in Kindergarten

The Pattern and Structure Mathematics Awareness Program

Joanne Mulligan

Abstract

The Australian Pattern and Structure project comprises a series of related studies that has developed an assessment interview and pedagogical program for children aged 4 to 8 years. Through several classroom and evaluation studies with young children an Awareness of Mathematical Pattern and Structure (AMPS) has been identified and measured and found to be predictive of mathematical achievement. In this chapter an overview of the learning pathways of the Pattern and Structure Mathematics Awareness Program (PASMAP), five structural groupings and the pedagogical approach are described so as to support teachers in noticing mathematical structure. The PASMAP pedagogy is articulated through two exemplars of children's representations of structuring grids and hundreds' charts. Implications for further research, teaching and learning, and pre- and in-service programs are raised.

Keywords

mathematical pattern – mathematical structure – PASMAP – young children

1   Introduction

Recent research on mathematical patterns and structures with young children has provided a more coherent picture of the common underlying bases of early mathematical development. A number of studies have investigated the relationship between patterning and structural skills and mathematical achievement including counting and numeracy (Aunio & Niemivirta, 2010; Burgoyne et al., 2017; Kidd et al., 2014; Lüken, 2017; Verdine et al., 2013) and spatial reasoning (Rittle-Johnson et al., 2017; Rittle-Johnson et al., 2019). The development of patterning competencies through intervention studies has shown that young children are capable of abstract thinking so that early mathematical learning can be scaffolded to promote the development of algebraic reasoning (Carraher et al., 2006; Clements & Sarama, 2007; Lüken & Suazet, 2020; Papic et al., 2011; Rittle-Johnson et al., 2013; Rittle-Johnson et al., 2019; Warren & Cooper 2008). New cross-disciplinary studies are providing strong evidence that spatial reasoning skills are malleable and are of critical importance in the early years, and that these skills impact on later mathematical development (Casey et al., 2008; Mulligan et al., 2020a; Sinclair & Bruce, 2015). Related studies have drawn attention to the explicit contribution of perceptual subitizing and the spatial structuring of groups in arrays (Starkey & McCandliss, 2014). Spontaneous focusing on number (SFON) has also been found related to spatial estimation skills (Hannula & Lehtinen, 2005). Such studies are informing pedagogical and curriculum initiatives that are centred on 'spatial' approaches involving patterning (Mulligan et al., 2020b; Tirosh et al., 2018). The study of spatial structuring has also drawn attention to the role of structure in developing units of measure in traditional studies of arrays (Battista et al., 1998; Outhred & Mitchelmore, 2000).

However, further research is needed to establish a more coherent picture of how the findings from related but different disciplines can contribute to a more coherent interdisciplinary picture of the influence of patterning ability on mathematical development.

In this chapter an overview of the Pattern and Structure project is provided with a description of the PASMAP components aligned with five structural groupings; i.e., the big ideas. Two exemplars of learning pathways are presented for the purpose of articulating the PASMAP approach in order to support professionals' content and pedagogical knowledge.

2   The Australian Pattern and Structure Project

The Pattern and Structure project has been transformative in the assessment of early mathematical development and advancement of teaching and learning. This has been realised through a suite of nine successive clinical, design-based and evaluation studies over the last decade (see Mulligan & Mitchelmore, 2013a; Mulligan et al., 2013b, 2020a). These studies have identified how children can develop connected mathematical knowledge leading to generalization – interrelated with spatial structuring. The outcomes include the development and validation of innovative psychometric techniques to link quantitative and qualitative measures of mathematical development. The Pattern and Structure Assessment (PASA) (Mulligan et al., 2015) comprising three interview-based assessments for children aged 4 to 8 years, and the aligned Pattern and Structure Mathematics Awareness Program (PASMAP) (Mulligan & Mitchelmore, 2016a, 2016b) have been trialled and evaluated in a range of educational settings and articulated in early numeracy and professional learning programs and resources (Australian Association of Mathematics Teachers [AAMT], 2015).

Research on pattern and structure developed from seminal work on multiplicative reasoning, mathematical imagery and the analysis of structural development in children's representations (Thomas et al., 2002). Building on this work, a new theoretical approach to researching mathematical development, *Awareness of Mathematical Pattern and Structure* (AMPS) was validated through a suite of studies focused on the relationship between children's mathematical structural development across concepts. The PASA interview measures AMPS by analysing the structural features of children's responses using qualitative descriptors. The methodology and psychometric measures integrate phenomenologically-based analytical techniques with Rasch modelling and the micro-genetic analysis of students' conceptual understanding (Mulligan et al., 2015). A quantitative measure and qualitative descriptor of AMPS is indicated on a Rasch scale, based on a scoring system aligned with one of five increasing levels of structural development that provides a continuum from "low" to "high" levels of AMPS (Mulligan et al., 2015).

Three early studies informed the development of the PASA and the PASMAP: a study of 103 first-graders (aged 6–7 years), a 15-week intervention with Kindergarten (aged 5–6 years) and a 6-month intervention with pre-schoolers (aged 4–5 years) (Mulligan & Mitchelmore, 2009, 2013a; Papic et al., 2011). These studies found young children more capable than previously considered – they could represent, abstract and generalize mathematical ideas, albeit in emergent forms. Pre-schoolers showed an understanding of *unit of repeat* and *spatial structuring*, retaining and expanding these skills to growing patterns when assessed one year later. Interventions with Kindergarten and first-grade students resulted in impressive growth in their patterning and spatial structuring skills including *partitioning, similarity and congruence, unitizing* and *identifying properties* of 2D and 3D shapes.

The evaluation of PASA and early forms of PASMAP were central to the evaluation study of 316 Kindergarten children in the project, *Reconceptualizing early mathematics learning: The fundamental role of pattern and structure.* The longitudinal study found that the 'patterns' approach was advantageous to early mathematics learning, sustained a year after the program had ceased, and that teachers could implement the program with professional training, appropriate resources and on-going support (Mulligan et al., 2013b; Mulligan et al., 2020a). A descriptive analysis indicated that students generally progressed through five levels of structural development (Mulligan et al., 2020). The upper third of students demonstrated emergent generalisations at the structural and advanced structural levels which supported early algebraic thinking. Half of the less-able students moved from pre-structural to at least emergent level over the duration of the program.

The scope of the study was extended through another project *Transforming children's mathematical and scientific reasoning* which included early science learning and data modelling, and a longitudinal study of young gifted boys (Mulligan, 2015).

3   Structural Groupings

These studies provided further development of the classification of students' responses into five individual structural groupings as follows:

Sequences: recognising a (linear) series of objects or symbols arranged in a definite order or using repetitions, i.e., repeating and growing patterns and number sequences.

Structured Counting and grouping: subitizing, counting in groups, such as counting by 2s or 5s or on a numeral track with the equal grouping structure recognised as multiplicative.

Shape and Alignment: recognising structural features of two- and three-dimensional (two-dimensional and three-dimensional) shapes and graphical representations, constructing units of measure, such as co-linearity (horizontal and vertical coordination), similarity and congruence, and such properties as equal sides, opposite and adjacent sides, right angles, horizontal and vertical, parallel and perpendicular lines.

Equal Spacing: partitioning of lengths, other two-dimensional or three-dimensional spaces and objects into equal parts, such as constructing units of measure. It is fundamental to representing fractions, scales and intervals.

Partitioning: division of lengths, other two-dimensional or three-dimensional spaces, objects and quantities, into unequal or equal parts, including fractions and units of measure. These groupings are articulated through PASMAP learning Pathways represented in Table 6.1.

4   The Pattern and Structure Pedagogical Approach

The PASMAP promotes a highly structured interrelated network of learning experiences. The pedagogical strategy is to scaffold experiences where children seek out and represent patterns and structural relationships across a

TABLE 6.1   PASMAP pathways, phases 1 and 2, aligned with structural groupings

Pathway	Structural groupings
Phase 1	
Repeating Patterns	Sequences, structured counting
Structured Counting	Structured counting, equal spacing
Grid Structure	Shape and alignment, structured counting
Structuring Shapes	Shape and alignment, partitioning
Partitioning and Sharing:	Partitioning, equal spacing
Base Ten Structure	Equal spacing, structured counting
Growing Patterns	Sequences, shape and alignment
Structuring Measurement	Equal spacing, partitioning
Structuring Data	Equal spacing, shape and alignment
Symmetry and transformation	Shape and alignment, partitioning
Phase 2	
Multiplication Patterns	Sequences, structured counting
Fitting Shapes Together	Shape and alignment, equal spacing
Partitioning and Fractions	Partitioning, equal spacing
Place Value	Equal spacing, structured counting
Metric Measurement	Shape and alignment, structured counting
Patterns in Data	Shape and alignment, equal spacing
Angles and Direction	Shape and alignment

wide range of concepts in an interconnected way. The goal is to promote emergent generalization in early mathematical thinking. Emergent generalizations develop from the process of seeking similarity and difference, and by looking for the common structural features of quantities and measures, patterns and relationships, objects and shapes and situations.

Some simple examples include recognizing the equal side lengths of a square, the unit of repeat in a simple repetition, equivalence and unit fractions respectively: "a square always has four equal sides no matter how big it is"; "the blue, red, blue pattern is the same as the triangle, square, triangle pattern and it's the same at each end"; "If I add two plus four equals six it's the same as four plus two so it doesn't matter which way you add them"; "When you cut the pieces into smaller and smaller bits the number of pieces gets bigger but you have to make them the same size" (Mulligan et al., 2013b).

The PASMAP pedagogical approach is represented as a sequence of mathematical concepts and relationships, but with a view to representing and abstracting core structural elements and interconnecting these. The use of visual memory to visualize, construct and represent mathematical patterns and structures is emphasized. The initial pedagogical processes of modeling, representing (including symbolizing) are typically found in traditional mathematical teaching. In PASMAP visualization and visual memory are encouraged to extend the modelling and representation processes to abstraction and generalization, albeit at an emergent level. The pedagogical approach is summarized as follows:

Modelling: Children copy, model or describe a pattern linked to a specified mathematical task, usually under teacher direction. The teacher ensures that children understand the essential features of the pattern or structural features that are the focus of the learning sequence.

Representing: Children record usually by drawing, the pattern or a model of the pattern using pictorial, iconic or emergent symbolic inscriptions while visible. This experience helps children to isolate the essential features of the pattern or structure from the particular example in which it occurs. Digital technologies may also be utilized.

Visualizing: Children draw or symbolize the pattern or structure when it is not visible. Comparing their productions with the original pattern or structure highlights its essential features. The process of visualizing and comparing can be repeated until children have internalized the pattern or structure.

Generalizing: The teacher supports children (either individually or as a group) to make the pattern or structure explicit, find similar examples in other contexts, and express what is 'general' about the pattern.

Sustaining: Some learning experiences are provided that reinforce or extend children's development and application of the patterns or structures.

4.1 Teacher Development and the PASMAP Implementation

In the classroom studies and longitudinal Kindergarten evaluation study (Mulligan et al., 2020) teachers and associated pre-service teachers of the PASMAP classes participated initially in a two-day professional learning (PL) program led by the research team on the theoretical approach, the content and scope, pedagogical approach and implementation strategies of the PASA assessment interview and the PASMAP. The PL program focused on supporting teachers to assess and identify students' level of AMPS across a range of mathematical concepts, and analysing lessons and student work samples illustrating the PASMAP components and levels of structural development. Critical to the training was that teachers discussed and categorised a number of examples of students' responses into one of five levels of structural development: pre-structural, emergent, partial structural, structural and advanced (see Mulligan et al., 2013a). Following this process, the teachers evaluated how PASMAP aligned with the *Australian F-10 Curriculum: Mathematics* (ACARA, 2015) and school mathematics programs.

The PASMAP was provided to the teachers in the form of lesson guidelines for each of the sub-components organised by the PASMAP pedagogical model described above. The teachers adapted the lessons to accommodate their individual teaching styles, to differentiate for learners' abilities and needs, and to integrate their classroom norms. The teachers were supported by a member of the research team who was a trained, experienced early childhood teacher and expert on the PASMAP, on a regular basis and assisted in interpreting student learning. De-briefing workshops were conducted throughout the evaluation study and follow up focus-group interviews with teachers provided insights into the teacher 'change' process.

In the following sections, two pertinent examples of learning pathways are exemplified for the purpose of articulating the PASMAP approach and the way that students' responses shape the teacher scaffolding and refinement of the lesson process.

5 Learning Pathways: Grid Structure

5.1 *Grid Structure*

Early experience of horizontal and vertical alignment and co-linearity is often encountered through embodied action during play. The role of gesture and movement is explored in current research about early geometric learning (Elia, 2018). For example, Figure 6.1 shows a child negotiating a climbing frame by recognizing that there are equal-sized spaces to estimate the position of the

FIGURE 6.1
A child plays on a climbing frame (Mulligan & Mitchelmore, 2016b, p. 41)

hands and feet in order to move upwards on the roped platform. Three pertinent questions can be raised from observing the process of the child's negotiation of space:
– How do children develop the process of noticing similarity and difference?
– How do children develop spatial structure?
– How do children develop co-linearity (horizontal and vertical coordination)?

Two examples of grid structure are drawn from the PASMAP pedagogical interventions: simple square grids and constructing hundred s' grids.

5.2   *Simple Square Grids*

Grids are a rich source of mathematical pattern and structure and they are central to many mathematical concepts such as area measurement. The rows and columns are aligned vertically and horizontally and exploration of these can promote understanding of congruence, co-linearity and juxtaposition. Constructing and interpreting grids also relies on equal spacing. Co-ordinating vertical and horizontal intersecting points was found to be a difficult process for children who were operating at the pre-structural and emergent stages of development in the PASMAP evaluation studies (Mulligan et al., 2013b).

The following example is drawn from the PASMAP longitudinal study with Kindergarten (Mulligan et al., 2013b). The children were shown a 2 × 2 grid pattern of squares and asked to draw it freehand from memory, calculating and representing the number of squares. Figures 6.2 and 6.3 show contrasting examples from Alison and Michael.[1]

The children were then asked to finish an incomplete 2 × 2 grid so that "it looked exactly like the 2 × 2 grid card" (see Figures 6.4 and 6.5).

From the discussion with the children about their drawings, it was evident that Alison had developed good spatial structuring and a high level of AMPS compared with Michael who had low AMPS. Alison was able to identify the unit of repeat immediately, explaining that the same sized square was being repeated and that it was repeated twice. Recognising the unit of repeat

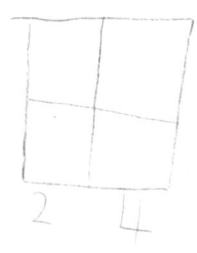

FIGURE 6.2   Alison's 2 × 2 grid pattern   FIGURE 6.3   Michael's 2 × 2 grid pattern

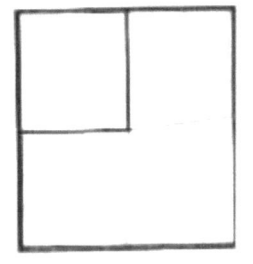

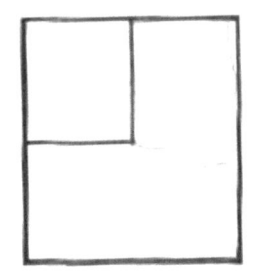

FIGURE 6.4   Alison's completion of   FIGURE 6.5   Michael's completion of
             the 2 × 2 grid pattern   the 2 × 2 grid pattern

involved the process of iteration of a square unit as well as the notion of symmetry and halving. Figure 6.2 demonstrates that Alison was able to draw the 2 × 2 grid from memory, and she understood that she could also complete the 2 × 2 grid by continuing the horizontal and vertical lines without drawing individual squares. It is also evident that Alison's structural development can be attributed to her ability to partition space into symmetrical and equal-sized parts (see Figure 6.4).

In contrast, when Michael was presented with the 2 × 2 grid, he identified four individual squares but he was not able to differentiate between a row and a column. In an intermittent activity, Michael was able to place four squares on another blank grid, in a clockwise, anticlockwise and diagonal pattern. However, he finished the incomplete grid by drawing "three more squares" (see Figure 6.5). These were neither connected to the vertical and horizontal lines, nor were they of equal size or covering the entire area. Michael was assessed at the emergent stage of structural development for this task. An underlying difficulty was that he did not perceive the grid formed by horizontal and vertical lines as partitioning the space into four equal-sized squares, although he does complete the space by drawing three irregular shapes. The notion of unequal sized squares may relate to lack of attention to the space as a whole, which also indicated poor spatial structuring skills.

5.3   Constructing a Hundreds' Chart

The application of structuring simple grids is extended in the construction of a hundreds' chart. The development of additive and multiplicative patterns, as well as base ten structure is advantaged by exploration of patterns on the hundreds' chart. In the PASMAP, the children were engaged in learning experiences that utilized parts of, or extensions of a hundreds' chart as a structured model for counting and exploring patterns to one hundred and beyond.

However, it is often assumed by the teacher that children automatically recognize and use grid structure. An important PASMAP learning experience is to scaffold the conceptual and representational of the hundred grid, beginning with one row of ten squares, and gradually building up the chart by coordinating rows or columns of ten as a pattern "down, across, down across".

An important step is the use of visual memory when the children reconstruct the hundreds' chart and draw it freehand from memory. The following excerpt provides a pertinent example of how James visualized the structure of the grid before drawing.

James: I made the square into ten rows and ten columns and made number patterns of twos, then fives then tens to fill it in.
Teacher: How did you know you need 10 rows and 10 columns?
James: We need 100 numbers, so 10 rows and 10 in each row ...
Teacher: What pattern are you using to fill in this column? [third column]
James: +10, all numbers on the column have to end with the same number, number 3. And the other numbers goes up by 1 [tenth place]. I know how to count by all patterns!

James demonstrated an advanced understanding of pattern and base ten structure for a Kindergarten child aged 5 years 3 months. He was able to identify patterns of five and ten easily, including on and off the decade and from various starting points.

In contrast, Michael was able to represent the grid with lines divided into smaller spaces but he was not able to visualize or represent the 10 × 10 grid structure. He filled the spaces with the unitary counting sequence until the spaces were exhausted (see Figure 6.6). Michael asked to see the hundreds' chart again after he had completed the first row as explained in the following interview excerpt.

Teacher: What can you see that is different from this hundreds' chart and yours?
Michael: My squares are different; they do not go down.

The use of the hundreds' grid as a model for structuring base ten was effective for children in the PASMAP studies who were advanced sufficiently in their spatial structuring skills so that they functioned at the partial and structural stages of development. For these children the grid structure encouraged development of number patterns and counting by fives and tens on and off the decade. However, for children who were clearly at the pre-structural and emergent stages, it would prove too complex for them to initially perceive the 10 × 10 grid structure related to grouping by tens. In the case of Michael, the

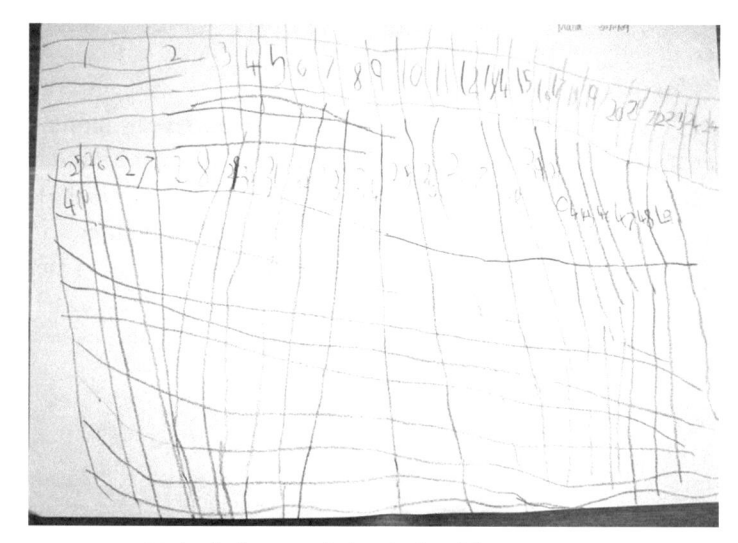

FIGURE 6.6   Michael's drawing of a hundred grid from memory

teacher might identify the underlying difficulties exhibited earlier in reproducing a simple 2 × 2 grid before expecting further development of co-linearity
and equal grouping or equal spacing structures.

6   Further Research

Further research aims to extend the PASA and PASMAP to accommodate children aged 8 to 12 years (elementary school in Australia). But longitudinal evaluation of the impact of the PASA on changes in pedagogy and improved student
achievement in mathematics generally would provide the necessary data to
inform review and further development of PASMAP. Larger and more diverse
samples that permit generalization could up-scale the existing research to the
wider population. Comparative cross-cultural studies would also be invaluable.

Tailoring PASA and the PASMAP approach to assist those students with special needs or those with learning difficulties in mathematics is also a priority
with some work already implemented for students in regular classrooms. Similarly, the assessment and teaching of students showing advanced AMPS, perhaps
those who are gifted and talented at mathematics, could provide a much more
challenging and conceptually-connected program of learning than that provided
by current curriculum content and sequence (English, 2012; Mulligan, 2015).

A new longitudinal study *Connecting spatial reasoning with mathematics
learning 2017–2021* has extended the PASMAP structural groupings by integrating AMPS with spatial reasoning. A *Spatial Reasoning Mathematics Program*

(*SRMP*) has been developed and evaluation of learning pathways with teachers and students from Grades 3 to 5 is in progress (Mulligan et al., 2020b). The potential benefit to teachers is that complex individual patterns of children's responses can be mapped as a visual diagram of networked concepts; this may have enormous potential for improved assessment and teaching, particularly for assisting children with learning difficulties, and children who are gifted and talented at mathematics. The significant implication for other domains and curriculum reform is that AMPS is transferable and can support an interdisciplinary approach to pedagogy and learning.

7 Implications for Teaching and Learning and Professional Development

The role of teacher pedagogical and content knowledge is critical for the improved teaching of mathematics. A grasp of patterning concepts is central to this knowledge. The recent studies of Tsamir and collegues point to a need to ensure that pre-service and practising teachers have developed robust and generalizable models of patterning knowledge. In a recent study they found that while teachers were able to identify repetitions and errors in patterns, continuations were more difficult to identify, especially those ending in mid-cycle (Tsamir et al., 2018).

Liljedahl (2004) draws attention to a more fundamental difficulty in students' limited conceptualization of patterns. He refers to students' inappropriate use of repeating patterns in the solving of number pattern problems and a propensity on the part of students towards repeating patterns. This may be a result of the students' conceptualization that patterns are always repeating patterns.

Pedagogical content knowledge must also be considered in an interrelated way when investigating teacher mathematical content knowledge. Teachers' deep understanding of pattern and structure needs to be aligned with pedagogical content knowledge (PCK). Thus professional learning opportunities would need to be provided and sustained, and the impact on teacher education programs ascertained. PASMAP pedagogy in early childhood and primary pre-service progams has already been integrated effectively with curricula objectives and mathematics pedagogy from inquiry-based perspectives. To achieve these changes new programs may need to investigate professionals' and pre-service teacher knowledge about patterns and structural relationships in mathematics. Teaching mathematics through a structural approach may require professionals to explore their own development of AMPS. This will surely impact on the way that mathematics learning, pedagogy, curriculum and assessment is conceptualised, structured and implemented. The PASMAP approach promotes conceptual knowledge that is interrelated and pedagogical strategies that scaffold these interrelationships. Thus for this approach to be effective, teachers will need to guide students in developing relational thinking by noticing connections within and between concepts. In contrast, many traditional mathematics programs shift attention regularly from one concept to another without focusing on interrelationships or extending the students towards generalization.

As a final remark, implementing a major shift in the scope and depth of mathematics education from the pre-school years will require consensus and collaboration at international level. The role of pattern and structure in mathematics learning must be highlighted in mathematics curriculum and assessment as an impetus for our future students to become deep mathematical thinkers.

Acknowledgements

The research reported in this paper was supported by Australian Research Council Discovery Grants No. DP0880394 and DP110103586 and the Australian Council for Educational Research (ACER). The author expresses her thanks to Mike Mitchelmore, Lyn English, Andrew Stephanou and John Lindsey.

Note

1   Pseudonyms have been used to preserve anonymity.

References

Aunio, P., & Niemivirta, M. (2010). Predicting children's mathematical performance in grade one by early numeracy. *Learning and Individual Differences, 20*, 427–435.

Australian Association of Mathematics Teachers (AAMT). (2015). *Top drawer teacher resources for teachers of mathematics: Patterns K-2.* AAMT. www://topdrawer.aamt.edu.au/Patterns

Battista, M. T., Clements, D. H., Arnoff, J., Battista, K., & Borrow, C. (1998). Students' spatial structuring of 2D arrays of squares. *Journal for Research in Mathematics Education, 29*, 503–532.

Burgoyne, K., Witteveen, K., Tolan, A., Malone, S., & Hulme, C. (2017). Pattern understanding: Relationships with arithmetic and reading development. *Child Development Perspectives, 11*(4), 239–244. doi:10.1111/cdep.2017.11.issue-4

Carraher, D. W., Schliemann, A. D., Brizuela, B. M., & Earnest, D. (2006). Arithmetic and algebra in early mathematics education. *Journal for Research in Mathematics Education, 37*, 87–115.

Casey, B. M., Andrews, N., Schincler, H., Kersh, J. E., Samper, A., & Copley, J. (2008). The development of spatial skills through interventions involving block building activities. *Cognition and Instruction, 26*(3), 269–309.

Clements, D. H., & Sarama, J. (2007). Effects of a preschool mathematics curriculum: Summative research on the Building Blocks project. *Journal for Research in Mathematics Education, 38*, 136–163.

Elia, I., (2018). Observing the use of gestures in young children's geometric thinking. In I. Elia, J. Mulligan, A. Anderson, A. Baccaglini-Frank, & C. Benz (Eds.), *Contemporary research and perspectives on early childhood mathematics education* (pp. 159–182). Springer.

English, L. D. (2012). Data modeling with first-grade children. *Educational Studies in Mathematics Education, 81*, 15–30.

Hannula, M. M., & Lehtinen, E. (2005). Spontaneous focusing on numerosity and mathematical skills of young children. *Learning and Instruction, 15*, 237–256.

Kidd, J. K., Pasnak, R., Gadzichowski, K., Gallington, D. A., McKnight, P., Boyer, C. E., et al. (2014). Instructing first-grade children on patterning improves reading and mathematics. *Early Education and Development, 25*(1), 134–151.

Liljedahl, P. (2004). Repeating pattern or number pattern: The distinction is blurred. *Focus on Learning Problems in Mathematics, 26*(3), 24–42.

Lüken, M. (2017). Repeating pattern competencies in three- and four-year old Kindergarteners. In I. Elia, J. Mulligan, A. Anderson, A. Baccaglini-Frank, & C. Benz (Eds.), *Contemporary research and perspectives on early childhood mathematics education* (pp. 35–54). Springer.

Lüken, M., & Sauzet, O. (2020). Patterning strategies in early childhood: A mixed methods study examining 3- to 5-year-old children's patterning competencies, *Mathematical Thinking and Learning.* doi:10.1080/10986065.2020.1719452

Mulligan, J. T. (2015). Moving beyond basic numeracy: Data modeling in the early years of schooling. *ZDM – International Journal on Mathematics Education, 47*(4), 653–663.

Mulligan, J. T., English, L. D., Mitchelmore, M. C., & Crevensten, N. (2013b). Reconceptualising early mathematics learning: The fundamental role of pattern and structure. In L. D. English & J. T. Mulligan (Eds.), *Reconceptualizing early mathematics learning* (pp. 47–66). Springer.

Mulligan, J. T., & Mitchelmore, M. C. (2013a). Early awareness of mathematical pattern and structure. In L. D. English & J. T. Mulligan (Eds.), *Reconceptualizing early mathematics learning* (pp. 29–46). Springer.

Mulligan, J. T., & Mitchelmore, M. C. (2016a). *Pattern and structure mathematics awareness program book 1*. ACER Press.

Mulligan, J. T., & Mitchelmore, M. C. (2016b). *Pattern and structure mathematics awareness program book 2*. ACER Press.

Mulligan, J. T., Mitchelmore, M. C., & Stephanou, A. (2015). *Pattern and Structure Assessment (PASA): An assessment program for early mathematics (Years F-2) teacher guide*. ACER Press.

Mulligan, J. T., Oslington, G., & English, L. D. (2020a). Supporting early mathematical development through a 'pattern and structure' intervention program. *ZDM – International Journal on Mathematics Education*. doi:10.1007/s11858-020-01147-9

Mulligan, J. T., Woolcott, G., Oslington, G., Busatto, S., Lai, J., Mitchelmore, M. C., & Davis, B. (2020). Evaluating the impact of a Spatial Reasoning Mathematics Program (SRMP) intervention in the primary school. *Mathematics Education Research Journal, Special Issue*, 32(2), 285–305.

Outhred, L., & Mitchelmore, M. C. (2000). Young children's intuitive understanding of rectangular area measurement. *Journal for Research in Mathematics Education*, 31, 144–68.

Papic, M. M., Mulligan, J. T., & Mitchelmore, M. C. (2011). Assessing the development of preschoolers' mathematical patterning. *Journal for Research in Mathematics Education*, 42, 237–268.

Rittle-Johnson, B., Fyfe, E. R., Hofer, K. G., & Farran, D. C. (2017). Early math trajectories: Low-income children's mathematics knowledge from age 4 to 11. *Child Development*, 88(5), 1727–1742. doi:10.1111/cdev.12662

Rittle-Johnson, B., Fyfe, E. R., McLean, L. E., & McEldoon, K. L. (2013). Emerging understanding of patterning in 4-year-olds. *Journal of Cognition and Development*, 14(3), 376–396.

Rittle-Johnson, B., Zippert, E. L., & Boice, K. L. (2019). The roles of patterning and spatial skills in early mathematics development. *Early Childhood Research Quarterly*, 46, 166–178.

Sinclair, N., & Bruce, C. (2015). New opportunities in geometry education at the primary school. *ZDM–International Journal on Mathematics Education*, 47(3), 319–329.

Starkey, G. S., & McCandliss, B. D. (2014). The emergence of "groupitizing" in children's numerical cognition. *Journal of Experimental Child Psychology*, 126, 120–137.

Thomas, N. D., Mulligan, J. T., & Goldin, G. A. (2002). Students' representations and cognitive structural development of the counting sequence 1–100. *The Journal of Mathematical Behavior*, 21, 117–133.

Tirosh, D., Tsamir, P., Barkai, R., & Levenson, E. (2018). Engaging young children with mathematical activities involving different representations: Triangles, patterns, and counting objects. *CEPS Journal, 8*(2), 9–30.

Tsamir, P., Tirosh, D., Levenson, E., & Barkai, R. (2018). Early childhood teachers' knowledge and self-efficacy for evaluating solutions to repeating pattern tasks. In I. Elia, J. Mulligan, A. Anderson, A. Baccaglini-Frank, & C. Benz (Eds.), *Contemporary research and perspectives on early childhood mathematics education* (pp. 291–312). Springer.

Verdine, B. N., Golinkoff, R., Hirsh-Pasek, K., Newcombe, N., Filipowocz, A. T., & Chang, A. (2013). Deconstructing building blocks: Preschoolers' spatial assembly performance relates to early mathematics skills. *Child Development, 85*(3), 1062–1076.

Warren, E., & Cooper, T. J. (2008). Generalising the pattern rule for visual growth patterns: Actions that support 8-year olds thinking. *Educational Studies in Mathematics, 67*, 171–185.

CHAPTER 7

Young Children's Recognition of Mathematical Structures and Its Relations to Mathematical Skills

Tal Sharir and Zemira Mevarech

Abstract

While much research has focused on young children's mathematics skills such as counting, subitizing, enumeration, and numerical cognition, much less is known at present on children's processing of more complex mathematical structures. The aim of the present study is, therefore, threefold: (a) to investigate young children's recognition of mathematical structures (ROMS) including multiplication patterns, arithmetic series and items presented in random orders; (b) to examine the differences between ROMS-verbal and nonverbal; and (c) to study the relationships between the different types of ROMS and mathematical reasoning. Participants were 113 Israeli children age 4–5 years old. Children's ROMS was assessed both verbally (describing cards that represent mathematical structures) and nonverbally (imitating the experimenter demonstration of mathematical structures). The verbal and nonverbal ROMS included the same mathematical structures. Results indicated that: (a) young children could focus not only on the exact number of objects, but also on; multiplication patterns and arithmetic series; (b) children's scores on the nonverbal ROMS were significantly higher than those on the verbal ROMS; and (c) the different types of ROMS explained 32% of the variance in mathematics reasoning, while children's age and mothers' education added an additional 15% to the explained variance. The theoretical and practical implications are discussed.

Keywords

recognize mathematical structures – multiplication patterns – arithmetic series – young children – mathematics reasoning

1 Introduction

Children tend to describe their everyday surroundings by focusing on different aspects. Some children focus on visual objects, others on auditory stimuli, and still others on mathematical features. For example, while traveling, there are children who say the numbers printed on cars' license plates or count aloud the number of children sitting in those cars. Others refer to the cars' color, and still others describe the environment around them. The present study explores the extent to which young children choose to describe their surroundings in mathematical terms, even though they were not asked to do so. In particular, we aim to test what kinds of mathematical structures are recognized by these young children and the extent to which children who recognize and describe the mathematical features that appear around them score higher on mathematical reasoning than children who focus on other features in their environments. These issues are addressed by focusing on numerosity, multiplication patterns and arithmetic series, each represented in both verbal and nonverbal modes.

Research on mathematical development indicates that children can recognize numerosity (Hannula & Lehtinen, 2001) from a very early age. Babies at the age of six months recognize small numbers of items (Wynn, 1998a, 1998b). By the age of two years, they can identify up to four objects (Baroody, Li, & Lai, 2008). In kindergarten and preschool, many children show interest in abstract mathematical ideas and mathematical reasoning (Ginsburg, Lee, & Boyd, 2008). They spontaneously explore numbers, count objects (Ginsburg & Amit, 2008), build bridges with blocks (Ginsburg et al., 2008), investigate forms of patterns (Ginsburg & Golbeckm 2004), perform the four basic arithmetic operations (addition, subtraction, multiplication, and division) in free play (Baroody & Ginsburg, 1990), and plan various strategies for solving mathematical problems (Greenes, Ginsburg, & Balfanz, 2004; Mevarech & Kramarski, 2014). These activities occur mostly spontaneously in accordance with the needs of the activity the children initiate, without adult direction (Ginsburg & Amit, 2008; Ginsburg & Golbeckm 2004; Greenes et al., 2004). Additionally, in a series of studies, Hannula and Lehtinen (2001, 2005) reported that kindergarten children (age of 3–5 years) can spontaneously focus on numerosity presented in imitation tasks, although the variability was very large (Hannula & Lehtinen, 2001; Hannula, Lepola, & Lehtinen, 2010). Hannula and Lehtinen (2001, 2005) coined a term of this phenomenon: Spontaneously Focusing on Numerosity (SFON). Furthermore, as part of a longitudinal study, Hannula and Lehtinen (2001, 2005) indicate that SFON is positively related to the development of enumeration, subitizing, and number sequence, and that children's SFON in preschool is positively related to mathematics achievement assessed later in school. Subsequent studies replicated these findings among at different age groups (McMullen, Hannula-Sormunen, & Lehtinen, 2014; Hannula, Grabner, & Lehtinen, 2009), in different countries (Potter, 2009), and by using various nonverbal tasks, such as imitating an experimenter performing activities expressing quantitative relations (McMullen et al., 2014; Potter, 2009 and in reading books (Rathe, Torbeyns, Hannula-Sormunen & Verschaffell, 2016). Another interesting series of studies was based on neuroscience using EEG and fMRI, found correlation between SFON and number recognition (De Smedt, Ansari, Grabner, Schneider, & Verschaffell, 2011; Hannula, Grabner, Lehtinen, Laine, Parkkola, & Ansari, 2009).

Previous studies on young children's Spontaneously Focusing on Numerosity (SFON) and on spontaneous Focusing of quantitative relations (SFOR) were based mainly on nonverbal settings. For example, in one of the first SFON studies (Hannula & Lehtinen, 2005), the researcher showed the child a toy parrot capable of 'swallowing' and some glass berries. Then, the experimenter told the child: "watch carefully what I do, and then you do just like I did". The experimenter put two berries, one at a time, into the parrot's mouth so that the sounds of the berries falling into the parrot's mouth were clearly heard. The child was then asked to imitate the experimenter. Whereas some children put the exact number of berries in the toy's mouth, others put a random number of berries, without paying attention to numerosity. in one of the first SFOR studies (McMullen, Hannula-Sormunen, & Lehtinen 2013) children were presented with two dolls and two plates with a flat circle dough. In the first plate the dough divided for halves, and in a second plate for quarters. The researcher fed his doll from the first plate and asked the child to feed his doll from the second plate with the four quarters, "exactly the same way I did". If the child fed his doll with two quarters he Spontaneously focused on the quantitative relations, if the child gave the doll one quarter he Spontaneously focused on Numerosity. In this study most kindergartners focused only on Numerosity (see also Hannula et al., 2010; McMullen et al., 2013). Since these studies were based on the child's imitation of the researcher, it remains unclear whether these observed findings reflect the encoding of the number of items or the recall of the experimenter's action, which largely depends on working memory (Holmes, Gathercole & Dunning, 2009; Collins & Laski, 2015) and executive functioning (Diamond & Lee, 2011). And to what extent can young children Spontaneously focus not only on numerosity, but also on mathematical structures such as multiplication patterns or arithmetic series. Patterns are defined as any predictable regularity involving number, space or measure; Multiplication pattern is prescribed as repetitive sets of equal number of items; arithmetic series refer to a sequence in which each term is obtained by the addition of a constant number to the preceding term (Mulligan & Mitchelmore, 2009). Recent studies have indicated that young children can be explicitly directed to look for multiplication patterns and arithmetic series (e.g., Mulligan &

Mitchelmore, 2013; Mulligan, Prescott, Papic, & Mitchelmore, 2006), but to the best of our knowledge no studies so far have assessed children's recognition of mathematical structure (ROMS) without being prompted by others to do so, both verbally and nonverbally.

Another open issue relates to possible differences between children's ability to recognize mathematical structures presented in their 'natural' environments vs those presented in a 'clear' background without any 'distractions' caused by the natural environments. One may argue that the 'natural environment' redirect the child's attention from the mathematical structures to other features in the environment and thus does not indicate that the child performs poorly on the ROMS task. The current study addresses also this issue by asking children to describe cards on which mathematical structures are presented by squares printed either on 'blank' background or on photos of items in their natural environments.

Finally, another interesting question regards the relationships between children's ROMS and mathematical reasoning. In the current study, the term mathematical reasoning refers to children's knowledge of mathematical facts (e.g., knowing the sequential order of numbers, counting up to 30, ordinal number, number recognition, and numerical sequence order) and higher order of mathematical skills (e.g., solving word problems). According to English (2004), children having a high level of mathematical reasoning skills evaluate mathematical situations, select problem-solving strategies, draw logical conclusions, and describe and reflect on their solutions (English, 2013). It is reasonable to suppose that children who pay attention to the mathematical structures that appear around them tend also to "play" with numbers and vice versa, children who are interested in numbers are more attentive to mathematical structures. We studied this issue by examining the correlations between the various types of ROMS and mathematical reasoning beyond the factors that were found to be related to mathematical achievement: gender (Lindberg, Hyde, Petersen, & Linn, 2010), age (Hannula & Lehtinen, 2005) and parents' education (Anders et al., 2012). The aim of the present study is, therefore, threefold: (a (to investigate young children's recognition of mathematical structures (ROMS). By presenting objects in a random order, in a multiplication patterns structure, and in an arithmetic series structure; (b) to examine the differences between ROMS-verbal and ROMS-nonverbal; (c) to study the contribution of the different types of ROMS to mathematical reasoning. We hypothesized that substantial differences would be found between objects presenting in a random order, in a multiplication patterns structure, and in an arithmetic series structure. Between the verbal versus nonverbal ROMS, assuming that the nonverbal ROMS is easier because it is based on imitation of the experimenter's actions (Hannula &

Lehtinen, 2005), while ROMS verbal description requires the child to transform the recognition of mathematical characterizations into words. In addition, we hypothesized that substantial differences would be found between describing cards on which mathematical structures are presented by squares printed on 'blank' background and cards presented photos of items in their natural environments. We hypothesized that a correlation would be found between ROMS types and mathematical reasoning.

2 Method

2.1 *Participants*

Participants were 113 Israeli children, 49 boys (43.4%) and 64 girls (56.6%), who studied in four kindergartens randomly selected from forty kindergartens located in the center of Israel. Children's ages ranged from 4.1–6.0 years ($M =$ 4. 9 years; SD = 0. 51). Children came from middle class families as indicated by their parents' education: 66.4% of the mothers and 60.2% of the fathers had an academic degree see. All tasks were administered in a familiar room in the child's kindergarten. The tasks were presented as follows: in the first week, the verbal tasks, ROMS-pictures and ROMS-squares were assessed. In the second week, ROMS-nonverbal was administered followed by the mathematical reasoning test. This administration order was determined in order to eliminate any clue that the ROMS tasks are related to numbers or mathematics. We would like to note that the instructions to all ROMS tasks did not include any phrase that suggests that the tasks were somehow related to numbers or mathematical structures. The experimenter presented the task and wrote down the child's responses.

2.2 *Measurements*

Two measurements were used in the present study: ROMS tendency and mathematical skills. ROMS tendency was assessed both nonverbally and verbally. Nonverbal ROMS assesses children's ability to imitate the experimenter demonstration of inserting discs into a saving box; Verbal ROMS was based on children's descriptions of cards that display items in their natural environment (ROMS-Pictures) and cards that display squares on blank background (ROMS-Squares). Each of the three ROMS representations (pictures, squares, and discs) displayed three mathematical structures, (random order, multiplication patterns, and arithmetic series). Thus, altogether the study assessed nine ROMS categories: three representations (verbal pictures, verbal squares, and nonverbal imitation tasks) for each of the three mathematical structures (random order, multiplication patterns, and arithmetic series). Only small numerosity that all children were able to handle was used.

Nonverbal ROMS: The nonverbal ROMS measurement included 7 items, for each of which children were asked to imitate the experimenter. A saving-box and discs (blue, green, yellow and red) were placed on the table in front of the child. The experimenter stated, "This is a saving-box and here are different discs: blue, green yellow and red. Watch carefully what I do, and then you do exactly just like I did". The experimenter then demonstrated various mathematical structures by putting the discs into the saving-box in a certain order. The sound of each disc falling into the box could be clearly heard. The demonstration included three different types of mathematical structures: random order (e.g., 3 discs put into the saving-box, one at a time) (see also Hannula & Lehtinen, 2005); multiplication patterns (e.g., 2 repetitive pairs of discs put into the saving-box with about 2 seconds pause between each pair); and arithmetic series (e.g., groups of 1, 2, and 3 discs put into the saving-box, with about 2 seconds pause between the groups).

Verbal ROMS: Verbal ROMS was based on a series of seven cards presenting items in their natural environments (see also Hannula et al., 2009) and seven cards showing squares (ROMS-Pictures and ROMS-Squares, respectively). Each card presents a different type of mathematical structure: random order (e.g., 4 items presented in a random order), multiplication patterns (e.g., 2 repetitive pairs of items), or arithmetic series (e.g., sets of 1, 2, and 3 items). The experimenter showed a card to the child and says, "Please look at the card and describe carefully in details what you see in the card". The researcher wrote down everything the child said. There was no time limit for children to respond. When the child finished the experimenter asked: "Is that everything?" When the child was ready to move on, the researcher introduced the next trial: "Let's look at the next picture".

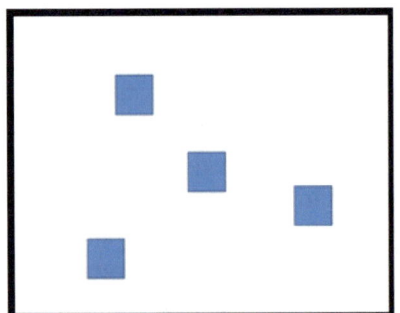 

FIGURE 7.1   Items presented in random order

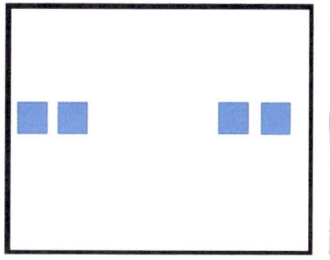

FIGURE 7.2   Items presented in pattern or series

Mathematical Test: A 15 item mathematical test was designed by the authors to assess children's mathematical skills. The test was based on the Israel Kindergarten Mathematics Curriculum (2009) and the NCTM the National Council of Teachers of Mathematics, that sets Principles and Standards for School Mathematics (2002). The test included recall of mathematical facts and mathematical reasoning tasks (7 and 8 items, respectively).

3   Results

3.1   *Mathematical Structure Recognition*

Table 7.1 presents the nine ROMS categories three ROMS types (random order, multiplication patters, and arithmetic series) by three ROMS representations (ROMS-verbal pictures, ROMS-verbal squares, and ROMS-nonverbal).

As can be seen from Table 7.1, children spontaneously focus on quantities presented in random order, both when the tasks were verbal or nonverbal. Almost 70% of the children focus spontaneously on the quantitative aspects

TABLE 7.1   Scores in percentage on ROMS types and representations (score range 0–1)

ROMS representations	ROMS types		
	Random order	Multiplication patterns	Arithmetic series
Verbal (pictures)	17.3	2.1	9.4
Verbal (squares)	69.6	20.6	15.9
Nonverbal	58.4	56.1	33.6

at the verbal squares task, Almost 60% of the children focus spontaneously on the quantitative aspects at the nonverbal task, and 17% of the children focus spontaneously on the quantitative aspects at the verbal picture task. Children spontaneously focus on multiplication structures and arithmetic series, especially in the nonverbal task. The percentage of children who focused on multiplication structures in nonverbal tasks was almost identical to the percentage of children who focused on quantities presented in random order (58% and 56%, respectively). On the other hand, only about a third of the children focus spontaneously on arithmetic series in the nonverbal task. In the verbal "squares" task, children tend to focus spontaneously on quantities presented in random order, then on multiplication structures and arithmetic series (21% and 16%, respectively). As for the "picture" tasks, less than 10% of the children spontaneously focused on the arithmetic series and only 2% in the multiplication structures.

3.2   The Relationships between ROMS Categories and Mathematical Reasoning

To gain insight into the relationships between ROMS categories and mathematical reasoning, we calculated Pearson correlations between recall of mathematical facts (number sequence production, counting and numerical sequence order) and mathematical reasoning (word problem solving) and

TABLE 7.2   Correlations between ROMS types, recall of mathematical facts and problem solving

ROMS types	Mathematical reasoning	Recall of mathematical facts
Random order	70**	.36***
– verbal (pictures)	.52***	.22*
– verbal (squares)	.44***	.31**
Nonverbal	.59***	.22*
multiplication patterns	.63***	.07
– verbal (pictures)	.48***	.13
– verbal (squares)	.62***	.14
nonverbal	.36***	.03
arithmetic series	.67***	.19*
– verbal (pictures)	.27**	.10
– verbal (squares)	.61***	.23*
Nonverbal	.59***	.11

*p < .05, **p < .01, ***p < .001

TABLE 7.3 Hierarchical regression analyses: Specific effects of ROMS types, age, gender and parental Education of Recall of mathematical facts

	Recall of mathematical facts	
	R^2	β
ROMS verbal	.15***	.39***
ROMS nonverbal	.00	.04
Age	.06**	.27**
Mother's education	.00	−.05
Father's education	.00	.08
Gender	.00	.09
Total R^2	.21	

*p < .05, **p < .01, ***p < .001

scores on ROMS categories. As can be seen in Table 7.2, whereas mathematical reasoning correlated significantly with all ROMS categories (r ranged from .18–.58), recall of mathematical facts correlated significantly only with ROMS random order (r ranges from −.08–.39). Tables 7.3 and 7.4 present the findings of the hierarchical regressions with recall of mathematical facts and mathematical reasoning as the dependent variables and children's ROMS, age, gender, and parents' education as the independent variables.

As can be seen from Table 7.3, the incremental R square for recall of mathematical facts is 21; Verbal ROMS explained 15% of the variance, age added 6%

TABLE 7.4 Hierarchical regression analyses: Specific effects of ROMS types, age, gender and parental education of mathematical reasoning

	Recall of mathematical facts	
	R^2	β
ROMS Verbal	.25***	.49***
ROMS Nonverbal	.07**	.25**
Age	.11***	.38***
Mother's education	.04**	.24**
Father's education	.00	.19
Gender	.00	−.06
Total R^2	.47	

*p < .05, **p < .01, ***p < .001

more to the explained variance in recall of mathematical facts. As can be seen from Table 7.4, the incremental R square for mathematical reasoning is 47; Verbal ROMS, and Nonverbal ROMS explained 32% of the variance, age and mother's education added 15% more to the explained variance in mathematical reasoning, whereas father's education and gender were not significant.

4   Discussion

The present study explores children's ROMS and its relationships to mathematical reasoning, focusing on the following mathematical structures: random order, multiplication patterns and arithmetic series each represented in verbal tasks (i.e., describing cards displaying pictures and squares), and nonverbal task (imitating the experimenter putting discs into a saving box). Results indicate that recognizing numerosity in random order is the easiest, followed by multiplication patterns, which in turn are easier than recognize arithmetic series. These findings are expected since the complexity of these tasks gradually increases: recognize the exact number of objects is strongly related to the development of counting skills, which are the building blocks for the formation of the other mathematical concepts (e.g., Wynn, 1998a; McMullen et al., 2014). In recognizing multiplication patterns, attention needs to be focused not only on the exact number of objects, but also on the way the items are organized (e.g., the 'structure'). In recognizing arithmetic series, the child must attend to the exact number of objects, the way the items are organized, and to the constant difference between two consecutive sets, in our case the sets increased by 1.

Interestingly, the present study also shows that the nonverbal tasks referring to multiplication patterns and arithmetic series were successfully performed by 50% and 27% of the children, respectively. These findings indicate that children at the age of 4–5 years acquire much more advanced mathematical insights than simply focusing on numerosity. As previous studies have shown, awareness of mathematical structures, such as patterns and series, is essential, since mathematics is based on pre-algebraic thinking, which develops through awareness of patterns and repetitive pattern (Mulligan & Mitchelmore, 2009; Mulligan & Mitchelmore, 2013). Thus, children at this age acquire rather complex mathematical knowledge, not only counting skills. For example, in recognizing multiplication patterns as those represented in Appendix 2, children have to know that it is not the shape of the items that constitutes a mathematical structure (e.g., dolls), but the mathematical configuration (e.g., repetitive sets, constant number of items in each set, order-irrelevance, and cardinality).

4.1 ROMS Representations

Within ROMS representations, recognize Mathematical structures represented in "squares on blank background" and in the imitation tasks were the easiest, whereas recognize Mathematical structures represented in "pictures" were the most difficult ones. Several factors may explain this finding. First, low scores on verbal ROMS pictures may result from the fact that pictures representing familiar surroundings might stimulate a response to the environment and by that may have acted as a powerful distraction from the mathematical structures (Lehman, Schraw, McCrudden & Hartley, 2007). Additionally, pictures that include many details distract the child attention more than pictures with few details as the cards displaying the squares on blank background. Third, there is reason to suppose that the imitation tasks which involved dual channels for processing information (e.g., visual and auditory) facilitate children ROMS compared to only the visual channel used in verbal ROMS-pictures. Finally, it is possible that verbal descriptions are more difficult for young children than nonverbal responses because of their limited verbal skills. We would like to note that when all items were factor analyzed, the data was classified according to the three ROMS representations (pictures, squares, and nonverbal), but not according to the mathematical configurations (random order, multiplication patterns, and arithmetic series). This finding may suggest that children's attention is directed to the appearance of the stimuli rather than to the structure presented within the different representation types.

The findings regarding the nonverbal ROMS are in line with those of Hannula and Lehtinen (2005) who used similar assessment to study Finnish children's spontaneous focusing on numerosities. In both the Israeli and Finnish studies, the same percentage of children at the age of 4–5 years was able to exactly imitate the experimenter putting the discs/berries in a saving-box/parrot mouth, respectively. This common phenomenon was observed in spite the fact that there were slight differences in the scoring procedure between the two studies, and the 'formal' mathematics learning, which begins in Israel at 4–6 years compared to 7 years at Finland. The very fact that the percentage of children who performed the tasks successfully was almost identical (about 40%) suggests that this phenomenon does not depend on specific culture. Repeated studies in different countries may shed light on early mathematical development regardless of culture or specific conditions in kindergartens and preschool education.

4.2 The Relationships between ROMS and Mathematics Achievement

Similar to previous studies (Hannula & Lehtinen, 2005) who studied the correlations between SFON, and mathematics achievement also reports positive correlations between children's mathematical reasoning and their recognition of numerosity represented in random order (r = .58). Yet, the present study went one-step further by classifying mathematics achievement into two categories: recall of mathematics fact and mathematical reasoning. By that, the present study was able to identify significant correlations between mathematical reasoning and multiplication patterns (r = .27) and between mathematical reasoning and arithmetic series (r = .25), but not between those factors and recall of mathematical facts. One possible explanation for the positive correlations between ROMS scores and mathematical reasoning is that children who have a higher ROMS tendency are more inclined to self-initiate practicing, using exact enumeration, and 'playing' with numbers, which in turn enhances their mathematical reasoning (Hannula, Mattinen & Lehtinen, 2005), while children with low ROMS tendency might be less interested in mathematics. Whether or not these correlations are mediated by general abilities or verbal competencies merits future research.

Another question concerns the role of the child's family background in developing mathematics skills in general and ROMS. A large number of studies have assessed the relationships between parents' education and children's mathematics development (Anders et al., 2012). Generally, research indicates that in contrast to fathers' education, mothers' education is significantly correlated with children's cognitive development (Schady, 2011). Also in the present study, mothers' education was significantly correlated with most ROMS types, whereas fathers' education was significantly correlated only with ROMS random order – though the correlation was rather low (r = .201).

Furthermore, beyond ROMS, only age and mothers' education were significantly correlated with mathematics reasoning (multiple R = .70), whereas gender and fathers' education did not enter the regression equation. The fact that gender does not have a significant role in predicting mathematics reasoning in young children is in line with current meta-analysis studies indicating small, insignificant gender differences in mathematics achievement (Lindberg, Hyde, Petersen, & Linn, 2010). Future research may examine the roles of each parent in developing their children's mathematical knowledge.

4.3   *Educational Implications*

Embedding mathematical concepts in everyday situations is one of the basic assumptions of early mathematics education. Children indeed show interest in abstract mathematical ideas that surround then, investigate patterns, and plan strategies for solving mathematical problems in a way that is relevant to their world. Educators might utilize the spontaneous and sometimes explicit interest in mathematical ideas that young children have (Ginsburg et al.,

2008). This phenomenon leads teachers to introduce new mathematical concepts by showing pictures of natural environments in which the mathematical concepts are represented. Yet, the findings of the present study call into question this assumption. It is quite possible that the rich details of the surroundings confuse the child and distract his/her attention from the essence of the mathematical concepts to be introduced. Thus, teachers must be very careful in using rich visual devices for enhancing mathematical reasoning. This is not to say that teachers have to detach mathematics ideas from the surrounding or avoid using visual and audio representations, but rather to be more sensitive to the distractive effects of the extraneous stimuli.

Studies in the area of neurosciences and education highlight the importance (and limitations) of dual channels for processing information compared to a single channel. According to Mayer (2010), people have separate processing channels for visually and audial represented materials, although people are able to convert the representation for processing from one channel to another. When information is presented to the eyes, such as watching pictures, humans begin by processing that information in the visual channels; when information is presented to the ears, such as hearing the sound of the discs falling into the saving-box, humans begin by processing that information in the auditory channels. Cross-channel representations of the same stimuli (e.g., the nonverbal tasks used in the present study) may facilitate active processing in both channels, thus leading the child to be aware of the mathematical configurations represented aurally and visually. Effective instruction might utilize dual channels for information processing and reduce extraneous stimuli.

This study raises many issues for future research, some of which will be presented here. Is there room to develop intervention programs focused on promoting the tendency to spontaneously focus on mathematical aspects of preschool children? If so, will this also have an impact on mathematics? Is the ROMS tendency stable over the years? Is it culturally dependent? Are there differences in the spontaneous focus on mathematical aspects between gifted children and non-gifted children or children with special needs? And what can brain research contribute to these issues? Here are some of the open questions. We hope that this fascinating subject will continue to be explored in the future as well.

References

Anders, Y., Rossbach, H. G., Weinert, S., Ebert, S., Kuger, S., Lehrl, S., & von Maurice, J. (2012). Home and preschool learning environments and their relations to the development of early numeracy skills. *Early Childhood Research Quarterly, 27*(2), 231–244.

Baroody, A. J., & Ginsburg, H. P. (1990). Children's mathematical learning: A cognitive view. In R. B. Davis, C. A. Maher, & N. Noddings (Eds.), *Constructivist views on the teaching and learning of mathematics* (Journal for Research in Mathematics Education, Monograph No. 4) (pp. 51–64). Morin of Teachers of Mathematics.

Baroody, A. J., Li, X., & Lai, M.-L. (2008). Toddlers' spontaneous attention to number. *Mathematical thinking and learning, 10*(3), 240–270.

Collins, M. A., & Laski, E. V. (2015). Preschoolers' strategies for solving visual pattern tasks. *Early Childhood Research Quarterly, 32*(3), 204–214.

De Smedt, B., Ansari, D., Grabner, R. H., Hannula-Sormunen, M., Schneider, M., & Verschaffel, L. (2011). Cognitive neuroscience meets mathematics education: It takes two to tango. *Educational Research Review, 6,* 232–237.

Diamond, A., & Lee, K. (2011). Interventions shown to aid executive function development in children 4 to 12 years old. *Science, 333*(6045), 959–964.

English, L. D. (2004). Promoting the development of young children's mathematical and analogical reasoning. In L. D. English (Ed.), *Mathematical and analogical reasoning of young learners* (pp. 201–213). Erlbaum.

English, L. D. (Ed.). (2013). *Mathematical reasoning: Analogies, metaphors, and images.* Routledge.

Fuson, K. C. (2009). Avoiding misinterpretations of Piaget and Vygotsky: Mathematical teaching without learning, learning without teaching, or helpful learning-path teaching? *Cognitive Development, 24,* 343–361.

Ginsburg, H. P., & Amit, M. (2008). What is teaching mathematics to young children? A theoretical perspective and case study. *Journal of Applied Developmental Psychology, 29*(4), 274–285.

Ginsburg, H. P., & Golbeck, S. L. (2004). Thoughts on the future of research on mathematics and science learning and education. *Early Childhood Research Quarterly, 19*(1), 190–200.

Ginsburg, H. P., Lee, J. S., & Boyd, J. S. (2008). Mathematics education for young children: What it is and how to promote it. *Social Policy Report of the Society for Research in Child Development, 22,* 3–22.

Greenes, C., Ginsburg, H. P., & Balfanz, R. (2004). Big math for little kids. *Early Childhood Research Quarterly, 19*(1), 159–166.

Hannula, M. M., Grabner, R., & Lehtinen, E. (2009). *Neural correlates of spontaneous focusing on numerosity (SFON) in a 9-year-longitudinal study of children's mathematical skills* [Paper presentation]. *EARLI Conference.*

Hannula, M. M., & Lehtinen, E. (2001). Spontaneous tendency to focus on numerosities in the development of cardinality. In M. Panhuizen-Van Heuvel (Ed.), *Proceedings of 25th Conference of the International Group for the Psychology of Mathematics Education* (Vol. 3, pp. 113–120). Drukkerij Wilco.

Hannula, M. M., & Lehtinen, E. (2005). Spontaneous focusing on numerosity and mathematical skills of young children. *Learning and Instruction, 15*(3), 237–256.

Hannula, M. M., Lepola, J., & Lehtinen, E. (2010). Spontaneous focusing on numerosity as a domain-specific predictor of arithmetical skills. *Journal of Experimental Child Psychology, 107*(4), 394–406.

Hannula, M. M., Mattinen, A., & Lehtinen, E. (2005). Does social interaction influence 3 year-old children's tendency to focus on numerosity? A quasi-experimental study in day-care. In L.Verschaffel, E. De Corte, G. Kanselaar, & M. Valcke (Eds.), *Powerful learning environments for promoting deep conceptual and strategic learning* (Studia Paedagogica, Vol. 41, pp. 63–80). Leuven University Press.

Hannula, M. M., Grabner, R., Lehtinen, E., Laine, T., Parkkola, R., & Ansari, D. (2009). Neural correlates of Spontaneous Focusing on Numerosity (SFON). *NeuroImage, 47*, S44.

Hannula-Sormunen, M., Lehtinen, E., & Räsänen, P. (2015). Children's preschool spontaneous focusing on numerosity, subitizing, and counting skills as predictors of mathematical performance 6–7 years later at school. *Mathematical Thinking and Learning, 17*, 155–177.

Holmes, J., Gathercole, S. E., & Dunning, D. L. (2009). Adaptive training leads to sustained enhancement of poor working memory in children. *Developmentalscience, 12*(4), 9–15.

Kindergarten Mathematics Curriculum. (2009). Ministry of Education, Jerusalem, Israel.

Kemler, D. G. (1983). Holistic and analytic modes in perceptual and cognitive development. In T. Tighe & B. E. Shepp (Eds.), *Perception, Cognition, and Development: Interactional Analyses* (pp. 77–102). Lawrence Erlbaum Associates.

Lehman, S., Schraw, G., McCrudden, M. T., & Hartley, K. (2007). Processing and recall of seductive details in scientific text. *Contemporary Educational Psychology, 32*(4), 569–587.

Lindberg, S. M., Hyde, J. S., Petersen, J. L.,& Linn, M. (2010). New trends in gender and mathematics performance: A meta-analysis. *Psyhcological Bulletin, 136*(6), 1123–1135.

Mayer, R. E. (2010). Learning with technology. In *The nature of learning: Using research to inspire practice* (pp. 179–198).

McMullen, J., Hannula-Sormunen, M. M., & Lehtinen, E. (2013). Young children's recognition of quantitative relations in mathematically unspecified settings. *Journal of Mathematical Behavior, 32*(3), 450–460.

McMullen, J., Hannula-Sormunen, M. M., & Lehtinen, E. (2014). Spontaneous focusing on quantitative relations in the development of children's fraction knowledge. *Cognition and Instruction, 32*(2), 198–218.

Mevarech, Z. R., & Kramarski, B. (2014). *Critical maths for innovative societies: The role of metacognitive pedagogies.* OECD Publishing.

Mulligan, J. T., & Mitchelmore, M. (2009). Awareness of pattern and structure in early mathematical development. *Mathematics Education Research Journal, 21*(2), 33–49.

Mulligan, J. T., & Mitchelmore, M. C. (2013). Early awareness of mathematical pattern and structure. In L. D. English & J. T. Mulligan (Eds.), *Reconceptualizing early mathematics learning* (pp. 29–45). Springer.

Mulligan, J. T., Prescott, A., Papic, M., & Mitchelmore, M. (2006). *Improving early numeracy through a pattern and structure mathematics awareness program.* PASMAP Proceedings of the 28th annual conference of the Mathematics Education Research Group of Australia.

NCTM, National Council of Teachers of Mathematics. (2002). *Principles and standards for school mathematics.* Author.

Potter, E. (2009). *Spontaneous focusing on numerosity: Motivational and skill correlates in young children in a public preschool and kindergarten program* [Paper presentation]. PME conference.

Rathé, S., Torbeyns, J., Hannula-Sormunen, M. M., & Verschaffel, L. (2016). Kindergartners' spontaneous focusing on numerosity in relation to their number-related utterances during numerical picture book reading. *Mathematical Thinking and Learning, 18*(2), 125–141.

Schady, N. (2011). Parents' education, mothers' vocabulary, and cognitive development in early childhood: Longitudinal evidence from Ecuador. *American Journal of Public Health, 101*(12), 2299.

Wynn, K. (1998a). Numerical competence in infants. In C. Donlan (Ed.), *The development of mathematical skills: Studies in developmental psychology* (pp. 3–25). Psychology Press.

Wynn, K. (1998b). Psychological foundations of number: Numerical competence in human infants. *Trends in Cognitive Sciences, 2*(8), 296–303.

PART 4

Early Childhood Mathematical Thinking and Cognition: Reasoning and Explanations

∴

CHAPTER 8

Decision Making and Logical Deductions in Early Childhood When Dealing with the Quantifier "For All"

Amal Sharif-Rasslan

Abstract

In natural language, there is a necessity for logical connectives, such as "and" and "or", and in quantifiers, such as "all" and "exists/there is/are". In this chapter, we investigate the decision-making and logical reasoning processes among young children, specifically when dealing with logical deduction based on the quantifier "all". Two hundred and seventy eight kindergarten and first- and second-grade pupils participated in the study, (age range 4–8 years). In this chapter, we report on a problem worded as follows: "All of Roni's red shirts are in the closet. Is Roni wearing a red shirt or a green shirt now?"

The findings of this study show that about fifty percent of the children arrived at the correct decision about Roni's shirt colour, with older children giving a higher percentage of correct answers: a reasonable expectation given that children are developing their cognitive abilities. In addition, the findings of this study do suggest that there is a very strong significant correlation between decision making and the rationale given by children, and this is influenced by three predominant factors: environmental, preferences, and intuition.

The principle conclusion from this study is that there are parameters that affect the logical reasoning in early childhood: environment, intuition, and preferences. In addition, young children may use abductive reasoning when required to deal with quantifier-based problems, but this only occurs in the case of an incorrect decision.

Keywords

quantifiers – "all" – logical reasoning – preferences – intuition – environment – young children

1   Introduction

1.1   *Logical Relationships and Quantifiers in Natural and Mathematical Language*

Mathematics as a language has been the province of many researchers in mathematics education (Pimm, 1987; Boulet, 2007; Jamison, 2000; Tamir, 2005). As Tamir (2005) has claimed, every language (not specifically mathematical) requires logical analysis to a certain extent, and the language of mathematics also makes use of "regular" language, both for the mathematical terms and for describing the relationships between those terms. Jamison (2000) discussed the use of language as a tool for teaching mathematical concepts; in particular, he referred to the conjunctions "and" and "or" (as logical connectives), "if ... then ...", which implies a specific meaning (i.e., making a decision based on logic), and the universal quantifiers "all" and "exists/there is/are". Note that there is a specific cognitive difference between the functions of "logical connectives" and "quantifiers", and this study focuses on the issue of the "quantifier".

Jamison (2000, p. 51) claimed that logical relations are a major source of difficulty for students due to their incorrect comparison to standard speech, that is to say, to their natural language. It must be emphasized that in natural language, there is a necessity for logical connectives, such as "and" and "or", and in quantifiers, such as "all" and "exists/there is/are". Some examples: "We must eat *and* drink", "You can go with Dad *or* Grandma", "*There is* a cat in the backyard", "*All* the children are playing in the playroom". Furthermore, in all existing natural languages, there are sentences that require logical deduction. For example, when the kindergarten teacher says to the children playing in the yard, "Now I want all the boys to play with jump ropes and all the girls to play with the balls", the children have to make a deduction: if the listener is a boy, he will jump rope and if the listener is a girl, she will play with the ball. Another example is a mother telling her child, "If you eat up all your food, I will have a surprise for you". From this sentence, the child deduces that in order to get the surprise, he must eat up all his food. According to Boulet (2007), communication is a key factor in building understanding in general and mathematical understanding in particular. It should be noted that native language is the basis of communication between people, and from the examples given, it is clear that natural language is permeated with logical connectives, quantifiers, and of course logical deductions.

Because such concepts are a part of natural language, we can conclude that by understanding the relationship between natural language and mathematical language (and through this, the way that children relate to quantifiers and logical deductions) may add an important facet to understanding how mathematical thinking develops, and thus impress upon parents, kindergarten teachers, and primary school teachers the importance of addressing the subject of quantifiers and logical deductions in the primary years.

1.2   *Logical Reasoning and Making Decisions*

Coping with logical deductions requires logical reasoning. Logical reasoning is defined as a process of thinking about a problem and finding the most effective solution (Çelik, 2017). Çelik adds that children begin using logical reasoning well before beginning formal studies at school; however, it is clear that the logical reasoning children use in early childhood is intuitive and based on previous knowledge and experiences. As Clemens and Sarama (2007) have claimed, the more knowledge and experience children get dealing with problems that require reasoning and logic *before* beginning formal education, the greater will be their ability to use logical reasoning in the mathematical sense.

The literature mentions four types of mathematical reasoning: deductive, inductive, abductive, and by analogy (see, for example, Reid & Knipping, 2010). They can be distinguished by using the terms "case", "rule", and "result". The term "case" refers to the existence of particular property for a particular object (e.g., "Sally is two years old"); the term "rule" implies that under certain conditions, another condition occurs (e.g., "Infants under the age of three years are beautiful"); and the term "result" is the observation that results from a given rule (e.g., "Sally is beautiful") The reason for this "result" is that since Sally is under the age of three, then according to the rule, she must be beautiful.

Deductive reasoning begins with the rule and the case to deduce the result. For example, the rule is "All the balls in Joseph's bag are white" and the case is "This ball comes from Joseph's bag". The (deductive) result will be "This ball is white".

Inductive reasoning begins with the case and the result to find the rule. For example, the case that "this ball is from Joseph's bag" and the result that "this ball is white" can lead us to inductively conclude that the rule is "all the balls in Joseph's bag are white". Note that a rule that arises from inductive reasoning is not necessarily correct.

Abductive reasoning begins with the rule and the result to arrive at the case. Continuing with the previous example, the rule is "all the balls in Joseph's bag are white" and the result is "this ball is white". This leads us to conclude that "this ball is from Joseph's bag". Again, it must be emphasized that abductive reasoning does not necessarily lead to a correct conclusion. Fischer (2001) claimed that abductive reasoning requires two stages: in the first stage, one must understand the "phenomenon" (i.e. the hypothesis) in terms that promote both the "rule" and the result that is the outcome of the rule; in the second stage, one presents the derived case (which is not necessarily true). In the example used, the abductive reasoning unfolds as follows: one must first understand the rule "all the balls in Joseph's bag are white" and the result that "this ball is white". In the second stage, one concludes that the (seemingly) appropriate case must be that "the ball is from Joseph's bag" (i.e., one concludes – perhaps falsely – that the white color is due to the color of the balls in Joseph's bag). Jøsang (2008) has claimed that abductive reasoning, in general, describes the process of determining a hypothesis or a set of rules that leads to a particular deduction, and that this reasoning allows one to estimate the likelihood that from one particular hypothesis one can arrive at a particular conclusion.

Reasoning by analogy, in contrast to deductive, inductive, and abductive reasoning, is based on comparing two objects or systems in some way that underscores some similarity between them. Reasoning by analogy is useful in daily life in addition to being used in mathematics (Magdas, 2015). It is interesting to note that many scholars have assumed that reasoning by analogy is the province only of children over eight years of age and that younger children are unable to explain events through analogy (Piaget, Montangero & Billeter, 1974; Gallagher & Wright, 1979; Nippold & Sullivan, 1987). However, some researchers have reported observing children between the ages of four and seven using analogical reasoning when given non-routine problems to solve. For example, in one study, young children were told a story where a genie uses a rolled-up carpet as a tube to transfer precious jewels from one bottle to another. Based on that story, the children elected to move some small rubber balls from one bowl to another using a sheet of paper in the same way as in the story (Gentner, 1977; Holyoak, Junn & Billman, 1984). (Interestingly, they often ignored the piece of paper and looked for a rug.)

1.3   *Decision Making*

Coping with logical deductions requires decision-making. Decision-making means choosing a preferred option in a given situation from among all the alternative options available (Wang, Wang, Patel, & Patel, 2004; Wilson & Keil, 2001). Clements and Sarama (2007) have pointed out that even very young children can make decisions. For example, babies between six and nine months may "decide" to pull a blanket toward them to obtain a doll that is far away. Other studies have shown that pre-school children can make decisions that lead to future benefits. For example, in a study by Mischel and colleagues (Mischel, Shoda, and Rodriguez, 1989) pre-school age children were given a choice: either receive an immediate reward or wait and get two rewards later.

The results showed that many kindergarten children will decide to wait for the larger prize even though this meant postponing gratification.

1.4   *Decision Making and Metacognition*

The classical definition of metacognition is "any conscious cognitive or affective experiences that accompany and pertain to an intellectual enterprise" (Flavell, 1979, p. 906) and include both experience and knowledge. This is usually understood to be "cognition of cognition" or "thinking about thinking". Metacognitive ability is very important for guiding an individual when making judgments and decisions. Metacognitive processes are influenced by emotions, judgments, and metacognitive knowledge. Strle (2012) and Yeung & Summerfield (2012) have both claimed that an individual's ability to come to a decision depends on having metacognitive skills. In other words, a person who wishes to answer a question or solve a problem must make judgments and decisions. If that person is then asked to rationalize his thinking (decision), he must go through a metacognitive process, as this requires thinking about thinking.

1.5   *Decision Making: Intuition and Preferences*

Decision making in early childhood is accompanied by two additional parameters: intuition and preferences. Intuition refers to a type of immediate, obvious knowledge, meaning that intuitions are cognitions that are accepted as they are without feeling the need for an additional scrutiny of its correctness. It should be noted that compulsion is a characteristic of intuition since intuition enforces itself on the thinking process and how to select solutions for a specific problem (Fischebein, Tirosh, & Barash, 1998; Fischebein, 2005). Abdillah and colleagues (2016) claimed that intuition is an initial basic component of decision-making; later, Ergül (2018, p. 3) added that children's reasoning (preschool age) is limited by simple and intuitive perceptions.

It should be emphasized that somewhere between the ages of four and seven, perhaps sooner, a child begins to develop his or her reasoning by asking questions like "why?" and "how?" This is how children develop intuitive thinking based on subjective impression rather than logic. This phase in a child's development is the second sub-stage in Piaget's pre-operational stage. Now, children think more logically than they did in the previous sub-stage (pre-language). Nevertheless, they do make errors in logic (Oswalt, 2008). Furthermore, according to Piaget's theory, the intuitive sub-phase in child development is characterized by egocentrism: children in this developmental stage believe that the whole world perceives the environment just as they do. In this context, children perceive themselves to be the center of their environment, which in turn affects a child's preferences. In other words, children at this age tend to explain things according to their preferences. In addition, Fawcet and Markson (2010) reported that children from age three on recognize the preferences of others who are close to them, and this influences their choices or decisions. Ergül (2014) also added that from age three onward, children can determine whether the preferences of others match their own, and this information is used by them when making their decisions.

2   Study Purpose and Research Questions

In this study, we investigate the decision-making and logical reasoning processes among young children, specifically when dealing with logical deduction based on the quantifier "all".

We focused on the following research questions. With respect to children in early childhood:

– To what extent are they able to come to a correct conclusion when dealing with logical deductions that focus on the quantifier "all"?
– What characterizes their reasoning?
– Is there any relationship between the decision-making process and their logical reasoning?
– Is there any relationship between decision-making and age, gender, and social strata?
– Is there any relationship between logical reasoning and age, gender, and social strata?

3   Methodology

We presented a problem specifically designed to test pupils' reasoning when faced with the quantifier "all". The children were asked to make their decision and then explain their reasoning behind their answer.

3.1   Study Population and the Sampling Method

The study population included a total of 278 kindergarten, and first- and second-grade pupils from Arab schools in Israel. (Age range: 4–8 years; 48–84 months.) These included 129 Negev Bedouin (southern region of the country, considered to be on a low socioeconomic level) and 149 pupils from the northern area of the country (medium socioeconomic level: the sample included all the Arab ethnic groups in this region). (With respect to defining the socioeconomic levels of the populations, see Lavi, 2016.) The classes in both areas were selected randomly. Table 8.1 shows the distribution by gender and grade.

TABLE 8.1   Sample distribution by gender and grade

		Entire sample (n = 278)	Area	
			North (n_1 = 149)	South (n_2 = 129)
Gender	Male	136 (48.9%)	75 (50.3%)	61 (47.3%)
	Female	142 (51.1%)	74 (49.7%)	68 (52.7%)
Grade	Kdgtn	129 (46.4%)	87 (58.4%)	42 (32.6%)
	1	78 (28.0%)	34 (22.8%)	44 (34.1%)
	2	71 (25.6%)	28 (18.8%)	43 (33.3%)

3.2   Designing the Problem

This current study reports on questions based on the quantifier "all". (The complete study dealt with a number of quantifiers and logical connectives, but we restrict the results here only to the quantifier "all", by presenting the findings for one daily life question that represents the other similar questions. by one daily life representative question.) The problem was written in a way that was appropriate for all the children, regardless of age, gender, or socioeconomic level. The problem is worded as follows:

"*All of Roni's red shirts are in the closet. Is Roni wearing a red shirt or a green shirt now?*" Note that this issue focuses on the quantifier "all", and the answer "red" is incorrect. However, even though the correct answer should be "green", we considered any other color (not red) acceptable.

3.3   Analysis of the Problem from the Viewpoint of Logical Reasoning

Using *deductive reasoning*, we can verify that the given rule is "all of Roni's red shirts are in the closet" and the given case is "now Roni is wearing a shirt". The result is therefore "the shirt that Roni is wearing *now* is not red". If we use *inductive reasoning*, we begin with the case "now Roni is wearing a shirt" and the results "the shirt that Roni is wearing now is green/other", and from this we derive the rule "all of Roni's red shirts are in the closet". It is clear that this rule is not necessarily true. Using *abductive reasoning*, we would begin with the rule "all of Roni's red shirts are in the closet" and from the result, "the shirt that Roni is wearing now is red", conclude that "the shirt is from Roni's closet".

According to the widely held belief given in the literature, there was no point in considering *analogical reasoning* since children under seven cannot deal with analogical reasoning when the task tends to be an abstract one similar to the problem shown here.

3.4   *Mathematical Analysis of the Problem*

We use P_1 to represent the property "Roni's shirt is red" and P_2 to represent the property "Roni's shirt is in the closet".

According to the given in the problem: If "the shirt is red" then "the shirt is in the closet". Mathematically, this is written:

$$\forall\, x,\, (P_1\,(x)) \Rightarrow x,\, (P_2\,(x));$$

which is equivalent to

$$\forall\, x,\, (\neg P_2\,(x)) \Rightarrow x,\, (\neg P_1\,(x)).$$

If y is a shirt that belongs to Roni, y has two possibilities: "the shirt is red" or "the shirt is not red". In symbols, it is written:

$$P_1\,(y) \vee \neg P_1\,(y).$$

Similarly, we also have "the shirt is in the closet" or "the shirt is not in the closet", written as:

$$P_2\,(y) \vee \neg P_2\,(y).$$

If x is the shirt that Roni is wearing **now**, the shirt is (obviously) not in the closet, that is to say $\neg P_2$, and the conclusion is that the shirt is *not* red, that is to say, $\neg P_1$. Mathematically:

$$\forall\, x,\, (\neg P_2\,(x)) \Rightarrow x,\, (\neg P_1\,(x)).$$

3.5   *Data Collection*

The problem was given to each participating pupil, individually, in a quiet area of the school or kindergarten where he/she learned. To ensure that the pupils' answers were not influenced by factors that would jeopardize the study results (e.g., an interviewer who was a stranger to the pupil) the pupil's mathematics teacher administered the questions and recorded the conversation. The pupil was first asked to state what color shirt Roni was now wearing, and then the pupil was asked to explain their reasoning for their answer.

After the interview, the teacher also wrote field notes with respect to her observations.

4 Results

We shall first present the general results (that is to say, decisions regarding the color of the shirt). Following this, we shall examine and analyze the children's reasoning for their decisions.

4.1 General Results: What Color Was the Shirt?

Overall results. Overall, of the *entire population* (n = 278), exactly 50% of the pupils answered correctly (Roni's shirt is green) and 2.2% (6 pupils) responded with a color other than red or green. In other words, 52.2% of the population gave what was considered a correct answer. Of the 47.8% remaining, 47.1% (131) answered "Roni's shirt is red" (incorrect) and 0.7% (2 pupils) could not answer at all.

Socioeconomic level. The answers, divided by socioeconomic level, are presented in Table 8.2.

TABLE 8.2   Distribution of answers based on socioeconomic level (region)

Area	Green (correct)	Other color (correct)	Red (incorrect)	No answer
North (n = 149)	48.3%	4%	47.7%	0
South (n = 129)	51.9%	0%	46.5%	1.6%

Based on a chi-square analysis, any correlation between the decision about the color and socioeconomic level seems to be borderline ($\chi 2(3$, n = 278) = 7.705, p = 0.053 > 0.05).

Results based on grade. In kindergarten, the answers "red", "green", "other color", "no answer" were given 48.8%, 46.5% 4.7%, and 0%, respectively; for grade 1, 51.3%, 46.2%, 0% and 2.6%; for grade 2: 39.4%, 60.6%, 0% and 0%, respectively (see Table 8.3).

TABLE 8.3   Distribution of answers given by pupils per grade

Area	Green (correct)	Other color (correct)	Red (incorrect)	No answer
Kindergarten (n = 129)	46.5%	4.7%	48.8%	0%,
Grade 1 (n = 78)	46.2%	0%	51.3%	2.5%
Grade 2 (n = 71)	60.6%	0%	39.4%	0%
Total population N = 278				

It is obvious that there is a strong correlation between answer and grade ($\chi^2(6, n = 278) = 15.445$, p = 0.017 < 0.05); (Cramer's V = 0.167).

Results based on gender. Table 8.4 shows the distribution of pupils in relation to gender.

TABLE 8.4   Distribution of answers based on gender, divided by socioeconomic level

		Green (correct)	Other color (correct)	Red (incorrect)	No answer
Total[a] (n = 278)	M (n = 136)	51.5% (70)	4.4% (6)	43.4% (59)	0.7% (1)
	F (n = 142)	48.6% (69)	0	50.7% (72)	0.7% (1)
North[b] (n = 149)	M (n = 74)	50.7% (38)	8% (6)	41.3% (31)	0
	F (n = 74)	45.5% (34)	0	54.1% (40)	0
South[c] (n = 129)	M (n = 61)	52.5% (32)	0	45.9% (28)	1.6% (1)
	F (n = 68)	51.1% (35)	0	47.1% (32)	1.5% (1)

a $\chi^2(3, n = 278) = 7.171$, p = 0.067; (Cramer's V = 0.161). Overall, no significant correlation between gender and answer.

b $\chi^2(2, n = 149) = 7.357$, p = 0.025 < 0.05; (Cramer's V = 0.222). In the north, a significant correlation between gender and answer.

c $\chi^2(2, n = 129) = 0.021$, p = 0.989; (Cramer's V = 0.013). In the south, no correlation between gender and answer.

4.2   Pupil Reasoning

After each pupil gave his or her answer, they were asked to explain why they decided on that particular answer. The reasons were divided into categories based on the various parameters that humans, particularly young children, use when arriving at decisions.

In the current study, we detected seven categories of reasoning associated with the correct answer: correct reasoning, personal preference, preferences of individuals close to the participant, environmental influence, intuition, other, and none. With respect to incorrect answers, the same categories were detected, except that "abductive reasoning" was used instead of "correct reasoning". The categories for each type of answer, with examples, are presented in Table 8.5.

It should be noted that 2.3% of the pupils gave the wrong answer ("*red*") yet justified it using the reason that should correspond to the correct answer, that is to say, "*because all his red shirts are in the closet*". This may be due to abductive reasoning based on the rule "*all of Roni's red shirts are in the closet*" with the

TABLE 8.5 Types of reasoning for correct and incorrect answers with examples

Response	Reasoning category	Examples	No.
Correct answer[a]	Correct	– Green because all his red shirts are in the closet.	29.5% (41)
	Pupil preference	– Green because I like the color green. – Green because I do not like red.	10.1% (14)
	Close preferences	– Green because my mother loves green.	0.7% (1)
	Environmental influence	– Green because Roni is a boy. – Green because the school uniform is green. – Green because the tree is green. – Green because it is the color of grass.	17.3% (24)
	"Intuition"	– Green because he wants to go to Grandma and is dressed in a shirt – Green because has many red shirts in the closet. – Green because he wore all the red shirts and now he wears the green.[b]	7.2% (10)
	Else	– Green because he is wearing green.	0.7% (1)
	None given		34.5% (48)
Wrong answer (red shirt)	"Abductive" Reasoning	– Red because all his closet is red. – Red because all his shirts are red.	29.8% (39)
	Pupil preferences	– Red because he's my friend. – Red because he loves the color red. – Red because red is beautiful.	8.4% (11)
	Close preferences	– Red because my mother has a red shirt.	0.8% (1)
	Environmental influence	– Red because of Santa Claus. – Red because it is a holiday and we have to wear red. – Red because it's winter. – Red because it's cold. – Red because we see red. – Red because he is going to a party.	11.5% (15)

(cont.)

TABLE 8.5   Types of reasoning for correct and incorrect answers with examples (*cont.*)

Response	Reasoning category	Examples	No.
	"Intuition"	– Red because you did not mention the green shirt in the question.	9.9% (13)
	Else	– Red and green because he is wearing, one above the other.	3% (4)
	None given		36.6% (48)

a   Refers only to the correct answer "The color of the shirt that Roni is now wearing is green".
b   This answer is considered intuitive response because the answer may have been decided upon immediately, since the child thinks that if all the red shirts are in the closet, he has worn them already, thus now he is wearing a green shirt.

result being "the shirt that Roni is wearing now is red", leading them to deduce that the situation is "the shirt comes from Roni's closet". That is to say, their reasoning was that since all his red shirts are in the closet and the shirt comes from the closet, the color of this shirt must be red.

Differences in reasoning: overall results. Considering all the participants as one group, the findings suggest that there is a significant relationship between the response (the decision made) to the category of reasoning used ($\chi^2(18$, n $= 278) = 84.998$, p $= 0.00001 < 0.05$). In this case, the association is very strong (Cramer's V $= 0.319$).

Differences in reasoning based on socioeconomic status: There seems to be a significant relationship between socioeconomic status and the reasoning the pupil gave: ($\chi^2(6$, n $= 278) = 32.009$, p $= 0.00001 < 0.05$; very strong association – Cramer's V $= 0.339$). With respect to the correct reasoning, 16.1% (24) of pupils from the north, gave the correct reasoning (although four gave an incorrect answer), whereas for pupils from the south, 18.3% (21) gave the correct reason (all of which were associated with the correct answer). However, a considerable difference is noted between the north and south with respect to reasoning regarding the preference of the child or people close to the child: in the north, 2% (3) of the pupils chose "red" because he/she preferred red, and 1.3% chose "red" because someone they were close to liked red (total 3.3%). However, in the south, 17.1% (22) of the pupils gave the first reason (none used the second). Similarly, a large difference is noted in intuition-based reasoning: 13.4% (20) of children from the north compared with only 2.3% (3) from the south. Environmental-based reasoning was evident in 12.1% (18) of answers from the north, and 16.3% (21) of answers in the south. Finally, abductive reasoning was used by 13.4% (20) of the children in the north and 15.5% (20) in the south. However, it is important to note that a large number of pupils, 41.6% (62) from the north and 32.6% (42) from the south were not able to provide any reasoning whatsoever for the decision (whether their answer was correct or incorrect).

Furthermore, in both sectors, a strong correlation was found between pupils' decisions and reasoning: in the north (χ^2(12, n = 149) = 37.953, p = 0.00001 < 0.05), that is to say, a very strong association (Cramer's V = 0.357); in the south (χ^2(10, n = 129) = 56.091, p = 0.00001 < 0.05), and the association is very strong (Cramer's V = 0.466).

Differences in reasoning based on gender. Gender did not seem to have any effect on results, both overall and by sector.

Differences in reasoning based on grade. Table 8.6 shows that, overall and specifically in the north, there was a very strong correlation between grade and reasoning; in the south, there was a strong correlation. The percentage of correct reasoning rises overall, with the highest percentage from grade-two pupils in the north.

Table 8.6 also indicates differences in how the pupils were influenced. For example, in the south, pupils were influenced by their own preferences and peer preference did not have any influence whatsoever. This is in contrast to pupils from the north, where the effect of personal preference or the preferences of those close to them (particularly their mother) were both very small. Environmental influence seems to be a very significant element in the pupils' reasoning: in the northern region, similar to the overall population, environmental impact decreased as grade level increased, whereas, in the south, environmental impact was expressed mostly in second grade. In addition, intuition affected the logical reasoning in the north in ascending order with class level, whereas in the south intuition was evident only in kindergarten. Abductive reasoning was observed in first-graders across the board, and a large percentage of second-graders used the abductive argument, but only a small percentage of kindergarteners used this type of reasoning.

It is noteworthy that, overall, about half of the kindergarten pupils did not provide a reason for their decision. In the north, the absence of a reason was highest in kindergarten and decreased with age: 60%, 30%, 0% (kindergarten, grade 1, grade 2, respectively, which might be considered reasonable since older children are becoming more articulate). In the south, however, there was a higher incidence of *first-graders* (45.5%) who did not justify their decisions compared to kindergarteners (31%) and second-graders (21%). This anomaly is discussed below.

TABLE 8.6 Distribution of reasoning categories based on grade

Response	Reasoning category	Kinder-garten	Grade 1	Grade 2	Correlation
Overall	Correct	9 (7%)	11 (14.1%)	25 (35.2%)	See note a
	Pupil preference	13 (10.1%)	5 (6.4%)	7 (9.9%)	
	Close preferences	2 (1.6%)	0 (0%)	0 (0%)	
	Environmental influence	20 (15.5%)	7 (9%)	12 (6.9%)	
	"Intuition"	13 (10.1%)	5 (6.4%)	5 (7%)	
	Abductive	7 (5.4%)	20 (25.6%)	13 (18.35%)	
	None given	65 (50.45%)	30 (38.5%)	9 (12.7%)	
North area	Correct	4 (4.6%)	4 (11.8%)	16 (57.1%)	See note b
	Pupil preference	2 (2.3%)	1 (2.9%)	0 (0%)	
	Close preferences	2 (2.3%)	0 (0%)	0 (0%)	
	Environmental influence	14 (16.1%)	3 (8.8%)	1 (3.6%)	
	"Intuition"	10 (11.5%)	5 (14.7%)	5 (17.9%)	
	Abductive	3 (3.4%)	11 (32.4%)	6 (21.4%)	
	None given	52 (59.8%)	10 (29.4%)	0 (0%)	
South area	Correct	5 (11.9%)	7 (15.9%)	9 (20.9%)	See note c
	Pupil preference	11 (26.2%)	4 (9.1%)	7 (16.3%)	
	Close preferences	0 (0%)	0 (0%)	0 (0%)	
	Environmental influence	6 (14.3%)	4 (9.1%)	11 (25.6%)	
	"Intuition"	3 (7.1%)	0 (0%)	0 (0%)	
	Abductive	4 (9.5%)	9 (20.5%)	7 (16.3%)	
	None given	13 (31%)	20 (45.5%)	9 (20.9%)	

a χ^2 (12, n = 278) = 61.229, p = 0.00001 < 0.05; (Cramer's V = 0.332). Over the entire population, there is a very strong significant correlation between class level and reasoning. The higher the grade, the higher the instances of correct reasoning. There was a tendency to avoid giving a reason in the lower grades. Kindergarten children were most affected by the environment, by their own preferences, and by intuition.

b χ^2 (12, n = 149) = 79.448, p = 0.0001 < 0.05; (Cramer's V = 0.516). In classes in the north, there was a very strong correlation between class level and rationale. As age increases (i.e. higher grade) the higher the instances of correct reasoning. As age increases (i.e. higher grade) the rationale is affected more by intuition. In lower classes, there is more tendency to be affected by the environment. In first grade, abductive reasoning stands out, but it still exists in second grade. Only a small percent were affected by personal preference in all grades. Younger children were more likely not to give any rationale.

c χ^2 (10, n = 129) = 20.522, p = 0.025 < 0.05; (Cramer's V = 0.282). In classes in the north, there is a strong correlation between class level and rationale. As age increases (i.e. higher grade) the higher the instances of correct reasoning. In kindergarten, the reason for the decision is mostly influenced by pupil's preferences in kindergarten, but not at all by close acquaintances. The environment has a greater influence in Grade 2. Abductive reasoning is most prominent in first grade. A large percentage of all grades gave an answer without rationale, and this was for most of first graders. Rationale based on intuition is almost negligible.

5   Discussion and Conclusions

This study examined an aspect of decision-making in children and pupils aged four to seven when dealing with an issue based on the quantifier "all" and examined their logical reasoning and deductions for the question: "*All* of Roni's red shirts are in the closet. Is Roni now wearing a red or green shirt?" This problem is representative of many issues in a child's day-to-day life, such as "All the children who are in Teacher Sara's class are five years old. Sam is in Sara's class, so this must mean that Sam is five years old". Another example: "All the apples in the refrigerator are in the top drawer. If you ask Sally to get an apple out of the fridge, then Sally should open the top drawer in the fridge to fetch an apple". Furthermore, similar quantifier problems can be found in mathematics in higher grades. For example, a well-known statement is "the unit digit in all even numbers is even. Is 217 an even number?" Another example: "In a quadrilateral, any two sides can meet at only at one single point (the vertex). Is the shape ⟍ a quadrilateral?"

It should be emphasized that the quantifier "all" is meaningful and understandable already from the age of four (Nel & Southwood, 2016; Roeper, 2007; Brooks & Braine, 1996). According to Chomsky's nativist theory, children in all the different cultures and languages have the same language acquisition skills (Chomsky, 2001). Based on this, our current research findings should be applicable to all children, regardless of language or culture.

The results of this study show that about 50% of the children arrived at the correct decision about Roni's shirt color, with older children giving a higher percentage of correct answers: a reasonable expectation given that children are developing their cognitive abilities. This result was irrespective of socioeconomic level (i.e. whether from the north or south of the country). Similarly, there was no clear *overall* correlation between gender and the correct answer, a finding which is consistent with previous studies that have shown that there is no clear correlation between gender and decision-making skills using logical reasoning (see, for example, Çelik, 2017). Nevertheless, the data did show a difference based on location: while there was no correlation with gender in the south, in the north, about 60% of the boys gave the correct answer, but only about 45% of the girls. This finding coincides with previous studies, such as that of Meland and Kaltvedt (2019), who reported that in some societies "boys and girls are treated differently: girls and boys challenge prevailing gender structures while kindergarten staff simultaneously conforms to gender stereotypes". In Arab families boys have greater status and thus obtain more attention than girls. Previous studies, such as one by Haj Yihya-Abu Ahmad (2006), have noted that "for the most part, parents educate boys to be dominant and leaders, whereas the girls are taught to surrender and be obedient to other family members". Apparently, this aspect can influence an individual's decision-making process, meaning that the girls tended to rely more on what "others" might prefer rather than trusting their own use of logic to come to their decision. The fact that there was no difference between the genders in the Bedouin sector (that is to say, the population in the south) can be attributed to the fact that a good portion of this population live in unrecognized towns with no infrastructure and no schools (LaVie, 2016; Rasslan & Sharif-Rasslan, 2018). As a result, young children in this environment, boys and girls alike, need to act similarly when making decisions, such as for example making a decision whether to go long distances every day to get to school.

Regarding the rationale given by the children, the findings of this study do suggest that there is a very strong significant correlation between decision making and the rationale given by children, and this is influenced by three predominant factors: environmental, preferences, and intuition. Regardless if the decision was correct or not, the environment influenced 17.3% and 11.5% of the answers (correct and incorrect, respectively), preferences influenced 10.8% and 9.2% of the answers, and intuition was the basis for 7.2% and 9.9% of correct and incorrect answers, respectively. Environmental influences included a number of different aspects: for example, some of the participants from the north answered the question during the Christmas holiday, and their reasoning (which led to an incorrect answer) was influenced by the red clothing that is typical of the season. On the other hand, the rationale given by one of the children from the south (also leading to the incorrect answer, "red") was "because one sees red". The explanation for this might be environment dependent because they took part in this survey during the winter, when many bonfires are lit in the south for warmth. It is clear that one "sees red" in the fire. In this context, one may assume that the impact from the environment depends both on individual preference and intuition. These findings can be interpreted based on Piaget's theory that the intuitive stage of a child's development (ages 4–7 years, which corresponds to the age of the population in this study) is characterized by egocentrism: thus the child's immediate environment, his own intuition and preferences are what affect his rationale (Cohen & Friedman, 2002; Oswalt, 2008). The dependence of rationale on preferences has also been observed in other studies (Fawcet & Markson, 2010; Ergül, 2014).

A correct answer substantiated with the correct rationale occurred for about 16% of the study participants. The correlation between rationale and decision was very strong. Furthermore, the incidence of correct rationale given to arrive at the correct answer increases with age (class level) irrespective of socioeconomic level. This result is supported by Piaget's theory of development as all the participants in this study were younger than seven. During this period, children are in the preoperational stage, where they are unable to learn complex concepts such as cause-and-effect relationships. Their intelligence is egocentric and intuitive, not logical (Piaget, 1977).

Approximately 35% of the pupils gave an answer without any rationale at all (for both correct and incorrect answers). Most of the pupils who gave answers without any rationale were in kindergarten, a result that is also supported by Piaget's theory: during the preoperational stage, children are beginning to use language and develop their memory and imagination, and many children find it difficult to clearly express their thoughts at this time.

One noteworthy result is that the percentage of pupils in the north who did *not* rationalize their answers decreased (as would be expected) as the grade level rose, whereas in the south, more grade-one than kindergarten pupils *did not* give any rationale for their decision (45% and 31%, respectively). However, this can be explained by the fact that about 21% of Negev Bedouin children do not attend kindergarten (Weisblay, 2017, p. 3). This suggests that any observation of a decrease in the tendency to give answers without any rationale will begin in grade one (and not from kindergarten) and will be observed only in grade two. This seems to be what has happened in this case.

Given the case "Roni is wearing a shirt", the child must first decide what color shirt Roni is wearing and then give the rationale for his answer. There are two cases: either the child decides on the correct answer and says that the shirt that Roni is now wearing is green (or another color other than red), or the child decides that the shirt that Roni is wearing is red. All the children gave an answer (correct or not). In other words, all the children were able to arrive at a decision on a specific color. If the child has decided on the correct color, the best case is the correct logical reasoning. However, they may have been influenced by other parameters (intuition, preferences, environmental, or no rationale at all). In the event that the child decided that Roni is wearing a red shirt, that is to say, the incorrect answer, the child's rationale may also have been influenced by intuition, preferences, environmental, or no rationale at all. But here, a type of reasoning may have been used that could not have been the case when the answer was correct, and that is abductive reasoning. In fact, of those who gave the incorrect answer ("red shirt") about 30% decided this due to abductive reasoning: "red because all of Roni's shirts are red". This can be interpreted in accordance with the mechanisms of abductive reasoning (Ried & Knipping, 2010), the rule being "if Roni is wearing a red shirt, then the shirt comes from the closet", and the results "the shirt that Roni is wearing is red" (which is the answer given by the child), and then the case may be deduced: "all of Roni's shirts are red" (an *incorrect* conclusion in the specific case here). In other words, using the rule and the results, they decide that Roni's shirts are red. Using this rationale, the child "snatches" the first part of the sentence "all of Roni's red shirts ..." and ignores the second part of the sentence, "... are in the closet". He thus jumps to the conclusion: "all of Roni's shirts are red", and decides that if, indeed, all his shirts are red, he must be wearing a red one.

The principle conclusion from this study is that there are parameters that affect the logical reasoning in early childhood: environment, intuition, and preferences. In addition, young children may use abductive reasoning when required to deal with quantifier-based problems, but this only occurs in the case of an incorrect decision. However, it must be emphasized that for the most part, kindergarteners seem to avoid use of logical reasoning and they avoid giving any rationale for their decisions (overall, just over 50% of kindergarteners could not explain their decision).

Based on our findings, it seems that it would be valuable to expose young children to activities and challenges that involve dealing with quantifiers, as well as having them explain their reasoning for quantifier-based problems. As we mentioned at the beginning of this discussion, life is full of situations that require using logical reasoning to arrive at some decision. Such exposure will help children develop the comprehension required to cope more effectively with daily situations of this type, but it will also prove beneficial when it comes to tackling problems in elementary mathematics.

References

Abdillah, A., Nusantara, T., Subanj, S., Susanto, H., & Abadyo, A. (2016). Student's decision making in solving discount problem. *International Educational Studies, 9*(7), 57–63.

A'mir, D. (2005). The language of mathematics. *Bulletin of Mathematics Teachers, 34,* 5–9. [in Hebrew]

Boulet, G. (2007). How does language impact the learning of mathematics? Let me count the ways. *Journal of Teaching and Learning, 5*(1), 1–12.

Brooks, P., & Braine, M. D. S. (1996). What do children know about the universal quantifiers all and each? *Cognition, 60,* 235–268. http://dx.doi.org/10.1016/0010-0277(96)00712-3

Çelik, M. (2017). Examination of children decision making using clues during the logical reasoning process. *Educational Research and Reviews, 12*(16), 783–788.

Chomsky, N. (2001). *Language and problems of knowledge: The Managua lectures.* The MIT Press.

Clements, D. H., & Sarama, S. (2007). Early childhood mathematics learning. In F. K. Lester (Ed.) *Second handbook of research on mathematics teaching and learning.* Information Age Publishing.

Ergül, A. (2014). *Erken matematiksel akıl yürütme becerileri değerlendirme aracı geliştirilmesi.* Hacettepe Üniversitesi Sağlık Bilimleri Enstitüsü.

Feischbien, A., Tirosh, D., & Brush, A. (1998). Intuitive knowledge and logical knowledge as components of mathematical activity. *Bulletin of Mathematics Teachers, 22,* 12–28. (Hebrew). https://www.scribd.com/doc/163196879/Intuition-in-Science-and-Mathematics-E-Fischbein-2005-WW

Fischebein, E. (2005). *Intuition in science and mathematics: An educational approach.* Retrieved February 16, 2019, from www.scribd.com/doc/163196879/Intuition-in-Science-and-Mathematics-E-Fischbein-2005-WW

Fischer, H. R. (2001). Abductive reasoning as a way of world making. *Foundations of Science, 6,* 361–383.

Flavell, J. H. (1979). Metacognition and cognitive monitoring: A new area of cognitive-developmental inquiry. *American Psychologist, 34*(10), 906–911. http://dx.doi.org/10.1037/0003-066X.34.10.906

Gallagher, J. M., & Wright, R. J. (1979). Piaget and the study of analogy: Structural analysis of items. In M. K. Poulsen & G. I. Lubin (Eds.), *Piagetian theory and the helping professions: Proceedings from the 8th interdisciplinary conference* (Vol. 2, pp. 100–104). University of Southern California.

Gentner, D. (1977). Children's performance on a spatial analogies task. *Child Development, 48,* 1034–1039.

Haj Yahia-Abu Ahmad, N. (2006). *Couplehood and parenting in the Arab family in Israel: Processes of change and preservation in three generations* [Doctoral dissertation]. School of Social Work, University of Haifa. [in Hebrew]

Holyoak, K. J., Junn, E. N., & Billman, D. O. (1984). Development of analogical problem-solving skill. *Child Development, 55,* 2042–2055.

Jamison, R. E. (2000). Learning the language of mathematics. Language and learning across the *Disciplines, 4*(5), 45–54.

Jøsang, A. (2008). Abductive reasoning with uncertainty. In *The proceedings of the international conference on information processing and management of uncertainty* (IPMU2008).

Kuhen, A., & Freidman, D. (2002). *Developmental psychology: Piaget's theory – The pre-operative stage.* CET – Center for Educational Technology. [in Hebrew] Retrieved May 16, 2018, from http://lib.cet.ac.il/pages/item.asp?item=13550

Lavie, A. (2016). *The Palestinian Arab society in the State of Israel: A time for strategic change in the process of change and equality.* The Institute for National Security Research. [in Hebrew].

Magdas, I. (2015). Analogical reasoning in geometry education. *Acta Didactica Napocensia, 8*(1), 57–65.

Meland, A. T., & Kaltvedt, E. H. (2019). Tracking gender in kindergarten. *Early Child Development and Care, 181*(1), 94–103.

Mischel, W., Shoda, Y., & Rodriguez, M. (1989). Delay of gratification in children. *Science, 244*, 933–938.

Nel, J., & Southwood, F. (2016). The comprehension and production of quantifiers in isiXhosa-speaking Grade 1 learners. *South African Journal of Communication Disorders, 63*(2), a138. http://dx.doi.org/10.4102/sajcd.v63i2.138

Nippold, M. A., & Sullivan, M. P. (1987). Verbal and perceptual analogical reasoning and proportional metaphor comprehension in young children. *Journal of Speech and Hearing Research, 30*, 367–376.

Oswalt, A. (2008). *Early childhood cognitive development: Intuitive thought.* Retrieved May 16, 2018, from https://www.mentalhelp.net/articles/early-childhood-cognitive

Piaget, J., Montangero, J., & Billeter, J. B. (1977). La formation des correlats. In J. Piaget (Ed.), *Recherches sur l'abstraction reflechissante: L'abstraction des relations logico-arithmetiques* (pp. 115–129). Presses Universitaires de France.

Pimm, D. (1987). *Speaking mathematically: Communication in mathematics classrooms.* Routledge & Kegan Paul.

Rasslan, S., & Sharif-Rasslan, A. (2018). Mathematics education in the Arabic-speaking sectors in Israel. In N. Movshovitz-Hadar (Ed.), *K-12 mathematics education in Israel* (pp. 67–78). Scientific World.

Reid, D., & Knipping, C. (2010). *Proof in mathematics education: Research, learning and teaching* (pp. 83–110). Sense Publishers.

Roeper, T. (2007). *The prism of grammar. How child language illustrates humanism.* The MIT Press.

Strle, T. (2012). Metacognition and decision making: Between first and third person perspective. *Interdisciplinary Description of Complex Systems, 10*, 284–297. doi:10.7906/indecs.10.3.6

Wang, Y., Wang, Y., Patel, S., & Patel, D. (2004). A Layered Reference Model of the Brain (LRMB). *IEEE Transactions on Systems, Man, and Cybernetics (C), 36*(2), 124–133. http://dx.doi.org/10.1109/TSMCC.2006.871126.

Weisblay, A. (2017). *Bedouin education in the Negev: A current situation.* The Knesset, Research and Information Center. [in Hebrew]

Wilson, R. A., & Keil, F. C. (2001). *The MIT encyclopaedia of the cognitive sciences.* MIT Press. http://dx.doi.org/10.1023/B:MIND.0000035500.35700.12

Yeung, N., & Summerfield, C. (2012). Metacognition in human decision-making: confidence and error monitoring. *Philosophical Transactions of the Royal Society B, 367*(1594), 1310–1321.

CHAPTER 9

On Explaining, Explanations and Second Graders

Rina Hershkowitz and Abraham Arcavi

Abstract

In an extensive survey on learning mathematics administered to 470 second graders from 17 classes throughout Israel, two problems were included that required students to write explanations (justifications) to their solutions. The purposes of these items were (a) to investigate the ability of second graders to provide explanations to their mathematical productions; (b) to characterize these explanations; and (c) to establish possible factors that may affect the characteristics of their explanations as well as their avoidance to offer them. We discuss a number of theoretical aspects of explanatory processes and explanations and we analyze and discuss students' written responses sequentially from several points of view. We include some teaching implications from the conclusions.

Keywords

explanations – mathematical explanations – justifications – explanatory processes – second graders

1 Theoretical Background: On Explanations and Explaining

The production of arguments and the process of argumentation have been the focus of intense theoretical and empirical scrutiny in the learning sciences literature in recent years. Argumentation is the process by which humans strive to reach conclusions based on premises and reasoning and it includes dialogues/debates in which explanations play a central role. Krummheuer (1995, p. 262), following Toulmin's (1958) scheme on the structure of an argument, claimed that "the warrant *explains* the soundness of the inferential step", and called this aspect "explanatory relevance". Schwarz and Asterhan (2009) concluded that argumentation and explanation have similar syntax and structure, but differ in at least one important aspect: their purpose. An explanation has a clarifying function.

Explanations have been studied as both instructional tools (e.g. Leinhardt, 1987; Leinhardt & Schwarz, 1997) and as key components of learning and understanding (e.g. Chi & Bassok, 1989). Alibali (2007) claims that:

> ... literature has focused on two types of explanations: (1) instructional explanations, which are explanations provided by teachers, tutors, or other agents that provide instruction (such as computer-based learning environments), and (2) self explanations, which are explanations generated by learners themselves. (p. 98)

In this study we engage in self explanations in mathematics.

1.1   *What Are Mathematical Explanations?*

In our view, a mathematical explanation is a description that addresses and unfolds the origins/sources, entailments and connections of a mathematical idea. It is often an answer to a 'why' question, or a justification within an argument to support a central claim (Means & Voss, 1996). "Explanations involve activities such as generating inferences, filling in details, articulating underlying principles ..." (Alibali, 2007, p. 98). The ability to provide a coherent and convincing (to oneself or to others) explanation of an idea is often taken as (a) an operative expression of the 'understanding' of that idea, and (b) as a sign for taking up individual responsibility for one's own claims or ideas, and thus it is taken as an indication of autonomic learning.

There are many studies concerning the resources on which learners provide a basis for their explanations. For example, Levenson, Tsamir & Tirosh (2007) investigated the explanation types produced by elementary school children in the context of multiplication by zero and distinguished between mathematically-based (MB) versus practically-based (PB) explanations.

1.2   *Why Explanations?*

Children's production of explanations has been considered as central to learning and to knowledge construction processes by both the cognitive and the socio-cultural perspectives (Chi, de Leeuw, Chiu, & La Vancher, 1994). While children listen to explanations or engage in producing explanations, a cognitive approach may, for example, examine how explaining "de-centers" egocentric thinking and reflects schemata or "mental images". A socio-cultural approach may study, for example, the role explanations play in argumentation, which is a main component in dialogues which may enhance the zone of proximal development, may promote internalization of ideas, and may strengthen the development of communication (e.g. Brown & Palincsar, 1989). Explaining may also enhance the awareness of the nuances of ideas raised and discussed, by highlighting, first and foremost to the "explainer" (but also to her audience), both the weak and strong points of her own reasoning with respect to a mathematical topic. Explanations may create opportunities for involvement and motivation, for listening, discussing, imitating, and legitimizing different approaches to the underlying concepts of a mathematical topic.

The "practice" of explaining can take several forms, for example, verbalizing, gesturing, acting upon objects (measuring, calculating), and it may include illustrations, examples, analogies, inferences and more.

Dreyfus (1999) sees explanation as a category on a mathematical reasoning continuum, on which argument and proof are other categories. Dreyfus claims that:

> For mathematics educators there appears to be a continuum reaching from explanation via argument and justification to proof, and the distinctions between the categories are not sharp. (p. 102)

Students' explaining processes provide teachers and researchers with a window into the mathematical knowledge and needs of the students, and into the development and expression of their autonomic thinking, and thus it can serve as a point of departure upon which to build onwards (e.g. Douek, 1999).

1.3   When to Engage in Explaining?

Given the important roles attributed to explaining, a simple and general reply to this question would be: anytime! However, one may argue that young children can rarely produce meaningful explanations, with the intended effects described above, without a certain knowledge base. On the other hand, one can view the production of explanations as an integral part of building such a knowledge base. This may lead us to a circularity and to a subsequent impasse: how can one build a knowledge base needed to explain if one needs explaining to build such knowledge? Paraphrasing Sfard (2001), we would argue that explanations are one of the building blocks which at times scaffolds knowledge building and at times is it scaffolded by knowledge, making knowledge construction possible. Moreover, young children also need to learn about and experiment with the "meta-level", namely what an explanation is all about, what are its desirable components, why is it needed, when an explanation or an argument indeed explains and convinces and why. If this is so, it would seem that the sooner children are exposed to and requested to engage in the practice of explaining, the richer and the more effective their learning would be. However, the production, exposition and discussion of mathematical explanations are sophisticated activities, especially for very young children, and thus not surprisingly, except for some notable exceptions (e.g. Levenson et al. 2007), have not been very widely studied. Thus, regardless of the theoretical lens adopted, and certainly if one advocates a more eclectic approach, the process of producing and communicating explanations is important and deserve effort to know them better.

2   The Study

In the present work, we study the production of explanations by second graders in the context of mathematical tasks in a test. In particular, we address the following interrelated research questions:
- To what extent can very young students engage in the practice of providing mathematical explanations?
- What are the characteristics of the explanations that young children are able to produce?
- Is there any relationship between students' production of explanations and the classroom practices they experienced, and to what extent?

These questions are addressed, based on data collected from a large survey conducted in Israel, with the participation of second grade students. The survey included a written test, administered (towards the end of the school year) to 17 second grade classes (N = 470), each one from a different school, spread over the country. All these classes studied according to the same official syllabus, and each used one of the six different curriculum packages available at the time. The school sample took into account a representation of these different curriculum packages, different regions across the country and the socio-economic background of the students' population.

In order to address the research questions, we analyzed in detail student responses to two of the test items in which explanations/justifications to solutions/claims were explicitly required. The classes sampled allowed us to access a large and heterogeneous population of individuals.

The decision to address these research questions within this context posed some challenges: not only that second graders were requested to explain, they were requested to do so in writing, which demands a greater effort than producing a verbal explanation (Pimm, 1987). Besides, each of the second graders had to work by herself (in an exam situation with no opportunities to engage in conversations with peers or adults), in order to provide explanations even if they lack a clear sense of what "to produce an explanation" may mean. In short, they had to engage in an "unbalanced communication situation" – to convince oneself and/or even to imagine a "virtual interlocutor" who silently listens to the explanation.

2.1 The Tasks

The following are the two tasks designed to address the research questions.

2.1.1 Task 1 (T1)

a. Insert in the empty space the right symbol: >, < or =

$$750 - 13 \ \square \ 750 - 25$$

b. Can you answer this question without calculating the results? Explain.

2.1.2 Analysis of Task 1

In order to compare between the two subtractions without performing the calculations, one should realize that:

(a) whereas the *minuends are the same* (Element 1),
(b) the *subtrahends are not the same* (Element 2), and to *infer and explain* that
(c) the *more you subtract from a number the less you are left with* (Element 3).

Thus 750 – 13 must be larger than 750 – 25, regardless of the exact result. A full ("correct") explanation has to contain the three elements. This task requires children to move away from calculations and to focus on observation and production of an explanation, based on the nature of the subtraction operation. In terms of the Realistic Mathematics Education (RME) approach, the students have to engage in *vertical mathematization,* i.e. the reorganization of knowledge *within mathematics itself,* finding connections between elements and strategies and applying them for constructing new knowledge (Treffers & Goffree, 1985; Freudenthal, 1991). Hershkowitz, Parzysz, and van Dormolen (1996) define vertical mathematization as "an activity in which mathematical elements are put together, structured, organized, developed, etc. into other elements, often more abstract or formal form than the original" (p. 177).

2.1.3 Task 2 (T2)

Second grade children built a diagram to describe how many books they have read during the last month. Each kid pasted a small square in the appropriate place in the following diagram.

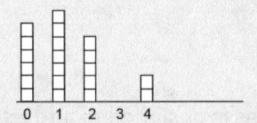

a. How many students in the class read one book? _____
b. How many students are there in this class? _____
c. Why do you think there are no squares above the number 3? Explain.

2.1.4 Analysis of Task 2

In order to explain the lack of squares above number 3, children have to refer back to the story, and infer that since nobody placed a square there, nobody had read three books during the last month. It is worth noting that, whereas in the first task students were familiar with the mechanism of subtraction, in this case they had only little experience in reading graphs of this kind. In terms of the Realistic Mathematics Education (RME) approach, students have to engage in *horizontal mathematization* (Treffers & Goffree, 1985, Freudenthal, 1991), namely, moving back and forth from the real world to the world of mathematical symbols and representations. Moreover, the interpretation of the particular feature of the representation requires two successive inferential steps: the absence of squares above the number 3 means that nobody placed a square there, which in turns indicates that nobody had read 3 books.

3 Results and Findings

In this section, we unfold the data analysis step by step from the more general to the more refined findings. In each step, the results build up so as to add information and insights enriching (and sometimes constraining) the findings presented in the previous step, in order to provide a complex and interesting set of answers to our research questions.

3.1 Step 1: The General Distribution of the Explanation Types for Both Tasks

At first, we categorized student explanations. Hence, the unit of analysis was the individual student and her explanations (or their absence). The categories emerged from the analysis of the explanations of about 100 students from four different classes, and then we used these categories to analyze the rest, and validate the categories. In the following, we present the categories illustrated by relevant quotes and their distribution.

In task 1, we found five categories: full correct explanations, partial explanations, non-mathematical explanations, incorrect explanations and no explanations.

3.1.1 Full Correct Explanations

As stated above, a full explanation includes three elements. We considered an explanation to be full (and correct) also when the first element was only implicit. For example:

Yoram: *Yes! Because we start in both exercises* (sides) *with the same number, but if you subtract a larger number, you get a smaller result.* (All three elements).

Dana: *Yes! Because 25 is a larger number, therefore the result is smaller.* (2nd and 3rd elements).

David: *Yes! Because if I do 750-13 and I do 750-25, it means that if I subtract less, the result will be larger.*

3.1.2 Partial Explanations

Gal: *Because there are 750 in both expressions and we subtract different numbers* (1st and 2nd elements).

Ruti: *Because the number 13, is smaller than 25* (2nd element only).

3.1.3 Non-Mathematical Explanations

This category includes:
– Explanations related to children's beliefs about the role of calculations. For example:
  Moshe: *No! Because one can't do an exercise without computing it.*
– Tautological explanations. For example:
  Miri: *One should not calculate without calculating.*
– Explanations not connected to mathematics. For example:
  Eli: *Yes! I trust myself and therefore I do not think.*

3.1.4 Incorrect Explanations

Neta: *Yes! When you subtract more, you get more.* (The inequality sign in a. was in the wrong direction).

This explanation is consistent with the widespread intuitive principle reported by Stavi & Tirosh (2000) which can be summarized as: 'more of A $\Rightarrow$ more of B'.

3.1.5   No Explanation
This category refers to the absence of any explanation.
     Table 9.1 presents the distribution of the above categories.

TABLE 9.1   Distribution of categories of explanations for T₁ (N = 470)

Full correct explanation	Partial explanation	Non-mathematical	Incorrect explanation	No explanation
17%	15%	13%	13%	42%

     Firstly, we note that 58% of the students in this research (aggregation of the
first four categories) at least attempted to engage in the production of a written
explanation, and more than half of them (32% of the whole sample) gave either
a partial or a full correct explanation. The responses in the third and fourth
categories (26% incorrect or non-mathematical explanations), represent those
students who did not know to explain correctly, but might have felt the responsibility to produce an explanation. It is worth noting that from those who gave a
wrong explanation (13%) only a few responded according to the intuitive principle "more of A ⇒ more B". However, there is a high percentage of students
(42%), who did not produce any explanation. As was hinted above, it is reasonable to assume that this category includes students who did not know how to
explain (and possibly aware of their lack of knowledge, decided not to answer)
and students who perhaps did not feel that explaining is their responsibility.
     In task 2, we found the same five categories.

3.1.6   Full Correct Explanations
As stated above, a full explanation includes explicit or implicit reference to the
two inferential steps. In some responses, the first inferential step is not mentioned (see David's example in the following).

Orna: *I think there are no squares above the number 3 because there are no stu-
          dents who read three books.*
David: *No one read three books.*

3.1.7   Partial Explanations
Mazal: *No one wanted three books* (the phrasing reflects a correct interpretation
          of the representation without alluding to the reading of the books).
Amos: *Because the children did not put any squares* (first inferential step only).

3.1.8 Non-Mathematical Explanation

Dina: *There are no squares above the number 3* (repetition of the question wording).

Naomi: *Because the boy or the girl were ill.*

3.1.9 Incorrect Explanations

Benny: *Three students did not read books* (the number 3 relates to the number of students and not to the number books).

Eyal: *The third student did not read books* (the absence of squares in the diagram is related to "no reading", but this answer refers to a certain student, as if students were numbered).

Table 9.2 shows the distribution of these categories

TABLE 9.2   Distribution of categories of explanations for T2 (N = 470)

Full correct explanation	Partial explanation	Non-mathematical	Incorrect explanation	No explanation
24%	8%	8%	16%	44%

The distribution of categories is similar to that of T1: 56% of students tried to provide an explanation (with a slight increase in the number of full explanations), and 44% of the students did not provide any explanation. We speculate that in spite of the novelty of this type of tasks for these second graders, the *horizontal mathematization* may be less demanding than the *vertical mathematization*.

What may this similarity between the distributions of categories in the two tasks be an indication of? We pursue these questions by further analyzing the data.

3.2   *Step 2: The Distribution of Explanation Types (Categories) Per Class*

A closer inspection of the data on T1 shows large differences among classes: in some of them, almost 80% of the students did not provide any explanation, with only up to 4% of correct explanations, whereas in others almost 50% of the students provided either a full or a partial explanation. A similar pattern of results was obtained for T2: in some classes, up to 70% of the students provided a full explanation, whereas in others less than 20% of the students did so.

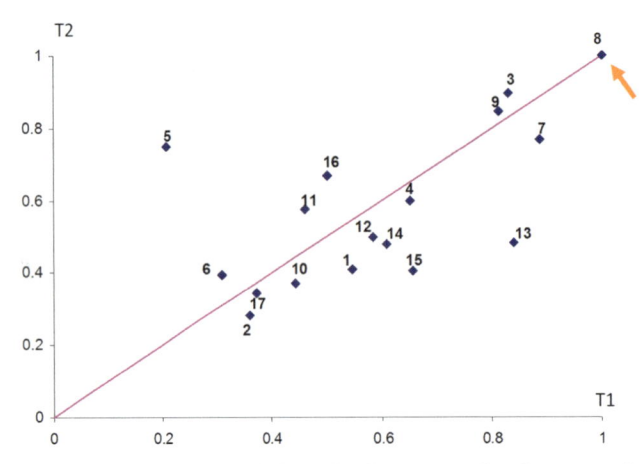

FIGURE 9.1   Distribution of classes by the percent of students providing any explanation in both tasks (Spearman r = 0.6; P < 0.011)

According to the results for both tasks, it would seem that the "explainers" cluster in certain classrooms. We found striking similarities between the pattern of responses to the two tasks in each class. For example, in class 17, 64% of the students did not provide any explanation for T1 and 72% did not provide it for T2. Only 12% produced a full explanation for T1 and 20% produced it for T2. It seems that for the students in this class there was almost no difference between the *vertical mathematization* required in T1 and the *horizontal mathematization* required in T2, both seemed equally foreign practices to most of the students.

Figure 9.1 shows the pattern of providing explanations (all categories except no explanation) for both tasks according to classes (N = 17).

The classes (represented by dots) are numbered, and the coordinates of each dot (class) represent the percentage of students providing an explanation for both tasks in a given class. For example: in class 8 (the point is highlighted by an arrow) 100% of the students provided some explanations to both, T1 and T2.

The graph shows a marked tendency of classrooms to support the production of an explanation regardless of the task. The correlation between the distribution per class for both tasks is quite high and significant (Spearman r = 0.6; P < 0.012). In addition, the classes spread along the diagonal rather than clustering in specific intervals, show the high variation among classes.

Similar findings emerge from the distribution of *correct or partial explanation* only (see Figure 9.2).

If we focus classes 2 and 8 (highlighted in the graph), we can see that 61% of the students in class 8 provided a full or a partial explanation for T1 and 78% for T2, while only 3% (one student) in class 2 provided it for T1 and 20% for T2.

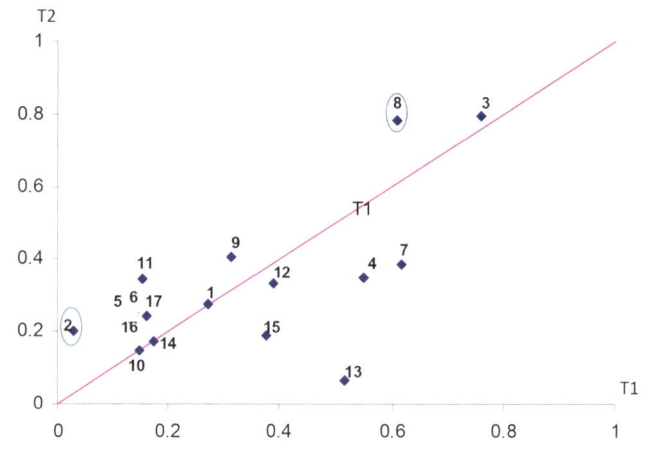

FIGURE 9.2   Distribution of classes by the percentage of correct or partially correct explanations in both tasks (Spearman r = 0.53; P < 0.05)

The differences between Figures 9.1 and 9.2 are due to those students who did not know how to explain correctly and/or mathematically, but still provided an explanation.

The above findings suggest that students' production of explanations (and/or their feeling of responsibility to produce explanations) may be related either to classroom practices and norms, or to some other variable, intrinsic to the specific class, like the socio-economic composition of the population. In order to confirm or dismiss this speculation we analyzed the data further.

3.3   Step 3: Correlation between Amount of "Explainers" and Socio-Economic Factors

As mentioned above, each of the 17 classes in our sample belongs to a different school. Since the schools participating in this study were sampled to include different socio-economic compositions of the population, we looked for possible relationships between this variable and the explanation patterns observed. Our analysis was based on an official indicator (MTT index) provided by the Ministry of Education and constructed on the basis of several socio-economical variables. The scale for this indicator ranges from 0 to 10, the highest the number the weaker the socio-economic status of the school measured. These measures are the basis upon which the government decides allocation of funds to schools.

Figures 9.3–9.6 show the distributions of classes according to both: the production of explanations (as the dependent variable) and the MTT indicator for both tasks (as the free variable).

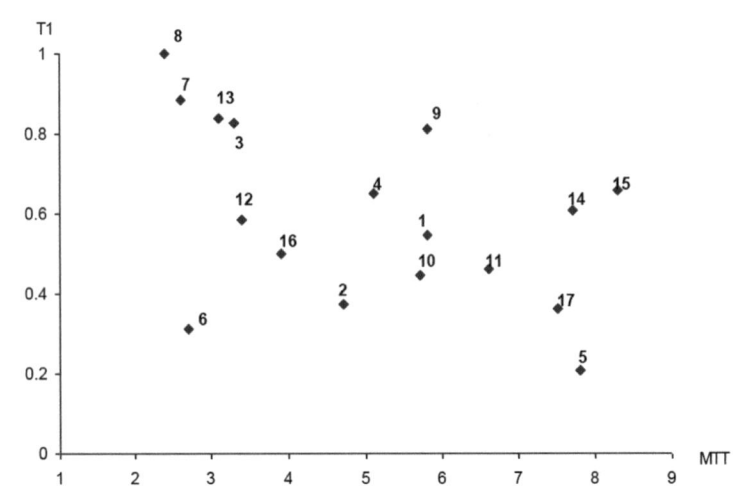

FIGURE 9.3   The distribution of classes relating the MTT indicator of the class to the percentage of students providing any explanation in T1 (Spearman r = −0.43; P < 0.1)

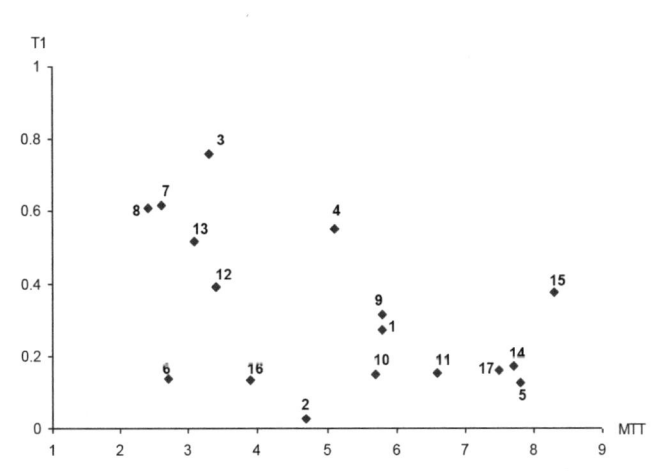

FIGURE 9.4   The distribution of classes relating the MTT indicator of the class to the percentage of students providing full/partial correct explanations in T1 (Spearman r = −0.4; P < 0.1)

The data show that the correlations between the MTT and the explaining patterns of each class are not significant. Thus, we propose that explanations might be closely related to the classroom culture and norms and how these norms regard the engagement with explanations as a central component of their mathematical practices. Due to the limitations of this study (which did not include long term observations of classroom habits and norms) we attempted to confirm this hypothesis by looking at "extreme cases".

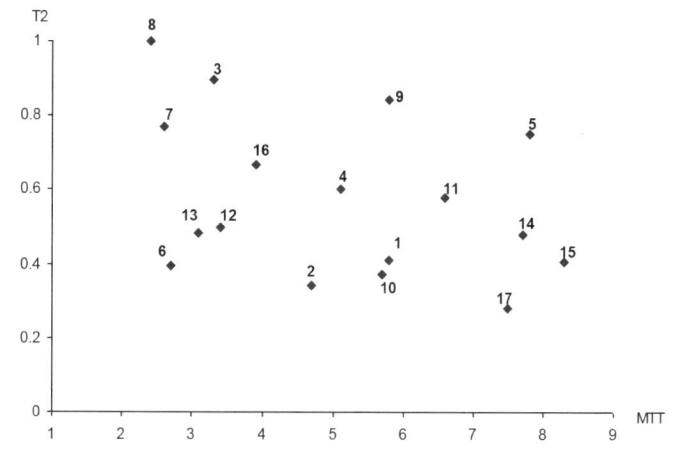

FIGURE 9.5   The distribution of classes relating the MTT indicator of the class to the
percentage of students providing explanations in T2 (Spearman r = −0.34; P < 0.2)

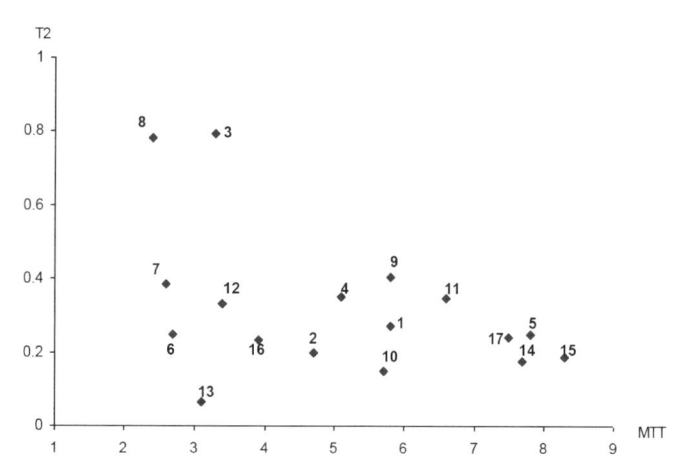

FIGURE 9.6   The distribution of classes relating the MTT indicator of the class to the
percentage of students providing full/partial explanations in T2 (Spearman
r = −0.35; P < 0.2)

3.4   *Step 4: Comparisons between the Explanation Categories of Two "Extreme Classes"*

As shown in Figures 9.1 and 9.2, classes 2 and 8 can be considered "extreme cases". The following figures display the distribution of the categories for each of them (see Figures 9.7 and 9.8).

The differences between the two classes are striking: whereas in class 8 there are no students who did not provide some kind of explanation, in class 2, more than 60% of the students did not provide any explanation. These data

T1: class 2 vs. class 8

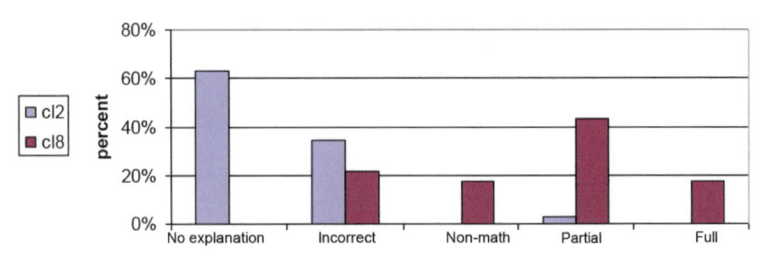

FIGURE 9.7   Comparison between the distribution of explanations' categories of classes 2 & 8 in T1 (Chi square, with 4 df = 39.45 (P < 0.0001))

T2: class 2 vs. class 8

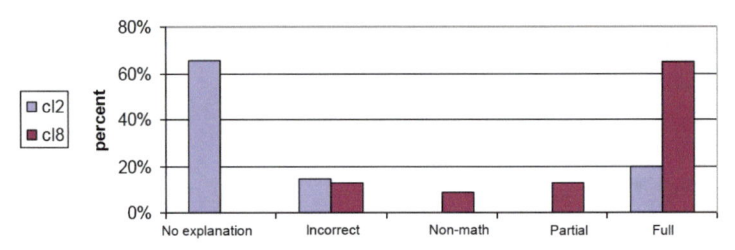

FIGURE 9.8   Comparison between the distribution of explanations' categories of classes 2 & 8 in T2 (Chi square, with 4 df = 30.22 (P < 0.0001))

led us to further scrutinize individual responses for each of the two tasks, in both classes, and to investigate whether (and if so how) we can tie differences to different classroom cultures which may nurture the production and communication of explanations.

3.5   Step 5: What Can We Learn from the Relationships between Individual Student Responses for Both Tasks?

We focused both on (a) the distributions of class 2 and class 8 students' individual responses to the two tasks, and on (b) each class in itself. The data for each class (see Tables 9.3 and 9.4 respectively), represent the patterns of responses for both tasks.

There are 17 students (almost half of the class) who did not provide explanations in the two tasks, either because they did not know how to explain or did not feel any responsibility to do so. A closer look at their written work provides more information: in T2 most of these 17 students just did not leave any "traces" of a response, except one girl who wrote explicitly: "I do not know". In T1 14 students, (out of the 17 who did not explain T2) responded to the first section of T1, by inserting the inequality sign (5 of them inserted it wrongly and 9 correctly), but did not respond to section *b*, i.e., they did not claim that they

TABLE 9.3   Class 2 (n = 35) cross-distribution of student responses in T1 & T2

	No expl	Incorrect	Non-math	Partial	Full	Total T2
No expl.	49% (17)	17% (6)				66% (23)
Incorrect	3% (1)	8.5% (3)		3% (1)		14.5% (5)
Non-math						
Partial						
Full	11% (4)	8.5% (3)				20% (7)
Total T1	63% (22)	34% (12)		3% (1)		100% (35)

can (or cannot) respond without a calculation, and they did not provide any explanation. These data are still not enough to conclude whether explaining is not a norm supported in this class or, alternatively, students just did not know how to explain.

Some more information is worth noticing in this table. For example, the cell showing that 4 students did not explain in T1 but provided a full-correct-explanation for T2. A student who is represented in this cell wrote the correct inequality sign in section *a* of T1, and added: "No, one cannot give an answer without calculating", but did not explain it. This student provided the full explanation for T2. Three more students, who gave wrong explanations in T1, provided a full explanation in T2.

These data imply that, at least for some students, the context and the type of the explanation required, makes a difference. Explanations, which are a result of horizontal mathematization may be easier to produce than those involving vertical mathematization. However, other issues may be at stake. For example, a student, who provided a correct explanation for T2 and who wrote the correct inequality sign in T1, claimed that he could not give an answer without calculating: "Because if we will not calculate the result than we will not have the answer". This may be consistent with the belief that calculations should always be performed, in order to compare results of operations. Similarly, another student (who wrote the wrong inequality sign) claimed: "if I will not calculate, I will not know, and I will not understand as well". Namely, the lack of explanation in some cases may have less to do with the ability or the norm of explaining and more with the sophistication of the arithmetic knowledge, which students are just learning at this stage.

In class 8, the distributions of individual students' responses for the two tasks, is completely different (see Table 9.4).

Whereas in class 2 (see Table 9.3) the most frequent category was no explanation for both tasks, this cell is empty for class 8. For class 8 the most populated

TABLE 9.4 Class 8 (N = 23) cross-distribution of students' responses in T1 & T2

	No expl	Incorrect	Non-math	Partial	Full	Total T2
No expl.						
Incorrect		4% (1)	4% (1)	4% (1)		13% (3)
Non-math			4% (1)	4% (1)		9% (2)
Partial		4% (1)	4% (1)	4% (1)		13% (3)
Full		13% (3)	4% (1)	30% (7)	17% (4)	65% (15)
Total T1		22% (5)	17% (4)	43% (10)	17% (4)	100% (23)

cell is not on the table's diagonal but quite close; the cell where the responses for T1 are partially correct and the responses for T2 are correct and full (7 students, 30% of the students' number in the class). It is worth noticing that also in this class we found some evidence of the belief (although less widespread) that only calculations can guarantee the answer in T1. A student wrote: "if we will not calculate we will not know who will be the biggest, the smallest".

4   Discussion and Implications

In our view, this paper offers a contribution in terms of the results themselves and in terms of their theoretical and practical implications regarding young student's productions of mathematical explanations.

Firstly, we stress our general finding: when given the opportunity, many young students (as young as second graders), are capable of engaging in generating explanations in mathematics, in different contexts and of different nature. In our study, the explanations generated are not mere repetitions of what they may have heard in class, especially when they explain the features of a graph, which were not explicitly taught to most of them. Moreover, we note that what can be considered an alienating setting (explaining in writing in an exam situation) did not prevent them from generating explanations.

Secondly, our data display salient differences among the classes concerning explanations and explaining. The generation of explanations is much more frequent in certain classes than in others (e.g. whereas most of the students in class 8 provided explanations for both tasks, most students in class 2 did not explain in either task).

In our attempt to uncover factors, which may explain these differences, we found that most of the 17 classes showed similar percentages of students who engaged in explanations in both tasks (see Figures 9.1 & 9.2). The classes are spread all over the range, from very small percentage of explainers and growing towards higher percentages. We consider this as a striking result given the marked differences between the two tasks (as pointed out by our task analysis using the constructs of horizontal and vertical mathematization) and given the novelty of task 2 for most students, who were not previously exposed to data graphs. We conjectured that this result is possibly due to an inherent characteristic of a class which either provides (explicit or implicit) support for generating explanations and explaining (regardless of the task), or alternatively these activities are absent from their practice. This interpretation of the findings suggests that the presence (or absence) of the underlying meta-knowledge driving the production of explanations may be strongly related to the norms and the culture of a classroom. Tautological answers or the absence of responses can be attributed to lacking the sense of what explanations are all about, which in turn reflects their possible absence from classroom's practices.

What factors might be related to classroom culture and norms? We decided to investigate the effect of socio-economic background of the population of each of the 17 schools. We found no significant correlation of this factor with the presence or absence of explanations in the classes (see Figures 9.3–9.6). This brought us back to the norms of teaching and learning mathematics of a class rather than to the socio-economic background of its population.

Therefore, given the capabilities of students to generate explanations in different mathematical tasks, and given that this seems to happen in certain classes and not in others regardless of their socio-economic background, the role of orchestrating a classroom culture to support explaining seems crucial. We conclude that students should be exposed to explanations, even at very early ages and should be required to engage themselves in explaining within all areas of mathematics and with different types of explanations. It is only through that exposure and engagement that students will build meta-level understandings and enrich their knowledge base, which in turn will foster their capabilities to develop explanations. Teaching should include modeling of explanations by the teacher, discussing partial explanations of students with the whole class, posing challenges and stimulating argumentative dialogues.

Orchestrating such classroom culture is by no means simple but should be a central issue in the professional development of teachers.

References

Alibali, M. W. (2007). Mechanisms of change in the development of mathematical reasoning. *Advances in Child Development and Behavior, 33,* 79–123.

Brown, A. L., & Palincsar, A. S. (1989). Guided, cooperative learning and individual knowledge Acquisition. In L. B. Resnick (Ed.), *Knowing, learning and instruction* (pp. 393–452). Lawrence Erlbaum Associates.

Chi, M. T. H., & Bassok, M. (1989). Learning from examples via self-explanations. In L. B. Resnick (Ed.), *Knowing, learning and instruction* (pp. 251–282). Lawrence Erlbaum Associates.

Chi, M. T. H., de Leeuw, N., Chiu, M. H., & LaVancher, C. (1994). Eliciting self-explanations improves understanding. *Cognitive Science, 18,* 439–477.

Douek, N. (1999). Argumentation and conceptualisation in context: A case study on sun shadows in primary school. *Educational Studies in Mathematics, 39,* 89–110.

Dreyfus, T. (1999). Why Johnny can't prove. *Educational Studies in Mathematics, 38*(1–3), 85–109.

Freudenthal, H. (1991). *Revisiting mathematics education. China lectures.* Kluwer Academic Publishers.

Hershkowitz, R., Parzysz, B., & van Dormolen, J. (1996). Shape and space. In A. J. Bishop, K. Clements, C. Keitel, J. Kilpatrick, & C. Laborde (Eds.), *International handbook of mathematics education* (pp. 161–204). Kluwer Academic Publishers.

Krummheuer, G. (1995). The ethnography of argumentation. In P. Cobb & H. Bauersfeld (Eds.), *Emergence of mathematical meaning interaction in classroom cultures.* Lawrence Erlbaum Associates.

Leinhardt, G. (1987). Developing of an expert explanation: An analysis of a sequence of subtraction lessons. *Cognition and Instruction, 4,* 225–282.

Leinhardt, G., & Schwarz, B. (1997). Seeing the problem: An explanation from Polya. *Cognition and Instruction, 15,* 295–434.

Levenson, E., Tsamir, P., & Tirosh, D. (2007). First and second graders use of mathematically-based and practically-based explanations for multiplication with zero. *Focus on Learning Problems in Mathematics, 29*(2), 21–40.

Means, M. L., & Voss, J. F. (1996). Who reasons well? Two studies of informal reasoning among children of different grade, ability, and knowledge levels. *Cognition and Instruction, 14,* 139–178.

Pimm, D. (1987). *Speaking mathematically communication in the classrooms.* Routledge.

Schwarz, B. B., & Asterhan, C. S. C. (2009). Argumentation and reasoning. In K. Littleton, C. Wood, & J. Kleine Staarman (Eds.), *The handbook of education: the psychology of teaching and learning* (pp. 137–176). Emerald.

Sfard, A. (2001). Learning mathematics as developing a discourse. In R. Speiser, C. Maher, & C. Walter, (Eds.), *Proceedings of 21st conference of PME-NA* (pp. 23–44). Clearing House for Science, mathematics, and environmental education.

Toulmin, S. (1958). *The uses of argument.* Cambridge University Press.

Traffers, A., & Goffree, F. (1985). Rational analysis of realistic mathematics education. In L. Streefland (Ed.), *Proceeding of the 9th International Conference for the Psychology of Mathematics Education* (Vol. II, pp. 97–123). OW&OC.

PART 5

Early Childhood Mathematics Teachers' Knowledge and Professional Development

∵

CHAPTER 10

Between Natural Language and Mathematical Symbols (<, >, =)

The Comprehension of Pre-Service and Preschool Teachers' Perspective of "Numbers" and "Quantity"

Bat-Sheva Ilany and Dina Hassidov

Abstract

Many activities for children in preschool and even higher grades ask them to compare non-mathematical objects using mathematical relational symbols (i.e. =, <, >). This can lead to incidents where a first-grade child will write "6 < **4**", for example, because the four looks bigger and thicker than the six, indicating that the child is relating to the numbers as graphical entities and not as mathematical ones. Such cases have led to studies on how pre-service preschool teachers and preschool teachers understand, use, and intend to teach this topic.

This paper reports on an ongoing, 15-year, quantitative-and-qualitative study about how groups of pre-service (n = 71) and preschool (n = 149) teachers understand the concepts that constitute part of symbolic thinking, in particular, their understanding and use of the mathematical relational symbols <, >, and = when comparing numbers, figures, and shapes of different sizes and thicknesses. While there was a significant difference between how the two groups validated their answers, the fact remained that the majority of participants did not answer the questions correctly, which indicates that they do not understand that mathematical symbols should be used only in the mathematical context.

Keywords

preschool teachers – pre-service teachers – mathematics education – early childhood – mathematical symbol

1   Theoretical Background

1.1   *Mathematical Language in Early Childhood*

Mathematical language in Early Childhood is a language of symbols, concepts, definitions, and theorems. It does not develop naturally like a child's natural language, but needs to be taught (Ilany & Margolin, 2010). Hiebert (1988) emphasizes the importance of the connection between advanced cognitive processes and understanding written mathematical symbols. His approach relies on, among other things, theories of mathematical psychology.

In essence, children are engaged in mathematics in daily life from birth, and today's global trend is to introduce "formal" mathematics at a young age. Preschool math practice aims to develop mathematical awareness and cultivate mathematical thinking from an early age, thus shaping the child's future mathematical thinking, general thinking, and cognitive abilities. Studies have shown that the volume and quality of preschool math practice predict a child's success in math in elementary school (Clements & Sarama, 2006, 2015).

According to the accepted Israeli curriculum, first skills include being able to use the concepts (not the actual symbols) of "bigger", "smaller", and "equal to" to recognize differences between objects. Some preschool teachers introduce the mathematical symbols =, <, and > already in preschool and, unfortunately, ask the children to use these mathematical relational symbols to compare non-mathematical objects. This leads children to believe that these symbols are not restricted to mathematical values and, moreover, even when comparing numbers, to use them incorrectly. For example, a child in grade one may write "6 < **4**" because the four looks bigger and thicker than the six, indicating that he is looking at the numbers as graphical entities and not mathematical ones. Such instances have led to the study of how pre-service teachers (PST) and preschool teachers (PT) themselves use these mathematical symbols.

1.2   *Mathematical Comparison and Relations of Order*

This paper deals with a study that relates to the understanding of the concepts that constitute part of symbolic thinking. We will present a mathematical reference to these concepts (Sinitsky & Ilany, 2016). Different quantities are compared through relations of order using various strategies based on the properties of these relations. According to Cantor's (Dauben, 1971) sorting principles, the set of real numbers has an intrinsic linear order. In other words, between any two quantities, one and only one of three following options holds true:

1.   The two values are equal to each other.
2.   The first is greater than the second.
3.   The first is smaller than the second.

If we plot real numbers on a number line, two numbers, a and b, are equal only if the points that represent them coincide. If b is greater than a, the point representing b will be to the right of a. Here, we can also say that a is less than b. It is useful to present the ways that a relationship between two quantities can be described by using three pairs of relations, where each proposition of the pair is the negation of the other:

$$a = b \qquad a \neq b$$
$$a > b \qquad a \leq b$$
$$a < b \qquad a \geq b$$

Recall that the strategies used to compare two quantities are based on the general properties of comparison relations. The relation of equality is an equivalence and maintains the three properties of any equivalence relation: reflexivity, $a = b$ (each value is equal to itself); symmetry, $a = b \Leftrightarrow b = a$; and transitivity, $a = b \& b = c \Rightarrow a = c$ (two values equal to a third are also equal to each other).

The relations of greater than and less than are strict ($a > a$ is never true) and asymmetric (there is no pair where both $a > b$ and $b > a$ are true it holds transitivity. This last property ($a < b$, $b < c \Rightarrow a < c$) is expressed in the well-known "rule of transition" (similar to equality): if one value is less than another, and that second value is less than a third, then the first is less than the third.

1.3   *The Development of Symbolic Understanding in Early Childhood*
The early development of symbolic reasoning in children should allow them to properly use mathematical symbols later in formal math.

Symbolic reasoning means the ability to grasp the meaning of a symbol representing an object or idea, without having an expression in the symbol itself (Bialystok, 1992). For example, an evolving ability and one of the developing expressions of thought (Thomas, Jolley, Robinson & Champion, 1999). Its development is characterized by changes that occur in the form of the mental representation of an object. Young children believe that the symbolic representation reflects the nature of the object it represents (Bialystok, 1992), For example, children may write the names of large objects using large letters (Thomas et al., 1999). Nemirovsky and Monk (2000) noted that young children do not distinguish between the symbol and the object that the symbol represents.

Many studies have examined how children of various ages comprehend the "equal" sign (e.g.: Mark-Zigdon & Tirosh, 2008). They show that children aged 5–12 tend to perceive the equal sign as an operational symbol and not as a sign of comparison. PST translate the symbols as a command to perform a mathematical operation. It is important to grasp that the meaning of a symbol cannot be changed by non-mathematical factors (such as a change in size or other physical factor).

1.4   Teaching Mathematics by Preschool Teachers

Teaching mathematics to preschoolers today requires professional knowledge on the part of the PT (Charalambous, Panaoura, & Philippou, 2009). Preschool teachers must have adequate knowledge of teaching mathematics in kindergarten and grades 1 and 2, and it is important that preschool teachers have appropriate mathematical background and knowledge (Mulligan, 2016). Unfortunately, studies conducted in recent years indicate that preschool teachers assigned with teaching preschool mathematics do not have adequate knowledge. This may stem from negative personal experiences or a lack of appropriate training in college (Hassidov & Ilany, 2014, 2015). They often use the knowledge and experience they bring from daily life, meaning that they might not always give the correct mathematical importance to the symbol. If the teachers incorrectly understand the use of mathematical symbols, it is reasonable to assume that they will subsequently pass this misinformation on to the children, leading to incorrect use in the future. It is thus crucial to teach the proper mathematical use of symbols from the preschool level (Hassidov & Ilany, 2017). Although young children can identify symbols and write them, this does not necessarily reflect an understanding of the symbols' mathematical meaning or their relationship to numbers. The concept of equality is an especially difficult concept to comprehend for children, since this term can be used both relationally and mathematically. Using the = symbol incorrectly with children makes it even harder for them to properly understand its concept.

2   Research Questions

This study examines how pre-service preschool (PST) and veteran preschool teachers (PT) understand the concepts of (>, <, and =). Its objectives were twofold:

1.   How do pre-service preschool teachers and preschool teachers comprehend and use the relational symbols (>, <, and =) in perspective of "Numbers" and "Quantity"?
2.   Is there any difference between how the two groups comprehend and use these symbols?

3 Methodology

3.1 *Population*

The study population comprised 71 second- or third-year PST participating in a year-long course dedicated to the teaching and learning of mathematics in early childhood and 149 veteran PT.

3.2 *Research Tools*

Data were collected via semi-structured interviews and a 25-item questionnaire designed by the authors. Of the 25 questions in the questionnaire, eight (questions 1, 2, 3, 17 and 7, 9, 10, 16) addressed the use of mathematical symbols between shapes and numbers that had some graphical difference (size, thickness, placement) (Table 10.1). Respondents were asked to either place a relational symbol between two figures or indicate "X" if they believed there was no appropriate answer, and then justify their answers. Analysis was both qualitative and quantitative.

Questionnaires were filled out by the PST before any formal study of the subject. The researchers interviewed a random sampling of 30 PST. This was followed by a class discussion on the use and meaning of mathematical symbols, and the subject's place in the preschool curriculum. Questionnaires were filled out by the preschool and then individual interviews were conducted to ascertain the PT reasoning for their answers. Relevant background information was collected.

4 Results

Overall, not one of the participants gave the correct answer and justification for questions 1, 2, 3, and 17. Even the very few who gave the correct answer ("X") gave flawed justifications, the correct one being that these symbols cannot be used for graphical objects and only for numerical entities. A significant difference was found between the two groups: a large number of PT did not supply any justification for their reasoning (58.4% for question 1, and 57.7%, 60.4%, and 66.4% for questions 2, 3, and 17, respectively) compared to the number of PST who did not (19.8%, 14.1%, 16.9%, 28.2%, respectively).

Questions for example: 2, 17 (Quantitative) asked which mathematical symbol, if any, should be placed between the shapes of different sizes and thickness.

Question 2: contained three smileys. The results were similar to question 1: most did not answer "X", and those who did, justified it incorrectly. Similarly, there was a significant difference (p < 0.001) between the groups (see Table 10.2). The vast majority of both PST and PT answered "=", indicating that they focused on the number of smileys (numerical properties). However, one pre-school teacher said:

There are the same numbers of smileys, but the area is different.

That is, her answer was based on quantity, but her justification also considered the shape. Another wrote:

I counted the smileys.

TABLE 10.1   Quantitative (questions 1, 2, 3, and 17) and numerical (questions 7, 9, 10, and 16) analysis of the responses of PST and PT (all values represent percentages, correct answer)

Question			Answers						
		<		>		=		X	
		PT	PST	PT	PST	PT	PST	PT	PST
1	☺☺ □ ☺☺☺	98	100	0	0	0	0	2	0
2	☺☺☺ □ ☺☺☺	5	0	16	6	74	94	4	0
3	(smileys figure) □ (smileys figure)	95.4	96	1.3	1	1.3	3	3	0
7	▼ + ▲ □ ◆	1.3	0	2.7	4	92	90	4	6
7	1/2 □ 1/4	14.1	0	*80.5	*97.2	0.7	0	4.7	2.8
9	5 □ 5	0	0	26.2	14.1	*70.5	*77.5	3.3	8.4
10	6 □ 4	17.4	2.8	*77.9	*91.6	0	0	4.7	5.6
16	2 × 3 □ 6	1.3	0	6	0	*86	*98.6	6.7	1.4

Notes: Differences between correct answers: Question 7 p* = 0.001, distribution p = 0.006; Question 10 p* = 0.01, distribution p = 0.01; Question 16 p* = 0.003, distribution p = 0.032.

TABLE 10.2   Quantitative analysis (value and percent) of the justifications given by PST and PT to questions: 1; 2; 3; 17

Justification for question 1		Graphic properties*	Numerical properties*	Both size and quantity*	No answer*	Number who gave correct justification
PST	N	1	56	0	14	0
N = 71	%	1.4	78.8	0	19.8	0
PT	N	6	53	3	87	0
N = 149	%	4	35.6	2	58.4	0
Justification for question 2						
PST	N	2	52	7	10	0
N = 71	%	2.8	73.2	9.9	14.1	0
PT	N	18	41	4	86	0
N = 149	%	12.1	27.5	2.7	57.7	0
Justification for question 3						
PST	N	1	57	1	12	0
N = 71	%	1.4	80.3	1.4	16.9	0
PT	N	3	54	2	90	0
N = 149	%	2.1	36.2	1.3	60.4	0
Justification for question 17						Another answer X	Number who gave correct justification
PST	N	10	36	4	20	1	0
N = 71	%	14.1	50.7	5.6	28.2	1.4	0
PT	N	4	44	1	99	1	0
N = 149	%	2.7	29.5	0.7	66.4	0.7	0

*$p < 0.001$

One wrote:

> Based on my experience, I would teach that the second is larger. But there can be different levels.

Indicating that she feels that different criteria can be used under different circumstances. One PST teacher wrote:

> I looked at the number of smileys. There is no importance to the length of the rectangle, only the number.

One PST teacher indicated "=" but wrote:

> There are the same quantities in each rectangle, although the left rectangle has a greater area.

Those who indicated "<" justified their answer by indicating either the size or thickness of the rectangles. One preschool teacher answered:

> They look to me to be the same, except that one rectangle is longer.

A PST teacher who marked "<" wrote "the rectangle on the right is thicker and coloured". Again, although 4% of the PT gave the correct answer ("X") their justifications were incorrect. For example:

> They cannot be compared because the shapes are not the same.

Question 17: Each side had two triangles, one being "upside down". On the left, they were in a single row with a plus sign ("+") between them. On the right, they were one on top of the other. Once again, the vast majority (94% of PST and 96% of PT) answered incorrectly and there was a significant difference ($p < 0.001$) between the justifications they gave (Table 10.2). One preschool teacher who indicated ">" said:

> There are two triangles and the addition operation, so that side is larger than the right side.

One who indicated "=" wrote, "We haven't learned this yet". Another gave an answer that seemed confused:

> They are equal from two standpoints. One is that on each side one triangle goes up, and one goes down. So, they make the shape of an equilateral diamond.

A teacher who indicated "=" said:

> The placement of the triangles is not important. What is important is their quantity.

One PST who answered "X" justified it and said:

There is no answer because I didn't know which symbol to use. There are two triangles on each side, but they are not arranged the same.

Some PT answered "X" because they did not know which of the others to use.

Questions for example: 7, 9, 10, 16 (Numerical) asked which mathematical symbol, if any, should be placed between numbers of different sizes and thickness.

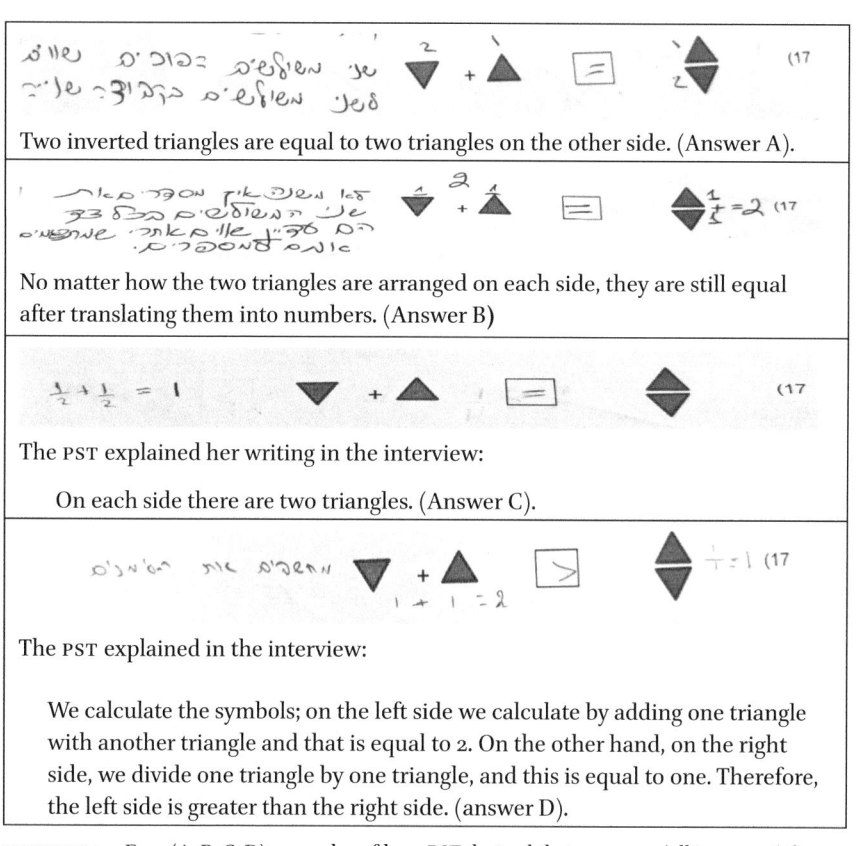

FIGURE 10.1   Four (A, B, C, D) examples of how PST derived their answers (all incorrect) for question 17

Question 9: Table 10.1 shows that 77.5% of the PST and 70.5% of the teachers answered correctly, but as can be seen in Table 10.3, only 45.1% of the PST and 16.1% of the teachers who answered correctly gave the correct explanation. Of those who gave an incorrect explanation, 2.8% of the PST and 13.4% of the teachers gave the reason to be the graphic form of the numbers, and 12.7% of PST and 4.7% of the teachers referred to the quantity of items (one numeral)

TABLE 10.3   Numerical analysis (value and percent) of the justifications given by PST and PT to questions: 7; 9; 10 and 16

	PST	N = 71	PT	N = 149
Justification for question 7: 1/2 □ 1/4	%	N	%	N
Justification for correct answers				
None given.	19.7	14	49.7	74
The sequence of numbers.	18.3	13	2.7	4
A quarter plus a quarter equals half.	11.3	8	2.0	3
Because half is greater than a quarter.	32.4	23	12.8	19
Based on number of items.	14.1	10	13.4	20
Justification for incorrect answers				
None given.	0	0	14.1	21
The ¼ is larger according to the picture but ½ is larger according to quantity.	4.2	3	0	0
Based on graphic property.	0	0	0.7	1
We never learned fractions.	0	0	4.7	7
Justification for question 9: 5 □ 5	%	N	%	N
Justification for correctly answered				
None given.	16.9	12	36.2	54
The sequence of numbers.	45.1	32	16.1	24
Incorrect reason (based on graphic property).	2.8	2	13.4	20
Based on number of items.	12.7	9	4.7	7
Justification for incorrect answers				
None given	2.8	2	16.8	25
Both have the same value but differ in size and thickness.	8.5	6	1.3	2
The left number is larger than that the right one.	11.3	8	11.4	17
Justification for question 10: 6 □ 4	%	N	%	N
Justification for correct answers				
None given.	19.7	14	47	70
The sequence of numbers.	63.4	45	24.8	37
Incorrect justification.	0	0	0.7	1
Based on number of items.	8.5	6	5.4	8
Justification for incorrect answers				
None given	0	0	14.1	21
There is no answer because 4 is graphically larger but 6 is numerically larger.	5.6	4	0.7	1
The 4 is larger because of the size.	2.8	2	7.4	11

(cont.)

TABLE 10.3   Numerical analysis (value and percent) of the justifications given by PST and PT to questions: 7; 9; 10 and 16 (*cont.*)

	PST	N = 71	PT	N = 149
Justification for question 16: 2 × 3 □ 6	%	N	%	N
Justification for correct answers				
None given.	22.5	16	55.7	83
The sequence of numbers.	53.5	38	28.9	43
Based on quantity.	22.5	16	1.3	2
Justification for incorrect answers				
None given	0	0	8.1	12
We didn't learn this subject	1.4	1	2	3
Because of the size of the numeral.	0	0	4	6

on each side. One reason given by a teacher indicated her deliberation between the graphic or numerical quality of the numbers:

> It depends on how one looks at the question: according to shape, one is larger than the other; according to numerical value, they are equal.

Of those who answered incorrectly, 8.5% of the PST and 1.3% of the teachers argued that no mark could be put between the digits because there can be multiple answers based on how one looked at the question ("Both numbers have the same value but not the same size and thickness"). 11.3% of the PST and 11.4% of the PT argued the number on the left is larger. One PST wrote:

> Looking at the numbers, they are equal in terms of quantity or value, but the type is bigger and it's confusing. (Figure 10.2)

Question 10: Table 10.1 shows that 91.6% of the PT answered correctly compared with 77.9% of PT (Table 10.3). This question deals with getting to know

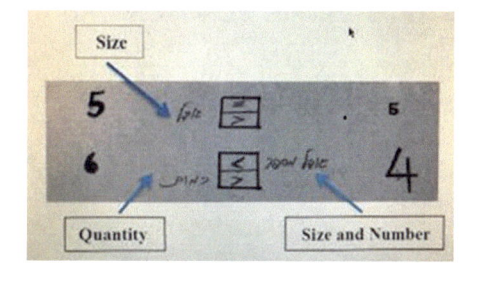

FIGURE 10.2
Example of how PT derived an answer

the first ten numbers. From Table 10.1 it could be seen that there is a significant difference in the scattering distribution between kindergarten PST to PT ($\chi^2_{(2)}$ = [9.271, p = 0.01]). It can also be seen that 91.6% of the PT answered correctly, compared to 77.9% of the kindergarten PT (($\chi^2_{(1)}$ = [6.19, p = 0.01]). In Table 10.3 we see that 63.4% of the PST and 24.8% of the PT correctly explained that it was due to the sequence of numbers. Some participants (8.5% of PST, 5.4% of PT) incorrectly based their answer on the number of items on each side and not their numerical value. Of the incorrect answers, 17.4% of the PT, but only 2.8% of the PST answered that "four" was larger than "six" based on the numbers' graphic properties.

Question 16: Table 10.1 shows that 98.6% of the PST answered correctly compared with 86% of PT (p < 0.01). Of the 21 (14.1%) of PT who answered incorrectly, 10 answered "X", claiming that a number of answers were possible, and 9 (6%) claimed that 3 × 2 was greater than 6 due to the graphic properties of the numerals (Tables 10.1 and 10.3).

Additional findings: Figure 10.3 shows an example of the answers given by one pre-service teacher to 7 questions (2, 3, 4, 5, 6, 7, and 8). His reasoning can be understood by observing that he translated each graphical object into a numeric quantity.

Another pre-service teacher showed inconsistencies between questions 1 and 2 although he indicated "X" (correct answer), he explained that:

The drawings do not represent numbers because they are inaccurate.

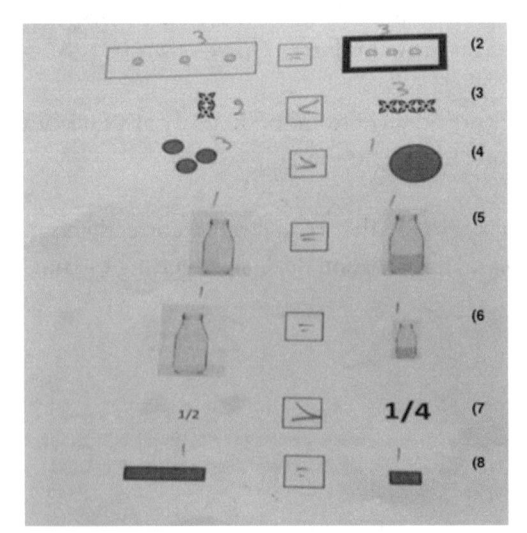

FIGURE 10.3
Example of how PT derived an
answer to questions 2–8

He indicated different symbols between the two sets of bottles based on quantity or size or volume.

One pre-service teacher who marked "=" for question 2 wrote that:

> The smileys are equal in both rectangles, what is different is length of the frame.

The same student referred to other criteria in other questions, for example, in question 3, he referred to the length of the design, and in question 4, he gave the correct symbol (X), but his reasoning was that:

> It is irrelevant in terms of size and volume.

Interviews and discussions with the PST and PT revealed that most of them thought it was possible to use more than one mathematical symbol, between numbers, as an answer.

5   Discussion and Conclusions

The conclusions arising from this study (derived from the explanations and the interviews) are that some preschool teachers and a large proportion of pre-service teachers do not correctly understand the meaning of the relational symbols $(<, >, =)$, and therefore they are or will be improperly teaching this concept to their pupils.

For example, the study showed that when asked to insert the correct symbol in the expression **5 □ 5**, some participants placed BOTH the "=":
- Because they are both the same number and also the ">":
- Because the size and thickness of the 5, on the left is greater.

This indicates that their frame of reference in the second case was graphic and not mathematical. In other words, they believed that either of the two relational marks is appropriate depending on their frame of reference (mathematical or graphical). This error is the result of a lack of understanding of the essence of both relational mathematical symbols and numerical digits, that is, that such symbols should only be used in the mathematical sense. Participants indicated this, since they often related to the graphical characteristic of the numerals and not to its mathematical one. Some participants even used two symbols simultaneously, such as using both the "=" and the ">" between the same numbers, as shown in the example. This error stems from a lack of understanding of the mathematical significance of both numerals and relational symbols. That is to say, they considered that these symbols could also be used in a non-mathematical sense.

> We teach children that in the case of **5** > 5, the size and thickness determine the answer, whereas in other cases the length or the height may determine the answer, and that it depends on the context.

The scientific literature describes a phenomenon known as the "Stroop effect", first described in England in 1935 by John Ridley Stroop, which is a demonstration of cognitive interference due to a mismatch of stimuli when an individual is performing a cognitive assignment. There is note in the scientific literature of a numerical Stroop effect, in which participants were asked to specify which digit of two is larger – once regarding the physical size of the numeral (font size) and then regarding the value of the numeral. Results showed that some participants erred, and the researchers claimed that this was a result of the Stroop effect (Algom, Dekel, & Pansky, 1996).

A situation may arise in which children may experience the numerical Stroop effect. Thus, it is important to ensure that children understand the precise meaning of numerals and the relational mathematical symbols, especially since, at the beginning of their mathematical journey, children tend to write the numerals in different sizes and shapes. If preschool teachers erroneously relate to numerals as graphical objects and do not emphasize the mathematical significance of the numeral, they can mislead the children; consequently the child may take it to understand that at times the size of the numerals, rather than their numerical value, will determine the appropriate relationship. This study found that most of the participants failed to answer the questions correctly. The justifications given to the questions show a significant difference between the PST and PT with respect to how many justified their answers, yet it is clear that all participants did not appreciate the significance of the mathematical symbols and how to use them, specifically, that mathematical symbols should be used only for mathematical symbols. This was clear since even when the answer given was correct ("X"), the justification was generally incorrect (Hassidov & Ilany, 2017; Ilany & Hassidov, 2018).

The results of this study show that pre-service teachers and preschool teachers feel that mathematical symbols may be used in different ways, depending on context: sometimes with respect to the quantity and sometimes to the shape or size of graphical images and they did not restrict them only to their mathematical significance. The conclusion is that the participants do not properly understand the significance of the symbols =, <, and > nor how to use them. This will, in all probability, mean that they will not teach the concepts properly to preschoolers. Indeed, studies have shown that PT believe the signs can be used in many ways.

Three types of misunderstandings were detected:
1. Misunderstanding that mathematical symbols relate only to numerical situations in primary mathematic.
2. Misunderstanding that a graphic object cannot be treated as a number.
3. Not understanding and knowledge of the mathematical conventions behind these symbols, that there is always one, and only one, unique symbol that can be placed between two numerals.

Even in cases where they answered correctly, the reasoning was incorrect. False perceptions regarding the meaning of the mathematical relational signs can be a result of using identical words in everyday life and in mathematics (Ilany & Margolin, 2010).

One way to lead teachers to understand the correct meaning and use of the relational symbols is by means of activities that exhibit the cognitive conflicts that can arise followed by a discussion of the subject.

It is important to emphasize that, like any language, the mathematical language has its own rules and symbols – numerals, operational symbols, relational symbols, and more – that allow the language to exist and this understanding must be strengthened among those involved in the teaching of mathematics.

Using the same words in everyday life and in mathematics, leads to misconceptions regarding the meaning of the mathematical signs. Examples of this are the use of the words "larger than", smaller than", and "equal" in natural language in everyday life for non-mathematical situations and their use as the mathematical language for the symbols $>$, $<$ and $=$.

Preschool teachers thus do not see any problem if a child writes "$5 > 5$", and have stated that they teach the child to use the symbol "$>$" between two objects, as

> In this case the size is important; in another case the length may be important. It depends on the context.

Preschool teachers may even believe it is correct to use two different signs at the same time; however, they must understand the cognitive conflict that this gives children and must understand that it is never possible to use two different signs between two numbers at the same time.

Some preschool teachers must be made aware that the signs $<$, $>$, and $=$ must be used only in the mathematical sense. Preschool teachers who incorrectly see quantity as a graphical concept and do not see the mathematical significance will, most likely, pass on this misconception to the children. This might lead the children to think that the size of the number or graphical object is what determines the relationship and which symbol to use.

It is important to emphasize that, like any language, the mathematical language has its own rules and symbols – numbers, operational symbols, relational symbols. It enables the language to exist and this awareness must be reinforced among those involved in the teaching of mathematics, "best practices" and what we should aim for as mathematics educators.

References

Algom, D., Dekel, A., & Pansky, A. (1996). The perception of number from the separability of the stimulus: The Stroop effect revisited. *Memory & Cognition, 24*(5), 557–572. https://doi.org/10.3758/BF03201083

Bialystok, E. (1992). Symbolic representation of letters and numbers. *Cognitive Development, 7*, 301–316.

Charalambous, C. Y., Panaoura, A., & Philippou, G. (2009). Using the history of mathematics to induce changes in pre-service teachers' beliefs and attitudes: Insights from evaluating a teacher education program. *Educational Studies in Mathematics, 71*, 161–180.

Clements, D. H., & Sarama, J. (2006). Young children's mathematical mind. *Scholastic Parent & Child*, 30–37.

Clements, D. H., & Sarama, J. (2015). Developing young children's mathematical thinking and understanding. In S. Robson & S. Flannery (Eds.), *The Routledge international handbook of young children's thinking and understanding* (pp. 331–344). Routledge.

Dauben, J. (1971). The trigonometric background to Georg Cantor's theory of sets. *Archive for History of Exact Sciences, 7*, 181–216.

Hassidov, D., & Ilany, B. (2014). A unique program ("Senso-Math") for teaching mathematics in preschool: Evaluating facilitator training. *Creative Education (CE), 5*(11), 976–988. https://www.scirp.org/journal/paperinformation.aspx?paperid=47205

Hassidov, D., & Ilany, B. (2015). The "Senso-Math" preschool program: Successful cooperation between mathematics facilitators and preschool teachers. In *Proceedings of the 39th Conference of the International Group for the Psychology of Mathematics* (Vol. 3, pp. 41–48). PME.

Hassidov, D., & Ilany, B. (2017). Between natural language and mathematical symbols (<, >, =): The comprehension of pre-service and preschool teachers-perspective of numbers. *Creative Education, 8*, 1903–1911. https://doi.org/10.4236/ce.2017.812130

Hiebert, J. (1988). A theory of developing competence with written mathematical symbols. *Educational Studies in Mathematics, 19,* 333–355.

Ilany, B., & Hassidov, D. (2018). Perspective of "quantity" – Between natural language and mathematical symbols $(<, >, =)$: The comprehension of pre-service and preschool teachers. Special issue "teaching and teacher education". *Creative Education (CE), 9*(10), 1525–1535. https://www.scirp.org/journal/paperinformation.aspx?paperid=86502

Ilany, B., & Margolin, B. (2010). Language and mathematics: Bridging between natural language and mathematical language in solving problems in mathematics. *Creative Education (CE), 1*(3), 138–148. https://www.scirp.org/journal/paperinformation.aspx?paperid=3360

Mark-Zigdon, N., & Tirosh, D. (2008). What counts and what does not count as legitimate arithmetic number sentences: The case of kindergarten and first grade children. In J. J. Kaput, M. Blanton, & D. Carraher (Eds.), *Algebra in the early grades* (pp. 201–210). Lawrence Erlbaum Associates.

Mulligan, J. T. (2016, July 24–31). Promoting early mathematical structural development though an integrated assessment and pedagogical program. In *Program of the 13th International Congress on Mathematical Education Topic Study Group 1: Early childhood mathematics education.*

Nemirovsky, R., & Monk, S. (2000). "If you look at it the other way …". An exploration into the nature of symbolizing". In P. Cobb, E. Yackel, & K. McClain (Eds.), *Symbolizing and communicating in mathematics classrooms: Perspectives on discourse, tools, and instructional design* (pp. 233–257). Lawrence Erlbaum.

Sinitsky, I., & Ilany, B. (2016). *Change and invariance – Algebraic insight into numbers and shapes.* Sense Publishers.

Thomas, G. V., Jolley, R. P., Robinson, E. J., & Champion, H. (1999). Realist errors in children's responses to pictures and words as representations. *Journal of Experimental Child Psychology, 74,* 1–20.

CHAPTER 11

Investigation of Mathematical-Pedagogical Knowledge among Prospective Teachers in the Early Childhood Program at the College for Arabic Speakers

Juhaina Awawdeh Shahbari

Abstract

This chapter examines whether the training given to first- and second-grade mathematics teachers provides them with an adequate level of mathematical and pedagogical content knowledge. The participants in the study consisted of 150 first- and second-grade in-service mathematics teachers and 150 pre-service mathematics teachers studying in the Early Childhood Education track. Mathematical and pedagogical content knowledge was examined via two tests relating to content taught in first and second grade. These tests included four sub-domains: numbers, arithmetic operations, geometry/measurements, and word problems. The findings indicate inadequate levels of both mathematical content and pedagogical knowledge among the three groups studied.

Keywords

mathematical content knowledge – pedagogical content knowledge – pre-service teachers – mathematics teacher

1 Introduction

Up until a few years ago, teachers for first and second grades were trained through the Department of Early Childhood Education. This training process is similar to the training process in various countries around the world and allows teachers to teach language, science, and mathematics (Akerson, 2004; Cheang et al., 2007; Horm-Wingerd, Hyson & Karp, 2000). The lack of specialized training in mathematics was highlighted in a comprehensive study conducted in the United States, in which all first and second grade mathematics teachers studied lacked a major specialization in mathematics or mathematics education (Malzan, 2002). In recent research Flower (2020) indicate that in the United States the most teachers in first and second grades with a qualification of general elementary education. Ginsburg, Lee and Boyd (2008) emphasized that the number of courses related to mathematics or mathematics education in early childhood training tracks in colleges and universities is very small or even nonexistent. The present study was conducted to examine whether training for prospective teachers in the first and second grades of the Early Childhood Education Program at the College for Arabic Speakers provides learners with the various knowledge components of mathematics needed in first and second grades.

2 Background

2.1 *Mathematical Content Knowledge and Pedagogical Content Knowledge*

Mathematical content knowledge includes knowledge about the structure of knowledge, facts, theories and principles related to the field (Shulman, 1986). Mathematical content knowledge is considered by Ball, Thame and Phelps (2008) as knowledge of common mathematical content and unique mathematical knowledge. Knowledge of common mathematical content refers to content knowledge shared by mathematically educated individuals who are not necessarily teachers, including basic algorithmic and procedural knowledge for problem solving and the ability to define and write mathematical concepts correctly (Delaney, Ball, Hill, Schilling & Hill, 2004). Knowledge of unique mathematical content for teachers includes the knowledge and skills required for teaching mathematics to students (Delaney et al., 2008). The component of content knowledge is expressed in knowledge and insight into the historical development of key mathematical concepts, which are considered an inseparable part of existing mathematics. It is also expressed in the interrelationship between ideas, analogies, and images related to different principles (Davis & Simmt, 2006).

Pedagogical content knowledge combines content knowledge with pedagogic knowledge, and it deals with adapting specific content and organizing it for students while understanding the reasons that make learning easy or difficult. In addition, pedagogic knowledge deals with the different ways of presenting the subject, building on the students' previous knowledge, and common mistakes related to the content or concept learned and the difficulties involved in learning it (Shulman, 1986). Pedagogical content knowledge is considered to be the core of the understanding of content and pedagogy (Ball, Lubinski & Mewborn, 2001). Ball and her colleagues (Ball et al., 2008) refer to two categories of pedagogical content knowledge: the first is knowledge of content and students that includes awareness of how students think and understand; the second category, knowledge of content and teaching, combines knowledge of mathematics and knowledge of instruction (Hill, Ball & Schilling, 2008). An extensive breakdown of pedagogic knowledge components has been proposed in the research literature, such as elements relating to the teachers' understanding of the structures and mathematical links, the teachers' knowledge of a variety of alternative representations of concepts for explanation, the ability of teachers to analyze cognitive demands of mathematical tasks, the ability of teachers to understand students' learning difficulties and abilities to take appropriate action to address them (Cheang et al., 2007). Additional components include knowledge related to the curriculum including teaching goals, knowledge of the design and teaching of mathematics, including the design of mathematics classes and the choice of different activities, the choice of evaluation patterns, the prediction of typical responses of students, including misconceptions, etc. Teachers must also have knowledge of the learning and teaching of mathematics within an action, including evaluation of student solutions and the discourse created and analyzed, analysis of the content of students' questions, diagnosis of student answers, explanation of mathematical concepts or procedures, and more (Tatto et al., 2008).

2.2 Knowledge of Mathematical Content and Pedagogical Knowledge among Prospective Mathematics Teachers

Mathematical content knowledge and pedagogical knowledge have been extensively studied and research findings (Livy & Vale, 2011; Venkat & Spaull, 2015) indicate limited and insufficient knowledge among prospective mathematics teachers. The limitations of knowledge among prospective mathematics teachers have been exposed regarding knowledge of one mathematical concept or subject (Tutak, 2009) in rational numbers (Depaepe, Torbeyns, Vermeersch, Janssens, Janssen, Kelchtermans, & Van Dooren, 2015), in ratios (Livy & Vale, 2011); in proportional problem (Burgos & Godino, 2020); in averages (De Haro & Moll, 2014); in number sense performances (Aktaş & Özdemir, 2017); and in number of components belonging to different topics (Cheang et al., 2007; Shirvani, 2015);

Despite the extensive review of mathematical content knowledge and pedagogical knowledge among prospective mathematics teachers, there is little reference to knowledge related to first and second grades and to prospective teachers who are supposed to teach in these classes (Mewborn, 2001). Mewborn (2001) suggests that the lack of reference to the lower grades stems from the assumption that teachers understand topics such as addition and subtraction, integers, and other basic subjects.

2.3 Methods of Testing Mathematic Content Knowledge and Mathematic Pedagogical Knowledge

The best way to test teachers' knowledge is not by the number of courses they have taken but by testing their knowledge in content of specific subjects (Ball et al., 2001). Indeed, research literature is rich in studies that examine content knowledge among students through the use of various tasks. Some of the studies used ready-made tests of students' knowledge, such as the TIMSS (Trends in International Mathematics and Science Study) for grades 4 and 8 (Tatto et al., 2008). Another approach to testing teachers' content knowledge proposes that the test should include the specific knowledge that teachers are supposed to teach in classrooms and at least two levels of knowledge above. Accordingly, it was proposed to examine elementary school teachers' content knowledge through basic concepts including the four arithmetic operations, comparison and arithmetic operations in simple fractions, decimal numbers, percentages, measurements, and word problems (Southwell, White, Way & Perry, 2006). In another study, Hill, Rowan and Ball (2005) examined teachers' mathematical knowledge with items relating to numbers and arithmetic operations up to grade 8, as well as items related to functions and amplification to that level. The scales that were selected by Goulding (2003) used questions in algebra, proofs, measurements, probability and statistics, to examine the knowledge of prospective primary school teachers.

Each study used a different index for testing pedagogical knowledge. Several studies used items representing different topics to test general content knowledge, for example, Chin et al. (2007), which examined pedagogical knowledge by means of items relating to four main topics: numbers, geometry, algebra, and data processing. Other research focused on testing pedagogical knowledge on specific mathematical subjects, for example Hill et al. (2005), which examined special mathematics knowledge of first and third grade teachers by analyzing strategies for students' solutions to exercises in four arithmetic operations.

3 Methodology

3.1 Research Questions

1. What is prospective teachers' in the Early Childhood Education track mathematical and pedagogical knowledge related to first and second grades in four areas (numbers, arithmetic operations, geometry, and word problems)?
2. How does the level of mathematical content knowledge and pedagogic knowledge in these four areas among prospective teachers in the early

childhood education track at the beginning of the training process differ from prospective teachers at the end of the training process?

3.2   *Sample*

The sample included 150 prospective teachers in the Early Childhood Track at the College for Teaching Training in Israel, 75 first-year prospective teachers and 75 third- and fourth-year prospective teachers. 97% of the participants indicated that they wanted to teach in first and second grades, and only 3% indicated that they intended to teach in kindergarten. 71% of the participants had completed a 3-unit mathematics secondary school matriculation program, 26% of them completed 4 units, and only 3% of the subjects studied at a level of 5 units.

3.3   *Research Process*

The questionnaires were distributed to the prospective teachers in their first year of study, at the beginning of the academic year. Prospective teachers in their third and fourth year of study were given the questionnaires at the end of same year.

3.4   *The Training Process in Mathematics for Prospective Teachers in the Early Childhood Track*

Colleges for Arabic speakers and Israeli colleges, in general, offer an average of three courses in mathematics and geometry and their instruction in the early childhood tracks. The syllabi of the courses relate to various subjects in mathematics and geometry and their teaching. The courses in mathematics and its teaching relate to topics that teaching in the primary school. The course in geometry relates to basic topics and concepts in geometry which teaching in primary and secondary schools.

3.5   *Research Tools*

The data were collected in a three-part questionnaire. Part A of the questionnaire included items relating to the background variables of the participants, such as the number of mathematics units they studied in the high school and information about participants' training at the college, including the mathematics courses taken. Part B of the questionnaire included items that examined mathematical content knowledge and part C included items that examined pedagogical knowledge. The items in Part B and C that examine mathematical and pedagogical content knowledge related to subjects and concepts studied in first and second grades. The study topics can be divided into four main categories, which reflect the first and second grade curriculum:

A.   Numbers: decimal structure, place value, zero features, numbers divisi-
      bility by 2, 5, and 10, even and odd.
B.   Arithmetic operations: addition, subtraction, multiplication and division.
C.   Geometry and measurements: Length measurements, time measure-
      ments, area measurements, polygons and polyhedrons.
D.   Word problems: solving word problems, writing word problems and sort-
      ing word problems.

Part B, the section examining mathematical content knowledge, was constructed
according to view that supports the examination of mathematical content
knowledge on subjects and concepts that participants learned or are supposed
to teach (Ball et al., 2001). This part included 25 items. The reliability measures
examining internal consistency (Cronbach's α) indicate high scores; the reliability coefficient in the mathematical content knowledge test was $0.89 = \alpha$.
The items were collected from various sources: from Ministry of Education
professional tests in Israel; from items used in similar studies and published
in the research literature (e.g. Ball & Hill, 2004); and from the researcher. Following are two examples of items included in the questionnaire. The following
item was suggested by the researcher and examines mathematical knowledge
in polygons.

> Divide a square into two parts using a section. What is the polygon with
> highest number of sides that you can obtain?

Prospective teachers with mathematical content knowledge can recognize
that the polygon with the highest number of sides can be obtained by creating
another side as in the example below:

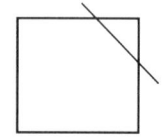

Another item that was taken from the Professionalization Test 2008/09
examines mathematical content knowledge regarding reflection.

> Samar drew a rectangle with a short side equal to half of its long side. Samar
> reflected this rectangle through one of its sides. The shape obtained from
> the rectangle and its reflection was a square. Was the reflection on the long
> side of the rectangle or on its short side? Explain your answer.

We expect that Prospective teachers with adequate content knowledge, will answer that the mirror should be on the long side.

Part C included items that examine pedagogical knowledge presented as important in the research literature (Cheang et al., 2007): understanding mathematical structures and mathematical relationships; understanding difficulties; misconceptions and strategies of student solution and responses; knowledge of alternative teaching methods of mathematical concept. Part C included 25 items. The reliability measures that examined internal consistency (α of Cronbach) indicate high scores, the reliability coefficient in the pedagogical knowledge test is $0.90 = \alpha$. The test items were collected from various sources: from the Ministry of Education's proficiency tests in Israel and from items used in similar studies (e.g., Ball & Bass, 2000; Lim, Teo, Chua, Cheang & Yeo, 2007). The following is an example of an item that examines pedagogical knowledge related to the number place value. The task was taken from Losq's (2005) study.

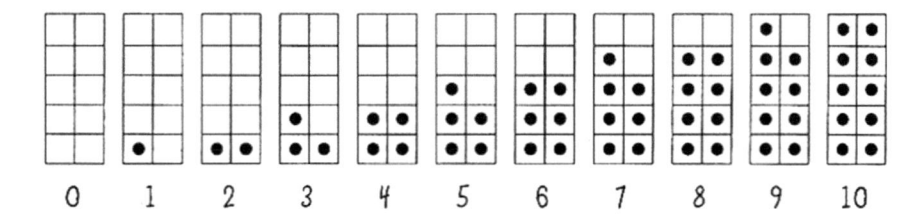

The teacher presented her students with ten patterns of numbers from zero to 10 (shown above) and requested students to represent the number 27 using these patterns. Rami chose two patterns and arranged them as follows:

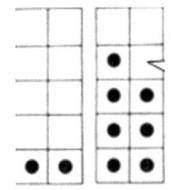

Explain Rami's choice in both patterns to represent the number 27.

We expect that teachers with adequate pedagogical knowledge about place value will indicate about the problematic nature of Rami's solution, which does not distinguish between the number of tens and their value and the amount represented.

Another example below of an item that examines pedagogical knowledge in a vertical subtraction is taken from (Learning Mathematics for Teaching [LTM], 2008).

> The teacher wants to divide her students into groups according to their type of errors in the subtraction operations. Following are three incorrect student solutions:

III	II	I

```
   4   12          4      15        6 9 8 15
   5 0 2          3 5 0 0 5         7 0 0 5
   -   6          -       6         -     7
   _____          _____        _____
   4 0 6          3 4 0 0 9         6 9 8 8
```

> Which ones have the same error? Circle the correct answer.
>
> a.   I and II
> b.   I and III
> c.   II and III
> d.   I, II and III

The item refers to one of the common mistakes among students in subtraction exercises that include zero in the internal digits of the number. In the conversion from one unit to the other, students skip the number zero. The student in example II only made the conversion from the thousand digit to units, while ignoring the numbers in the hundreds and tens digits. The student in example I did the same thing. Prospective teachers with pedagogical knowledge in subtraction will indicate that option A includes the same error.

4   Findings

In order to conduct the statistical analyzes, each participant was given five scores for each questionnaire (overall score, numbers score, operations score, geometry and measurement score and word problems score) and a total of 10 scores. The score for each questionnaire was determined so that the correct answer was one point and the wrong answer was zero points. The mean scores for each questionnaire were calculated separately. In addition, the scores for each field (numbers, account operations, geometry and measurements, and word problems) were calculated separately among the two study groups. In addition, a comparison was made between the average scores in the different fields in each of the two questionnaires.

4.1   *Knowledge of Mathematical Content among prospective Teachers in the Early Childhood Track*

The findings relating to mathematical content knowledge indicate an average grade of 46 (on a scale of 0–100) among prospective teachers studying in the third and fourth years and a lower average grade of 36 (on a scale of 0–100) among first-year prospective teachers. This hierarchy among the two research groups was observed in each of the areas examined in mathematical content knowledge (MCK): numbers, arithmetical operations, geometry and measurements, and word problems. In addition, the findings indicate that in both of the groups there was higher average knowledge related to numbers and that the lowest average was in geometry and measurements. The averages and standard deviations in the areas examined for mathematical content knowledge are presented in Table 11.1.

In order to compare the level of knowledge and mathematical content between the two research groups, a *t* test for independent samples was conducted in mathematical content knowledge as a whole and for each knowledge component (numbers, arithmetical operations, geometry and measurements, and word problems) separately. The findings indicate that the mean of third and fourth-year prospective teachers is higher than the mean of first year prospective teachers and the differences is significant in MCK $(t = 148) = -3.52, p <$ 0.05 and in content knowledge in geometry $t(148) = -3.05, p < 0.05$. Regarding content knowledge in arithmetic operations and in word problems, there was no significant difference between the two groups.

The mean of content knowledge in geometry and measurements, as seen in Table 11.1, is lower than the means in the other fields of mathematical content knowledge for both of the two research groups. In order to examine whether the difference between the means is significant in the various knowledge components, a paired-samples *t*-test was conducted. The findings indicate that among the first-year prospective teachers group, the mean of geometry and measurements was significantly lower than the mean of numbers

TABLE 11.1   Means and standard deviations for mathematical content knowledge and for each component

		M	SD	N
First year prospective teachers	MCK	35.96	14.84	75
Third/fourth-year prospective teachers		46.05	19.86	75
Total		41.00	18.19	150
First year prospective teachers	Numbers	48.38	21.83	75
Third/fourth-year prospective teachers		60.19	16.48	75
Total		54.29	19.93	150
First year prospective teachers	Arithmetic operations	46.67	22.81	75
Third/fourth-year prospective teachers		55.02	31.43	75
Total		50.48	27.69	150
First year prospective teachers	Geometry	21.33	16.25	75
Third/fourth-year prospective teachers		31.66	24.34	75
Total		26.50	21.27	150
First year prospective teachers	Word problems	43.56	27.92	75
Third/fourth-year prospective teachers		52.00	26.63	75
Total		47.78	29.00	150

$t(74) = -10.40$, $p < 0.001$; the mean of arithmetic operations $t(74) = -9.25$, $p < 0.001$ and the mean of word problems $t(74) = -7.03$, $p < 0.001$. Similarly among the third/fourth-year prospective teachers, the mean in geometry was lower and statistically significant than the mean in numbers $t(74) = -10.33$, $p < 0.001$, the mean in arithmetic operations $t(74) = -7.00$, $p < 0.001$, and the mean in word problems $t(74) = -7.28$, $p < 0.001$.

In order to identify more specific difficulty points in mathematical content knowledge in geometry and measurements, separate examinations were conducted in the individual subjects in the field of geometry and measurements, which included measurements of length, time, area, weight, transformations, polygons, and *polyhedrons*. It was found that the participants in both groups have more difficulties in transformation and in *polyhedrons*. Figure 11.1 presents the mean of the content knowledge in the various subjects examined.

Figure 11.1 shows that the difficulty in transformations and *polyhedrons was found* in both groups. Analysis of the questionnaires further indicates common mistakes among the subjects. The following are examples of the common mistakes among the participants.

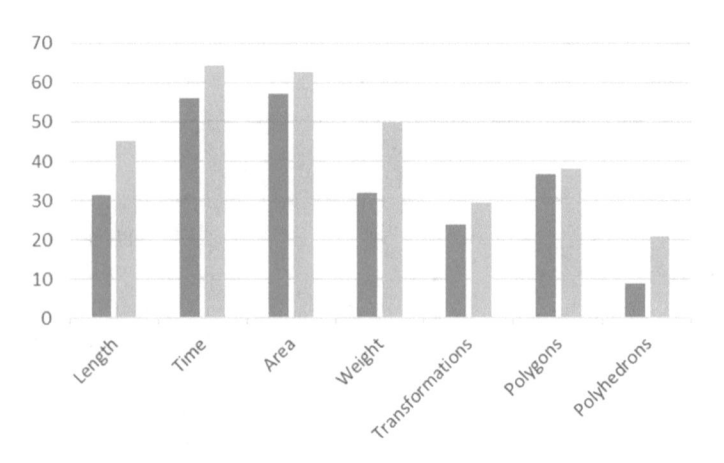

■ First year prospective teachers ▪ Third/fourth-year prospective teachers

FIGURE 11.1   The mean of the two research groups in mathematical knowledge of selected
subjects in geometry

In a task that requires the participants to divide a square into two parts using a section and to find the polygon with highest number of sides that can be obtained:

The participant drew a square and divided it into two rectangles as depicted below.

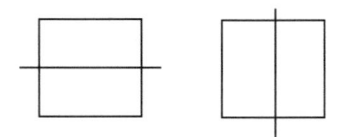

It is important to note that in all the answers which chose the rectangle as a solution to the task, the most common division of the given square was by crossing it into two overlapping rectangles, either through a vertical or horizontal line. Another example that examines content knowledge is shown in the following *polyhedrons*.

The box is given below

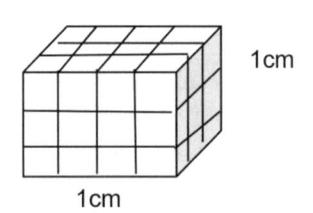

1cm

1cm

a.   What is the volume of the box drawn? _____ (cm^3)

b.   Write the dimensions of a box that is three times larger than the size of the drawn box.

Half of the prospective teachers who answered item a correctly did not succeed in answering item b and set correct measurements for a box that was three times larger than the volume of the given box. The most common error was to increase the three dimensions of the drawn box by 3 times, by recording the dimensions as 3, 3 and 3.

Another example of the errors was in an item that examined the layout of *polyhedrons*: According to the layouts of surfaces (the facades without the bases) of three *polyhedrons*. What are the *polyhedrons*?

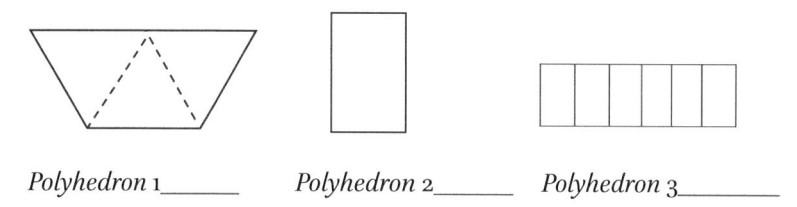

*Polyhedron 1*_____   *Polyhedron 2*_____   *Polyhedron 3*_____

The task was considered difficult for the prospective teachers, with 80% of them failing to recognize the first *polyhedron* as a pyramid and the second *polyhedron* as a cylinder. In addition, 70% failed to identify *polyhedron* 3 as a prism.

4.2   *Pedagogical and Content Knowledge among Early Childhood Prospective Teachers*

The findings related to pedagogical knowledge in each of the areas examined: numbers, arithmetical operations, geometry and measurements, and word problems indicate means lower than those obtained in mathematical content knowledge between the two groups. However, similar to the findings regarding mathematical content knowledge, the findings indicate a mean of 21 (on a scale of 0–100) among third/fourth-year prospective teachers and a lower mean of 16 (on a scale of 0–100) among first-year prospective teachers. This hierarchy among the research groups was maintained in all fields of pedagogical knowledge. As with mathematical content knowledge, pedagogical knowledge of numbers was the highest among each group. In contrast to the findings obtained on mathematical knowledge, the lowest mean in pedagogical knowledge was in word problems. The means and standard deviations in all components of pedagogical knowledge examined are presented in Table 11.2.

To compare the level of pedagogical knowledge between the two research groups, an independent sample was conducted for pedagogical knowledge as a

TABLE 11.2   Means and standard deviations in content pedagogical knowledge

		M	SD	N
First year prospective teachers	MPCK	16.81	16.34	75
Third/fourth-year prospective teachers		21.57	21.72	72
Total		19.14	19.52	147
First year prospective teachers	Numbers	23.33	27.97	75
Third/fourth-year prospective teachers		40.28	49.21	72
Total		31.63	40.75	147
First year prospective teachers	Arithmetic operations	20.38	19.39	75
Third/fourth-year prospective teachers		23.02	22.81	72
Total		21.67	21.10	147
First year prospective teachers	Geometry	15.33	20.91	75
Third/fourth-year prospective teachers		21.64	27.96	72
Total		18.42	24.37	147
First year prospective teachers	Word problems	10.38	17.06	75
Third/fourth-year prospective teachers		9.13	16.49	72
Total		9.77	16.47	147

whole and for each of the fields of knowledge separately: numbers; arithmetical operations; geometry and measurements; and word problems. The findings indicate that there is no significant difference between the two groups in general pedagogical knowledge, in pedagogical knowledge in arithmetic operations, in pedagogical knowledge in geometry and measurement, and in pedagogical knowledge in word problems ($p > 0.05$). It was found that the mean pedagogical knowledge in numbers among third/fourth-year prospective teachers was significantly higher than mean of first year prospective teachers $t(145) = -2.57, p < 0.05$.

The mean of the pedagogical knowledge in word problems as observed in Table 11.2 was lower than the means in the other components of pedagogical knowledge in both of the research groups. To examine whether the differences between the means is significant, a paired simple t-test was conducted. The findings indicate that among the first year prospective teachers, word problems were significantly lower than the mean of numbers $t(74) = 4.04, p < 0.05$, lower than the mean of arithmetic operations $t(74) = 4.48, p < 0.05$, and lower than the mean of geometry and measurements $t(74) = 2.13, p < 0.001$. For the third/fourth-year prospective teachers, the mean of word problems was statistically significant and lower than the mean of numbers $t(71) = -80, p < 0.05$,

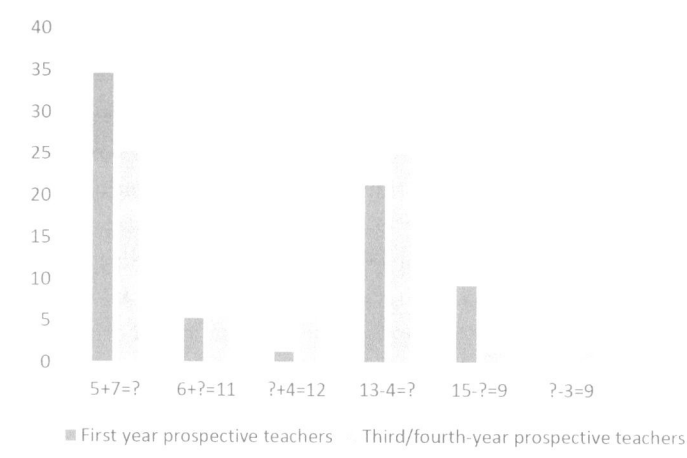

FIGURE 11.2   Average success in composing word problems is appropriate for exercises

lower than the mean of arithmetic operations $t(71) = -4.91, p < 0.05$, and lower than the mean of geometry and measurements $t(71) = -4.41, p < 0.001$.

To identify specific difficulty points in pedagogical knowledge of word problems, reference was made to each item that relates to word problems separately. It was found that most of the participants made mistakes on items that request to classify division problems into partitioning and division problems. In addition, they had trouble composing word problems that fit a specific exercise. The most common errors among the participants in both groups were in composing word problems in addition in which the initial group was not known, and in contrast, they were more successful in composing problems in which the final group was not known. Figure 11.2 shows the mean in composing word problems for addition and subtraction exercises among the two groups.

Figure 11.2 shows that the participants in both groups were more successful in constructing word problems in which the question relates to the sum and less successful in composing word problems in which the question relates to the initial group.

4.3   *Comparing the Level of Mathematical and Pedagogical Knowledge*
The mean of mathematical content knowledge was higher than the mean of pedagogical knowledge in the two research groups, as illustrated in Tables 11.1 and 11.2. In order to examine whether the differences were significant, a paired sample t-test was conducted between the means of the two research groups. The findings indicated a higher mean in mathematical content knowledge than in the pedagogical knowledge and the differences were significant among third/fourth-year prospective teachers $t(71) = 9.411, p < .001$ and among first year prospective teachers $t(74) = 11.37, p < .001$.

5 Discussion

The purpose of this study is to provide a snapshot of the mathematical content knowledge and pedagogical knowledge among prospective teachers in the early childhood education at a teacher training college. Mathematical content knowledge and pedagogical knowledge is examined in the context of the topics that the research subjects are supposed to teach and according to the mathematics curriculum for first and second grades. The content was divided into four main areas: numbers, geometry and measurements, arithmetic operations, and word problems.

There are low achievements on tasks aimed at measuring mathematical content knowledge among prospective teachers studying in the early childhood education track, both among those at the beginning of their studies and those at the end of the training process. The mean of third/fourth-year prospective teachers in mathematics content knowledge is 46 (on a scale of 0–100) and in the pedagogical knowledge of content is 21 (on a scale of 0–100). Lower scores were observed among first year prospective teachers. The differences between the third/fourth-year prospective teachers and the first year prospective teachers were significant only in some of the components of mathematical content knowledge and in pedagogical knowledge. This can indicate that the process for training prospective teachers to teach math in first and second grades is incomplete. This picture differs from the findings of Chein et al. (2007), which showed a significant improvement in the pedagogical knowledge of mathematics students in the first year and after completion of the mathematics training in Singapore. Hamlet (2007) attributed the low achievements on tasks aimed at measuring mathematical content knowledge among first-year prospective teachers in the Early Childhood Education Track to the fact that they had forgotten the math they learned in school. The findings indicate that the level of knowledge of mathematical content in the field of geometry and measurements is lowest among both of the research groups. The knowledge of geometry and measurement has also been identified as the weakest field among students from different countries who participated in the Times test (Tatsuoka, Corter & Tatsuoka, 2004). Similar findings have been reported in studies among teachers (Jones, 2000; Baturo & Nason, 1997). Also, among pre-service primary school teachers who intended to teach mathematics to lower grades as reported by Romano (2017). In the area of pedagogical knowledge, the findings indicate that word problems were the most difficult for participants. The participants were able to solve word problems and but had less success in composing word problems to fit a given exercise, especially when the unknown was in the initial group. Other research also found that composing problems was a difficult task for prospective mathematics teachers when they were required to compose word problems corresponding to a given symbolic structure in fractions (Luo, 2009). Word problems are considered a difficult topic among students (Rogers, 2004). Low achievements in the tasks that aimed to measuring pedagogical knowledge regarding word problems was also revealed in a study of first-grade teachers (Carpenter, Fennema, Peterson & Cary, 1988). Similarly, Ball (1988) reported that teachers were successful in performing an algorithm correctly, but they found it difficult to explain the underlying principle and the relationship to the place value of the number.

It is important to note that the findings indicate a difference between the levels of mathematical content knowledge and the level of pedagogical knowledge. The level of mathematical content knowledge was higher than the level of pedagogical knowledge in both research groups. This finding is consistent with reports in the research literature (Turnuklu & Yesildere, 2007). The gap between the components of content knowledge and the elements of pedagogical knowledge is reasonable, because pedagogical knowledge includes not only mathematical content knowledge, but also analysis of solution strategies, misconceptions, teaching methods, and other components. The difference between the levels of knowledge and the higher level of mathematics content knowledge can be attributed to two factors. One is the greater exposure of the two groups to content knowledge throughout their years of study, especially in high school and during academic training at the college. Another reason for the difference is exposure to mathematical content knowledge components and the use of this knowledge in daily life, in contrast to pedagogical knowledge, which is used only while teaching.

6 Conclusion

The main conclusion of the study is that teacher training for the first and second grades in the Early Childhood Education Track is incomplete in imparting mathematical content and pedagogical knowledge for prospective teachers. It is important to note that there has been a change in the teachers' training process for the first and second grades, so that according to the new guidelines of the Ministry of Higher Education in Israel, the early childhood education track has been canceled. Training for elementary school teaching offers a major specialization in mathematics. However, it is still possible for prospective teachers in the kindergarten track to expand their training in math instruction for first and second grades, while completing only a limited number of courses in mathematics and mathematics education. This is similar to the training of the prospective teachers in this study. In light of this situation, it is recommended to enrich the curriculum for prospective teachers in the kindergarten program who wish to teach mathematics in first and second grades by expanding the number and variety of courses in mathematics and mathematics education that emphasize the content for these grades in mathematical and pedagogical aspects. The contents must emphasize first and second grades mathematics curriculum such as: Numbers decimal structure, place value, zero features, numbers divisibility by 2, 5, and 10, even and odd. Arithmetic operations: Addition, subtraction, multiplication and division. Geometry and measurements: Length measurements, time measurements, area measurements, polygons and polyhedrons. And Word problems: solving word problems, writing word problems and sorting word problems. The pedagogical aspects could include how to teach the earlier topics and about specific mistakes, difficulties and solving strategies. These can be done in different tools such as video clips of children thinking aloud as they work on mathematics tasks as similar to Kuennen and Beam's (2020) suggestions. Finally, it is important to note that special intervention programs should address widely the geometry and measurement and word problems, which were found to be two weak areas among participants.

Acknowledgment

This study was conducted in accordance with the recommendation of the Inter-Academic Committee of the Mofet Institute and with the support of the Department of Teacher Education in the Ministry of Education.

References

Akerson, V. L. (2004). Designing a science methods course for early childhood pre-service teachers. *Journal of Elementary Science Education, 16*(2), 19–32.

Aktaş, M. C., & Özdemir, E. T. (2017). An examination of the number sense performances of preservice elementary school mathematics teachers. *European Journal of Education Studies.*

Ball, D. L., & Bass, H. (2000). Interweaving content and pedagogy in teaching and learning to teach: Knowing and using mathematics. In J. Boaler (Ed.), *Multiple perspectives on mathematics teaching and learning* (pp. 83–104). Ablex.

Ball, D. L., Hill, H., & Bass, H. (2004). *Knowing and using mathematical knowledge in teaching: Learning what matters* [Invited plenary address]. Southern African Association of Mathematics, Science, and Technology Education, Cape Town, South Africa.

Ball, D. L, Lubienski, S., & Mewborn, D. (2001). Research on teaching mathematics: The unsolved problem of teachers' mathematical knowledge. In V. Richardson (Ed.), *Handbook of research on teaching* (4th ed., pp. 433–456). Macmillan.

Ball, D. L., Thames, M. H., & Phelps, G. (2008). Content knowledge for teaching what makes it special? *Journal of Teacher Education, 59*(5), 389–407.

Baturo, A., & Nason, R. (1996). Student teachers' subject matter knowledge within the domain of area measurement. *Educational Studies in Mathematics, 31*(3), 235–268.

Burgos, M., & Godino, J. D. (2020). Prospective primary school teachers' competence for analysing the difficulties in solving proportionality problem. *Mathematics Education Research Journal,* 1–23.

Carpenter, P. T., Fennema, E., Peterson, P. L., & Cary, A. D. (1988). Teachers' pedagogical content knowledge of students' problem solving in elementary arithmetic. *Journal for Research in Mathematics, 19*(5), 385–401.

Cheang, W. K., Yeo, J. K. K., Chan, M. E., Lim-Teo, S. K., Chua, K. G., & Ng, L. E. (2007). Development of mathematics pedagogical content knowledge in student teachers. *The Mathematics Educator, 10*(2), 27–54.

Davis, B., & Simmt, E. (2006). Mathematics-for-teaching: An ongoing investigation of the mathematics that teachers (need to) know. *Educational Studies in Mathematics, 61*(3), 293–319.

De Haro, J. J. O., & Moll, V. F. (2014). Pre-service teachers' common content knowledge regarding the arithmetic mean. *Journal of Research in Mathematics Education, 3*(3), 192–219.

Delaney, S., Ball, D. L., Hill, H. C., Schilling, S. G., & Zopf, D. (2008). "Mathematical knowledge for teaching": Adapting US measures for use in Ireland. *Journal of Mathematics Teacher Education, 11*(3), 171–197.

Depaepe, F., Torbeyns, J., Vermeersch, N., Janssens, D., Janssen, R., Kelchtermans, G., & Van Dooren, W. (2015). Teachers' content and pedagogical content knowledge on rational numbers: A comparison of prospective elementary and lower secondary school teachers. *Teaching and Teacher Education, 47*, 82–92.

Fowler, R. C. (2020). Credentials of teachers in states where elementary and early childhood education licenses overlap in grades K, 1, 2, and/or 3. *Journal of Research in Childhood Education, 34*(2), 238–250.

Ginsburg, H. P., Lee, J. S., & Boyd, J. S. (2008). Mathematics education for young children: What it is and how to promote it. *Social Policy Report – Giving Child and Youth Development Knowledge Away, 22*(1), 1–24.

Goulding, M. (2003). An investigation into the mathematics knowledge of primary teacher trainees. *Proceedings of the British Society for Research into Learning Mathematics, 23*(3), 73–78.

Hamlet, B. (2007). Mathematics content knowledge of pre-service primary teachers: Developing confidence and competence. *Proceedings of the British Society for Research into Learning Mathematics, 27*(3), 43–48.

Hill, H. C., Ball, D. L., & Schilling, S. G. (2008). Unpacking pedagogical content knowledge: Conceptualizing and measuring teachers' topic-specific knowledge of students. *Journal for Research in Mathematics Education, 39*(4), 372–400.

Hill, C. H., Rowan, B., & Ball, D. L. (2005). Effects of teachers' mathematical knowledge for teaching on student achievement. *American Educational Research Journal, 42*(2), 371–406.

Horm-Wingerd, D. M., Hyson, M., & Karp, N. (2000). *New teachers for a new century: The future of early childhood professional preparation* [Abstract]. In U.S. Department of Education (Ed.), *ED 438* 954 (pp. 1–13). U.S. Government Printing Office.

Jones, K. (2000). Teacher knowledge and professional development in geometry. *Proceedings of the British Society for Research into Learning Mathematics, 20*(3), 109–114.

Kuennen, E. W., & Beam, J. E. (2020). Teaching the mathematics that teachers need to know: Classroom ideas for supporting prospective elementary teachers' development of mathematical knowledge for teaching. In A. Appova, R. M. Welder, & Z. Feldman (Eds.), *Supporting mathematics teacher educators' knowledge and practices for teaching content to prospective (grades K-8) teachers* (Special issue: *The Mathematics Enthusiast, 17*(2–3)) (pp. 771–805). ScholarWorks, University of Montana. https://scholarworks.umt.edu/tme

Learning Mathematics for Teaching (LMT). (2008). Mathematical Knowledge for Teaching (MKT) measures: Mathematics released items 2008. www.sitemaker.umich.edu/lmt/files/LMT_sample_items.pdf

Lee, J. (2010). Exploring kindergarten teachers' pedagogical content knowledge of mathematics. *International Journal of Early Childhood, 42*(1), 27–41.

Luo, F. (2009). Evaluating the effectiveness and insights of pre-service elementary teachers' abilities to construct word problems for fraction multiplication. *Journal of Mathematics Education, 2*(1), 83–98.

Mewborn, D. (2001). Teachers content knowledge, teacher education, and their effects on the preparation of elementary teachers in the United States. *Mathematics Education Research Journal, 3*, 28–36.

Rogers, J. (2004). Autonomy and mathematical problem-solving: The early years, education. *International Journal of Primary, Elementary and Early Years Education, 32*(3), 24–31.

Romano, D. A. (2017). Prospective B&H elementary school teachers' understanding of processes with basic geometric concepts. *Imvi-Open Mathematical Education Notes, 7*(1), 49–42.

Sharyn, L., & Colleen, V. (2011). First year pre-service teachers' mathematical content knowledge: Methods of solution for a ratio question. *Mathematics Teacher Education and Development, 13*(2), 22–43.

Shirvani, H. (2015). Pre-service elementary teachers' mathematics content knowledge: A predictor of sixth graders' mathematics performance. *International Journal of Instruction, 8*(1), 133–142.

Shulman, L. (1986). Those who understand: Knowledge growth in teaching. *Educational Researcher, 15*(2), 4–14.

Southwell, B., White, A. L., Way, J., & Perry, B. (2006). Attitudes versus achievement in pre-service mathematics teaching. In *Refereed proceedings of the Australian Association for Research in Education Annual Conference*.

Tatsuoka, K. K., Corter, J. E., & Tatsuoka, C. (2004). Patterns of diagnosed mathematical content and process skills in TIMSS-R across a sample of twenty countries. *American Educational Research Journal, 41*(4), 901–926.

Tatto, M. T., Schwille, J., Senk, S., Ingvarson, L., Peck, R., & Rowley, G. (2008). *Teacher Education and Development Study in Mathematics (TEDS-M): Policy, practice, and readiness to teach primary and secondary mathematics – conceptual framework.* Teacher Education and Development International Study Center, College of Education, Michigan State University.

Turnuklu, E. B., & Yesildere, S. (2007, October). The pedagogical content knowledge in mathematics: Pre-service primary mathematics teachers perspectives in Turkey. *IUMPST: The Journal 1 (Content Knowledge)*. www.k-12prep.math.ttu.edu

Tutak, F. A. (2009). *A study of geometry content knowledge of elementary pre-service teachers: The case of quadrilaterals* [PhD dissertation]. University of Florida. http://etd.fcla.edu/UF/UFE0041186/tutak_f.pdf

Venkat, H., & Spaull, N. (2015). What do we know about primary teachers' mathematical content knowledge in South Africa? An analysis of SACMEQ 2007. *International Journal of Educational Development, 41*, 121–130.

CHAPTER 12

Professional Development of Kindergarten Teachers through Collaboration with Preschool Math Education Expertise

Dina Hassidov and Bat-Sheva Ilany

Abstract

This chapter presents a mixed-methods study of the innovative "Senso-Math" preschool program and the reactions of both the facilitators, who underwent a special training program, and the preschool teachers in whose classes the program was implemented. The goal of the program is to enhance mathematical development in preschool children through the intervention of trained facilitators who bring the adjunct program into preschools. The results indicated a positive change in the attitudes of the facilitators to their professional calling and, after an adjustment period, a positive attitude overall regarding the facilitators' contribution to mathematics education in the preschool as evidenced by the significant relationships that developed between the facilitators and the preschool teachers.

Keywords

facilitators – mathematics education – preschool – kindergarten – "Senso-Math" Preschool Program-SMP

1 Introduction

Today's preschool teachers are expected to have sufficient knowledge to teach early mathematics in preschools, in keeping with the global trend that advocates familiarity with mathematical concepts as early as preschool so as to build mathematical readiness for primary school. Research has established that children at preschool age are able to understand concrete mathematical processes – sometimes even abstract ones – and the earlier the children acquire mathematical experience, the more impact the experience has on their future development and abilities (Baroody, 2000).

It has been shown that teachers' attitudes are one of the main factors affecting children's attitudes towards mathematics (Philippou & Christou, 1998; Plucker, 1996) since teachers serve as a model for their students (Charalambous et al., 2009; Philipp, 2007). "Attitudes" are effective structures, sustainable over time, through which people react to certain things in a particular way (Fiske & Taylor, 2008; McLeod, 1992). When dealing with mathematics, the teachers' attitudes are reflected in the way learners study, feel, and think (Philipp, 2007; Charalambous et al., 2009).

Unfortunately, studies conducted in recent years indicate that teachers assigned to teach mathematics in preschool find themselves challenged, feeling they lack competency for the job. In part, this may stem from the teachers' negative personal experiences, but it is also due to a want of professional knowledge, since relevant training in teaching preschool mathematics is not often acquired in college (Ben-Yehuda & Ilany, 2008; Guo et al., 2011; Tirosh & Graeber, 1990), meaning that teachers lack adequate knowledge to teach mathematics in preschool. Thus, in addition to the preschool teachers' normally heavy commitment load, they find themselves additionally burdened with the responsibility of creating and enabling positive experiences in foundation mathematics for young learners without adequate training.

These studies and others have led to the realization that suitable support programs must be developed to strengthen teachers' sense of competence for teaching mathematics in preschool. Such support programs should be structured along current teaching principles: to develop quantitative, critical, and creative understanding; to direct towards thinking and understanding; and to encourage mathematical discourse (Pimm, 1987) and metacognitive processes (NCTM, 2000).

2 Preschool Children and Mathematics

According to one of Piaget's (1972) principles, toddlers are at a stage approaching readiness for formal and abstract learning. This is the period when a child's thought structures are constructed, and visual and verbal representations are built. The child's activity at this age is essentially intuitive, combining imitation and imagination. Perry and Dockett (2013) emphasize that young children can be powerful mathematicians and suggest ways for stimulating mathematical comprehension.

Developmental constraints mean that children adhere to sensory impressions and experience subjective vision that is considered egocentric. This leads to restrictions in the child's ability to reach generalizations (Vygotsky, 1962), hampering their natural ability in math unless these abilities are nurtured, either in the home or in the school environment. In Australia, for example, one in four young children growing up in disadvantaged communities enter formal schooling without the necessary mathematical skills (Australian Early Development Census, 2012).

However, preschool children do have the ability to build concrete mathematical – sometimes even abstract – processes, and the earlier that children are exposed to the experience, the greater the child's mathematical development will be later on. In fact, there is indication that, through mediation, a change can be achieved in a child's ability to use basic logical reasoning. Developmental psychology emphasises that a suitable change in the physical-social environment of the child that provides opportunities to experience physical objects, speculate, argue, and explain (Kilpatrick et al., 2001) can encourage cognitive development, including in the areas of mathematics and mathematical language.

However, for this to happen, it is important for the child to solve problems that are relevant to his or hers individual needs as a learner (Carpenter et al., 1998). In other words, children must be able to find and apply the relationship between the understanding of mathematics as abstract knowledge, and its relevance to their everyday world.

3   Teaching Mathematics to Preschoolers: Training the Teachers

Since young children are essentially engaged in mathematics in daily life from birth (NAEYC & NCTM, 2002), preschool mathematics practice should develop their awareness, so as to cultivate mathematical thinking at an early age. Indeed, preschool mathematics practice helps shape the child's future cognition, mathematical thinking, general thinking, and cognitive abilities (Clarke, Clarke & Cheeseman, 2006). In addition, the volume and quality of mathematics practice during preschool predict a child's success in math in primary school (Clements & Sarama, 2006, 2009). Neuroscience research shows that preschool mathematics activity is important. Clements (2001) maintains that the structure and organization of the brain of developing preschoolers is affected by their learning experience, and that complex activities lead to increased brain development.

In fact, many early childhood mathematics curricula aim to place more emphasis on mathematics in early learning (see, for example, Australian Curriculum, Assessment and Reporting Authority (ACARA), 2009; Clements, 2007). An example is the Australian program "Let's Count" (2016), for children aged three to five, that aims to develop children's skills by encouraging them to notice, explore, and talk about numbers, counting, measurement, shapes, and patterns in everyday life.

Mulligan (2016) emphasizes that the important question is how educators can effectively understand, and consequently promote, deep mathematical structural development from an early age. It is clear that teaching mathematics to preschoolers requires appropriate professional knowledge on the part of the preschool teacher. However, preschool teachers are not always prepared for such a task, due to the minimal (or lack of) training they may receive in college in the realm of preschool teaching in general, and preschool mathematics in particular. Without sufficient, appropriate knowledge, the teacher, already overburdened, is hard-pressed to teach mathematics effectively. Furthermore, if the preschool teacher feels unequipped for the role of teaching mathematics, she may not present mathematics in a cheerful and pleasant manner to the children.

The teacher's attitude is a key factor influencing students' attitudes toward mathematics (Philippou & Christou, 1998), since teachers serve as role models for their students (Charalambous et al., 2009), and recent studies in various countries point to the difficulties that preschool teachers have regarding mathematics in general. Such personal, negative feelings may increase feelings of ineptitude regarding teaching the subject, especially if the teachers have not received adequate training for the role (Guo et al., 2011; Ilany et al., 2021).

The conclusion, therefore, is that there is a need to construct appropriate adjunct programs to encourage and empower preschool teachers to teach mathematics. Such programs should be based upon new pedagogical principles regarding the development of quantitative, creative, and analytic understanding; teaching for the purpose of constructing knowledge and understanding; and encouraging mathematical discourse and meta-cognitive thought processes (NCTM, 2000). Children thus develop the numerous skills needed for the successful transition to primary school.

Based on these principles, the Australian "Let's Count" program is an example of a program that provides training for early childhood educators, including how to support parents in developing the maths skills of their child using the take-home resource pack that is part of the kit (Figure 12.3). The "Senso-Math" preschool (SMP) program (Hassidov & Ilany, 2014) is also based on these principles.

4   The "Senso-Math" Preschool Program

Based on the understanding that a change was needed in teacher-training methods, and taking into account the unique character of preschool learning, the "Senso-Math" program was developed (2004–2005). One of its main goals was to train facilitators to supplement the teaching of mathematics in the preschool. The "Senso-Math" program is based upon the definition of the curriculum of the Israel Ministry of Education for mathematics in early childhood (2009). It aims to give preschool children the chance to experience math.

The "Senso-Math" Preschool program (SMP) is unique in that it promotes the professional mathematical knowledge of the preschool teacher by introducing into the classroom professional facilitators who model methods by which mathematics can be taught to preschoolers. SMP facilitators come to the preschool and work with the children in small groups. They provide the teachers with formal, didactic information regarding how children learn, demonstrate to the teacher how to work with the material, and engage the children. They are available to answer any questions the teacher may have. The preschool teacher observes the facilitator and becomes a partner in the teaching process. By providing guidance and assistance in presenting mathematics, the facilitators reduce the responsibility placed on preschool teachers to achieve the afore-mentioned goals.

The SMP approach teaches math using hands-on materials and experiential activities that encourage mathematical learning through dynamic experiences that encourage mathematical reflective discourse. Children investigate mathematical aspects of day-to-day life using all their senses and are thus able to assimilate and shape mathematical concepts and models (Figure 12.2).

Special educational materials were designed and created for the SMP program to present varied, graduated exercises that follow the already established preschool curriculum. The mathematical concepts are taught through a combination of sensory and motoric activities, utilizing their everyday experiences in a way that is appealing and engaging.

Three kits were produced for the facilitators to use in the classroom, one for each year of preschool, to accompany children from the ages of three to six years according to their cognitive maturity. Each kit consists of 30 learning units that correspond to the ten topics covered over the year as suggested by the Ministry of Education (seasons, holidays, etc.). Each topic is further divided into three customized units corresponding to three "styles" of learning: creative, structured, and motoric. Each unit includes detailed task cards and assistive materials that allow the teacher to create a rich, experiential, authentic mathematical learning environment and provide activities to allow the children to explore familiar concepts mathematically, learn the correct mathematical terms, and develop mathematical thinking. The task cards specify the purpose of the activity, number of participants, level of activity, and recommended accessories.

In addition, each child receives an individual kit that includes special teaching materials such as worksheets, "fun pages", card games, board games, and specially designed accessories and props. Some of the activities are meant to be taken home and shared with parents and siblings.

In each preschool, learning groups of up to ten children were set up, based on the teacher's recommendation. The small size of the group allows them to work individually, in pairs, or in a group activity. The children can successfully express themselves in the group but also work independently without giving up individual attention. The facilitator worked with the children once or twice a week, either during formal preschool hours, or in the afternoon, within the framework of after-school enrichment classes. Each session lasted for a period of 40 minutes for children aged four to six, and 30 minutes for children aged three to four.

The pedagogical and mathematical rationale of the "Senso-Math" teaching kits were initially tested in 20 preschools. The results of the initial program were validated through observation, data collection, and accompanying research, then were revised to further enrich the curriculum framework. After final approval by the Israel Ministry of Education, several hundred preschools were chosen to implement the program.

5 Facilitator Training

SMP facilitators undergo a two-year program that qualifies them to work independently teaching and promoting mathematics in preschools. The first year,

FIGURE 12.1   Facilitator's and children's kits

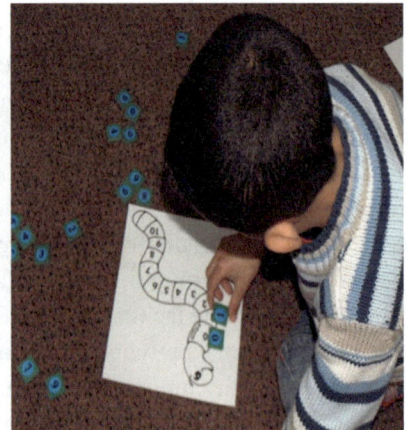

FIGURE 12.2   Children investigating mathematical objects

FIGURE 12.3   Parents investigating mathematical objects

qualified women (see below), participate in a 128-academic-hour program (20 meetings): 40 hours focus on the organizational aspect of naturally integrating the SMP into preschools, and 88 hours are devoted to mathematical content in early childhood education and practical work administering and facilitating the SMP in preschools. It was focused on mathematical education in early childhood and hands-on experimentation and application of the SMP program in preschools. They were also taught to coach the preschool teachers in teaching mathematics, by modelling and demonstrating the method.

Content covered includes teaching and learning methods, mathematics education, cognitive abilities of primary school children, and more. During the program, they are familiarized and shown how to use the unique "Senso-Math" kit (Figure 12.1), which includes all the paraphernalia needed for teaching the 30 extended activities each year, as an activity centre. In the second year of training, facilitators undergo 28 hours of practical experience in primary schools, accompanied by one-on-one mentoring, as required. In addition, they receive 15 hours of professional guidance when they commence formal work. After completing the course, participants were qualified to work as autonomous teachers in the field.

6　Purpose of Study

The purpose of this study was to track the progress and attitudes of the facilitators as they implemented their training in preschool classrooms alongside preschool teachers, to discover any insights regarding the preschool teachers' acceptance and appreciation of the SMP program, and to determine how the SMP affected how they taught and related to mathematics in their classrooms.

7　Methodology

7.1　*Population*

All the preschool teachers were graduates of teacher training colleges, with more than three years of experience teaching in preschools. The preschool teachers had little or no background in early childhood mathematics, since few college students are trained to teach preschool mathematics. All the preschools in the study were under the supervision of the Israeli Ministry of Education. The SMP activities in the preschools took place with approval of the Ministry of Education supervisors.

Of the 500 women who participated in the facilitator training program, 49 were chosen at random to take part in this study (Hassidov, 2014). The average education level of the study group participants was 14.5 years of schooling. Each participant had a requisite diploma or training certificate from a teachers' college or other school of higher education, were mathematically oriented, and could work as mathematical facilitators in preschool. Although all had a background in early childhood education, none of the participants had ever worked in preschool education. The average age of the participants was about 34 years old. The women were of diverse marital status, and came from various socio-economic, demographic sectors around the country (Israel Ministry of Education, 2009).

7.2　*Research Tools*

Research methods were both quantitative and qualitative. Data was collected via questionnaires and semi-structured interviews designed and conducted by the researchers. The questionnaire comprised 22 statements (see Table 12.1) to ascertain the participants' attitudes to teaching mathematics in preschool and to the "Senso-Math" program. Fifteen facilitators (who were not included in the study group) validated the questionnaires. The 49 study participants were asked to rate the statements from 1 (not at all) to 5 (to a great extent). Negative statements were highlighted and were not included in the questionnaire. After filling in the questionnaires, semi-structured interviews were conducted with all the study participants (n = 49) to clarify their attitudes. Relevant background information was also collected at this time, such as age, education, place of residence, occupation, and socioeconomic status. Data collection was carried out three times: at the beginning of this study, at the completion of training, and a year post-training. Statements were divided into four categories: attitudes toward learning mathematics, development of professional confidence, self-confidence in teaching mathematics in particular, and evaluation of the program.

8 Results and Discussion

8.1 Summary of Quantitative Results

The results of the survey carried out a year post-training are presented in Table 12.1, and a summary of the overall results regarding the study participants' attitudes regarding mathematics in preschool, how the facilitator training course developed their professional confidence and their self-confidence in teaching mathematics, and their satisfaction with the program is shown in Table 12.2. It shows that, overall, the 49 participants viewed the course favourably and considered it a viable career alternative.

Table 12.1 presents a detailed picture of the participants' responses. The 22 statements are divided according to categories. The number of responses for each level, rated from 1 (not at all) to 5 (to a great extent), are listed, along with the average rating.

Statements 1–7 related to teaching mathematics in preschool. The highest average rating was the statement regarding the importance of having children learn mathematics already in their preschool years, and the statement that received the lowest rating was "Anyone can enjoy learning mathematics". However, the average ratings for all the statements are in the range of 4 and above, implying that most facilitators were aware of the importance of early mathematics education for developing a positive attitude to math and making math a subject that everyone can learn. The results show that the facilitators thought that having children learn mathematics as early as preschool was important (average 4.65) and would help them develop a positive attitude to the subject (average 4.51), and that anyone can learn mathematics (average 4.15).

Statements 8–15 examine the attitudes regarding professional confidence. The statement that received the highest average score was "Anyone who aspires to succeed can do it at any age", whereas the statement "I am considering making mathematics teaching my main profession" received the lowest score. So although the results indicate that training encouraged facilitators to begin teaching mathematics in preschool, and that teaching preschool mathematics requires readiness, knowledge and professional maturity (statement 10), they did not necessarily show readiness to continue in this area. So although the results indicate that the training encouraged the facilitators to begin teaching mathematics in preschool (average 3.67), and gave them the ability to integrate the SMP into the preschool (average 3.57). The facilitators realised that teaching preschool requires readiness, knowledge and professional maturity (average 3.79).

Statements 16–17 show the participants' attitude towards their self-confidence in teaching mathematics. The results shows that the participants were convinced that the course gave them confidence to teach mathematics, which implies a high level of self-confidence.

Statements 18–22 show the results of the questions dealing with the participants' satisfaction with the SMP and the course itself. An examination of the averages indicates that the SMP was considered valuable for teaching mathematics in preschool. In general, it can be seen that most of the statements relating to the program and accompanying kit won scores of over 4. Participants showed satisfaction with the tools they were given for teaching mathematics in preschool (average 4.15), with the training for facilitating mathematics in preschools (average 4.18), with the teaching materials (average 4.19), and with the facilitator kits (average 4.30). In addition, the participants felt that the course was conducted in a professional manner (average 4.19) and most indicated that they would recommend the program to a friend (average 3.96).

The values presented in Table 12.2 were determined based on a statistical factor analysis of the questions that appeared on the questionnaire (see Table 12.1).

The statements are divided by category:
- *Attitude regarding the study of mathematics*: It is important that children start learning mathematics in preschool; Children of preschool age can learn mathematics; If the basics of mathematics are learned before first grade, the child will develop a positive attitude towards the subject; Anyone can learn mathematics; I see my future in teaching children mathematics; Anyone can enjoy learning mathematics.

TABLE 12.1   Responses to the questionnaire

Statement	5	4	3	2	1	Av.
Attitudes regarding the study of mathematics						
1 It is important for children to start learning mathematics in preschool.	33	13	2	–	–	4.65
2 Children of preschool age can learn mathematics.	29	15	4	–	–	4.52
3 If the basics of mathematics are learned before first grade, the child will develop a positive attitude towards the subject.	27	20	2	–	–	4.51
4 If the basics of mathematics are learned before first grade, the child will develop a positive attitude towards the subject.	27	20	2	–	–	4.51
5 Anyone can learn mathematics.	18	18	11	–	–	4.15
6 I see my future in teaching children mathematics.	19	15	13	1	–	4.08
7 Anyone can enjoy learning mathematics.	16	14	14	4	–	3.88
Development of professional confidence						
8 Anyone who aspires to succeed can do so at any age.	20	18	9	1	1	4.40
9 Unemployed women should be concerned about their professional development.	2	11	10	10	16	4.12
10 Teaching mathematics in preschool requires readiness, knowledge, and professional maturity.	6	11	13	11	7	3.79
11 The training encouraged me to start teaching mathematics in preschool.	6	10	15	7	4	3.67
12 I feel I can incorporate the smp into the preschool.	14	17	11	2	3	3.57
13 The training gave me professional confidence.	23	20	4	–	–	3.17
14 The training encouraged me to pursue my professional aspirations.	11	16	13	2	3	2.96
15 I am considering making mathematics teaching my main profession.	8	15	19	3	1	2.45
Statements about self-confidence in teaching mathematics						
16 The training gave me confidence to teach mathematics.	6	10	15	7	4	3.17
17 Had I not participated in the smp; I would not have confidence to teach mathematics.[a]	1	2	9	5	29	1.72
Statements about satisfaction with the program						
18 The smp facilitators' kit is a valuable aid for facilitating mathematics in preschool.	17	15	4	1	–	4.30

(*cont.*)

TABLE 12.1   Responses to the questionnaire (*cont.*)

Statement	5	4	3	2	1	Av.
19 The SMP activity pages were valuable for teaching mathematics in the preschool.	19	14	9	1	–	4.19
20 The course was conducted professionally.	20	14	7	1	1	4.19
21 The training gave me tools to facilitate mathematics in preschool.	19	14	11	–	–	4.18
22 The training gave me tools to teach mathematics in preschool.	19	18	7	1	1	4.15

a   The overall low score to this question could have been due to its having been presented as a negative statement.

TABLE 12.2   Attitudes of participants towards various aspects of the SMP

Attitudes of participants	Average	(sd)
Attitude regarding the study of mathematics	4.34	(0.40)
Development of professional confidence	3.46	(0.56)
Developing self-confidence in teaching mathematics	2.19	(0.90)
Evaluation of the program	4.29	(0.64)
Would you recommend participating in the SMP program to a friend?	4.04	(1.19)

– *Development of professional confidence*: Anyone who aspires to succeed can do so at any age; Unemployed women should be concerned about their professional development; Teaching mathematics in preschool requires readiness, knowledge, and professional maturity; The training encouraged me to start teaching mathematics in preschool; I feel I can incorporate the SMP into the preschool; The training gave me professional confidence; The training encouraged me to pursue my professional aspirations; I am considering making mathematics teaching my main profession.
– *Statements about self-confidence in teaching mathematics*: The training gave me confidence to teach mathematics; had I not participated in the SMP program, I would not have confidence to teach mathematics.
– Statements about evaluation of the program: The training gave me tools to teach mathematics in preschool; The training gave me tools to facilitate

mathematics in preschool; The SMP activity pages were valuable for teaching mathematics in the preschool; The SMP facilitators' kit was a valuable aid for facilitating mathematics in the preschool; The course was conducted professionally.

The attitudes of the participants regarding the study of mathematics were, on the whole, favourable: the average ratings for all the statements are in the range of 4 and above. The statement that received the highest average rating was the one regarding the importance of having children learn mathematics as early as preschool (4.65, average). The statement that received the lowest rating was "Anyone can enjoy learning mathematics", but was still close to 4. The results indicate that the facilitators thought it was important for children to learn mathematics as early as preschool, and that this would help the children develop a positive attitude to the subject (4.51).

Regarding professional confidence, the statement that received the highest average score was "Anyone who aspires to succeed can do it at any age". Moreover, while the answers indicate that the training was successful (statements 11, 12, and 13), statement 15, "I am considering making mathematics teaching my main profession", received the lowest score.

Regarding the participants' satisfaction with the SMP program and the training course: Results (average of all statements over 4, with a clear majority of answers at levels 5 or 4) indicate that the SMP was considered significant for teaching mathematics in preschool. Participants indicated satisfaction with the tools, kit, and activity pages, as well as with the professional way in which the course was conducted.

Other aspects of our study examined the participants' satisfaction with the course correlated with factors such as number of years of education and age and the number of children in their preschool groups. See Table 12.3. A Pearson correlation was used in which the coefficients can be in the range of zero to 1 or zero to -1. The closer the coefficient is to zero, the weaker the correlation. A negative correlation indicates an inverse relationship between the variables. Table 12.3 indicates that higher education is correlated with lower satisfaction with the program and with less positive attitudes towards the program itself. Moreover, more educated women showed less support for professional development. These correlations convey an expression of criticism that may be due to the women's level of education. Perhaps highly educated women are more critical in general, and this criticism is expressed by the attitudes they expressed towards the program. More detailed results can be found in Hassidov and Ilany (2014).

Table 12.3 presents correlations between the satisfaction of the participants with the course and factors regarding education, number of children, and age.

TABLE 12.3   Correlation between variables and statements regarding satisfaction with the program

	No. of children	Age	Years studied
Would you recommend the SMP to a friend?	−0.26	−0.17	−0.40**
Participants attitudes towards teaching mathematics in preschool	−0.13	−0.03	−0.31*
Professional development	0.03	−0.12	−0.47**
Development of self-confidence	−0.05	−0.07	−0.13
Program evaluation	−0.29	−0.36*	−0.42**

*p < 0.05; **p < 0.01

8.2   Summary of Qualitative Results

Policy changes regarding teaching mathematics beginning as early as preschool and with the need to prepare children mathematically for the transition from preschool to primary school place a great deal of responsibility on the preschool teacher. The SMP qualifies facilitators by training them specifically to be adjunct mathematics teachers in preschool, thus expanding the options and educational resources available for teaching preschool mathematics.

A year after the SMP pilot program, a large proportion of the 500 course participants (75%) had been integrated into preschools as facilitators. In interviews conducted at this time, their experiences regarding their integration into the preschool system were recorded. The qualitative results support, strengthen, and clarify the quantitative data.

The facilitators felt that the teachers realised the profound need to teach mathematics as early as preschool. The general impression was that the facilitators created a rich, diverse environment for learning mathematics in the preschool, and that teachers benefitted from the presence of a professional colleague who came once or twice weekly to take responsibility for mathematics instruction. The facilitator brought learning materials for the children, and the teacher received guidance as to how to continue the experience during the week. The facilitators reported that the teachers observed their activities with the children and repeated them during the course of the week.

Often, the considerable task load placed on a preschool teacher over the course of the academic year does not allow her sufficient time to teach mathematics in her classes. On the other hand, the facilitators' only task is to teach mathematics. This lifts a huge load of responsibility from the preschool teacher's shoulders.

However, accounts indicated that the relationship between the facilitator and teacher did not always start out smoothly. Some of the preschool teachers seemed to feel threatened:

> Why do I need someone else – an "expert" in mathematics – to come every week? What can they explain that I can't?

Some teachers initially suspected that the facilitators represented the Department of Education, and were there to observe the teacher's ability to teach mathematics. Since the program was implemented in the preschools through mathematics teaching inspectors affiliated with Ministry of Education, the preschool teachers were under the impression that the facilitators would be initiating a specific program to advance the teachers' efficacy and professionalism vis-à-vis teaching mathematics in the preschool. The teachers were suspicious of the process, and lacked a clear idea of what would occur regarding teaching mathematics in their classes. They did not realise that the facilitators were there to lighten their load, not to add to it.

Thus, at the beginning of the program the teachers tended to be uncooperative, and did not give the facilitators freedom to carry out the program as they wished. For example, one of the facilitators reported:

> I was anxiously looking forward to working in a preschool .... I had a good feeling that I could contribute and collaborate with the teacher ... However, it seemed I was received with some trepidation, and there was a sense of contrariness on the part of the teacher ... She couldn't find a suitable spot for me to work ... or she would say that the children were busy doing some other activity ... Every time I got started, I would hear mumbling that made me feel she wasn't thrilled to have me in the class.

After a period of adjustment, once the facilitators had received guidance to deal with the teachers' reluctance, the situation changed. The facilitator continued her account:

> The course instructor accompanied me and gave me some advice, and I understood the teacher's apprehension about the situation ... After several weeks, during which I had been teaching and the teacher had been observing, things started to change for the better. At the end of the year, the teacher asked me to explain the models to her, and she asked me to help her prepare a mathematics program for next year. ... She also asked

me to come to the parents-teachers' meeting to update the parents on what we had done in the class, and to explain how mathematics learning-aids had been incorporated into the play area.

One preschool teacher who taught 4–6 year olds reported:

> After a few lessons during which I had not been asked to do anything, I understood how much simply observing her and her way of working with the materials contributed to me ... After the facilitator left the preschool, I, myself, used the teaching materials that she had left, and I saw how easy it was to teach the children with them.

Another teacher reported:

> After a few weeks ... I started to look forward to her arrival. Believe me, I stood at the door and waited for her. I was keen to tell her what had happened the day before, when I taught the children about pattern: the children told me that Nadine's socks are also patterned because they have stripes – blue, red, green, blue, red, green. Then all the children started looking for patterns on their classmates' clothes. It made me so happy!

A third preschool teacher said:

> I never had anyone with whom I could discuss how to teach mathematics in my classes; now, I have someone to talk to every week, and I can consult with her. My supervisor is aware of this too.

As time passed, the instruction of mathematics in the preschools bloomed into full cooperation between the teacher and facilitator. The facilitator taught the children mathematics once or twice a week, while the teacher observed the activity. The teacher continued the facilitator's activities during the week, to reinforce the studies for the children.

As one of the facilitators reported:

> At first, the teacher objected to having me in her preschool teaching mathematics. But after several months, we were collaborating nicely, and she told me that she now realised that teaching preschool mathematics is important and requires professional training; something that I, the facilitator, had attained and that she lacked.

9   Conclusions

The global trend today favours access to mathematics at a young age. Changes regarding teaching mathematics from preschool age and the need to prepare the child for the transition to school impose a heavy responsibility on the preschool teachers (Baroody, 2000).

Recent years have seen a change regarding the importance of the learning environment and the teacher's role, with a change from the traditional environment, where the teacher transmits knowledge, to an active and constructivist learning environment (Cobb, 1996). This change has led to a transformation in the teacher's role and responsibilities. In this new environment, the teacher serves more as a facilitator or mediator who encourages learning by enabling opportunities for the students to engage in interesting activities. The students take on the responsibility for constructing their learning experience from the knowledge available. Fostering such experience requires a teacher to have professional knowledge.

The unique SMP provides a solution for a clearly-defined need in the current education system, where mathematics must be taught to children at a young age to prepare them for their mathematics studies in primary school.

This study indicates that the SMP has had a great impact on both populations: those who studied to be facilitators as a means of professional development, and the heavily burdened preschool teachers who do not have enough knowledge or training to adequately provide mathematical instruction in their classes. The presence of facilitators in the preschool transformed mathematics into a subject that is interesting and appealing.

The SMP program comes as an answer to this demand, expands the range of possibilities, and increases teaching resources by providing professional facilitators who are specially trained to teach mathematics in preschool using specially created exercises to allow children to experience math in a unique learning program.

This study shows that the SMP program seems to be successful in this aspect, as can be seen from the fact that the majority of the participants in the program (75%) had, a year later, been integrated into mathematics teaching in preschools.

Furthermore, according to the response, in preschools where facilitators were integrated, the mathematical learning environment became rich and diverse. The teacher benefited from a professional colleague (the facilitator) who came once or twice a week to the preschool, and who had the responsibility for teaching mathematics to the children. The teacher received training in teaching preschool math from the facilitators, and also learned through observation (modelling) of the facilitators' activities in the class. Facilitators reported that the teachers observed their activities with the children and repeated them during the week.

As one of the facilitators reported during her interview, her activity affected the preschool mathematical progression:

> The teacher told me that since I had begun coming to the preschool, her attitude towards teaching mathematics changed. She told me that she is integrating daily mathematical activities into her program.

In addition, the introduction of facilitators in the preschools gave new prominence to mathematical instruction: The many tasks imposed upon the preschool teacher do not always allow her to devote sufficient time to teaching mathematics. Because the facilitators are engaged only in teaching mathematics, this aspect of preschool education becomes standard. It was found that the facilitators who participated in the program recognized that children should and can learn mathematics in preschool. It was also found that the SMP training contributed to their professional development and gave them confidence to facilitate mathematics teaching in preschool. Interviewees reported that the training and the accompanying materials were of a professional calibre and thus considerably contributed to their success in the program and, subsequently, to the preschool teachers and the children learners. One of the conclusions drawn from this study was that the facilitators training program had a positive effect on the professional development of the participants. Teaching mathematics in preschool became a key area of interest to them that was intriguing and challenging. In addition, their addition became accepted as a positive contribution to the learning environment. The introduction of facilitators into the preschool also impressed upon the teachers that teaching mathematics to preschool children requires professional understanding and training. For example, one of the facilitators said in an interview:

> In the beginning, the teacher objected to having me in her preschool and teaching mathematics. After several months, though, we were collaborating nicely. The teacher told me that now she realizes that teaching mathematics in the preschool is a very important area and that I, the facilitator, have received training that she lacks.

In time, the facilitated mathematics teaching in the preschools was carried out in full cooperation between the teacher and the facilitator. The teacher observed the facilitators' methods, and used the activities to teach mathematics on the days when the facilitator was not present. The structure and organization of the mathematical knowledge of developing preschoolers is affected by their learning experience (Clements, 2001). Complex activities lead to increased brain development.

The conclusion indicates that the SMP program is the way to answer the current needs of an educational system that demands the introduction of mathematics education in preschool so as to prepare children for the transition to mathematics education in school.

Acknowledgments

We thank Marganit Klugman for her contribution to the SMP program. The program was developed and the facilitators were trained by Dina Hassidov and Marganit Klugman.

References

Australian Curriculum, Assessment and Reporting Authority [ACARA]. (2009). *Australian curriculum: Papic, Mulligan, and Mitchelmore mathematics.* www.australiancurriculum.edu.au/Mathematics/Curriculum/F-10

Australian Early Development Census 2012 Summary. (2013).

Baroody, A. J. (2000). Does mathematics instruction for three- to five-year-olds really make sense? *Young Children, 55*(4), 61–67.

Ben-Yehuda, M., & Ilany, B. (2008). *Pituach Chushiva matematit bagil harach: teoria, mechkar, uma'aseh behachsharat morim [The development of mathematical thinking in young children: theory, research and practice in training teachers].* Machon Mofet Publications.

Carpenter, T. P. (1988). Teachers' pedagogical content knowledge of students' problem solving in elementary arithmetic. *Journal for Research in Mathematics Education, 19*(5), 385–401.

Charalambous, C. Y., Panaoura, A., & Philippou, G. (2009). Using the history of mathematics to induce changes in preservice teachers' beliefs and attitudes: Insights from evaluating a teacher education program. *Educational Studies in Mathematics, 71*(2), 161–180. http://doi.org/10.1007/s10649-008-9170-0

Clarke, B., Clarke, D., & Cheeseman, J. (2006). The mathematical knowledge and understanding young children bring to school. *Mathematics Education Research Journal, 18*(1), 78–103.

Clements, D. H. (2001). Mathematics in the preschool. *Teaching Children Mathematics, 7,* 270–277.

Clements, D. H., & Sarama, J. (2006). Your child's mathematical mind. *Scholastic Parent & Child*, 30–37.

Clements, D. H., & Sarama, J. (2009). *Learning and teaching early math: The learning trajectories approach*. Routledge.

Cobb, P. (1966). *Accounting for mathematical learning in social context of the classroom* [Paper presentation]. ICME 8.

Fiske, S. T., & Taylor, S. E. (2008). *Social cognition: from brains to culture*. McGraw-Hill Higher Education.

Guo, Y., Justice, L. M., Sawyer, B., & Tompkins, V. (2011). Exploring factors related to preschool teachers' self-efficacy. *Teaching and Teacher Education*, *27*(5), 961–968. http://doi.org/10.1016/j.tate.2011.03.008

Hassidov, D. (2014). *Evaluating facilitator training for the "Senso-Math" preschool mathematics program* [Paper presentation]. IICE-2014.

Hassidov, D., & Ilany, B. S. (2014). A Unique program ("Senso-Math") for teaching mathematics in preschool: Evaluating facilitator training. *Creative Education*, *5*(11), 976–988. http://doi.org/10.4236/ce.2014.511112

Ilany, B., & Ben-Yehuda, M. (2021). Developing mathematics teaching in kindergarten. *Creative Education (CE)*, *12*(2).

Israel Ministry of Education. (2009). *Curriculum for the education of mathematics in early childhood* (*core mathematics program*). The Department for the Development of School Curricula.

Kilpatrick, J., Swafford J., & Findell, B. (Eds.). (2001). *Adding it up: Helping children learn mathematics*. National Academy of Sciences – National Research Council, Center for Education.

Let's Count. (2016). www.thesmithfamily.com.au/campaigns/lets-count-program

McLeod, D. B. (1992). Research on affect in mathematics education: a reconceptualization. In D. A. Grouws (Ed.), *Handbook of research on mathematics teaching and learning* (pp. 575–596). Macmillan.

Mulligan, J. T. (2016, July 24–31). *Promoting early mathematical structural development though an integrated assessment and pedagogical program*. Program of the 13th international congress on mathematical education topic study group 1: Early childhood mathematics education.

National Council of Teachers of Mathematics. (2000). *Principles and standards for school mathematics*. National Council of Teachers of Mathematics.

NCTM. (2002). Position statement early childhood mathematics: Promoting good beginnings. *Teaching Children Mathematics*, *9*, 24–25.

Perry, B., & Dockett, S. (2013). Reflecting on young children's mathematics learning. In L. English & J. Mulligan (Eds.), *Reconceptualising early mathematics learning* (pp. 149–161). Springer.

Philipp, R. A. (2007). Mathematics teachers' beliefs and affect. In F. K. Lester (Ed.), *Second handbook of research on mathematics teaching and learning* (pp. 257–315). Information Age Publishing.

Philippou, G. N., & Christou, C. (1998). The effects of a preparatory mathematics program in changing prospective teachers' attitudes towards mathematics. *Educational Studies in Mathematics, 35,* 189–206. http://doi.org/10.1023/A:1003030211453

Piaget, J. (1972). *The psychology of the child.* Basic Books, Inc.

Pimm, D. (1987). *Speaking mathematically: Communication in mathematics classroom.* Routledge & Kegan Paul.

Plucker, J. A. (1996). Secondary science and mathematics teachers and gender equity: Attitudes and attempted interventions. *Journal of Research in Science Teaching, 33*(7), 737–751. http://doi.org/10.1002/(SICI)1098-2736(199609)33:7<737:AID-TEA3>3.0.CO;2-O

Tirosh, D., & Graeber, A. O. (1990). Evoking cognitive conflict to explore preservice teachers' thinking about division. *Journal for Research in Mathematics Education, 21*(2), 98. http://doi.org/10.2307/749137

Vygotsky, L. (1962). *Thought and language* (E. Hanfmann & G. Vakar, Eds.). MIT Press. http://content.apa.org/books/11193-000

PART 6

Conclusion

∵

Special Issues in Early Childhood Mathematics Education

A Wrap-up of Topics in the Book

Amal Sharif-Rasslan

The twelve chapters in this book, authored by twenty-three prominent mathematicians, mathematics educators, psychologists, and researchers, covered a multitude of different aspects and approaches related to early-childhood mathematical education: some on issues of learning and teaching, some on children's mathematical knowledge, and others on teacher development. Together, they contribute to the expanding number of studies on this topic. The following topics were addressed and can be found in various places in the book:

- Literature reviews of early childhood mathematics education (Sharif-Rasslan, Chapter 1; Clements, Sarama & Joswick, Chapter 4; Markovitz, Hershkowitz, Rosenfeld, Ilani & Eylon, Chapter 5; Mulligan, Chapter 6).
- An overview on learning and teaching geometry in early childhood (Clements, Sarama & Joswick, Chapter 4).
- A report about a program for developing visual thinking (Markovitz, Hershkowitz, Rosenfeld, Ilani & Eylon, Chapter 5).
- Theoretical essays about early-childhood mathematics education and the history of mathematics, including focus on the origin of numbers (Sharif-Rasslan, Chapter 1; Ventura, Santamaria & Scheuer, Chapter 2, Clements, Sarama & Joswick, Chapter 4; Markovitz, Hershkowitz, Rosenfeld, Ilani & Eylon, Chapter 5).
- An analysis of young children's metacognitive processes when dealing with a variety of challenging number tasks (Ventura, Santamaria & Scheuer, Chapter 2) and analyses of the mathematical structures used by young children to describe their surrounding in mathematical terms, especially numerosity (Sharir & Mevarach, Chapter 7; Mulligan, Chapter 6).
- An analysis of mathematical terms in daily life concepts, with a focus on quantifiers (Sharif-Rasslan, Chapter 8).
- Descriptions and investigations of how technology applications are used in early childhood for dealing with mathematical concepts (numbers and geometry) (Barki, Levenson, Tsamir & Tirosh, Chapter 3; Clements, Sarama & Joswick, Chapter 4).

- Reports about empirical investigations on the mathematical knowledge of pre-service and in-service kindergarten teachers (Hassidov & Ilany, Chapter 10; Shahbari, Chapter 11).
- A report about empirical investigations on the professional development of in-service kindergarten teachers (Ilany & Hassidov, Chapter 12).
- Analyses of young children's mathematical reasoning and their ability of provide explanations (Sharif-Rasslan, Chapter 8; Hershkowitz & Arcavi, Chapter 9).
- A research report and overview on patterns of spontaneous thinking (Mulligan, Chapter 6; Sharir & Mevarech, Chapter 7).

Despite the wide range of topics, all the authors share the common belief that it is important to educate children early in life to use mathematical terms accurately and rigorously. Moreover, it is important to design curricula that will make learning enjoyable and offer a learning environment that encourages exploration, creativity, and a desire to learn and understand mathematics. Also important is to ensure that kindergarten teachers participate in professional development courses to improve their mathematical and pedagogical knowledge.

To wrap up this book and attempt to consolidate the myriad topics covered, this chapter offers closing information about some important prevailing concepts and curricula issues of early-childhood mathematics education and reminds the readers how and where they were addressed in the various chapters in this book.

1   Early Childhood Mathematics Concepts and Curricula Issues

The first step was to determine exactly what "early childhood" refers to, as there is no consensus on how different researchers and educators define the term. Some believe that early childhood mathematics education involves children between the ages of three to six. Indeed, in many countries, young toddlers are sent to early childhood centers (Impact.Upenn, 2021). Others define it more inclusively as the period from birth to age eight (Björklund, van den Heuvel-Panhuizen & Kullberg, 2020; Goodwin University). In this book, we adopted the second definition, that is, the period from birth to eight years.

Next, a basic agreement regarding core topics and basic requirements needed to be established. The National Association for the Education of Young Children and the National Council of Teachers of Mathematics (NAEYC/NCTM 2002/2010) have highlighted six principles to guide curricula preparation for school mathematics, and these can also apply to early childhood: equity, curriculum, teaching, learning, assessment, and technology. Moreover, they reported that "a curriculum is more than a collection of activities; it must be coherent, focused on important mathematics, and well-articulated across the grades" (NAEYC/NCTM, 2002/2010, p. 2).

Research in mathematics education began to develop in the last century (Kilpatrick, 2014), and investigating mathematical learning and teaching in early childhood mathematics education came later (Björklund et al., 2020), although previous studies have investigated developmental psychology and cognitive sciences.

Almost the world over, the core of mathematics curricula is based on four basic standards: *problem solving, communications, reasoning,* and *connections.* In early childhood, fundamental content must include the following five specific components: *number sense and numeration, geometry, measurement and spatial sense, mathematical situations in daily life,* and *mathematical patterns* (see for example NCTM, 1989, 2000, 2010; DfE, 2013; Kaur et al., 2015; Israel Ministry of Education, 2009).

Figure 13.1 illustrates the relationship between the four basic standards (outer circle) and the early-childhood components (inner circle) and how they intersect into the concept of pattern (center).

In more recent times, several mathematics education conferences have focused on early-childhood mathematics education. These conferences include CERME 11 (Congress of the European Society for Research in Mathematics Education), PoEM4 (Practice of Enterprise Modelling), and ICME 13 (International Congress on Mathematical Education) (Björklund et al., 2020). Worthy of note are the five key themes listed in the ICME 13 monograph

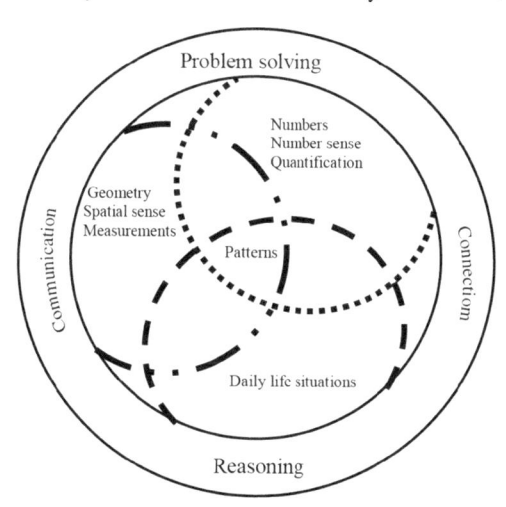

FIGURE 13.1
Components of early childhood mathematics curriculum

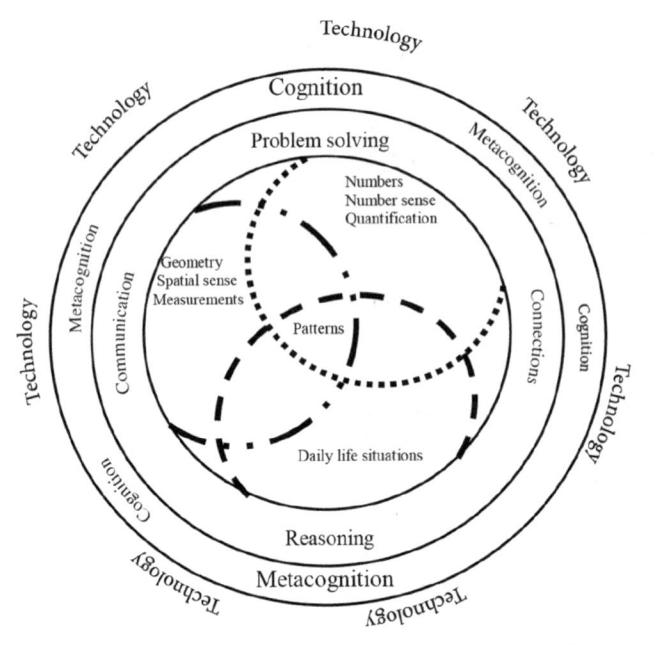

FIGURE 13.2   The spectrum of research in early childhood mathematics education

"Contemporary research and perspectives on early childhood mathematics education" (Elia et al., 2018), some of which correspond to those listed above: *patterns and structures, number sense, embodied action and context, technology,* and *early childhood educators' professional issues and education.* These may be added to the diagram to present a more complete and complex illustration of the spectrum of concepts and topics in this field (see Figure 13.2).

2   Spectrum of Themes Presented in This Book

Following, we present an overview of seven of the above-mentioned themes that make up the intrinsic spectrum of early-childhood mathematics education research, present some background research, and note how and where they are addressed in this book. As will be seen, no chapter stands on its own, and various issues are found in more than one place, linking all the chapters in this book into a comprehensive web of information. For example, chapters dealing with "number" and "geometry" also present suggestions on how technology can be employed to enhance teaching.

2.1   *Component Theme 1: "Number"*
The NCTM has stated that understanding numbers, the relationships between numbers, what numbers represent, and foundations in number systems should

be areas of focus for pupils from pre-kindergarten to grade two (NCTM, 2000). Thus, numbers, number sense, and quantitative competence provide a basic core for research on early childhood education.

Various studies have examined different aspects of these core topics. In 1978, Gelaman and Gallistel suggested five basic counting principles: stable order, one-to-one correspondence, and cardinality ("how-to-count"), along with abstraction and order irrelevance ("what-to-count"). These are considered basic concepts when analyzing children's mathematical counting behavior. Sharif-Rasslan (Chapter 1) and Barki, Levenson, Tsamir, and Tirosh (Chapter 3) based their studies on these principles to analyze children's mathematical behavior when coping with counting activities: Sharif-Rasslan to compare children's behavior with that of primitive man, and Barki et al. to investigate the three "how-to-count" principles and then analyzing the presentation of objects on a screen while taking into account the two "what-to-count" principles.

Some studies (e.g., Rinvold, 2016) have focused on how children use their body (e.g., their fingers) for communicating numbers and to facilitate the learning process. This was discussed in Chapters 1 and 2: Sharif-Rasslan discussing numerical forms used around the age of about three years; and Ventura, Santamaria and Scheuer discussing numerical forms used by children aged five to six. These include diverse counting procedures supported by parts of the body, speech, and tallies; finger patterns to convey quantity; number words; and written number signs (i.e., numerals).

Chapter 6 (Mulligan) and Chapter 7 (Sharir and Mevarech) relate to the term "number" in another sense. These chapters presented some perspective regarding spontaneous focus on numerosity, particularly regarding children's recognition of mathematical structures. (The term "spontaneous" implies that the process of "focusing attention on numerosity" is self-initiated and non-guided.)

Finally, Chapters 10 and 11 (Hassidov & Ilani and Shahbari, respectively) dealt with educators' and pre-service teachers' knowledge of the term "number" and suggest advanced thinking and problem-solving strategies that support conceptual growth.

2.2 Component Theme 2: "Geometry"

Geometry is important for understanding the world around us. Children develop and operate in an environment filled with geometrical bodies and shapes, and an acquaintance with geometrical concepts helps them to orient themselves in space. In addition, familiarity with the connections between shapes and bodies is a foundation for logical thinking.

Geometry is a basic component of the mathematics curricula in all levels, no less than in early childhood. Several studies have indicated the importance of geometry in children's development. For example, Freudenthal (1973) emphasized that "geometry is grasping space. And since it is about the education of children, it is grasping that space in which the child lives, breathes, and moves" (p. 403). Nevertheless, as Clements and Sarama (2009) have claimed, geometry and spatial thinking are often ignored or minimized in early childhood education. Several early-childhood mathematics education researchers (e.g., Geist, 2001; Pound, 2006; Willis, 2001) have explored the knowledge and conceptual understanding that children four years of age and older have about geometrical shapes, geometrical properties, and the names of shapes. Instilling this knowledge is a common feature of academic program designers.

Concepts related to shape (as well as most mathematical concepts) are not commonly mentioned in the literature as being appropriate for infants or toddlers. Yet some researchers, Halat and Dağlı (2016), for example, have observed that preschool children *do* have a conceptual understanding of geometric shapes, the square in particular. (In their study, more than half of the children successfully drew a square, selected a square from among three other geometric shapes, identified a picture of a square-like real life object among a selection of pictures, differentiated three different-sized squares among five geometric shapes, and identified rotated squares).

Chapters 4 and 5 both emphasized the importance of geometry for spatial and visual thinking in children's mathematical development.

In Chapter 4, Clements, Sarama and Joswick reviewed several studies about young children's "skills" in geometry, especially with respect to several unique projects based on such research: the Agam Program for the Development of Visual Thinking, the Building Blocks curriculum, Educational Technology for Early Geometry (e.g. Shape's software, the Geometric Turtle), and dynamic geometry environments (e.g. ShapeMakers).

In Chapter 5, Markovitz, Hershkowitz, Rosenfeld, Ilani and Eylon presented their definition of visual thinking and the importance of developing visual thinking at a young age. They reviewed in detail the unique "visual pedagogy" approach of the Agam program and described the program's unique potential for developing visual thinking and language in young children. They discussed the program's aims and content and how they are contextualized into teaching units for kindergarten and elementary school.

In Chapter 11, Shahbari addressed the lack of geometrical knowledge among pre-service teachers.

2.3   Component Theme 3: "Basic Mathematical Concepts in Daily Life"

Fuson (2004) has suggested that mathematics is too important to be "left to chance". Effective preschool teaching (by parents and kindergarten teachers) must build on children's informal knowledge and mathematical experience, always considering the children's cultural background and language. Furthermore, cognitive research has shown that young children can develop an extensive understanding of "everyday mathematics" and are capable of learning and understanding mathematics that is more complicated than usually assumed (Ginsgurg et al., 2008). Another study that observed and assessed the extent to which young children are engaged in "natural" mathematics in the course of their everyday activities found that children varied considerably in the extent to which they engaged in mathematical activities (Tudge & Doucet, 2004). The NCTM (2000) has suggested engaging children in daily activities that can engage them in "mathematics" such as sorting objects by color, size, shape, etc.; comparing quantities in groups; making simple numerical summaries (e.g., tables and bar graphs to compare data); and so forth.

One important idea that is sometimes overlooked is the importance of having children learn to use accurate mathematical quantifiers and conjunctions in their daily communications, as it will enhance future mathematical performance. One such aspect was explored in Chapter 8 by Sharif-Rasslan, who examined an aspect of decision-making in children aged four to seven when dealing with an issue based on the quantifier "all" and their logical reasoning and deductions for a representative problem in day-to-day life. Note that this is a new issue in mathematics education, particularly in early childhood education.

2.4   Component Theme 4: "Pattern and Structure"

Recent research in mathematics education has focused upon the development and knowledge of patterning, which has been found to influence children's reasoning and their ability to generalize patterns (e.g. Mulligan et al., 2006; English, 2004). In this context, was Mulligan's overview of the learning pathways of the Pattern and Structure Mathematics Awareness program in Chapter 6. This is a pedagogical approach by which five structural groupings help teachers notice mathematical structures that are articulated through two exemplars of children's representations of structuring grids and hundreds charts. Implications regarding further research, teaching and learning, and pre- and in-service programs were raised.

Also in this context is Chapter 7, in which Sharir and Mevarech investigated young children's "recognition of mathematical structures" (ROMS) when presented with objects in random order, in a multiplication pattern structure, and in an arithmetic series structure. They examined the differences between verbal and nonverbal ROMS and studied the contribution that different types of ROMS make to mathematical reasoning. Their findings indicated that recognizing numerosity in random order is easiest, followed by multiplication patterns. Recognizing arithmetic series is the hardest.

2.5   Component Theme 5: "Reasoning and Explanation"

The NCTM has (2000) emphasized that problem solving, reasoning, communication, connections, and representation are basic skills that ought to be acquired in early childhood to enhance content knowledge. (These are clearly illustrated in Figure 13.1 and are components of all mathematics curricula.) Dreyfus (1999) considers "explanation" to be a skill on the mathematical reasoning continuum that also includes argument and proof. Çelik (2017) defined "logical reasoning" as a process of thinking about a problem to find the most effective solution.

In Chapter 9, Hershkovitz and Arcavi defined mathematical "explanation" as "a description that addresses and unfolds the origins/sources, entailments, and connections of a mathematical idea". They studied explanations given by second-graders in the context of mathematical tasks in a test and concluded that "the explanations generated [by the students] are not mere repetitions of what they may have heard in class, especially when they explain the features of a graph, which were not explicitly taught to most of them". Hence, they suggested that children should be exposed to explanations even at very early ages and should be encouraged to not only "do" math but also to "explain" what they are doing.

Chapter 8 is also relevant to this theme. In it, Sharif-Rasslan examined decision-making and logical reasoning processes among young children, specifically when dealing with logical deductions based on the quantifier "all". She concluded that various parameters – environment, intuition, and preferences – can affect logical reasoning in early childhood.

Chapter 8 also dealt with new visions of early-childhood research that relate to quantifiers and mathematical explanations in early childhood (respectively). This vision relates to communication (which is one of the basic standards of mathematics curricula, see Figures 13.1 and 13.2). Moreover, both chapters 8 and 9 refer to the "reasoning" standard and reached the conclusion that, even at very early ages, children should be exposed to explanations and reasoning, be encouraged to engage in "explaining", and be taught to use and understand terms related to quantifiers.

2.6   Component Theme 6: "Technology"

This theme addresses the use of technology in learning and teaching mathematics in early childhood, both at home and at school. It is interesting to note that in their 2008 paper, Clements and Sarama pointed out that some researchers (e.g., Cordes & Miller, 2000) criticize the use of computers in childhood, claiming that they pose serious physical, emotional, intellectual, and developmental hazards to children and that computers have no place in the early childhood classroom. Clements and Sarama, however, countered that claim and argued that computers can make significant contributions to learning mathematics. The NCTM also highlighted the use of technology: "technology is essential to teaching and learning mathematics; it influences the mathematics that is taught and enhances students' learning" (NAEYC/NCTM, 2002/2010, p. 2).

"Technology" for learning and teaching mathematics in early childhood includes computers, iPads, tablets, touch-screens, and more. There have been numerous studies in this context, including how they can be used to teach counting (Sinclair & SedaghatJou, 2013; Tucker & Johnson, 2020) and geometry (Clements & Sarama, 2008).

In Chapter 3, Barkai et al. analyzed the visual, auditory, and gestural aspects of 18 tablet applications in terms of their affordances and limitations when promoting object counting. Their findings indicated that verbal counting and one-to-one correspondence are given more attention than cardinality. In Chapter 4, Clements et al. reviewed the use of technology in learning and teaching geometry in early childhood by reviewing several applicable programs such as the Building Blocks curriculum, ShapeMakers, and others. They emphasized that children can enrich their learning about shape if their educational environment includes various examples and nonexamples, a wide variety of shape types, a broad array of geometric tasks, progress from "sensory-concrete" to "integrated-concrete" cognition, discussions about shapes and their attributes, the use of learning trajectories, and the appropriate inclusion of educational technology.

In fact, some chapters in this book make at least some reference to the use of technology as an aid to teaching and learning. For example, Chapter 3 mention the use of iPads and the like for understanding and perceiving the term "number". Chapter 4 touches upon how computer environments can enhance children's visual skills, help them progress from "naïve thinking" to empirical and logical thinking, encourage them to make and test conjectures, and promote a problem-solving approach. The authors of these chapters pointed out that the use of computers in education appear to have benefits for the development of both mathematical concepts and processes (e.g., reasoning, connecting, problem-solving, communicating, and representing) and are especially beneficial for developing student competence in solving complex problems.

2.7 Component Theme 7: "Early Childhood Educators' Knowledge and Professional Issues"

Ginsburg et al. (2008) reported that, typically, early-childhood educators are poorly trained to teach mathematics, are afraid of the subject, feel that it is not an important one to teach to preschoolers, and/or teach it badly or not at all.

In Chapter 10, Ilany and Hassidov demonstrated how some pre-service teachers see nothing wrong in using mathematical symbols in ways that are not mathematical in context. For example, they may use the "greater than" symbol to indicate a "non-mathematical" larger object. The study indicated that, indeed, some teachers do not properly understand the significance of the symbols =, <, and, > nor how to use them, which may mean that their young learners will start out confused about these concepts.

In Chapter 11, Shahbari examined whether the training provided in early childhood education courses for prospective first- and second-grade teachers adequately prepares them to teach mathematics in these grades. Her main conclusion was that mathematical content and pedagogical training is indeed lacking, but this can be remedied by providing teachers a deeper understanding of the features of good pedagogy to affect the ways in which they engage children in mathematically-related activities such as play, story/picture-book reading, project work, the arts, and physical education. In Chapter 12, Hassidov and Ilany proposed another way to meet this goal and investigated an innovative "Senso-Math" preschool program designed to enhance mathematical development in preschool children. In it, specially trained facilitators bring this adjunct program into preschools and "model" effective teaching behavior for the teachers, who continue the program during the week. The Senso-Math program is one way to address the current needs of an educational system that demands the introduction of mathematics education in preschool to prepare children for the transition to mathematics education in school.

3 Final Words

We, the editors of this book, firmly believe that this book offers a comprehensive and representative – if not all-encompassing – spectrum of research in the field of early-childhood mathematics education and we fervently hope that you, the reader, have obtained some valuable information on the various themes and issues in the field.

We also hope that reading the book will encourage exploration, creativity, and a desire to learn and understand mathematics and mathematic pedagogy. We hope you, whether teacher, educator, school principal, or parent now understand how important it is to educate children early in life about mathematical terms and concepts through the provision of enjoyable activities in different learning environments and the importance of having preschool and kindergarten teachers participate in professional courses to improve their mathematical and pedagogical knowledge.

References

Björklund, C., van den Heuvel-Panhuizen, M., & Kullberg, A. (2020). Research on early childhood mathematics teaching and learning. *ZDM Mathematics Education, 52,* 607–619. doi:10.1007/s11858-020-01177-3

Çelik, M. (2017). Examination of children decision making using clues during the logical reasoning process. *Educational Research and Reviews, 12*(16), 783–788.

Clements, D. H., & Sarama, J. (2008). Mathematics and technology: Supporting learning for students and teachers. In O. N. Saracho & B. Spodek (Eds.), *Contemporary perspectives on science and technology in early childhood education* (pp. 127–147). Information Age.

Cordes, C., & Miller, E. (2000). *Fool's gold: A critical look at computers in childhood.* https://files.eric.ed.gov/fulltext/ED445803.pdf

Department for Education (DfE). (2013). *The national curriculum in England: key stages 1 and 2 framework document.* Retrieved August 11, 2021, from https://www.gov.uk/government/publications/national-curriculum-in-england-primary-curriculum

Dreyfus, T. (1999). Why Johnny can't prove. *Educational Studies in Mathematics, 38*(1–3), 85–109.

Elia, I., Mulligan, J., Anderson, A., Baccaglini-Frank, A., & Benz, C. (Eds.). (2018). *Contemporary research and perspectives on early childhood mathematics education* (ICME-13 monograph). Springer Nature.

English, L. D. (2004). Mathematical and analogical reasoning in early childhood. In L. D. English (Ed.), *Mathematical and analogical reasoning of young learners* (pp. 1–22). Lawrence Erlbaum Associates.

Freudenthal, H. (1973). *Mathematics as an educational task.* Reidel Publishing Company.

Fuson, K. C. (2004). Pre-K to grade 2 goals and standards: Achieving 21st century mastery for all. In D.H. Clements, J. Sarama, & A.-M. DiBiase (Eds.), *Engaging young children in mathematics: Standards for early childhood mathematics education* (pp. 105–48). Lawrence Erlbaum.

Geist, E. (2001). Children are born mathematicians: Promoting the construction of early mathematical concepts in children under five. *Young Children, 56*(4), 12–19.

Goodwin University. (2019). *What is early childhood education, and is it the right career for you?* https://www.goodwin.edu/enews/what-is-early-childhood-education/

Halat, E., & Dağlı, U. Y. (2016). Preschool students' understanding of a geometric shape, the square. *Bolema, Rio Claro (SP), 30*(55), 830–848. doi:10.1590/1980-4415v30n55a25

Impact.Upenn. (2021). *What is early childhood?* The Center for Hight Impact Philanthropy. https://www.impact.upenn.edu/early-childhood-toolkit/what-is-early-childhood/

Israel Ministry of Education. (2009). *Curriculum for the education of mathematics in early childhood (Core mathematics program).* The Department for the Development of School Curricula, Israel Ministry of Education. Rretrieved August 11, 2021, from https://meyda.education.gov.il/files/tochniyot_limudim/kdamyesodi/math1.pdf

Kaur, B., Soh, C. K., Wong, K. Y., et al. (2015). Mathematics Education in Singapore. In S. Cho (Ed.), *The proceedings of the 12th International Congress on Mathematical Education*. doi:10.1007/978-3-319-12688-3_21

Kilpatrick, J. (2014). History of research in mathematics education. In S. Lerman (Ed.), *Encyclopedia of mathematics education*. Springer. doi:10.1007/978-94-007-4978-8_71

Mulligan, J. T., Mitchelmore, M. C., & Prescott, A. (2006). Integrating concepts and processes in early mathematics: The Australian Pattern and Structure Mathematics Awareness Project (PASMAP). In J. Novotná, H. Moraová, M. Krátká, & N. Stehlíková (Eds.), *Proceedings of the 30th annual conference of the International Group for the Psychology of Mathematics Education* (Vol. 4, pp. 209–216). Program Committee.

NAEYC/NCTM – National Association for the Education of Young Children and the National Council of Teachers of Mathematics. (2002/2010). *Early childhood mathematics: promoting good beginnings.* Joint position paper adopted in 2002, updated in 2010. www.naeyc.org/files/naeyc/file/positions/psmath.pdf

National Council of Teachers of Mathematics (NCTM). (1989). *Curriculum and evaluation standards for school mathematics.* Author.

National Council of Teachers of Mathematics (NCTM). (2000). *Principles and standards for school mathematics.* Author.

Pound, L. (2006). *Supporting mathematical development in the early years* (2nd ed.). Open University Press.

Rinvold, A. R. (2016). *The difficulty of learning the three first numerosities* [Poster]. 13th International Congress on Mathematical Education.

Seo, K.-H., & Ginsburg, H. P. (2004). What is developmentally appropriate in early childhood mathematics education? Lessons from new research. In D. H. Clements, J. Sarama, & A.-M. DiBiase (Eds.), *Engaging young children in mathematics: Standards for early childhood mathematics education* (pp. 91–104). Erlbaum.

Sinclair, N., & SedaghatJou, M. (2013). Finger counting and adding with TouchCounts. In In B. Ubuz, C. Haser, & M. A. Mariotti (Eds.), *Proceedings of the Eighth Congress of the European Society for Research in Mathematics Education* (*CERME 8*) (pp. 2198–2207). Middle East Technical University and ERME.

Tucker, I. S., & Johnson, N. T. (2020). Developing number sense with Fingu: a preschooler's embodied mathematics during interactions with a multi-touch digital game. *Mathematics Education Research Journal.* doi:10.1007/s13394-020-00349-4

Tudge, J. R. H., & Doucet, F. (2004). Early mathematical experiences: Observing young Black and White children's everyday activities. *Early Childhood Research Quarterly, 19,* 21–39.

Willis, S., (2001, May 31). *Becoming numerate: Who's at risk and why?* [Paper presentation]. Early years numeracy conference.

Index